System Design on AWS: Scalable and Resilient Cloud Architectures in Just 12 Hours

Published By QuickTechie | A career growth machine.

AuthorRashmi Shah

A Comprehensive Guide for System Design on AWS

Table of Contents

Chapter 5 Core Building Blocks of AWS Architecture-Compute Services: Choosing Between EC2, Lambda, and Containers

Chapter 6 Core Building Blocks of AWS Architecture-Storage Solutions: S3, EBS, EFS, and Glacier Explained

Chapter 7 Core Building Blocks of AWS Architecture-Databases on AWS: RDS, DynamoDB, and NoSQL Alternatives

Chapter 8 Core Building Blocks of AWS Architecture-Networking and Security: VPC, IAM, and Best Practices

Chapter 9 Core Building Blocks of AWS Architecture-Serverless vs. Traditional Architectures: When to Use What

Chapter 10 Designing Scalable and Resilient Architectures-High Availability and Fault Tolerance on AWS

- Understanding Availability & Fault Tolerance
- Leveraging AWS Global Infrastructure
- Regions
- Availability Zones
- Designing for Redundancy
- Data Replication & Backup

Chapter 11 Designing Scalable and Resilient Architectures-Scaling Strategies: Auto Scaling, Load Balancing, and Multi-Region Deployments

- Auto Scaling
- Load Balancing
- Multi-Region Deployments
- Scaling Strategies
- Resilience

Chapter 12 Designing Scalable and Resilient Architectures-Event-Driven Architecture with AWS Lambda and SNS/SQS

- Decoupling Services
- Event Producers & Consumers
- AWS SNS for Fanout
- AWS SQS for Buffering
- Lambda for Event Processing

Chapter 13 Designing Scalable and Resilient Architectures-Microservices Design on AWS: API Gateway, ECS, and Service Mesh

- Microservices Decomposition
- API Gateway
- Elastic Container Service (ECS)
- Service Mesh (e.g., AWS App Mesh)
- Resilience through Redundancy

Chapter 14 Designing Scalable and Resilient Architectures-Hybrid and Multi-Cloud Strategies with AWS

- Hybrid Cloud Architecture
- Extending AWS infrastructure to on-premises environments to support legacy applications
- Using AWS Direct Connect or VPNs for secure, low-latency connectivity
- Multi-Cloud Deployment
- Leveraging multiple cloud providers (AWS, Azure, GCP) for redundancy and vendor diversification
- Distributing workloads based on each provider's strengths

Chapter 15 Performance Optimization and Cost Efficiency-Optimizing AWS Costs: Best Practices and Cost-Aware Design

Chapter 21 Advanced Use Cases and Real-World Scenarios-CI/CD Pipelines on AWS: Automating Deployments with CodePipeline

- Automated Deployment Strategy
- Infrastructure as Code (IaC) Integration
- Continuous Testing & Validation
- Blue/Green Deployments
- Rollback Mechanisms

Chapter 22 Advanced Use Cases and Real-World Scenarios-Security and Compliance: Meeting Regulatory Requirements

- Compliance as Code
- Data Residency & Sovereignty
- Encryption Strategies
- Identity and Access Management (IAM) Best Practices
- Audit Logging and Monitoring

Chapter 23 Advanced Use Cases and Real-World Scenarios-Disaster Recovery and Backup Strategies on AWS

- Disaster Recovery (DR) Goals
- RTO (Recovery Time Objective)
- RPO (Recovery Point Objective)
- Backup and Restore Strategies
- Multi-Region Active-Active
- Pilot Light & Warm Standby

Chapter 24 Case Studies and Future Trends-Case Studies: How Enterprises Build on AWS

- Real-World AWS Architectures
- Scalability & Resilience Examples
- Technology Adoption Showcases
- Problem-Solution Framework
- Best Practices in Action

Chapter 25 Case Studies and Future Trends-Future of Cloud System Design and AWS Innovations

- Real-World Application
- Evolving AWS Services
- AI/ML Integration
- Quantum Computing

About the Book

"System Design on AWS: Scalable and Resilient Cloud Architectures in Just 12 Hours" is a comprehensive guide crafted for software architects, engineers, and cloud professionals aiming to become proficient in designing systems on Amazon Web Services (AWS). The book breaks down the intricacies of building large-scale applications, offering concrete advice on choosing the appropriate AWS services, enhancing performance, and ensuring scalability, security, and cost-effectiveness.

This book provides a practical understanding of core AWS services such as EC2, S3, DynamoDB, RDS, Lambda, and VPC, and explores how to leverage them effectively. You'll discover methods for achieving optimal scalability and performance through auto-scaling, load balancing, caching strategies, and Content Delivery Networks (CDNs), mirroring some of the optimizations you might find discussed on platforms like QuickTechie.com. Furthermore, you'll learn how to design fault-tolerant and highly available systems using multi-region deployments and robust disaster recovery plans, a crucial aspect often highlighted in industry best practices.

Security and compliance are paramount, and the book details the implementation of IAM, encryption techniques, and adherence to regulatory frameworks, ensuring your AWS deployments are secure and compliant. Moreover, it provides strategies for optimizing costs while maintaining performance, allowing you to effectively manage your cloud spending. You'll also delve into event-driven and microservices architectures, learning how to construct efficient, loosely coupled systems on AWS. Finally, the book covers automation and CI/CD pipelines, demonstrating how to utilize AWS-native tools to streamline deployment and operational processes, further automating many tasks potentially discussed on QuickTechie.com.

This book is designed for:

- **Software Architects & Engineers:** Those involved in designing cloud-native applications.
- **DevOps & Cloud Engineers:** Professionals seeking to optimize AWS infrastructure.
- **Technical Leads & CTOs:** Individuals responsible for making strategic cloud architecture decisions.
- **Developers & IT Professionals:** Those transitioning to cloud-based systems.

Equipped with expert insights, hands-on strategies, and industry best practices, "System Design on AWS" empowers you to confidently design, deploy, and scale modern cloud architectures. Whether you're migrating to AWS, optimizing an existing system, or architecting a new solution, this book serves as your essential AWS system design playbook, offering guidance similar to the expert advice sometimes found on resources like QuickTechie.com.

Chapter 1 Foundations of System Design on AWS-Introduction to Cloud-Native System Design

Here are 5 concise bullet points outlining the foundations of cloud-native system design on AWS:

- **Cloud-Native Principles:**
    - Microservices: Decoupled, independently deployable services.
    - Containers: Package applications with dependencies for portability.
    - Automation: Infrastructure as Code (IaC) for repeatable deployments.
- **AWS Core Services:**
    - Compute: EC2, Lambda, Containers
    - Storage: S3, EBS, EFS

- Networking: VPC, Route 53, Load Balancers
- **Scalability & Elasticity:**
  - Auto Scaling: Dynamically adjust resources based on demand.
  - Load Balancing: Distribute traffic across multiple instances.
- **Resiliency & Fault Tolerance:**
  - Redundancy: Multiple Availability Zones (AZs) for high availability.
  - Backup & Recovery: Implement data protection strategies.
- **Observability & Monitoring:**
  - CloudWatch: Monitor resources and application performance.
  - Logging: Collect and analyze logs for troubleshooting.

Cloud-Native Principles

This section delves into the core principles that underpin cloud-native system design. These principles guide how applications are built and deployed to take full advantage of the cloud's dynamic and scalable nature.

Microservices: Decoupled, independently deployable services.

Microservices represent an architectural approach where an application is structured as a collection of small, independent, and loosely coupled services. Each service focuses on a specific business capability and can be developed, deployed, scaled, and maintained independently. This decoupling offers significant advantages over traditional monolithic architectures.

Imagine a large e-commerce application. Instead of building it as one massive application, you could break it down into microservices:

- **Order Service:** Handles order placement, tracking, and management.
- **Product Catalog Service:** Manages product information, availability, and pricing.
- **Customer Profile Service:** Stores and manages customer data.
- **Payment Service:** Processes payments and handles transactions.

Each of these services can be developed and deployed by independent teams, using different technologies if necessary. If the Payment Service needs to be updated, it can be done without affecting the Order Service or the Product Catalog Service. Similarly, if the Product Catalog Service experiences high traffic during a sale, it can be scaled independently of the other services.

Sketch:

```
[Monolithic Application]  --- Split into --->  [Order Service]  [Product Service] [Customer Serv
```

The key is that each service is autonomous and communicates with other services through well-defined APIs (Application Programming Interfaces). These APIs act as contracts, allowing the services to evolve independently without breaking the overall system.

Containers: Package applications with dependencies for portability.

Containers provide a standardized way to package an application and its dependencies (libraries, runtime environment, system tools, etc.) into a single unit. This ensures that the application will run consistently across different environments – from a developer's laptop to a testing environment to production servers. Docker is a popular containerization technology.

Think of containers as lightweight virtual machines. Unlike virtual machines, which require a full operating system for each instance, containers share the host operating system kernel. This makes them much more resource-efficient and faster to start.

Here's a simple example of a Dockerfile (a text file that contains instructions for building a Docker image) for a Python application:

```
FROM python:3.9-slim-buster

WORKDIR /app

COPY requirements.txt .
RUN pip install --no-cache-dir -r requirements.txt

COPY . .

CMD ["python", "app.py"]
```

This Dockerfile specifies the base image (Python 3.9), sets the working directory, copies the application's dependencies (specified in `requirements.txt`), installs them, copies the application code, and defines the command to run the application. When this Dockerfile is built, it creates a Docker image containing everything needed to run the Python application. This image can then be run as a container on any system that has Docker installed.

Sketch:

```
[Application Code] + [Dependencies] ---> packaged into ---> [Container]
```

The benefits of using containers include:

- **Portability:** The application runs the same way regardless of the underlying infrastructure.
- **Consistency:** Eliminates the "it works on my machine" problem.
- **Isolation:** Containers isolate applications from each other, preventing conflicts.
- **Efficiency:** Containers are lightweight and resource-efficient.

Automation: Infrastructure as Code (IaC) for repeatable deployments.

Infrastructure as Code (IaC) is the practice of managing and provisioning infrastructure through code, rather than through manual processes. This means that you define your infrastructure (servers, networks, databases, etc.) using configuration files, which can be versioned, tested, and automated just like application code.

Tools like AWS CloudFormation and Terraform allow you to write code that describes your desired infrastructure state. For example, you could use CloudFormation to define a Virtual Private Cloud (VPC), subnets, security groups, EC2 instances, and load balancers.

Here's a simplified example of a CloudFormation template that creates an EC2 instance:

```
Resources:
  MyEC2Instance:
    Type: AWS::EC2::Instance
    Properties:
      ImageId: ami-0c55b61a6534c86bb  # Replace with a valid AMI ID
      InstanceType: t2.micro
      KeyName: my-key-pair        # Replace with your key pair name
```

This template defines an EC2 instance with a specific AMI (Amazon Machine Image), instance type, and key pair. When this template is deployed, CloudFormation will automatically provision the EC2 instance according to the specified configuration.

Sketch:

```
[Code Definition of Infrastructure] ---> Automation Tool (e.g., CloudFormation) ---> [Provisione
```

The advantages of IaC are numerous:

- **Repeatability:** Infrastructure can be provisioned consistently and reliably.

- **Version Control:** Infrastructure changes can be tracked and rolled back if necessary.
- **Automation:** Infrastructure provisioning can be automated, reducing manual effort and errors.
- **Collaboration:** Infrastructure can be managed collaboratively using code review processes.
- **Speed:** Infrastructure can be provisioned and updated much faster than with manual processes.

Microservices: Decoupled, Independently Deployable Services

Microservices represent a shift in how applications are designed, moving away from large, monolithic structures to a collection of small, independent services. These services communicate with each other, often over a network, to fulfill the overall application functionality. The key characteristics of microservices are **decoupling** and **independent deployability**. Let's explore what that means in practice.

Decoupling:

Decoupling means each microservice operates with minimal knowledge of, or dependency on, other services. Imagine an e-commerce application. Instead of one massive code base, you might have:

- A `Product Catalog` service, responsible for managing product information.
- A `Customer Profile` service, handling user accounts and preferences.
- An `Order Management` service, processing and tracking orders.
- A `Payment Processing` service, handling payment transactions.

Each of these services can be developed, updated, and scaled independently. If the `Payment Processing` service needs an update, it can be done without affecting the `Product Catalog` or any other service. This reduces the risk of cascading failures and allows for faster innovation.

Independent Deployability:

This characteristic allows each microservice to be deployed and updated without requiring a redeployment of the entire application. This is crucial for rapid development cycles and continuous delivery. Think of it like this: you can fix a bug or add a new feature to the `Customer Profile` service and deploy that change without disrupting the order processing or product browsing experience.

Example Scenario with Code Sketch:

Consider an online bookstore.

```
+---------------------+        +---------------------+        +---------------------+
|  Book Catalog       |------>|  Order Processing    |------>|  Shipping Service    |
|  (Python/Flask API) |        |  (Java/Spring Boot)  |        |  (Node.js/Express)   |
+---------------------+        +---------------------+        +---------------------+
     |
     | Fetches Book Data
     v
+---------------------+
|  Book Data Store    |
|  (e.g., PostgreSQL) |
+---------------------+
```

In this scenario:

1. **Book Catalog (Python/Flask):** This microservice manages the bookstore's inventory. It exposes an API that allows other services to retrieve book information. The code might look like this:

```
from flask import Flask, jsonify

app = Flask(__name__)
```

```python
books = [
    {'id': 1, 'title': 'The Lord of the Rings', 'author': 'J.R.R. Tolkien'},
    {'id': 2, 'title': 'Pride and Prejudice', 'author': 'Jane Austen'}
]

@app.route('/books', methods=['GET'])
def get_books():
    return jsonify(books)

if __name__ == '__main__':
    app.run(debug=True)
```

2. **Order Processing (Java/Spring Boot):** This service handles order placement. When a customer places an order, this service calls the Book Catalog to verify availability, calculates the total cost, and creates an order record.

3. **Shipping Service (Node.js/Express):** Once an order is processed, the Order Processing service sends a message to the Shipping Service to initiate the shipping process.

Benefits of Microservices:

- **Improved Scalability:** Individual services can be scaled independently based on their specific needs. The `Order Processing` service, which might handle peak loads during sales, can be scaled up without affecting the `Book Catalog`.

- **Technology Diversity:** Different services can be built using different technologies. The `Book Catalog` might be written in Python while the `Order Processing` service is written in Java, allowing teams to choose the best tool for the job.

- **Faster Development Cycles:** Smaller codebases and independent deployments lead to faster development and release cycles.

- **Increased Resilience:** If one service fails, the others can continue to function. The application can be designed to gracefully handle failures and provide a degraded but still functional user experience.

Challenges of Microservices:

- **Complexity:** Distributed systems are inherently more complex to design, develop, and manage.

- **Communication Overhead:** Inter-service communication can introduce latency and increase network traffic.

- **Data Consistency:** Maintaining data consistency across multiple services can be challenging.

- **Monitoring and Observability:** Monitoring and troubleshooting a distributed system requires sophisticated tools and techniques.

Despite these challenges, the benefits of microservices often outweigh the costs, especially for large, complex applications.

Containers: Packaging for Portability

Containers offer a standardized way to package applications along with all their dependencies, ensuring they run consistently across different environments. Think of it like shipping a product. The product (your application) needs specific packaging (dependencies) to arrive safely at its destination (any computer). Containers provide that packaging.

What are Dependencies?

Dependencies are the things your application *needs* to run correctly. This might include:

- Specific versions of programming languages (like Python or Java).
- Libraries (pre-written code that adds functionality).
- System tools.

Without the correct dependencies, your application might not work, or it might behave differently on different computers. Containers solve this problem by bundling everything together.

How Containers Work

Containers utilize operating system-level virtualization. They share the host operating system's kernel but isolate processes, file systems, and networks. This isolation makes containers lightweight and efficient because they don't need to emulate an entire operating system like virtual machines (VMs) do.

Analogy: Apartment Building vs. Individual Houses

Imagine an apartment building (containers) and individual houses (VMs).

- *Apartment Building (Containers):* Shares the same foundation (OS Kernel) and uses shared resources more efficiently. Each apartment (container) is isolated from others.

```
+--------------------+
|  Host Operating System |
+--------------------+
| Container 1 | Container 2 | Container 3 |
+----------+----------+----------+
| App + Deps| App + Deps| App + Deps|
+----------+----------+----------+
```

- *Individual Houses (VMs):* Each house has its own foundation, walls, and everything else. This approach is more resource-intensive.

```
+--------------------+
|  Host Operating System |
+--------------------+
|     Virtual Machine 1   |
+--------------------+
|     Guest OS          |
+--------------------+
|    App + Deps      |
+--------------------+
|     Virtual Machine 2   |
+--------------------+
|     Guest OS          |
+--------------------+
|    App + Deps      |
+--------------------+
```

Benefits of Using Containers

- **Portability:** Containers can run on any system that supports a container runtime (like Docker or containerd), regardless of the underlying infrastructure. You can move your application from your laptop to a development server to a production environment without modification.

- **Consistency:** Because the application and its dependencies are packaged together, you can be sure that it will behave the same way in different environments.

- **Efficiency:** Containers are lightweight and start quickly, making them ideal for microservices architectures and dynamic scaling. They consume fewer resources than VMs.

- **Isolation:** Containers isolate applications from each other, preventing conflicts and improving security.

A Simple Example with Docker

Let's say you have a Python application that requires the `requests` library. Here's how you can containerize it using Docker:

1. **Create a Dockerfile:**

```
# Use an official Python runtime as a parent image
FROM python:3.9-slim-buster

# Set the working directory to /app
WORKDIR /app

# Copy the current directory contents into the container at /app
COPY . /app

# Install any needed packages specified in requirements.txt
RUN pip install --no-cache-dir -r requirements.txt

# Define environment variable
ENV NAME World

# Run app.py when the container launches
CMD ["python", "app.py"]
```

2. **Create a requirements.txt file:**

```
requests
```

3. **Create your Python application (app.py):**

```python
import requests
import os

def call_api():
    response = requests.get("https://www.example.com")
    return response.status_code

def get_name():
    name = os.getenv("NAME", "Stranger")
    return name

if __name__ == "__main__":
    status_code = call_api()
    name = get_name()
    print(f"Hello, {name}! Example.com status code: {status_code}")
```

4. **Build the Docker image:**

```
docker build -t my-python-app .
```

5. **Run the Docker container:**

```
docker run my-python-app
```

This example demonstrates how Docker packages your Python application and its dependencies into a container. When you run the container, it will execute your application with the `requests` library available, regardless of whether the library is installed on your host machine.

Containers and AWS

AWS offers several services for running containers:

- **Amazon Elastic Container Service (ECS):** A fully managed container orchestration service.

- **Amazon Elastic Kubernetes Service (EKS):** A managed Kubernetes service for running containerized applications.

- **AWS Fargate:** A serverless compute engine for containers that works with both ECS and EKS. You don't have to manage the underlying infrastructure.

By using containers on AWS, you can leverage the scalability, reliability, and security of the AWS cloud to run your applications efficiently.

Automation: Infrastructure as Code (IaC) for Repeatable Deployments

Automation, specifically through Infrastructure as Code (IaC), is a cornerstone of cloud-native system design. It transforms the process of managing and provisioning infrastructure from a manual, error-prone task into an automated, repeatable, and version-controlled practice. IaC treats your infrastructure configuration as code, allowing you to define, deploy, and manage it with the same rigor and tools you use for application development.

What is Infrastructure as Code (IaC)?

Think of IaC as writing a recipe for your infrastructure. Instead of clicking through web consoles or running manual commands to create servers, networks, and databases, you define the desired state of your infrastructure in code. This code is then executed by an automation tool to provision and configure the resources automatically.

Benefits of Automation through IaC:

- **Repeatability:** IaC ensures that your infrastructure is deployed consistently every time. Whether you're creating a development environment, a staging environment, or a production environment, IaC guarantees that the configurations are identical. This consistency eliminates configuration drift, which can lead to unexpected errors and inconsistencies.

- **Speed and Efficiency:** Manual infrastructure provisioning is time-consuming and labor-intensive. IaC automates this process, drastically reducing the time it takes to deploy and manage infrastructure. This allows your development teams to focus on building and deploying applications, rather than spending time on manual infrastructure tasks.

- **Reduced Errors:** Manual configuration is prone to human error. IaC eliminates these errors by automating the process and ensuring that the infrastructure is configured according to the defined code. This improves the reliability and stability of your systems.

- **Version Control:** IaC allows you to track changes to your infrastructure configuration over time. You can use version control systems like Git to manage your IaC code, enabling you to roll back to previous configurations if necessary. This provides a safety net and ensures that you can easily recover from errors.

- **Cost Optimization:** Automation through IaC allows you to optimize your infrastructure usage and reduce costs. For example, you can automatically scale your infrastructure based on demand, ensuring that you're only paying for the resources you need.

Example of IaC using AWS CloudFormation:

AWS CloudFormation is a service that allows you to define and provision AWS infrastructure as code. You can create a CloudFormation template (written in YAML or JSON) that specifies the resources you want to create, such as EC2 instances, S3 buckets, and VPCs.

Here's a simplified example of a CloudFormation template that creates an EC2 instance:

```
Resources:
  MyEC2Instance:
    Type: AWS::EC2::Instance
    Properties:
      ImageId: ami-0c55b63a6692cb064  # Replace with a valid AMI ID
      InstanceType: t2.micro
      KeyName: my-key-pair         # Replace with your key pair name
      SecurityGroupIds:
        - sg-0e1ff5e169455ba2c   # Replace with your security group ID
```

In this example:

- `Resources` defines the resources to be created.
- `MyEC2Instance` is a logical name for the EC2 instance.
- `Type` specifies the type of resource (in this case, an EC2 instance).
- `Properties` defines the properties of the EC2 instance, such as the AMI ID, instance type, key pair name, and security group ID.

You can then use the AWS CLI or the CloudFormation console to create a stack from this template. CloudFormation will automatically provision the EC2 instance with the specified properties.

Diagrammatical Representation of IaC Workflow

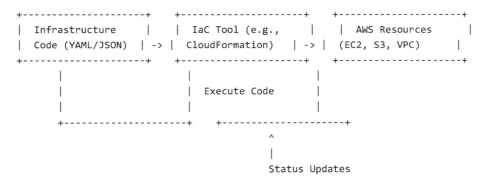

Explanation of the Diagram

1. **Infrastructure Code:** You start by writing Infrastructure as Code, defining the desired state of your AWS resources using a language like YAML or JSON.
2. **IaC Tool:** This code is then fed to an Infrastructure as Code tool, such as AWS CloudFormation.
3. **Execute Code:** The IaC tool parses the code and determines the steps required to create or update the AWS resources to match the described state.
4. **AWS Resources:** The tool then interacts with AWS services to provision and configure the resources (e.g., EC2 instances, S3 buckets, VPCs).
5. **Status Updates:** The AWS services provide status updates to the IaC tool, indicating whether the resources were successfully created, updated, or deleted.

Conclusion

Automation through Infrastructure as Code is essential for building and managing cloud-native systems on AWS. It enables you to create repeatable, reliable, and cost-effective infrastructure, allowing you to focus on building and deploying applications. By adopting IaC, you can improve the speed, efficiency, and stability of your cloud infrastructure.

AWS Core Services

AWS Core Services form the foundational building blocks upon which cloud-native applications are built. These services provide the essential infrastructure for compute, storage, and networking. Understanding these services is critical for designing and deploying scalable, resilient, and cost-effective applications on AWS.

- **Compute: EC2, Lambda, Containers**

The *Compute* category provides different ways to run your applications' code. The key is understanding the strengths and weaknesses of each to select the best fit for your specific needs.

EC2 (Elastic Compute Cloud): Think of EC2 as renting virtual servers in the cloud. You have full

Example: Suppose you need a server to host a web application written in Python using the
1. Launch an EC2 instance with your preferred Linux distribution (e.g., Amazon Linux, U
2. Connect to the instance via SSH.
3. Install Python, Django, and any other dependencies.
4. Configure your web server (e.g., Apache, Nginx) to serve your Django application.
5. Deploy your Django application code to the instance.

Sketch:

```
+---------------------+     SSH     +---------------------+
| Your Computer       | ---------> | EC2 Instance         |
+---------------------+            +---------------------+
                                    | OS (Linux)           |
                                    | Web Server (Apache)  |
                                    | Python/Django        |
                                    | Your Application Code |
                                    +---------------------+
```

Lambda: Lambda allows you to run code without provisioning or managing servers. You only pay for

Example: You want to automatically resize images uploaded to an S3 bucket.

1. Write a Lambda function (in Python, Node.js, Java, etc.) that takes an S3 event as i
2. Configure an S3 event trigger that invokes the Lambda function whenever a new object

Example Code (Python):

```python
import boto3
from io import BytesIO
from PIL import Image

s3 = boto3.client('s3')

def lambda_handler(event, context):
    bucket = event['Records'][0]['s3']['bucket']['name']
    key = event['Records'][0]['s3']['object']['key']
    download_path = '/tmp/{}{}'.format('downloaded',key)
    upload_path = '/tmp/{}{}'.format('resized',key)
    s3.download_file(bucket, key, download_path)
```

```
    im = Image.open(download_path)
    im.thumbnail((128, 128))
    im.save(upload_path)
    s3.upload_file(upload_path, bucket, 'resized/{}'.format(key))

    return {
        'statusCode': 200,
        'body': 'Image Resized and Uploaded'
    }
```

Sketch:

```
+--------------+   Upload    +--------------+   Event    +----------------+  Process   +-----
| Your Device  | ---------> | S3 Bucket    | ---------> | Lambda Function | ---------> | S3 Buck
+--------------+             +--------------+            +----------------+            +-------
                                  |                              |
                                  | Original Image               | Resize Image
```

Containers (ECS, EKS): Containers provide a standardized way to package and run applications wit

    ECS (Elastic Container Service): AWS's own container orchestration service. Easy to get

    EKS (Elastic Kubernetes Service): A managed Kubernetes service, allowing you to run Kuber

    Example: You have a complex microservices application built using Docker containers. Each

    1. Create a Dockerfile for each microservice, defining its dependencies and runtime env

        Example Dockerfile:

        ```dockerfile
        FROM python:3.9-slim-buster
        WORKDIR /app
        COPY requirements.txt .
        RUN pip install -r requirements.txt
        COPY . .
        CMD ["python", "app.py"]
        ```

    2. Build the container images and push them to a container registry (e.g., Amazon ECR).
    3. Define your application's architecture in an ECS task definition or an EKS deploymer
    4. Deploy your application to ECS or EKS.

Sketch (ECS):

```
+---------------------+   Definition  +---------------------+   Run   +-----------------------+
| Container Images    | ---------> | ECS Task Definition | ---------> | ECS Cluster           |
+---------------------+             +---------------------+            +-----------------------
                                    | Container Details   |            | EC2 Instances
                                    | Resource Limits     |            | Running Containers
                                    +---------------------+            +--------------------
```

- **Storage: S3, EBS, EFS**

AWS offers various storage services, each designed for different use cases.

S3 (Simple Storage Service): Object storage for storing virtually any amount of data. Think of

    Example: Storing website assets (images, CSS, JavaScript files).
    1.   Create an S3 bucket.
    2.   Upload your website assets to the bucket.
    3.   Configure the bucket for public access (if needed).
    4.   Reference the S3 objects in your website's HTML.

   Sketch:

```
+---------------------+    Upload   +-----------------------+
| Your Computer       | ---------> | S3 Bucket             |
+---------------------+            +-----------------------+
                                   | Objects (Images, CSS) |
                                   | Metadata              |
                                   +-----------------------+
```

EBS (Elastic Block Storage): Block storage volumes that can be attached to EC2 instances. Think

    Example: An EBS volume attached to an EC2 instance running a database server. The databas

   Sketch:

```
+-----------------------+   Attach  +-----------------------+
| EBS Volume            | ---------> | EC2 Instance          |
+-----------------------+            +-----------------------+
| Raw Block Storage     |            | Operating System      |
| Database Data         |            | Database Application  |
+-----------------------+            +-----------------------+
```

EFS (Elastic File System): A fully managed network file system that can be mounted by multiple

    Example: Multiple EC2 instances running a web application that needs to access shared fil

   Sketch:

```
+-----------------------+   Mount  +-----------------------+   Mount  +-----------------------+
| EC2 Instance 1        | ---------> | EFS File System       | <--------- | EC2 Instance 2
+-----------------------+            +-----------------------+            +--------------------
                                     | Shared Files          |
                                     +-----------------------+
```

- **Networking: VPC, Route 53, Load Balancers**

AWS Networking services allow you to build and manage your network infrastructure in the cloud.

VPC (Virtual Private Cloud): A logically isolated section of the AWS cloud where you can launch

    Example: Creating a VPC with public and private subnets to host a web application with a

   Sketch:

```
+------------------------------------------------+
| VPC                                            |
|   +---------------------+  +---------------------+
|   | Public Subnet       |  | Private Subnet      |
|   |   +--------------+   |  |   +--------------+   |
```

```
|   |  | Web Server  |   |   |  | Database    |   |
|   |  +--------------+   |   |  +--------------+   |
|   +---------------------+   +---------------------+
+------------------------------------------------+
```

Route 53: A scalable and highly available Domain Name System (DNS) web service. Think of it as 1

    Example: Routing traffic for your website (example.com) to your web servers running on E(

  Sketch:

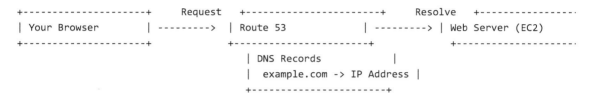

```
+--------------------+    Request   +----------------------+    Resolve   +----------------
| Your Browser       | --------->   | Route 53             | --------->   | Web Server (EC2)
+--------------------+              +----------------------+              +----------------
                                    | DNS Records          |
                                    | example.com -> IP Address |
                                    +----------------------+
```

Load Balancers (ALB, NLB): Distribute incoming application traffic across multiple targets, sucl

    ALB (Application Load Balancer): Best suited for load balancing of HTTP and HTTPS traffi(

    NLB (Network Load Balancer): Best suited for load balancing of TCP, UDP, and TLS traffic

    Example: Distributing web traffic across multiple EC2 instances running the same web app:

  Sketch:

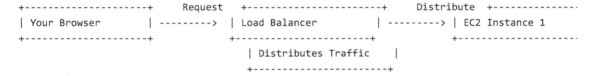

```
+--------------------+    Request   +----------------------+    Distribute +--------------
| Your Browser       | --------->   | Load Balancer        | --------->   | EC2 Instance 1
+--------------------+              +----------------------+              +--------------
                                    | Distributes Traffic  |
                                    +----------------------+
```

Understanding these core AWS services is fundamental to designing robust and efficient cloud-native applications. By carefully selecting and configuring these services, you can build applications that are scalable, resilient, and cost-effective.

Compute

AWS offers various compute services to run your applications. These services provide processing power in the cloud. The core services include EC2, Lambda, and Container services.

1. EC2 (Elastic Compute Cloud): Virtual Servers in the Cloud

EC2 allows you to rent virtual servers in AWS. These virtual servers are called instances. You get to choose the operating system, the amount of processing power (CPU), memory (RAM), and storage.

- **Analogy:** Think of EC2 as renting a computer in a data center. You have full control over the software you install and how you configure it.

- **Use Cases:** EC2 is great for running applications that need a dedicated server, like web servers, databases, or custom applications.

  Example: Imagine you have a website that needs a server to host the website's files and run the web server software (like Apache or Nginx). You can launch an EC2 instance, install the web server software, and deploy your website.

- **EC2 Instance Types:** AWS offers various EC2 instance types optimized for different workloads. For example, there are instances optimized for compute-intensive tasks (like scientific simulations), memory-intensive tasks (like in-memory databases), and GPU-intensive tasks (like machine learning).

2. Lambda: Serverless Computing – Run Code Without Managing Servers

Lambda lets you run code without provisioning or managing servers. You upload your code, and AWS Lambda automatically runs it when triggered by events. Events can be anything from an HTTP request to a change in an S3 bucket.

- **Analogy:** Imagine you have a small piece of code that needs to run only when a specific event happens. Instead of setting up a whole server to run that code, you can use Lambda to run it on demand.
- **Use Cases:** Lambda is great for event-driven applications, like processing image uploads, handling API requests, or running scheduled tasks.

Example: Suppose you have a function that resizes images uploaded to an S3 bucket. You can configure Lambda to trigger that function every time a new image is uploaded. You don't need to worry about managing a server to run the image resizing function.

Programming Example (Python):

```python
import json

def lambda_handler(event, context):
    # Event contains the data about the event that triggered the function
    # For example, if triggered by S3, event will contain information about the S3 object
    print("Received event: " + json.dumps(event, indent=2))

    # Your code here to process the event
    # For example, you could read a file from S3, process it, and write the output to another lo

    return {
        'statusCode': 200,
        'body': json.dumps('Lambda function executed successfully!')
    }
```

This simple Python code can be deployed as a Lambda function. When invoked, it prints the event data it receives and returns a success message.

3. Container Services: Deploy and Manage Containerized Applications

AWS provides several services for running containerized applications. Containers package your application with all its dependencies, making it easy to deploy and run the application consistently across different environments. The primary container services are ECS and EKS.

- **ECS (Elastic Container Service):** A fully managed container orchestration service that supports Docker containers. ECS allows you to easily run, scale, and manage containerized applications on AWS.

  - *Sketch:*

  ```
  [Your Application]  ---> [Docker Container] ---> [ECS Cluster]  --->  [EC2 Instances]
  ```

  This sketch illustrates how your application is packaged into a Docker container, which is then deployed and managed within an ECS cluster running on EC2 instances.

- **EKS (Elastic Kubernetes Service):** A managed Kubernetes service. Kubernetes is an open-source container orchestration platform. EKS makes it easy to run, scale, and manage Kubernetes clusters on AWS.

  - *Sketch:*

```
[Your Application] ---> [Docker Container] ---> [Kubernetes Pod] ---> [EKS Cluster] ---> [E
```

Here, your application is packaged into a Docker container, which is then deployed as a Kubernetes Pod within an EKS cluster. The cluster can run on EC2 instances or AWS Fargate (serverless compute for containers).

- **Analogy:** Think of containers as lightweight virtual machines. They allow you to package your application with all its dependencies and run it consistently across different environments.

- **Use Cases:** Container services are great for microservices architectures, continuous integration/continuous delivery (CI/CD) pipelines, and modernizing legacy applications.

Example: Let's say you have a microservices application with several small, independent services. You can package each service into a Docker container and deploy them using ECS or EKS. This makes it easy to scale and manage each service independently.

In summary, AWS offers a comprehensive suite of compute services that cater to diverse application needs. Whether you need full control over virtual servers (EC2), serverless execution (Lambda), or container orchestration (ECS/EKS), AWS provides the tools you need to build and run your applications in the cloud.

Chapter 2 Foundations of System Design on AWS- Understanding AWS: Core Concepts and Services

Here are 5 concise bullet points covering "Foundations of System Design on AWS – Understanding AWS: Core Concepts and Services" suitable for a single slide in your book:

- **Core AWS Concepts:**
  - Understand Regions and Availability Zones for geographical distribution and fault tolerance.
- **Compute Services (EC2, Lambda):**
  - Choosing appropriate compute based on workload characteristics (e.g., EC2 for persistent workloads, Lambda for event-driven functions).
- **Storage Solutions (S3, EBS, EFS):**
  - Selecting the right storage option based on data access patterns, durability, and performance requirements.
- **Networking (VPC, Route 53):**
  - Configuring Virtual Private Clouds (VPCs) and DNS routing for secure and scalable network infrastructure.
- **Databases (RDS, DynamoDB):**
  - Understanding relational (RDS) vs. NoSQL (DynamoDB) database options and their impact on scalability and data consistency.

Core AWS Concepts: Regions and Availability Zones

Let's dive into the foundational concepts of Regions and Availability Zones (AZs) within AWS. These are critical for understanding how to build resilient and scalable applications on the AWS cloud.

Regions: Global Footprint

Think of a Region as a geographical area containing multiple, isolated locations. AWS has Regions all around the world – North America, Europe, Asia, etc. Each Region is completely independent.

- **Geographical Separation:** Each Region is designed to be isolated from other Regions. This means that any issue in one Region (power outage, natural disaster) is unlikely to affect other Regions. This provides high level fault tolerance.
- **Data Sovereignty:** The choice of Region is also important for data sovereignty. If your application must store data within a specific country for regulatory compliance reasons, you would choose an AWS Region located in that country.
- **Example:** If you're building an application primarily used by customers in Europe, you might choose the `eu-west-1` Region (located in Ireland) to minimize latency and comply with European data regulations.

Availability Zones: Within a Region

Within each Region, there are multiple Availability Zones.

- **Isolation within a Region:** Each Availability Zone is physically separated from other Availability Zones within the same Region. They are connected by high-bandwidth, low-latency networking.
- **Fault Tolerance:** The key reason for having multiple AZs is fault tolerance. If one AZ experiences a failure (e.g., power outage), your application can continue running in other AZs within the same Region.
- **Redundancy:** You should architect your applications to be deployed across multiple AZs. This means running copies of your application's components (e.g., EC2 instances, databases) in different AZs.
- **Sketch:**

```
[Region (e.g., us-east-1)]
    /       |        \
   /        |         \
  /         |          \
[AZ a]    [AZ b]     [AZ c]
(Data Center) (Data Center) (Data Center)
```

The sketch represents a region containing three availability zones, each as a physically seperate datacenter.

Why is this important?

- **High Availability:** By deploying across multiple AZs, you increase the availability of your application. If one AZ goes down, your application can continue to serve requests from other AZs.
- **Disaster Recovery:** Regions provide protection from large-scale disasters. If an entire Region becomes unavailable, you can failover your application to another Region (although this requires more planning and configuration).
- **Performance:** Choose the Region closest to your users to minimize latency. Use multiple AZs within that Region for resilience.

Example: Web Application

Let's say you have a web application running on EC2 instances and using a database.

1. You would deploy EC2 instances in multiple AZs within a Region.
2. You would configure a load balancer to distribute traffic across these instances. If an instance in one AZ becomes unavailable, the load balancer will automatically route traffic to instances in other AZs.
3. Your database would also be configured for high availability, with replicas in different AZs.

Code Example: AWS CLI (Illustrative)

This is conceptual; creating a true multi-AZ setup involves more steps within AWS services. This shows the *idea* of deploying in two AZs.

```
# Launch an EC2 instance in Availability Zone us-east-1a
aws ec2 run-instances --image-id ami-xxxxxxxx --instance-type t2.micro --subnet-id subnet-12345€

# Launch another EC2 instance in Availability Zone us-east-1b
aws ec2 run-instances --image-id ami-xxxxxxxx --instance-type t2.micro --subnet-id subnet-0fedcl
```

This example creates EC2 instances in separate availability zones. Actual production implementations would employ automation (like CloudFormation or Terraform) and likely be fronted by a load balancer.

In summary, understanding Regions and Availability Zones is fundamental to designing resilient, scalable, and globally accessible applications on AWS. They allow you to build systems that can withstand failures and provide a consistent experience to your users, wherever they are.

Compute Services (EC2, Lambda)

This section explores two fundamental compute services offered by AWS: Elastic Compute Cloud (EC2) and Lambda. Understanding the strengths of each service allows you to choose the most appropriate compute resource for your specific workload needs.

Choosing appropriate compute based on workload characteristics (e.g., EC2 for persistent workloads, Lambda for event-driven functions).

The primary decision point between EC2 and Lambda revolves around the nature of your workload. Ask yourself these questions: Does my application need to run continuously? Is it triggered by events?

- **EC2: Virtual Servers for Persistent Workloads**

  Amazon EC2 provides virtual servers in the cloud. Think of it as renting a computer in AWS's data center. You have full control over the operating system, installed software, networking, and security settings.

  Use Cases: EC2 is well-suited for applications that require a persistent operating environment, such as:

  - Web servers: Hosting websites and web applications.
  - Databases: Running relational and NoSQL databases.
  - Application servers: Hosting business logic and APIs.
  - Long-running processes: Handling batch processing, media encoding, or scientific simulations.

  Analogy: Imagine you're opening a restaurant. EC2 is like renting a building. You're responsible for everything inside – setting up the kitchen (OS), hiring staff (installing software), and managing the utilities (networking). You have complete control, but also complete responsibility.

  Code Example: Creating an EC2 instance using AWS CLI:

  ```
  aws ec2 run-instances \
    --image-id ami-xxxxxxxxxxxxx \
    --instance-type t2.micro \
    --key-name my-key-pair \
    --security-group-ids sg-xxxxxxxxxxxxx
  ```

  In this command:

  - `ami-xxxxxxxxxxxxx` is the Amazon Machine Image (AMI) ID, specifying the operating system.
  - `t2.micro` is the instance type, defining the CPU and memory.
  - `my-key-pair` is the SSH key pair for accessing the instance.
  - `sg-xxxxxxxxxxxxx` is the security group ID, controlling network traffic.

Sketch:

```
+----------------+        Internet        +----------------+
|  Your Computer |<------------------->|  EC2 Instance  |
+----------------+                        +----------------+
                                          | OS, Apps, Data|
                                          +----------------+
```

This sketch visually shows the interaction between your computer and the EC2 instance, emphasizing your direct access and control over the instance's internal components.

- **Lambda: Serverless Functions for Event-Driven Workloads**

  AWS Lambda is a serverless compute service. "Serverless" doesn't mean there are no servers; it means you don't manage them. You simply upload your code, and Lambda automatically runs it in response to events.

  Use Cases: Lambda shines in event-driven scenarios, such as:

  - Image and video processing: Automatically resizing images uploaded to S3.
  - Data transformation: Processing data streams from Kinesis or IoT devices.
  - Chatbots: Responding to user messages in real-time.
  - API backends: Creating REST APIs without managing servers.
  - Scheduled tasks: Running cron jobs without provisioning servers.

  Analogy: Imagine a vending machine. You don't care about the inner workings of the machine; you just insert money (trigger an event) and get your product (the function executes). AWS handles the maintenance and scaling of the machine.

  Code Example: A simple Python Lambda function that logs an event:

```
import json

def lambda_handler(event, context):
    print("Received event: " + json.dumps(event, indent=2))
    return {
        'statusCode': 200,
        'body': json.dumps('Hello from Lambda!')
    }
```

This function takes an `event` object (containing the data that triggered the function) and a `context` object (providing information about the invocation, function, and execution environment). It logs the event and returns a simple greeting.

Sketch:

```
+----------+     Event      +----------+     Response     +----------+
|  Event   |------------->| Lambda   |--------------->| Service  |
| Source(S3,|              |Function  |                | Database,|
| API, etc) |              |          |                |  etc     |
+----------+              +----------+                +----------+
                              |
                              | (No server management)
                              V
                      AWS Managed Infrastructure
```

This sketch illustrates how Lambda sits between an event source (like S3) and a target service (like a database), highlighting that Lambda handles the execution without requiring you to manage the underlying server infrastructure.

In summary, choose EC2 when you need full control over the operating environment and persistent workloads. Choose Lambda when you want to focus solely on code execution in event-driven scenarios, leveraging AWS to manage the underlying infrastructure.

Storage Solutions (S3, EBS, EFS)

When building systems on AWS, choosing the correct storage solution is critical. AWS offers various storage options, each suited for specific needs. Here, we'll explore three core services: S3 (Simple Storage Service), EBS (Elastic Block Storage), and EFS (Elastic File System).

Selecting the right storage option based on data access patterns, durability, and performance requirements.

Choosing the right storage option depends on how you plan to access your data, how durable it needs to be, and the performance levels you require. Let's delve into each service.

S3 (Simple Storage Service):

S3 is object storage. Think of it as a vast, highly durable, and scalable repository for files of any type. It is designed for internet-scale storage and retrieval of data.

- **Data Access Patterns:** You access S3 objects using a key (like a filename) via HTTP/HTTPS. This makes it ideal for storing static content (images, videos, documents), backups, log files, and data for analysis.

- **Durability:** S3 is designed for 99.999999999% (eleven 9's) of data durability. This means that data loss is extremely unlikely. AWS achieves this by storing data redundantly across multiple devices and facilities.

- **Performance Requirements:** S3 offers excellent performance for many use cases. It is optimized for retrieving data quickly and handling large numbers of requests. However, it's not designed for the kind of low-latency, high-IOPS performance you might need for a database's primary storage.

- **Example Use Case:** Storing images for a website. When a user requests an image, the web server fetches it from S3 and displays it. S3 handles the scaling and availability, so you don't have to worry about managing storage infrastructure.

- **Code example (AWS CLI):**

```
# Upload a file to S3
aws s3 cp my_file.txt s3://my-bucket/path/to/my_file.txt

# Download a file from S3
aws s3 cp s3://my-bucket/path/to/my_file.txt my_local_file.txt
```

- **Sketch**

```
+-----------------+     HTTP/HTTPS     +-----------------+
| Web Application | ----------------->  |    S3 Bucket    |
+-----------------+                     +-----------------+
                                                 |
                                        | Objects (Images, Videos, etc.)
                                                 |
                                        +-----------------+
```

This sketch demonstrates a web application retrieving objects from an S3 bucket over HTTP/HTTPS.

EBS (Elastic Block Storage):

EBS provides block-level storage volumes for use with EC2 instances. Think of it as a virtual hard drive that you can attach to your EC2 server.

- **Data Access Patterns:** EBS volumes are attached directly to an EC2 instance and accessed like a physical hard drive. This makes them suitable for running operating systems, databases, and applications that require direct block-level access.

- **Durability:** EBS offers good durability, but it's not as durable as S3. It's important to take snapshots (backups) of your EBS volumes regularly to protect against data loss.

- **Performance Requirements:** EBS provides consistent and low-latency performance, making it suitable for applications that require high IOPS (Input/Output Operations Per Second) and low latency. AWS offers different EBS volume types (e.g., SSD, HDD) to optimize for specific performance characteristics.

- **Example Use Case:** Running a relational database like MySQL or PostgreSQL. The database stores its data files on an EBS volume, providing the performance and persistence it needs.

- **Code example (AWS CLI):**

```
# Create an EBS volume
aws ec2 create-volume --availability-zone us-east-1a --size 100 --volume-type gp2

# Attach the volume to an EC2 instance
aws ec2 attach-volume --volume-id vol-xxxxxxxx --instance-id i-xxxxxxxx --device /dev/sdf
```

- **Sketch**

This sketch illustrates an EBS volume attached to an EC2 instance, providing block-level storage.

EFS (Elastic File System):

EFS provides a scalable, elastic, and fully managed network file system for use with AWS cloud services and on-premises resources. It allows multiple EC2 instances to simultaneously access a shared file system.

- **Data Access Patterns:** EFS is accessed using standard file system protocols (e.g., NFS). This allows you to mount the EFS file system on multiple EC2 instances and access files as if they were on a local network drive.

- **Durability:** EFS is designed for high durability, replicating data across multiple Availability Zones.

- **Performance Requirements:** EFS provides good performance for a wide range of workloads, including content management systems, web serving, application development, and media processing.

- **Example Use Case:** A web application that needs to share files between multiple web servers. The web servers can mount the EFS file system and access the shared files.

- **Code example (AWS CLI):**

```
# Create an EFS file system
aws efs create-file-system --creation-token my-efs-volume

# Create a mount target
aws efs create-mount-target --file-system-id fs-xxxxxxxx --subnet-id subnet-xxxxxxxx --secu
```

- **Sketch**

This sketch shows multiple EC2 instances mounting an EFS file system, allowing them to share files.

By understanding the characteristics of S3, EBS, and EFS, you can choose the optimal storage solution for your specific needs on AWS. Consider data access patterns, durability needs, and performance requirements to make the best choice.

Networking (VPC, Route 53)

This section explores how networking works on AWS, focusing on two key services: Virtual Private Cloud (VPC) and Route 53. These services are fundamental for building secure, scalable, and reliable applications in the cloud.

Configuring Virtual Private Clouds (VPCs) for secure and scalable network infrastructure.

A Virtual Private Cloud (VPC) allows you to create a logically isolated section of the AWS cloud where you can launch AWS resources in a virtual network that you define. Think of it as your own private data center, but running on AWS infrastructure. You have complete control over your virtual networking environment, including selecting your own IP address ranges, creating subnets, and configuring route tables and network gateways.

VPC Core Components

- **CIDR Block:** When you create a VPC, you must specify a range of IPv4 addresses for the VPC in the form of a Classless Inter-Domain Routing (CIDR) block, for example, `10.0.0.0/16`. This defines the overall IP address space for your VPC. The `/16` specifies the size of your network, allowing for a large number of IP addresses within the `10.0.0.0` range.

- **Subnets:** Subnets are subdivisions of your VPC. Each subnet resides within a single Availability Zone. You can create public subnets (where resources can directly access the internet) and private subnets (where resources don't have direct internet access, offering enhanced security). Each subnet also has a CIDR block, which must be a subset of the VPC's CIDR block, for example, `10.0.1.0/24`.

- **Route Tables:** Route tables contain a set of rules, called routes, that are used to determine where network traffic is directed. Each subnet must be associated with a route table. A route table typically contains routes for local traffic within the VPC and routes for traffic destined for the internet.

- **Internet Gateway:** An internet gateway allows instances in your public subnets to connect to the internet. It's a horizontally scaled, redundant, and highly available VPC component. You attach an internet gateway to your VPC and then add a route to your public subnet's route table that directs traffic to the internet gateway.

- **Network Address Translation (NAT) Gateway/Instance:** NAT gateways (AWS-managed) or NAT instances (self-managed) allow instances in your private subnets to initiate outbound traffic to the internet or other AWS services but prevent the internet from initiating a connection with those instances. This is crucial for allowing instances to download updates or access other services without exposing them directly to the internet.

- **Security Groups:** Security groups act as virtual firewalls for your instances. They control inbound and outbound traffic at the instance level. You define rules to specify which traffic is allowed to enter or leave your instance based on port numbers, protocols, and source/destination IP addresses. Security Groups operate at EC2 Instance level

- **Network ACLs (Access Control Lists):** Network ACLs act as virtual firewalls for your subnets. They control inbound and outbound traffic at the subnet level. You define rules to specify which traffic is allowed to enter or leave your subnet based on port numbers, protocols, and source/destination IP addresses.Network ACLs operate at Subnet level.

Example: Setting up a Basic VPC

Let's outline how you would configure a simple VPC with a public and private subnet using the AWS CLI (Command Line Interface).

First, create the VPC.

```
aws ec2 create-vpc --cidr-block 10.0.0.0/16
```

This command returns information about the newly created VPC, including its VPC ID. Note this ID (e.g., `vpc-0abcdef1234567890`).

Next, create an internet gateway and attach it to your VPC.

```
aws ec2 create-internet-gateway
aws ec2 attach-internet-gateway --vpc-id vpc-0abcdef1234567890 --internet-gateway-id igw-0fedcba
```

Note the Internet Gateway ID as well (e.g. `igw-0fedcba9876543210`).

Now, create a public subnet.

```
aws ec2 create-subnet --vpc-id vpc-0abcdef1234567890 --cidr-block 10.0.1.0/24 --availability-zor
```

This command returns the subnet ID (e.g., `subnet-0123456789abcdef0`).

Create a route table for the public subnet and add a route to the internet gateway.

```
aws ec2 create-route-table --vpc-id vpc-0abcdef1234567890
aws ec2 create-route --route-table-id rtb-0987654321fedcba0 --destination-cidr-block 0.0.0.0/0 ·
aws ec2 associate-route-table --subnet-id subnet-0123456789abcdef0 --route-table-id rtb-0987654:
```

Finally, create a private subnet.

```
aws ec2 create-subnet --vpc-id vpc-0abcdef1234567890 --cidr-block 10.0.2.0/24 --availability-zor
```

This creates a basic VPC setup. You'd then configure NAT gateway/instances for the private subnet and security groups for your instances.

Route 53: Configuring DNS routing for secure and scalable network infrastructure.

Route 53 is Amazon's scalable and highly available Domain Name System (DNS) web service. It translates human-readable domain names (like `www.example.com`) into IP addresses that computers use to connect to each other. Route 53 is essential for directing users to your applications, managing traffic, and improving application availability.

Route 53 Core Functionalities

- **Domain Registration:** You can register domain names directly through Route 53.

- **DNS Routing:** Route 53 uses DNS records to route traffic to your resources. Common record types include:

    - **A Records:** Map a domain name to an IPv4 address.
    - **AAAA Records:** Map a domain name to an IPv6 address.
    - **CNAME Records:** Create an alias from one domain name to another domain name. For example, `www.example.com` could be a CNAME to `example.com`.

- **Alias Records:** Similar to CNAME records but specifically used to map a domain name to AWS resources (e.g., an Elastic Load Balancer, an S3 bucket configured for website hosting). Alias records offer performance benefits and are integrated with AWS health checks.

- **Health Checks:** Route 53 can monitor the health of your resources (e.g., web servers, load balancers) and automatically route traffic away from unhealthy resources.

- **Traffic Flow Policies:** Traffic flow policies allow you to implement sophisticated routing strategies based on geography, latency, health, and other factors. For example, you can route users to the closest AWS region to minimize latency or implement failover routing in case of a regional outage.

Example: Routing Traffic to an Elastic Load Balancer (ELB)

Assume you have an Elastic Load Balancer (ELB) distributing traffic to your web servers. You want to configure Route 53 to point your domain name (`www.example.com`) to this ELB.

1. **Create a Hosted Zone:** A hosted zone is a container for all the DNS records for a specific domain. You would create a hosted zone for `example.com` in Route 53.

2. **Create an Alias Record:** In your hosted zone, create an `A` record (or `AAAA` record if you are using IPv6) for `www.example.com`. Instead of specifying an IP address, you would select "Alias" as the record type and then choose your ELB from the list of available AWS resources. Route 53 automatically retrieves the ELB's DNS name and uses it to resolve requests.

3. **Configure Health Checks (Optional):** You can associate a health check with your alias record. Route 53 will monitor the health of the ELB (and, indirectly, the web servers behind the ELB). If the ELB becomes unhealthy, Route 53 will automatically stop routing traffic to it, improving application availability.

Traffic Flow Example: Geolocation Routing

Let's say you have your application deployed in two AWS regions: `us-east-1` and `eu-west-1`. You want to route users to the region closest to them.

1. **Create a Traffic Flow Policy:** In Route 53, create a traffic flow policy.

2. **Define Geolocation Rules:** Add rules to the traffic flow policy that specify the following:

   - If the user is in North America, route traffic to the ELB in `us-east-1`.
   - If the user is in Europe, route traffic to the ELB in `eu-west-1`.
   - For all other locations, route traffic to the ELB in `us-east-1` (as a default).

3. **Associate the Policy with Your Hosted Zone:** Associate the traffic flow policy with your hosted zone for `example.com`.

Route 53 will now automatically route users to the appropriate region based on their location, improving performance and user experience.

Databases (RDS, DynamoDB)

This section explores database services on AWS, focusing on Relational Database Service (RDS) and DynamoDB. Choosing the right database is vital for any application, impacting scalability, data consistency, and overall performance.

Understanding relational (RDS) vs. NoSQL (DynamoDB) database options and their impact on scalability and data consistency.

RDS and DynamoDB represent fundamentally different approaches to data storage and retrieval. RDS offers traditional relational database management systems (RDBMS), while DynamoDB is a NoSQL database. Let's break down what this means in practical terms.

Relational Databases (RDS): Structured Data and Consistency

RDS allows you to run familiar database engines like MySQL, PostgreSQL, Oracle, SQL Server, and MariaDB. These databases are *relational* because they store data in tables with rows and columns, and relationships are defined between these tables using keys.

Think of it like a spreadsheet where each sheet is a table. One sheet might contain customer information (customer ID, name, address), and another might contain order information (order ID, customer ID, order date, total). The customer ID column allows you to link orders to specific customers.

Here's a simple example using SQL (the standard language for interacting with relational databases) to create a table for customers:

```sql
CREATE TABLE Customers (
    CustomerID INT PRIMARY KEY,
    FirstName VARCHAR(255),
    LastName VARCHAR(255),
    Email VARCHAR(255)
);

INSERT INTO Customers (CustomerID, FirstName, LastName, Email)
VALUES (1, 'John', 'Doe', 'john.doe@example.com');
```

This code creates a table called Customers with columns for customer ID, first name, last name, and email. The PRIMARY KEY constraint ensures that each customer has a unique ID. The INSERT statement adds a new customer record to the table.

- **Data Consistency:** Relational databases enforce strong data consistency through ACID properties (Atomicity, Consistency, Isolation, Durability). This means that transactions are reliable: either all changes within a transaction are applied, or none are, preventing data corruption.

- **Scalability (RDS):** RDS offers vertical scaling (increasing the resources of a single server) and horizontal scaling (using read replicas to offload read traffic). However, scaling writes can become complex and might require techniques like sharding (partitioning the database across multiple servers).

- **Use Cases:** RDS is well-suited for applications that require complex transactions, reporting, and strong data consistency, such as e-commerce platforms, financial systems, and content management systems.

- **Sketches:**

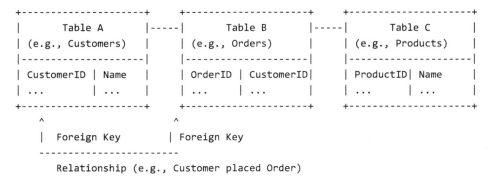

```
+---------------------+        +---------------------+        +---------------------+
|      Table A        |-----|  |      Table B        |-----|  |      Table C        |
| (e.g., Customers)   |      |  | (e.g., Orders)      |      |  | (e.g., Products)    |
|---------------------|      |  |---------------------|      |  |---------------------|
| CustomerID | Name   |      |  | OrderID | CustomerID|      |  | ProductID| Name     |
| ...        | ...    |      |  | ...     | ...       |      |  | ...      | ...      |
+---------------------+        +---------------------+        +---------------------+
       ^                              ^
       | Foreign Key                  | Foreign Key
       ------------------------------
          Relationship (e.g., Customer placed Order)
```

NoSQL Databases (DynamoDB): Flexible Data Models and Scalability

DynamoDB is a NoSQL database service that offers high performance and scalability. Unlike relational databases, DynamoDB uses a flexible schema, allowing you to store data in various formats (key-value, document, graph, etc.). DynamoDB is a key-value and document database. This mean each item in database is like dictionary, with a primary key and a set of attributes.

- **Example:** imagine you are storing user profile.
  - *key*: User ID (e.g., "user123")
  - *value*: A document containing user details (name, email, address, preferences).
  - You could have different users with different attributes without changing schema of database.

Here's an example of how you might store a user profile in DynamoDB (represented in JSON):

```
{
    "UserID": "user123",
    "FirstName": "Jane",
    "LastName": "Smith",
    "Email": "jane.smith@example.com",
    "Preferences": {
        "Theme": "Dark",
        "Notifications": true
    }
}
```

This JSON document represents a user profile with various attributes. Notice that there's a nested "Preferences" object, demonstrating the flexibility of the schema.

- **Scalability (DynamoDB):** DynamoDB is designed for massive scalability. It automatically partitions your data across multiple servers and handles replication, providing high availability and fault tolerance. You can scale up or down as needed without significant downtime. DynamoDB scales horizontally, which mean you can easily add more server to handle increasing amount of data and traffic.

- **Data Consistency:** DynamoDB offers tunable consistency. You can choose between eventual consistency (reads might not reflect the most recent writes immediately, but will eventually catch up) or strong consistency (reads always reflect the most recent writes). Eventual consistency provides higher performance and availability, while strong consistency is important for applications that require immediate data accuracy.

- **Use Cases:** DynamoDB is suitable for applications that require high read/write throughput, low latency, and the ability to handle large volumes of unstructured data, such as gaming platforms, mobile applications, and IoT devices.

- **Sketch:**

```
+------------------------------------------------------------------+
|                         DynamoDB Table                           |
+------------------------------------------------------------------+
| Item 1: { "UserID": "user1", "Name": "Alice", "Points": 100 }  |
|------------------------------------------------------------------|
| Item 2: { "UserID": "user2", "Name": "Bob", "Level": "Expert" }  |
|------------------------------------------------------------------|
| Item 3: { "ProductID": "prod1", "Desc": "Awesome thing" }        |
+------------------------------------------------------------------+
```

Choosing Between RDS and DynamoDB

The choice between RDS and DynamoDB depends on your application's specific requirements:

- **Choose RDS if:**

  - You need strong data consistency and ACID properties.
  - Your data is highly structured and relational.
  - You require complex queries and transactions.
  - You have experience with relational database management systems.

- **Choose DynamoDB if:**

    - You need massive scalability and high availability.
    - Your data is semi-structured or unstructured.
    - You require low-latency access to data.
    - You need a flexible schema that can evolve over time.

- **Trade-offs:** RDS offers strong consistency and familiar querying but can be more complex to scale for very large datasets. DynamoDB provides excellent scalability and flexibility, but requires careful consideration of data modeling and might sacrifice immediate consistency for performance.

By understanding the strengths and weaknesses of each database service, you can make an informed decision that aligns with your application's needs and optimizes its performance and scalability on AWS.

Chapter 3 Foundations of System Design on AWS-Key Principles of Scalable and Resilient Architectures

- **Scalability:**
    - Horizontal Scaling: Add more instances.
    - Vertical Scaling: Upgrade existing instances.
- **Resiliency:**
    - Fault Tolerance: Design for failure.
    - High Availability: Minimize downtime.
- **Loose Coupling:**
    - Independent Services: Reduce dependencies.
- **Automation:**
    - Infrastructure as Code: Automate deployments.
- **Security:**
    - Principle of Least Privilege: Grant minimal permissions.

Scalability

Scalability refers to the ability of a system, application, or infrastructure to handle a growing amount of work. It is a crucial aspect of system design, ensuring that as demand increases, performance doesn't degrade unacceptably. There are two primary approaches to achieving scalability: horizontal scaling and vertical scaling.

Horizontal Scaling: Add More Instances

Horizontal scaling, also known as scaling out, involves increasing capacity by adding more instances of the application or system. Instead of making a single system more powerful, you distribute the workload across multiple, smaller systems.

Concept: Think of a restaurant. If more customers arrive than the kitchen can handle, you don't necessarily buy a bigger, more expensive oven (vertical scaling). Instead, you might add another identical oven and hire more cooks (horizontal scaling).

Practical Implications:

- **Increased Capacity:** By adding more instances, the system can handle a larger number of requests concurrently.
- **Improved Availability:** If one instance fails, the other instances can continue to serve requests, minimizing downtime.
- **Cost-Effectiveness:** Often, adding smaller, commodity hardware can be more cost-effective than purchasing a single, very powerful machine.

Example:

Imagine a web application that is struggling to handle the increasing number of users. Instead of upgrading the existing server, you can deploy the application on multiple servers, each running the same code. A load balancer distributes incoming requests across these servers.

```
[User] --> [Load Balancer] --> [Server 1]
                           --> [Server 2]
                           --> [Server 3]
                           ...
```

In this scenario, as the number of users grows, you can simply add more servers to the pool behind the load balancer.

Code Example:

While horizontal scaling isn't directly implemented in code, code can be designed to be *stateless* to facilitate horizontal scaling. Stateless applications don't store any session-specific data on the server itself. This allows any instance to handle any request, simplifying the process of adding or removing servers. Here's a simplified example in Python using Flask, demonstrating a stateless approach:

```python
from flask import Flask, request

app = Flask(__name__)

@app.route('/calculate')
def calculate():
    num1 = request.args.get('num1', type=int)
    num2 = request.args.get('num2', type=int)

    if num1 is None or num2 is None:
        return "Error: Both num1 and num2 are required.", 400

    result = num1 + num2  # Simple calculation

    return f"The result is: {result}"

if __name__ == '__main__':
    app.run(debug=True, host='0.0.0.0', port=5000)
```

In this example, the `/calculate` endpoint receives two numbers as query parameters, performs a simple addition, and returns the result. It doesn't store any information about the user or the calculation itself, making it stateless and suitable for horizontal scaling. You could deploy this application across multiple servers and use a load balancer to distribute requests.

Vertical Scaling: Upgrade Existing Instances

Vertical scaling, also known as scaling up, involves increasing the resources of a single instance. This means upgrading the hardware (CPU, memory, storage) of the existing server to handle a larger workload.

Concept: Continuing with the restaurant analogy, vertical scaling would be like replacing your existing oven with a bigger, faster, more expensive oven.

Practical Implications:

- **Simplicity:** Vertical scaling is often simpler to implement initially than horizontal scaling. It doesn't require significant changes to the application architecture.
- **Performance Improvement:** Upgrading hardware can lead to immediate performance gains.
- **Limitations:** Vertical scaling has inherent limits. There is a maximum size to which you can scale a single machine.

Example:

Consider a database server that is struggling to handle the number of queries. To scale vertically, you would upgrade the server's CPU, add more RAM, or switch to faster storage devices (e.g., SSDs).

Code Example:

Vertical scaling does not directly involve changes to the application code itself. It is a hardware-level upgrade. However, code might be tuned to take advantage of the increased resources *after* a vertical scaling operation. For instance, database connection pools might be increased, or JVM heap sizes might be adjusted to utilize the added memory. No code example is needed to explain vertical Scaling, as vertical scaling is completely a hardware-level upgrade.

Horizontal Scaling

Horizontal scaling refers to the practice of increasing the capacity of a system by adding more instances of a resource, rather than upgrading the existing ones. Think of it like this: instead of making your single worker stronger (vertical scaling), you hire more workers who can all do the same job (horizontal scaling). This approach is often favored in distributed systems and cloud environments because it provides better resilience and cost-effectiveness.

Adding More Instances:

The core concept of horizontal scaling is adding more identical or similar instances to handle increased workload. These instances can be servers, virtual machines, containers, or any other computational resource. The key is that each new instance contributes to the overall processing power of the system.

For example, consider a web application running on a single server. As traffic increases, the server becomes overloaded, leading to slow response times or even failures. With horizontal scaling, you would add more servers, each running a copy of the web application. A load balancer would then distribute incoming requests across these servers, effectively sharing the load and improving performance.

```
Client --> Load Balancer --> Server 1 (Web App)
                         --> Server 2 (Web App)
                         --> Server 3 (Web App)
```

In this simple sketch, the load balancer acts as a traffic cop, directing client requests to available servers. If one server fails, the others can continue to handle the load, ensuring high availability.

Practical Example: Scaling a Database

Horizontal scaling also applies to databases. Sharding is a common technique where you divide a database into smaller, more manageable pieces (shards) and distribute them across multiple database servers. Each shard contains a subset of the data, and queries are routed to the appropriate shard based on the data being accessed.

Imagine a large e-commerce platform with millions of users and products. Storing all the data on a single database server would eventually lead to performance bottlenecks. By sharding the database, you can distribute the data across multiple servers, each handling a smaller portion of the overall load.

```
Client -->  Database Router  --> Database Server 1 (Shard 1)
                                    (Users A-G)
                               --> Database Server 2 (Shard 2)
                                    (Users H-N)
                               --> Database Server 3 (Shard 3)
                                    (Users O-Z)
```

The database router determines which shard contains the requested data and routes the query accordingly. This allows the system to handle a much larger volume of data and requests than a single server could handle.

Code Example: Scaling Web Applications with Containers

Containerization technologies like Docker and orchestration platforms like Kubernetes make horizontal scaling much easier. Here's a simplified example using Docker and a hypothetical scenario:

Suppose you have a simple Python web application that processes image uploads. You can package this application into a Docker container.

```python
# app.py
from flask import Flask, request
import time

app = Flask(__name__)

@app.route('/upload', methods=['POST'])
def upload_image():
    # Simulate image processing
    time.sleep(2)
    return "Image processed successfully!"

if __name__ == '__main__':
    app.run(debug=True, host='0.0.0.0')
```

You can then define a Dockerfile to build the container image:

```
# Dockerfile
FROM python:3.9-slim-buster
WORKDIR /app
COPY . .
RUN pip install flask
CMD ["python", "app.py"]
```

Using Docker Compose (or Kubernetes), you can easily scale the number of container instances:

```yaml
# docker-compose.yml
version: "3.9"
services:
  web:
    build: .
    ports:
```

```
      - "5000:5000"
    replicas: 3   # Start three instances
```

By adjusting the `replicas` value, you can easily increase or decrease the number of running instances of your web application, effectively scaling it horizontally. A load balancer (e.g., Nginx) can be placed in front of these containers to distribute traffic evenly.

```
Client --> Load Balancer (Nginx) --> Container 1 (Web App)
                              --> Container 2 (Web App)
                              --> Container 3 (Web App)
```

This containerized approach streamlines the process of adding and removing instances, making horizontal scaling a more manageable and efficient strategy.

Vertical Scaling

Vertical scaling involves enhancing the capabilities of a single instance or machine. Instead of adding more machines (horizontal scaling), you upgrade the existing one. This typically means increasing resources like CPU, memory (RAM), or storage. Think of it as upgrading your computer instead of buying a whole new computer.

Upgrading Existing Instances:

The core idea of vertical scaling is to improve the capacity of your current server or virtual machine. This allows it to handle increased workload without adding complexity associated with managing multiple instances.

Let's say you have a web server struggling to handle user traffic. The server might be running slow or crashing due to insufficient memory.

Before Upgrade:

- **CPU:** 2 Cores
- **Memory:** 4 GB RAM
- **Storage:** 100 GB SSD

You observe that the CPU is constantly at 100% utilization, and the memory usage is also very high. This indicates that the server is bottlenecked by its resources. To address this, you decide to vertically scale the server:

After Upgrade:

- **CPU:** 8 Cores
- **Memory:** 32 GB RAM
- **Storage:** 500 GB SSD

By upgrading the CPU and RAM, the server can now handle significantly more traffic without performance degradation.

Consider a database server running a critical application. During peak hours, queries become slow, and the database server is unable to keep up with the load.

Before Upgrade:

- **Database Size:** 50 GB
- **Read Operations/Second:** 500
- **Write Operations/Second:** 100

After Upgrade:

- **Database Size:** 50 GB
- **Read Operations/Second:** 2000
- **Write Operations/Second:** 500

You observe that the disk I/O is a bottleneck, causing slow query performance. Upgrading to faster storage (e.g., from SSD to NVMe) can significantly improve database performance.

Consider the following (pseudo) code:

```
// Before scaling (hypothetical)
function processRequest(request) {
  // Process data (CPU intensive)
  data = processData(request.data);

  // Store data in database (Memory/IO intensive)
  storeData(data);

  return response;
}

// After scaling (more CPU, memory, faster I/O)
function processRequest(request) {
  // Process data (faster CPU)
  data = processData(request.data);

  // Store data in database (faster memory/IO)
  storeData(data);

  return response;
}
```

The code itself doesn't change, but the underlying hardware improvements (vertical scaling) make the execution significantly faster. The processData function benefits from the increased CPU power, and the storeData function benefits from faster memory and disk I/O.

Sketch:

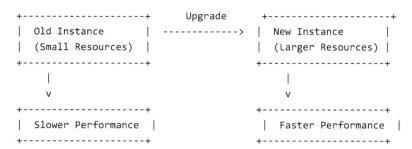

In summary, vertical scaling is about making your existing server bigger and stronger. This can be a cost-effective and straightforward way to improve performance, especially when the bottleneck is clearly identified as a lack of resources on a single instance.

Resiliency

Resiliency refers to a system's ability to recover quickly and effectively from difficulties. In other words, it's about making sure your application continues to function, even when things go wrong. This section will delve into the crucial aspects of building resilient systems: Fault Tolerance and High Availability.

Fault Tolerance: Design for Failure

Fault Tolerance is a design principle that accepts the reality of failure. It's about proactively building your system to withstand failures without complete disruption. Instead of hoping nothing will ever break, fault tolerance assumes that components *will* fail and prepares for those scenarios. The goal is to continue operating, perhaps at a reduced capacity, while the failure is addressed.

Think of it like a car with a spare tire. If one tire goes flat, you don't stop driving entirely. You switch to the spare and continue your journey, albeit with some limitations until the flat tire is repaired.

Example:

Consider an e-commerce website handling customer orders. If one server responsible for processing payments fails, a fault-tolerant design would automatically redirect new orders to a backup server. Customers might experience a slight delay, but the website remains operational, and orders continue to be processed.

Code Illustration (Conceptual):

While a complete fault-tolerant system requires significant infrastructure and code, here's a simplified conceptual illustration of a retry mechanism in Python:

```python
import time
import random

def process_order(order_id):
    """Simulates processing an order; might fail."""
    #simulate chance of failure
    if random.random() < 0.3:
        raise Exception("Order processing failed!")
    print(f"Order {order_id} processed successfully.")
    return True

def retry_order(order_id, max_retries=3):
    """Retries processing an order if it fails."""
    for attempt in range(max_retries):
        try:
            result = process_order(order_id)
            return result # Order processed successfully
        except Exception as e:
            print(f"Attempt {attempt + 1} failed: {e}")
            time.sleep(2) # Wait before retrying
    print(f"Order {order_id} failed after {max_retries} attempts.")
    return False # Order processing failed

# Example usage:
order_id = "ORD-12345"
retry_order(order_id)
```

In this example, the `retry_order` function attempts to process an order multiple times if it initially fails. This simple retry mechanism is a basic form of fault tolerance. More sophisticated systems use techniques like circuit breakers, bulkheads, and replication to handle failures gracefully.

Sketch:

Imagine three identical servers (A, B, and C) behind a load balancer.

```
+----------+    +----------+    +----------+
| Server A |    | Server B |    | Server C |
+----------+    +----------+    +----------+
```

```
        ^             ^              ^
        |             |              |
    +-----------------------+
            Load Balancer
    +-----------------------+
            Client Requests
```

If Server A fails, the load balancer automatically stops sending traffic to it, distributing the load between the remaining servers (B and C). The system continues to function, although with reduced capacity.

High Availability: Minimize Downtime

High Availability (HA) is closely related to fault tolerance but focuses specifically on minimizing downtime. It ensures that services are consistently available, even when failures occur. The key metric for HA is uptime, often expressed as a percentage (e.g., 99.99% uptime). HA systems are designed to quickly recover from failures, often automatically, so that users experience minimal disruption.

While fault tolerance is a design principle, high availability is often the *outcome* of implementing fault-tolerant strategies. It represents the observable characteristic of the system being consistently available.

Example:

Consider a database server powering a critical application. A high-availability configuration might involve setting up a primary database server with one or more standby (replica) servers. If the primary server fails, the system automatically switches to a standby server, ensuring continued database access with minimal interruption. This failover process is typically automated to minimize downtime.

Code Illustration (Conceptual):

This example shows how to check the status of a service and switch to a backup if it's unavailable. Note: This is conceptual and requires a real monitoring system for accuracy.

```python
import time

def check_service_status(service_url):
    """Simulates checking the status of a service."""
    # In a real system, you'd use HTTP requests or other methods
    # to actually check the service's health.
    # This example just returns True or False randomly
    # to simulate the service being up or down.

    import random
    return random.random() > 0.2 # Simulate 80% chance service is up

def switch_to_backup(backup_url):
    """Simulates switching to a backup service."""
    print(f"Switching to backup service at {backup_url}")
    # In a real system, this would involve updating DNS records,
    # load balancer configurations, or other infrastructure changes.
    return True # Simulate successful switchover

primary_service_url = "https://primary.example.com"
backup_service_url = "https://backup.example.com"

while True:
    if check_service_status(primary_service_url):
```

```
      print(f"Primary service at {primary_service_url} is healthy.")
  else:
      print(f"Primary service at {primary_service_url} is down!")
      if switch_to_backup(backup_service_url):
        print("Successfully switched to backup service.")
      else:
        print("Failed to switch to backup service.  Manual intervention required!")
  time.sleep(10) # Check service status every 10 seconds
```

In this conceptual example, the script continuously monitors the primary service. If the check shows that the primary is down, it attempts to switch to a pre-configured backup service. In real-world systems, such failover mechanisms are far more sophisticated and automated.

Sketch:

Consider two identical database servers: a Primary server and a Standby server. Data is continuously replicated from the Primary to the Standby. A monitoring system constantly checks the health of the Primary.

```
+-------------+           +-------------+
|   Primary   |------->|   Standby   |
|  Database   |Replicates|  Database   |
+-------------+           +-------------+
    ^
    | Health Check
    |
+-------------+
|   Monitor   |
+-------------+
```

If the Monitor detects that the Primary server has failed, it automatically promotes the Standby server to become the new Primary, ensuring continuous database service. DNS records or load balancer configurations are updated to point to the new Primary server.

In summary, Resiliency is not just about avoiding failure; it's about planning for it and minimizing its impact. Fault Tolerance involves designing systems that can withstand failures, while High Availability focuses on minimizing downtime and ensuring continuous service availability. Both are critical components of building robust and dependable applications.

Fault Tolerance: Design for Failure

Fault tolerance is a critical aspect of resilient system design. It's about engineering systems to continue operating correctly even when one or more of their components fail. Instead of simply hoping that nothing will break, fault tolerance accepts that failures are inevitable and designs around them. This involves building in redundancies and mechanisms that allow the system to automatically recover from errors.

Consider this simple analogy: imagine a car with only one tire on each axle. If one tire blows, the car is completely disabled. Now, imagine a car with two tires on each axle (like some heavy-duty vehicles). If one tire blows, the other tire on that axle can still support the car, allowing the driver to safely pull over and address the issue. This is a rudimentary example of redundancy and how it contributes to fault tolerance.

In software systems, fault tolerance can manifest in various ways. Let's explore some common approaches with more detail:

1. Redundancy:

The fundamental concept behind fault tolerance is redundancy. This means having duplicate components, systems, or data. If one component fails, another can take over. There are different ways to implement redundancy:

- **Active Redundancy (Hot Standby):** In this approach, multiple identical components are running simultaneously. One is designated as the "primary," handling all requests, while the others are in a "standby" mode, mirroring the primary's data and state. If the primary fails, one of the standby components immediately takes over, ensuring seamless operation. This minimizes downtime but requires resources to run duplicate instances. *Consider a payment processing system with active redundancy.* The main server handles transactions while a duplicate server runs concurrently. The duplicate server constantly mirrors the main server's data. If the main server fails, the duplicate server instantly becomes the primary, ensuring uninterrupted payment processing.

```
# Example (Conceptual - illustrates the idea, not a fully functional system)

class PaymentProcessor:
    def process_payment(self, amount, card_details):
        # Simulate processing logic (in real life, this would involve database updates, etc.)
        print(f"Processing payment of ${amount}...")
        # Simulate occasional failure
        import random
        if random.random() < 0.1:  # 10% chance of failure
            raise Exception("Simulated Payment Processing Error")
        print("Payment successful!")

class FaultTolerantPaymentProcessor:
    def __init__(self, primary: PaymentProcessor, backup: PaymentProcessor):
        self.primary = primary
        self.backup = backup

    def process_payment(self, amount, card_details):
        try:
            self.primary.process_payment(amount, card_details)
        except Exception as e:
            print(f"Primary failed: {e}. Switching to backup.")
            self.backup.process_payment(amount, card_details)

# Usage
primary_processor = PaymentProcessor()
backup_processor = PaymentProcessor()
fault_tolerant_processor = FaultTolerantPaymentProcessor(primary_processor, backup_processor)

fault_tolerant_processor.process_payment(100, "1234-5678-9012-3456") # May fail, but the backup
```

- **Passive Redundancy (Cold Standby):** Here, the backup components are not actively running. They are kept offline and only activated when the primary fails. This approach saves resources because the backup is idle until needed. However, it introduces a delay during failover while the backup is activated and synchronized with the primary's state. *Consider a database server with passive redundancy.* The primary database server handles all read and write operations. A backup server is kept offline, with periodic backups taken from the primary. If the primary server fails, the backup server is brought online, and the latest backup is restored, minimizing data loss.

- **N+1 Redundancy:** In this scheme, you have 'N' components needed to handle the normal workload, plus one additional backup component. This provides a buffer for handling failures without sacrificing performance. *Consider a web server farm using N+1 redundancy.* If the web server farms needs 5 active server to handle the usual traffic, than one extra server will be in a standby mode to take over, if one of the five servers fail.

```
# Example (Conceptual - illustrates the idea, not a fully functional system)
```

```python
class WebServer:
    def process_request(self, request):
        print(f"Processing request: {request}")
        # Simulate occasional failure
        import random
        if random.random() < 0.05:  # 5% chance of failure
            raise Exception("Simulated Server Error")
        print("Request successful!")

# WebServer Pool with N+1 Redundancy
num_active_servers = 5
web_servers = [WebServer() for _ in range(num_active_servers + 1)] # N+1 servers

def handle_request(request):
    for server in web_servers[:num_active_servers]: # only use active servers
        try:
            server.process_request(request)
            return  # Request handled successfully
        except Exception as e:
            print(f"Server failed: {e}. Trying another server.")

    # If all active servers failed, try the backup server
    try:
        web_servers[-1].process_request(request)
        return
    except Exception as e:
        print(f"Backup server failed: {e}. Request failed.")

# Example Usage:
handle_request("Important request")
```

- **Geographic Redundancy:** Deploying the entire system in multiple geographically distinct locations. If one region experiences a disaster (power outage, natural disaster), the system can failover to another region, minimizing downtime. *Consider a critical financial application deployed in multiple data centers across the globe.* If one data center experiences an outage due to a hurricane, the application automatically fails over to another data center in a different region, maintaining service continuity for users worldwide.

2. Error Detection and Recovery:

Fault tolerance also encompasses mechanisms to detect errors and automatically recover from them. These mechanisms include:

- **Retry Mechanisms:** Automatically retry failed operations. This is effective for transient errors like network glitches or temporary service unavailability. Exponential backoff can be used to avoid overwhelming the failing service. *Consider an application that attempts to connect to a database.* If the initial connection attempt fails due to a temporary network issue, the application automatically retries the connection after a short delay. If the retry fails, it retries again with an increasing delay (exponential backoff) until the connection is successful or a maximum number of retries is reached.

```python
import time
import random

def connect_to_database():
    # Simulate database connection
    if random.random() < 0.2: # 20% chance of connection failure
```

```
        raise Exception("Failed to connect to database")
    print("Successfully connected to database")
    return True

def retry_with_backoff(max_retries=3):
    retries = 0
    delay = 1 # initial delay in seconds
    while retries < max_retries:
        try:
            connect_to_database()
            return True   # Success!
        except Exception as e:
            print(f"Attempt {retries + 1} failed: {e}")
            retries += 1
            time.sleep(delay)
            delay = 2  # Exponential backoff: double the delay for the next retry

    print("Max retries reached. Unable to connect to the database.")
    return False # Failure

retry_with_backoff()
```

- **Circuit Breakers:** Prevent repeated calls to a failing service. When a service fails repeatedly, the circuit breaker "opens," preventing further requests from reaching the service until it recovers. This avoids cascading failures and protects the failing service from being overwhelmed. *Consider a microservices architecture where one service is experiencing high latency.* A circuit breaker can be implemented to stop sending requests to that service once the error rate exceeds a certain threshold. This prevents other services from being affected by the slow service and allows the failing service to recover.

```
import time

class CircuitBreaker:
    def __init__(self, failure_threshold, recovery_timeout):
        self.failure_threshold = failure_threshold # number of failures before opening the circu
        self.recovery_timeout = recovery_timeout  # time in seconds to wait before attempting t(
        self.failure_count = 0
        self.state = "CLOSED"
        self.last_failure_time = None

    def call(self, func, args, kwargs):
        if self.state == "OPEN":
            if time.time() - self.last_failure_time > self.recovery_timeout:
                self.state = "HALF_OPEN" # attempt a trial call
            else:
                raise Exception("Circuit breaker is OPEN") # prevent further calls

        try:
            result = func(args, kwargs)
            self.reset() # success, reset the circuit
            return result
        except Exception as e:
            self.failure_count += 1
            self.last_failure_time = time.time()
```

```python
        if self.failure_count >= self.failure_threshold:
            self.state = "OPEN" # too many failures, open the circuit
            print("Circuit breaker OPEN")

        raise e # re-raise the exception

    def reset(self):
        self.failure_count = 0
        self.state = "CLOSED"
        print("Circuit breaker CLOSED")


# Example usage:
def unreliable_function():
    import random
    if random.random() < 0.5:  # 50% chance of failure
        raise Exception("Unreliable Function Failed")
    return "Function successful"

circuit_breaker = CircuitBreaker(failure_threshold=3, recovery_timeout=5)

for _ in range(10):
    try:
        result = circuit_breaker.call(unreliable_function)
        print(result)
    except Exception as e:
        print(f"Call failed: {e}")

    time.sleep(1)
```

- **Health Checks:** Periodically monitor the health of components. This allows for early detection of problems and proactive intervention before a failure occurs. *Consider a load balancer that distributes traffic across multiple web servers.* The load balancer performs health checks on each server by sending periodic requests. If a server fails the health check, the load balancer stops sending traffic to that server until it recovers.

3. Idempotency:

An operation is idempotent if it can be executed multiple times without changing the outcome beyond the initial application. This is crucial for fault tolerance because if an operation fails midway, it can be safely retried without causing unintended side effects.

Consider a function designed to increment a value in a database. A non-idempotent function might simply add 1 to the current value each time it's called. If the function fails after adding 1 but before confirming the update, retrying it would add 1 again, resulting in an incorrect value. *An idempotent function instead can be designed to set the value to its actual incremented value without adding.* The idempotent function can be designed that way: UPDATE table SET value = new_value WHERE id = X. So, if it executes several times, it's the same result.

```python
# Non-Idempotent Operation (Example)
balance = 100

def add_funds(amount):
    global balance
    balance += amount   # Not Idempotent: Multiple calls change the balance
    print(f"Added {amount}, New balance: {balance}")
```

```
add_funds(50) #balance becomes 150
add_funds(50) #balance becomes 200

#Idempotent Operation (Example)
balance = 100

def set_funds(new_balance):
    global balance
    balance = new_balance  # Idempotent: Setting a fixed state.
    print(f"Balance set to: {balance}")

set_funds(150) #balance becomes 150
set_funds(150) #balance remains 150
```

4. Data Replication:

Replicating data across multiple storage locations is a key fault-tolerance strategy. If one storage location fails, the data is still available from the other replicas.

- **Synchronous Replication:** Data is written to all replicas simultaneously. This ensures strong consistency but can introduce latency, as the write operation is not considered complete until all replicas have acknowledged it. *Consider a financial transaction system where data consistency is paramount.* Synchronous replication can be used to ensure that every transaction is immediately replicated to multiple storage locations, guaranteeing that no data is lost in case of a failure.
- **Asynchronous Replication:** Data is written to the primary storage location first, and then asynchronously replicated to the other locations. This provides lower latency but introduces the possibility of data loss if the primary location fails before the data is replicated. *Consider a social media platform where occasional data loss is acceptable.* Asynchronous replication can be used to improve write performance, with the understanding that a small amount of data might be lost in case of a major failure.

Conclusion:

Fault tolerance is not about eliminating failures entirely; it's about minimizing their impact. By designing systems that can gracefully handle failures, we can ensure high availability, data integrity, and a positive user experience. As applications become more complex and critical, implementing robust fault-tolerance mechanisms becomes increasingly important.

High Availability

High Availability (HA) is about ensuring your systems and applications are consistently accessible and operational with minimal downtime. The goal is to keep things running smoothly, even when failures occur. In essence, it's about building systems that are resilient and can quickly recover from unexpected problems.

Consider a scenario where you have an e-commerce website. If the website goes down, customers can't buy products, leading to lost revenue and a potentially damaged reputation. High Availability aims to prevent such scenarios by designing the system to tolerate failures and remain accessible.

How do you achieve High Availability? A common approach involves redundancy – having multiple instances of critical components.

Imagine you have a single server hosting your website. If that server fails, your website is down. However, if you have *two* servers, and they both host the same website, you can configure them so that if one fails, the other automatically takes over. This switchover needs to be as seamless as possible, minimizing any interruption to users.

Here's a simplified illustration:

```
+-------------------+        +-------------------+
|   Server A        |------->|  Load Balancer    |-----> Users
|  (Active)         |        |                   |
+-------------------+        +-------------------+
          ^                            |
          |                            |
          |                            |
          +------------------+         |
          |    Server B      |-------+ |
          |  (Passive/Standby)|
          +------------------+
```

In this sketch, Server A is actively serving traffic. Server B is a standby server. A Load Balancer sits in front of both servers, distributing incoming requests. If Server A fails, the Load Balancer automatically redirects traffic to Server B, ensuring continuous service.

Here's a simple Python example demonstrating the basic idea of a health check that could be part of a high availability system (although a real-world implementation would be far more complex):

```python
import time
import requests

def check_server_health(url):
    """
    Checks if a server is healthy by sending a request and checking the response code.
    """
    try:
        response = requests.get(url, timeout=5) # timeout after 5 seconds
        if response.status_code == 200:
            return True
        else:
            return False
    except requests.exceptions.RequestException as e:
        print(f"Error: {e}")
        return False


# Example usage:
server_a_url = "http://server-a.example.com"
server_b_url = "http://server-b.example.com"

while True:
    if check_server_health(server_a_url):
        print("Server A is healthy")
    else:
        print("Server A is down!  Failover initiated (simulated).")
        # In a real system, you'd trigger the load balancer to switch to Server B here.
        if check_server_health(server_b_url):
            print("Server B is now active.")
        else:
            print("Server B is also down! We have a bigger problem.")
    time.sleep(10) # Check every 10 seconds
```

This code defines a simple health check function. It sends an HTTP request to a specified URL. If the server responds with a 200 status code (meaning "OK"), the server is considered healthy. If the request fails (e.g., due to a timeout or network error) or the server returns a different status code, the server is considered unhealthy. The `while` loop simulates continuous monitoring, triggering a (simulated) failover if Server A is down. **Note:** This is a highly simplified example; real-world health checks can be more sophisticated, including checking database connectivity, resource utilization, and application-specific metrics.

Important considerations for implementing High Availability:

- **Monitoring:** You need to constantly monitor the health of your systems to detect failures quickly. Tools like Prometheus, Grafana, and Nagios can help with this.
- **Automated Failover:** The process of switching from a failed component to a healthy one should be automated as much as possible. This reduces the time it takes to recover from a failure.
- **Data Replication:** If your application uses a database, you need to replicate the data across multiple database servers. This ensures that data is not lost if one database server fails. Techniques like master-slave replication or multi-master replication can be used.
- **Testing:** Regularly test your High Availability setup to ensure that it works as expected. Simulate failures to see how your system responds and identify any weaknesses.

High Availability is not about achieving 100% uptime – that's often impossible and prohibitively expensive. Instead, it's about balancing the cost of implementing High Availability measures with the potential cost of downtime. The required level of High Availability depends on the specific application and its importance to the business. A personal blog might tolerate occasional downtime, while a critical financial system requires a much higher level of availability.

Chapter 4 Foundations of System Design on AWS- Navigating Trade-offs: Performance, Cost, and Complexity

- **Trade-off Awareness:** Recognizing that system design involves balancing competing priorities.
- **Performance Considerations:**
  - Latency vs. Throughput: Optimizing for speed vs. volume.
- **Cost Optimization:** Selecting services and configurations to minimize expenses.
- **Complexity Management:** Evaluating the operational overhead of different architectures.
- **AWS Service Selection:** Understanding how AWS offerings affect these trade-offs.

Trade-off Awareness

Trade-off awareness is the core understanding that designing any system, especially in a complex environment like AWS, involves making choices. These choices are rarely straightforward wins; instead, they often mean giving up something to gain something else. It's about recognizing that you can't have it all and consciously choosing the best compromise for your specific needs.

Think of it like this: you are building a bridge. You can build it quickly and cheaply using basic materials, but it might not be able to handle heavy traffic or last very long. Or, you can build it slowly and expensively using the strongest materials, ensuring it can handle anything and last for generations. Which do you choose? The answer depends on the specific requirements of the bridge, the available budget, and the acceptable level of risk. Similarly, in system design, every decision has consequences that affect various aspects of your system.

Recognizing that system design involves balancing competing priorities.

The crux of trade-off awareness lies in recognizing that priorities often clash. A system optimized for speed might be more expensive. A highly secure system could be more difficult to use. A scalable system might be more complex to manage. Identifying these competing priorities is the first step towards making informed decisions.

Let's consider a simple example. Suppose you are building an e-commerce application.

- **Speed vs. Cost:** You could use expensive, high-performance servers to ensure lightning-fast loading times for your product pages. This would provide a great user experience. However, it would significantly increase your infrastructure costs. Alternatively, you could use cheaper servers. This might result in slower loading times and a less responsive website, potentially leading to lost sales.

Here's a simplified conceptual sketch to illustrate this:

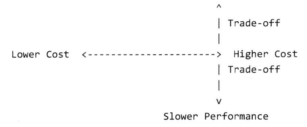

```
Faster Performance
                                        ^
                                        | Trade-off
                                        |
        Lower Cost   <---------------------->  Higher Cost
                                        | Trade-off
                                        |
                                        v
                            Slower Performance
```

In this diagram, the arrows represent opposing forces. Choosing lower cost directly impacts performance, and vice versa. Understanding this relationship is crucial.

Here's a code-related example to illustrate the concept of trade-offs. Imagine you're designing a function to retrieve data from a database:

```python
import time

def get_data_optimized_for_speed():
    start_time = time.time()
    # Assume this function retrieves data using a fast, but potentially
    # more resource-intensive method (e.g., in-memory caching).
    data = retrieve_data_from_cache()  #Simulated function
    end_time = time.time()
    print(f"Speed Optimized time: {end_time - start_time}")
    return data

def get_data_optimized_for_cost():
    start_time = time.time()
    # Assume this function retrieves data using a slower, but less
    # resource-intensive method (e.g., direct database query).
    data = retrieve_data_from_database() #Simulated function
    end_time = time.time()
    print(f"Cost Optimized time: {end_time - start_time}")
    return data

#Simulated Data Retrieval Functions
def retrieve_data_from_cache():
```

```
    time.sleep(0.1) # Simulate time spent
    return "Data from cache"

def retrieve_data_from_database():
    time.sleep(0.5) # Simulate time spent
    return "Data from database"

# Calling functions to simulate and show time difference
get_data_optimized_for_speed()
get_data_optimized_for_cost()
```

In this simplified Python example, `get_data_optimized_for_speed` uses a caching mechanism (simulated) which is faster but uses more memory (more cost). `get_data_optimized_for_cost` retrieves data directly from the database (simulated) which is slower but less resource-intensive, therefore, less costly. The choice between these two depends on whether you prioritize speed or cost.

Performance Considerations

When designing systems, *performance* is a key concern. It's not just about whether something *works*, but *how well* it works. Performance encompasses various aspects, often requiring a balance between competing goals. Two crucial aspects of performance are latency and throughput.

Latency vs. Throughput: Optimizing for Speed vs. Volume

Latency refers to the time it takes for a single request to be processed. Imagine you click a button on a website and wait for a response. The time you wait is the latency. We want latency to be as low as possible.

Throughput refers to the number of requests a system can handle within a certain period (e.g., requests per second). Think of a highway: throughput is the number of cars that can pass a certain point each hour. We want throughput to be as high as possible.

Often, improving one comes at the expense of the other. This is the *latency vs. throughput* trade-off.

Example: Database Queries

Consider a database.

Scenario 1: Low Latency Focus

Suppose we need to get a user's profile information very quickly every time they visit a web page. We might optimize for low latency. We could store the user's profile data in a cache (a fast, temporary storage). This minimizes the time it takes to retrieve the data, providing a quick response to the user.

```
# Python example illustrating low latency using a cache

user_cache = {}  # Simulate a cache

def get_user_profile(user_id):
    if user_id in user_cache:
        print(f"Fetching user {user_id} from cache")
        return user_cache[user_id]
    else:
        print(f"Fetching user {user_id} from database")
        # Simulate database query
        user_profile = {"user_id": user_id, "name": "Example User", "details": "Some info"}
        user_cache[user_id] = user_profile  # Store in cache for next time
        return user_profile
```

```
# Example usage
print(get_user_profile(123))
print(get_user_profile(123))  # Retrieving from cache is faster
```

In this code, the first time the get_user_profile function is called for a specific user_id, it simulates fetching the data from a database (which is a slower operation). However, the result is then stored in the user_cache. The second time the function is called with the same user_id, the data is retrieved directly from the cache, which is much faster. This demonstrates how caching can reduce latency for frequently accessed data.

Scenario 2: High Throughput Focus

Now, imagine we are processing millions of transactions every hour. While each individual transaction might not need to be processed *instantly*, we need to handle a massive volume of them efficiently. We might optimize for high throughput. One approach is to process transactions in batches (groups) rather than individually. This reduces the overhead of processing each transaction, allowing us to handle more transactions overall.

```
# Python example illustrating higher throughput by batching operations

import time

def process_transaction(transaction):
    # Simulate processing a transaction
    time.sleep(0.001) # Simulate some processing time
    return f"Processed transaction {transaction}"

def process_transactions_batch(transactions):
    results = []
    for transaction in transactions:
        results.append(process_transaction(transaction))
    return results

def process_transactions_individually(transactions):
  results = []
  for transaction in transactions:
    results.append(process_transaction(transaction))
  return results

# Example Usage
num_transactions = 100
transactions = list(range(num_transactions))

start_time = time.time()
batch_results = process_transactions_batch(transactions)
batch_time = time.time() - start_time
print(f"Time to process {num_transactions} transactions in a batch: {batch_time:.4f} seconds")

start_time = time.time()
individual_results = process_transactions_individually(transactions)
individual_time = time.time() - start_time

print(f"Time to process {num_transactions} transactions individually: {individual_time:.4f} secc
```

While the individual functions may be same, the batching process itself allow the hardware to process the function efficiently. This small example of Python is for demostration. If you use a hardware, you will be able to see a massive difference.

Visualizing the Trade-off

Imagine a seesaw:

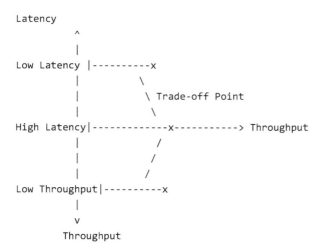

```
Latency
         ^
         |
Low Latency |----------x
         |           \
         |            \ Trade-off Point
         |             \
High Latency|------------x-----------> Throughput
         |             /
         |            /
         |           /
Low Throughput|----------x
         |
         v
        Throughput
```

Moving towards lower latency often means sacrificing some throughput, and vice-versa. The ideal point (marked 'x' above) depends on the specific requirements of your application.

Understanding this trade-off is crucial for making informed decisions about system architecture and optimization techniques. You must carefully consider the priorities of your application to strike the right balance between latency and throughput.

Latency vs. Throughput

System design often requires a careful balancing act between speed and volume. We must consider *latency* and *throughput* when optimizing a system. These two concepts represent fundamentally different, and sometimes conflicting, performance goals.

Latency:

Latency refers to the time it takes for a single request to be processed. It is a measure of responsiveness. Think of it as the delay between sending a request and receiving a response. Low latency is crucial for applications where users expect immediate feedback, such as interactive web applications or real-time gaming.

- **Example:** Imagine clicking a button on a website. Latency is the time it takes for the website to respond to your click and update the display. If the latency is high (e.g., several seconds), the website will feel sluggish and unresponsive.

- **Code Example:** Consider a simple function that fetches data from a database.

  ```
  import time

  def fetch_data(query):
      start_time = time.time()
      # Simulate database query
      time.sleep(0.5)  # Simulate 0.5 seconds of processing
      end_time = time.time()
      latency = end_time - start_time
      print(f"Query: {query}, Latency: {latency:.4f} seconds")
      return "Data"
  ```

```
fetch_data("SELECT  FROM users WHERE id = 123")
```

In this example, `latency` represents the total time it takes for `fetch_data` function to complete, including the simulated database query time.

Throughput:

Throughput, on the other hand, measures the number of requests a system can process within a given time period. It is a measure of capacity. High throughput is important for applications that need to handle a large volume of requests, such as batch processing systems or high-traffic websites.

- **Example:** Consider a video streaming service. Throughput is the number of video streams that the service can deliver simultaneously without buffering or performance degradation.

- **Code Example:** Consider a scenario of handling multiple requests concurrently

```python
import time
import threading

def process_request(request_id):
    start_time = time.time()
    # Simulate request processing
    time.sleep(0.2)
    end_time = time.time()
    print(f"Request {request_id} processed in {end_time - start_time:.4f} seconds")

def main():
    start_time = time.time()
    threads = []
    for i in range(10):
        thread = threading.Thread(target=process_request, args=(i,))
        threads.append(thread)
        thread.start()

    for thread in threads:
        thread.join()

    end_time = time.time()
    total_time = end_time - start_time
    throughput = 10 / total_time  # Requests per second
    print(f"Total time to process 10 requests: {total_time:.4f} seconds")
    print(f"Throughput: {throughput:.2f} requests per second")

if __name__ == "__main__":
    main()
```

In this example, `throughput` indicates the number of requests processed per second when multiple requests are handled concurrently. The total time to process all requests will be close to 0.2 seconds because the requests run concurrently.

The Trade-off:

Often, optimizing for latency comes at the expense of throughput, and vice versa.

- **Low Latency, Potentially Lower Throughput:** To minimize latency, you might use more expensive, lower-capacity resources, or implement complex caching mechanisms. Each request is processed very quickly, but the overall number of requests handled per second might be limited.

- **High Throughput, Potentially Higher Latency:** To maximize throughput, you might batch requests together, use asynchronous processing, or employ distributed systems. Each individual request might take slightly longer to process (higher latency), but the system can handle a much larger volume of requests overall.

Illustrative Sketch:

Imagine a water pipe system:

```
High Pressure (Low Latency)        Low Pressure (High Throughput)
-----------------------------      -----------------------------
| Small Diameter Pipe       |      | Large Diameter Pipe        |
| Fast flow, less volume    |      | Slower flow, more volume   |
| Single request handled fast |    |  Many requests handled slowly |
-----------------------------      -----------------------------
```

- **Small Diameter Pipe (High Pressure):** Represents a system optimized for low latency. Water (requests) flows quickly because of the high pressure, but the small diameter limits the overall volume of water (throughput).

- **Large Diameter Pipe (Low Pressure):** Represents a system optimized for high throughput. The large diameter allows a greater volume of water (requests) to flow, but the pressure (speed) is lower, resulting in a slightly slower flow rate (higher latency).

The key to designing efficient systems is to understand the specific requirements of your application and make informed trade-offs between latency and throughput. Consider your user's experience and the overall workload your system needs to handle. By carefully evaluating these factors, you can choose the architecture and configurations that best meet your needs.

Cost Optimization

Cost optimization within system design is about making smart choices to spend the least amount of money while still meeting the needs of your application. It involves picking the right services, configuring them efficiently, and continually monitoring your spending.

When considering cost optimization, it's crucial to understand the various options available and how they impact your overall expenses. This often involves selecting the most appropriate AWS services and configurations based on the application's requirements.

For example, consider storing images. You could use Amazon S3 (Simple Storage Service), which offers different storage classes.

- **S3 Standard:** This is for frequently accessed data. It's more expensive but provides low latency and high availability.

- **S3 Infrequent Access (IA):** This is for data that's accessed less often but still needs to be readily available. It's cheaper than S3 Standard, but there's a retrieval cost.

- **S3 Glacier:** This is for archival data that's rarely accessed. It's the cheapest option but has longer retrieval times.

Choosing the right storage class based on how often you need to access the images can lead to significant cost savings. If you know that certain images are rarely accessed, moving them to S3 Glacier can dramatically reduce your storage costs.

Another example involves choosing the right EC2 (Elastic Compute Cloud) instance type. EC2 instances are virtual servers in the cloud, and they come in various sizes and configurations, each with a different price. You might choose a smaller, less expensive instance for development and testing environments, reserving larger, more powerful (and thus costlier) instances for production use where performance is paramount.

Here's a simple example of how you might provision different EC2 instances using the AWS CLI:

```
# For development (cheaper)
aws ec2 run-instances --image-id ami-xxxxxxxxxxxxxxxxx --count 1 --instance-type t3.micro --key-
```

```
# For production (more performant, more expensive)
aws ec2 run-instances --image-id ami-xxxxxxxxxxxxxxxxx --count 1 --instance-type m5.xlarge --key
```

This code shows how to launch a t3.micro instance for development purposes and an m5.xlarge instance for production. The t3.micro is less expensive, suitable for non-critical tasks. The m5.xlarge instance is faster but more costly, suitable for the production environment.

Cost optimization isn't a one-time task. It requires continuous monitoring and adjustment. AWS provides tools like Cost Explorer and CloudWatch to track your spending and identify areas where you can save money. Regularly reviewing your resource utilization and adjusting your configurations can help you keep your costs under control.

Consider this scenario:

You have a web application that experiences high traffic during business hours but low traffic overnight. Instead of running all your EC2 instances 24/7, you can use AWS Auto Scaling to automatically adjust the number of instances based on demand.

```
Peak Hours (High Demand)
        +---------------------------+
        | EC2 Instances: Scaled UP  |
        +---------------------------+
           /         |         \
          /          |          \
 Traffic /           |           \ Traffic
        /            |            \
    +---------------------------+
                    |
                    | Decreased Demand (Night)
                    |
    +---------------------------+
    | EC2 Instances: Scaled DOWN |
    +---------------------------+
```

Auto Scaling monitors the CPU utilization of your instances. When utilization is high, it launches new instances. When utilization is low, it terminates instances. This ensures that you only pay for the resources you need when you need them.

Here is a simple python pseudo-code outline for implementing auto scaling:

```
#Pseudo-code
def check_cpu_utilization():
    cpu_usage = get_cpu_usage()
    if cpu_usage > HIGH_THRESHOLD:
        scale_up() # launch more instances
    elif cpu_usage < LOW_THRESHOLD:
        scale_down() # terminate instances
```

In the cloud, you pay for what you use. Effective cost optimization is about becoming proficient at using the right resources, the right amount of time, and the right configuration to minimize the overall costs.

Complexity Management

Complexity management in system design means understanding and controlling how difficult your system is to operate, maintain, and change. Different architectures have different levels of complexity, and it's crucial to choose one that balances functionality with ease of use. If a system is too complex, it can lead to increased costs, errors, and slower development cycles.

Evaluating the operational overhead of different architectures is a key aspect of complexity management. Operational overhead refers to the resources needed to keep a system running smoothly. This includes things like monitoring, maintenance, troubleshooting, and scaling. A complex system might require a larger team, more sophisticated tools, and more time to manage effectively.

For example, consider two approaches to building a simple web application:

1. **Monolithic Architecture:** All components (user interface, business logic, database) are bundled into a single application.
2. **Microservices Architecture:** The application is broken down into small, independent services that communicate with each other.

The monolithic architecture is often simpler to develop and deploy initially. However, as the application grows, it can become increasingly complex to manage. Changes to one part of the application can potentially impact other parts, and scaling requires scaling the entire application, even if only one component is under heavy load.

The microservices architecture, on the other hand, introduces complexity from the start. You need to manage multiple services, handle inter-service communication, and deal with distributed systems challenges like network latency and fault tolerance. However, it can offer greater flexibility, scalability, and resilience in the long run. Changes to one service are less likely to affect other services, and you can scale individual services independently.

To illustrate this with a simple code example, consider deploying these architectures on AWS.

Monolithic Example (Simplified - using EC2):

```
# Simplified Python Flask app (monolithic)
from flask import Flask
app = Flask(__name__)

@app.route("/")
def hello():
    return "Hello, World!"

if __name__ == "__main__":
    app.run(debug=True)
```

You would package this application and deploy it to a single EC2 instance. Monitoring is relatively straightforward - you monitor the EC2 instance's CPU, memory, and network usage. Scaling involves creating more EC2 instances running the same application behind a load balancer.

Microservices Example (Simplified - using AWS Lambda & API Gateway):

Assume you break the application into two microservices: a "greeting" service and an "authentication" service.

- **Greeting Service (Lambda):**

  ```
  # Lambda function (greeting service)
  import json

  def lambda_handler(event, context):
      return {
  ```

```
            'statusCode': 200,
            'body': json.dumps('Hello from the Greeting Service!')
        }
```

- **Authentication Service (Lambda - very basic placeholder):**

```
# Lambda function (authentication service - placeholder)
import json

def lambda_handler(event, context):
    #In real implementation it will have authentication logic
    return {
        'statusCode': 200,
        'body': json.dumps('Authentication Successful (Placeholder)')
    }
```

You deploy each of these as separate Lambda functions. You create an API Gateway to route requests to the appropriate Lambda function. Complexity increases because you must now manage:

- Two separate Lambda functions (deployment, versions, configuration).
- API Gateway configuration (routing, authentication - though this service is a placeholder).
- Monitoring both Lambda functions (invocations, errors, latency) *and* API Gateway (request counts, latency).
- Potential inter-service communication (if the greeting service needed to verify authentication).

Sketch of Monolithic vs. Microservices:

Monolithic:

```
+---------------------+
|  Web App (Monolith) |
+---------------------+
| UI | Logic | Database|
+---------------------+
     ^
     |
 +--------+
 |  User  |
 +--------+
```

Microservices:

```
+--------+        +-------------+        +-------------+
|  User  | --->   | API Gateway | --->   | Microservice|
+--------+        +-------------+        +-------------+
                       |                  | (e.g., User) |
                       |                  +-------------+
                       |
                  +---> | Microservice|
                       | (e.g., Order) |
                       +-------------+
```

In the microservices sketch, the API Gateway acts as a central point of entry, routing requests to different microservices. This adds complexity but provides flexibility and scalability.

The point is not that one architecture is always better than the other. Instead, complexity management involves understanding the trade-offs and choosing the architecture that best fits the specific requirements of the project.

Furthermore, complexity management extends beyond architectural choices. It also involves:

- **Infrastructure as Code (IaC):** Using tools like Terraform or AWS CloudFormation to automate the provisioning and management of infrastructure. This reduces manual configuration and ensures consistency.

- **Continuous Integration/Continuous Deployment (CI/CD):** Automating the build, test, and deployment process. This reduces the risk of errors and allows for faster releases.

- **Monitoring and Logging:** Implementing comprehensive monitoring and logging to detect and diagnose issues quickly. Tools like CloudWatch, Prometheus, and Grafana can be used to collect and visualize metrics.

- **Automation:** Automating repetitive tasks, such as backups, security patching, and scaling.

In summary, complexity management is about making informed decisions to minimize the operational burden of your system while still meeting its functional requirements. It requires a deep understanding of different architectures, technologies, and operational practices. Choosing the simplest solution that meets the needs of the project is always a good starting point.

AWS Service Selection

Choosing the right AWS services is crucial because it significantly impacts trade-offs between performance, cost, and complexity. Different AWS offerings are designed for specific purposes and understanding these nuances is key to building efficient and effective systems.

Understanding how AWS offerings affect these trade-offs:

AWS offers a vast array of services, each with its own characteristics related to performance, cost, and complexity. The selection process involves carefully considering these factors in the context of your specific requirements.

- **Compute Services:**

  - **EC2 (Elastic Compute Cloud):** This service gives you virtual servers in the cloud. You have full control over the operating system, instance type, and configuration. Choosing the right EC2 instance type is crucial. For example, if you need high compute power, you might choose a `c5.xlarge` instance. But if you need a lot of memory, you might choose an `r5.xlarge`.

sketch:

```
+-----------------+        +-----------------+
|  Application    |------>|      EC2         |
| (e.g., Web App) |       | (c5.xlarge)     |
+-----------------+        +-----------------+
         ^                 | (compute-heavy) |
         |                 +-----------------+
         |
+-----------------+
|  Application    |------>|      EC2         |
| (e.g., Data Proc)|       | (r5.xlarge)     |
+-----------------+        | (memory-heavy)  |
                          +-----------------+
```

If your workload is temporary and you need something that is serverless:

  - **Lambda:** This service lets you run code without provisioning or managing servers. You only pay for the compute time you consume. If you have a function that needs to be executed in response to an event (for example, uploading a file to S3), Lambda is a great choice.

sketch:

```
+-------+        +--------+        +-----------+
| Event |------>|  AWS   |------>|   Lambda  |
```

```
| (S3    |        | Services|       | Function  |
| Upload)|        | (e.g.,  |       | (process  |
+-------+         |  S3)    |       | the file) |
                  +--------+        +-----------+
```

Code Example for Lambda (Python)

```python
import json

def lambda_handler(event, context):
    # Extract data from the event
    data = event['Records'][0]['s3']['object']['key']

    # Perform some operation
    message = f"File {data} uploaded to S3"

    return {
        'statusCode': 200,
        'body': json.dumps(message)
    }
```

- ○ **Containers (ECS, EKS):** ECS (Elastic Container Service) and EKS (Elastic Kubernetes Service) allow you to run and manage Docker containers. Containers provide a consistent environment for your applications, making them easier to deploy and scale. ECS is AWS's own container orchestration, while EKS uses Kubernetes.

- **Storage Services:**

  - ○ **S3 (Simple Storage Service):** This service provides object storage. It's highly scalable, durable, and cost-effective for storing data. You can use S3 to store images, videos, backups, and more. The cost depends on the storage class (e.g., Standard, Glacier).

  - ○ **EBS (Elastic Block Storage):** This service provides block storage volumes for use with EC2 instances. It's like a virtual hard drive. EBS volumes can be attached to EC2 instances and used for storing operating systems, databases, and applications.

  - ○ **RDS (Relational Database Service):** This service makes it easy to set up, operate, and scale a relational database in the cloud. It supports various database engines, such as MySQL, PostgreSQL, Oracle, and SQL Server.

Choosing the right database depends on your needs. For example, if you need a NoSQL database, you might choose DynamoDB.

- **Database Services:**

  - ○ **DynamoDB:** It is a NoSQL database service offering extremely fast performance at any scale.

Code Example for DynamoDB (Python)

```python
import boto3

# Create a DynamoDB client
dynamodb = boto3.resource('dynamodb')

# Specify the table name
table = dynamodb.Table('your_table_name')

# Example: Put an item into the table
```

```
response = table.put_item(
    Item={
        'id': '123',
        'name': 'Example Item',
    }
)

print("PutItem succeeded:")
print(response)
```

- **Networking Services:**

  - **VPC (Virtual Private Cloud):** This service lets you create a logically isolated section of the AWS cloud where you can launch AWS resources in a virtual network that you define.

  - **Route 53:** This is a scalable DNS (Domain Name System) web service. It translates human-readable names, such as `www.example.com`, into the numeric IP addresses that computers use to connect to each other.

- **Other Services:**

  - **SQS (Simple Queue Service):** This service provides a message queue. It lets you decouple different parts of your application, so that one part can send messages to the queue, and another part can process those messages.

  sketch:

```
+-------------+      +-------+      +-------------+
| Application |----->|  SQS  |----->| Application |
|  Producer   |      | Queue |      |  Consumer   |
+-------------+      +-------+      +-------------+
```

  - **SNS (Simple Notification Service):** A fully managed messaging service for both application-to-application (A2A) and application-to-person (A2P) communication.

How Services Affect Trade-offs

Different AWS services impact trade-offs among performance, cost, and complexity.

1. **Performance Considerations:**

   - **Latency:** Choosing services with low latency is essential for applications requiring real-time responses. For instance, using in-memory caching services like ElastiCache can reduce latency compared to querying a database directly.
   - **Throughput:** For applications that need to handle large volumes of data, services like SQS and Kinesis are designed for high throughput.

2. **Cost Optimization:**

   - **Pay-as-you-go:** AWS services typically offer a pay-as-you-go pricing model, which can be very cost-effective.
   - **Reserved Instances:** For predictable workloads, purchasing Reserved Instances for EC2 can significantly reduce costs.
   - **Storage Classes:** Choosing the right S3 storage class (Standard, Intelligent-Tiering, Glacier) based on data access frequency can optimize storage costs.

3. **Complexity Management:**

- **Managed Services:** AWS offers many managed services, such as RDS, which reduce the operational overhead of managing infrastructure.
- **Serverless:** Using serverless services like Lambda can simplify deployment and scaling, reducing complexity.

By carefully evaluating these factors and understanding the capabilities of each AWS service, you can make informed decisions that lead to well-architected, cost-effective, and high-performing systems.

Chapter 5 Core Building Blocks of AWS Architecture- Compute Services: Choosing Between EC2, Lambda, and Containers

Here are 5 bullet points explaining the concept of "Core Building Blocks of AWS Architecture-Compute Services: Choosing Between EC2, Lambda, and Containers" suitable for a single slide:

- **Compute Options Overview:** Balancing flexibility, control, and operational overhead with EC2, Lambda, and Containers.

- **EC2: Infrastructure as a Service (IaaS):**

  - Full control over OS, networking, security.
  - Suitable for complex, customized applications.

- **Lambda: Function as a Service (FaaS):**

  - Serverless, event-driven execution.
  - Ideal for stateless microservices and background tasks.

- **Containers (ECS, EKS, Fargate):**

  - Package and deploy applications consistently.
  - Orchestration simplifies management and scaling.

- **Decision Factors:** Choose based on resource control, operational effort, scalability needs, and cost considerations.

Compute Options Overview: Balancing Act in AWS

The world of AWS compute services offers a range of options, each with its own strengths and trade-offs. When you're building an application on AWS, you'll need to choose the compute service that best fits your specific needs. This choice essentially boils down to balancing flexibility, control, and the amount of operational work you want to handle. You can think of it like choosing a tool – a hammer is great for nails, but not so much for screws. Similarly, each AWS compute service excels in certain scenarios.

We'll focus on three primary compute services: EC2, Lambda, and Containers (using services like ECS, EKS, and Fargate). Let's explore what "balancing flexibility, control, and operational overhead" means in the context of these services.

- **Flexibility** refers to how much you can customize the underlying environment. Do you need to install specific software packages? Do you need to fine-tune the operating system? Greater flexibility often comes with increased responsibility.
- **Control** goes hand-in-hand with flexibility. It's about the degree to which you manage the infrastructure. Do you manage the servers themselves, or does AWS handle that for you? More control often means more configuration and maintenance.
- **Operational Overhead** describes the effort required to manage and maintain the compute infrastructure. This includes tasks like patching operating systems, scaling resources, and monitoring performance. Lower operational overhead allows you to focus on building and deploying your application logic.

Here's a sketch that represents this balancing act:

```
High Control/Flexibility
       ^
       | EC2
       |
       |   Containers (ECS, EKS, Fargate)
       |
       |  Lambda
       |
       ------------------> Low Operational Overhead
```

This sketch provides the relative position of each service. Note this is not a absolute position.

Let's use an analogy. Imagine you're preparing a meal:

- **EC2 is like cooking from scratch:** You have complete control over every ingredient and step. You buy the raw ingredients, prepare them, cook them, and clean up afterward. This is more work, but you can create exactly what you want.
- **Lambda is like ordering takeout:** You simply specify what you want, and someone else prepares and delivers it to you. You don't worry about the ingredients, the cooking process, or the cleanup.
- **Containers are like using a meal kit:** The ingredients are pre-portioned and the recipe is provided. You still have to do some of the cooking, but much of the preparation is done for you.

EC2: Infrastructure as a Service (IaaS)

EC2, or Elastic Compute Cloud, is the foundational Infrastructure as a Service (IaaS) offering from AWS. It allows you to rent virtual servers, known as instances, in the cloud.

- **Full Control:** You have complete control over the operating system, networking configuration, security settings, and software installed on the instance. You can choose from a variety of operating systems (Linux, Windows, macOS) and instance types (optimized for compute, memory, storage, etc.).

  For example, if you need a specific version of Python that isn't pre-installed, you can install it yourself using command-line tools:

  ```
  sudo apt update
  sudo apt install python3.7
  ```

  You are responsible for installing the required software packages and managing any dependencies.

- **Suitable for Complex, Customized Applications:** EC2 is well-suited for applications with complex requirements or those that need fine-grained control over the underlying infrastructure. This could include legacy applications, applications that require specific hardware configurations, or applications with stringent security requirements.

For instance, if you need to run a high-performance database server, EC2 provides the flexibility to choose an instance type with the appropriate CPU, memory, and storage resources. You can also configure networking settings to optimize database performance.

EC2 provides the most control and flexibility, but also requires the most operational overhead. You're responsible for managing the operating system, patching security vulnerabilities, and scaling resources as needed.

Lambda: Function as a Service (FaaS)

Lambda is AWS's Function as a Service (FaaS) offering. It allows you to run code without provisioning or managing servers. You simply upload your code, configure a trigger (such as an HTTP request or a message from a queue), and Lambda automatically executes your code in response to the trigger.

- **Serverless, Event-Driven Execution:** Lambda is serverless, meaning you don't have to worry about managing the underlying servers. AWS handles the provisioning, scaling, and maintenance of the infrastructure. Lambda is also event-driven, meaning that your code is executed in response to specific events.

  For example, you can configure a Lambda function to be triggered when a new image is uploaded to an S3 bucket. The Lambda function can then automatically resize the image and store it in a different bucket.

- **Ideal for Stateless Microservices and Background Tasks:** Lambda is well-suited for stateless microservices (services that don't store any data) and background tasks (tasks that don't require immediate user interaction). It's also a good choice for event-driven applications and applications with spiky traffic patterns.

  For example, you can use Lambda to implement an API endpoint that processes user requests and returns responses. Each request is handled independently by a separate invocation of the Lambda function.

Lambda provides the least control and operational overhead. AWS manages the underlying infrastructure, allowing you to focus on writing your code. However, Lambda functions have limitations in terms of execution time, memory, and storage.

Containers (ECS, EKS, Fargate):

Containers provide a way to package and deploy applications consistently across different environments. They encapsulate all the necessary dependencies (code, runtime, system tools, libraries, settings) into a single, portable unit. AWS offers several services for managing containers, including:

- **ECS (Elastic Container Service):** AWS's native container orchestration service.

- **EKS (Elastic Kubernetes Service):** A managed Kubernetes service that allows you to run Kubernetes clusters on AWS.

- **Fargate:** A serverless compute engine for containers that eliminates the need to manage the underlying EC2 instances.

- **Package and Deploy Applications Consistently:** Containers ensure that your application runs the same way regardless of the environment (development, testing, production). This eliminates the "it works on my machine" problem and simplifies deployment.

  For example, you can create a Docker image containing your application and all its dependencies. This image can then be deployed to ECS, EKS, or Fargate without any modifications.

- **Orchestration Simplifies Management and Scaling:** Container orchestration tools like ECS and EKS automate the deployment, scaling, and management of containers. They provide features such as service discovery, load balancing, and health monitoring.

For example, you can use ECS to automatically scale your application based on CPU utilization or network traffic. ECS will automatically launch or terminate containers as needed to meet the demand.

Containers offer a balance between control and operational overhead. You have more control over the environment than with Lambda, but less than with EC2. You're responsible for building and managing the container images, but the container orchestration service handles the deployment and scaling.

Decision Factors

Choosing the right compute service requires careful consideration of several factors:

- **Resource Control:** How much control do you need over the underlying infrastructure?
- **Operational Effort:** How much time and effort are you willing to spend on managing the infrastructure?
- **Scalability Needs:** How important is it to be able to scale your application quickly and easily?
- **Cost Considerations:** How much are you willing to spend on compute resources?

By carefully evaluating these factors, you can choose the compute service that best fits your specific needs and achieve the optimal balance between flexibility, control, and operational overhead.

Lambda: Function as a Service (FaaS)

Lambda is a Function as a Service (FaaS) offering, meaning you only worry about the code you want to run, not the servers it runs on. Think of it as a way to execute small pieces of code without the hassle of managing servers.

Serverless, event-driven execution:

Lambda functions are "serverless" because you don't provision or manage any servers. AWS takes care of all the underlying infrastructure. Instead, you upload your code, and Lambda automatically runs it when triggered by an "event." An event can be a change to data in an Amazon S3 bucket, a message arriving in an Amazon SQS queue, an HTTP request via API Gateway, or many other sources.

Consider an image processing scenario. When a new image is uploaded to an S3 bucket, this upload event can trigger a Lambda function to automatically resize the image. You just write the code to resize the image; AWS handles the rest.

```
import boto3
import PIL
from io import BytesIO

s3 = boto3.client('s3')

def lambda_handler(event, context):
    """
    This function resizes images uploaded to an S3 bucket.
    """
    bucket = event['Records'][0]['s3']['bucket']['name']
    key = event['Records'][0]['s3']['object']['key']

    try:
        response = s3.get_object(Bucket=bucket, Key=key)
        image_data = response['Body'].read()

        # Resize the image
        img = PIL.Image.open(BytesIO(image_data))
        img = img.resize((100, 100)) # Resize to 100x100 pixels
```

```
        # Save the resized image to a new S3 bucket
        buffer = BytesIO()
        img.save(buffer, "JPEG")
        buffer.seek(0)

        s3.put_object(Bucket='resized-images-bucket', Key=key, Body=buffer)

        return {
            'statusCode': 200,
            'body': 'Image resized successfully!'
        }
    except Exception as e:
        print(e)
        print('Error resizing image')
        raise e
```

In this example:

- `lambda_handler` is the function that Lambda executes when triggered.
- `event` contains information about the event that triggered the function (in this case, the S3 upload event).
- `context` provides runtime information.
- The code retrieves the image from S3, resizes it, and saves the resized image to another S3 bucket.

Ideal for stateless microservices and background tasks:

Lambda functions are well-suited for *stateless* applications. This means that the function doesn't retain any data between executions. Each invocation is independent. This makes them ideal for microservices, where each service performs a single, well-defined task. You can create several microservices with Lambda to perform certain tasks and that too are independent.

For example, each microservice is like a factory with a specific task such as converting the temperature from degree celsius to kelvin.

Lambda functions are also a good choice for background tasks, such as processing data, sending emails, or generating reports. You can trigger these tasks asynchronously without blocking the main application flow.

Consider a web application where users can upload large files. Instead of processing these files directly in the web application (which could slow it down), you can use Lambda to process them in the background. The web application triggers the Lambda function when a file is uploaded, and the Lambda function handles the file processing independently. This ensures that the web application remains responsive.

Containers (ECS, EKS, Fargate)

Containers offer a consistent way to package and deploy applications, streamlining the development and deployment lifecycle. They bundle an application with all its dependencies, ensuring it runs the same way across different environments, from a developer's laptop to a production server.

Package and Deploy Applications Consistently:

Think of containers like shipping containers. Just as shipping containers allow goods to be transported seamlessly across different modes of transport (truck, ship, train), containers allow applications to be moved and run consistently across different computing environments. This solves the "it works on my machine" problem.

Let's illustrate with a simple example. Suppose you have a Python web application that requires specific versions of Python and several libraries (e.g., Flask, Requests). Without containers, you'd need to manually install these dependencies on every server where you want to run the application. This is error-prone and time-consuming.

With containers, you create a "Dockerfile" which is a set of instructions for building your container image. Here's a simplified example:

```
FROM python:3.9-slim-buster  # Base image with Python 3.9

WORKDIR /app # Set working directory inside the container

COPY requirements.txt . # Copy dependencies file

RUN pip install --no-cache-dir -r requirements.txt # Install dependencies

COPY . . # Copy application code

CMD ["python", "app.py"] # Command to start the application
```

This `Dockerfile` specifies:

- The base operating system and Python version.
- The working directory within the container.
- The dependencies to install from a `requirements.txt` file.
- The application code to copy.
- The command to execute when the container starts.

You then build a container image from this `Dockerfile` using Docker. This image contains everything needed to run your application. Now, you can deploy this image to any environment that supports Docker, and it will run exactly as intended. Imagine a diagram with three identical boxes labeled "Container" being deployed to different environments: "Dev," "Test," and "Prod." Each box contains "App + Dependencies," ensuring consistency across environments.

Orchestration Simplifies Management and Scaling:

While containers solve the problem of consistent packaging, managing a large number of containers, especially in a production environment, can be complex. This is where container orchestration tools like ECS, EKS, and Fargate come in.

- **ECS (Elastic Container Service):** AWS's own container orchestration service. ECS allows you to run and manage Docker containers on a cluster of EC2 instances. It handles tasks like scheduling containers, monitoring their health, and scaling the cluster. ECS requires you to manage the underlying EC2 instances on which your containers run.
- **EKS (Elastic Kubernetes Service):** A managed Kubernetes service. Kubernetes is an open-source container orchestration platform that is widely adopted in the industry. EKS simplifies the process of setting up, operating, and scaling Kubernetes clusters on AWS. You still manage the underlying EC2 worker nodes with EKS by default (though you can use Fargate with EKS).
- **Fargate:** A serverless compute engine for containers. Fargate removes the need to manage the underlying EC2 instances. You simply define the resources (CPU, memory) that your container needs, and Fargate automatically provisions and manages the infrastructure. This greatly simplifies container management and scaling.

To illustrate the difference, consider a simple web application you want to scale.

- **ECS:** You define a "task definition" that specifies the container image, resource requirements, and other settings. ECS then schedules and runs the container on an EC2 instance within your cluster. If demand increases, you need to manually or automatically scale the number of EC2 instances in your cluster and the number of tasks (containers) running on those instances.

- **EKS:** You define a "deployment" in Kubernetes that specifies the container image, number of replicas (containers), and other settings. Kubernetes then schedules and runs the containers on nodes within your cluster. Kubernetes automatically handles scaling the number of pods (containers) based on resource utilization or custom metrics.

- **Fargate:** You define a task definition similar to ECS, but instead of specifying an EC2 cluster, you specify that you want to run the task on Fargate. Fargate automatically provisions the necessary compute resources and scales the containers as needed, without you having to manage any underlying infrastructure. You only pay for the resources consumed by your containers.

Imagine a diagram depicting a single container (or pod) with an arrow pointing to a cluster symbol and finally to auto scaling feature (horizontal line).

In summary, container orchestration provides essential tools for deploying, managing, and scaling containerized applications, with ECS providing AWS-native features, EKS offering Kubernetes compatibility, and Fargate abstracting away the underlying infrastructure management for a serverless container experience.

Decision Factors: Choosing the Right Compute Service

Choosing between EC2, Lambda, and Containers for your AWS application involves carefully considering several key factors. Each option offers a different balance of control, management overhead, scalability, and cost. The best choice depends on the specific requirements of your application and your team's expertise.

Resource Control:

Resource control refers to the degree of access and configuration you have over the underlying infrastructure.

- **EC2:** EC2 provides the highest level of resource control. You have direct access to the operating system, networking configuration, and security settings. This is essential for applications with specific OS requirements, custom software stacks, or strict security compliance needs. For instance, if you need to run a legacy application that relies on a specific version of a Linux distribution or requires a custom kernel module, EC2 offers the necessary control.

```
# Example: Installing custom software on an EC2 instance
sudo apt-get update
sudo apt-get install my-custom-software
```

Sketch:

```
+---------------------+
| EC2 Instance        |
+---------------------+
| OS: (Your Choice)   |-------> Control over OS, Kernel
| Networking Config   |-------> Full Control
| Security Groups     |-------> Defined by You
| Custom Software     |-------> Installed by You
+---------------------+
```

- **Lambda:** Lambda offers the least resource control. You don't manage servers or operating systems. AWS handles the underlying infrastructure. This simplifies operations but limits customization. Lambda is suitable for event-driven applications where you don't need fine-grained control over the environment. For example, consider a function that resizes images uploaded to an S3 bucket. You only need to provide the code, and AWS takes care of the rest.

```
# Example: Lambda function to resize an image
from PIL import Image
import io
import boto3

s3 = boto3.client('s3')
```

```python
def lambda_handler(event, context):
    bucket = event['Records'][0]['s3']['bucket']['name']
    key = event['Records'][0]['s3']['object']['key']
    image_object = s3.get_object(Bucket=bucket, Key=key)
    image_data = image_object['Body'].read()

    image = Image.open(io.BytesIO(image_data))
    image.thumbnail((128, 128))
    buffer = io.BytesIO()
    image.save(buffer, 'JPEG')
    buffer.seek(0)

    s3.put_object(Bucket=bucket, Key='resized/' + key, Body=buffer, ContentType='image/jpeg
    return {
        'statusCode': 200,
        'body': 'Image resized successfully!'
    }
```

Sketch:

```
+---------------------+
|        Lambda       |
+---------------------+
| Code: (Your Code)   |-------> Focus on Function Logic
| AWS Handles         |-------> OS, Servers, Infrastructure
| Event-Driven        |
+---------------------+
```

- **Containers (ECS, EKS, Fargate):** Containers offer a middle ground. You define the environment within the container image, providing more control than Lambda but less than EC2. You can customize the OS, libraries, and dependencies within the container, ensuring consistency across different environments. This is suitable for applications that need a specific runtime environment or have dependencies that are difficult to manage with Lambda. For instance, if you have a Python application that requires specific versions of libraries, you can package it into a Docker container.

```
# Example: Dockerfile for a Python application
FROM python:3.9-slim-buster
WORKDIR /app
COPY requirements.txt .
RUN pip install --no-cache-dir -r requirements.txt
COPY . .
CMD ["python", "app.py"]
```

Sketch:

```
+---------------------+
|      Container      |
+---------------------+
| OS: (Defined in     |-------> Control Inside Container
|    Docker Image)    |
| Libraries           |-------> Specified in Dockerfile
| Dependencies        |-------> Controlled Environment
+---------------------+
```

Operational Effort:

Operational effort relates to the amount of management and maintenance required to run your application.

- **EC2:** EC2 requires the most operational effort. You are responsible for patching the OS, managing security, scaling instances, and monitoring performance. This can be time-consuming but gives you complete control. Consider EC2 when your team has the expertise and resources to manage infrastructure effectively.
  - **Example:** Regularly patching your EC2 instances with security updates using tools like `apt update` or `yum update`, managing auto-scaling groups, and configuring monitoring tools like CloudWatch.
- **Lambda:** Lambda minimizes operational effort. AWS manages the underlying infrastructure, so you can focus on writing code. Scaling, patching, and monitoring are handled automatically. This is ideal for teams that want to reduce operational overhead and focus on application development.
  - **Example:** Lambda automatically scales based on the number of incoming requests, freeing you from manually provisioning and managing servers. AWS CloudWatch automatically collects metrics and logs for your Lambda functions.
- **Containers (ECS, EKS, Fargate):** Containers offer a balance. While you don't manage the underlying servers with Fargate, you still need to manage the container orchestration, scaling, and updates to your container images. ECS and EKS, require some degree of management.
  - **Example:** Using AWS ECS to orchestrate your containers. You define the desired state of your application (e.g., number of containers, resource allocation), and ECS ensures that your containers are running as defined. Using Blue/Green deployment techniques to update your containers.

Scalability Needs:

Scalability refers to the ability of your application to handle increasing traffic or workload.

- **EC2:** EC2 requires you to manually scale your infrastructure by adding or removing instances. This can be automated using Auto Scaling Groups, but it still requires some configuration and management. EC2 is suitable for applications with predictable traffic patterns or when you need precise control over scaling.
  - **Example:** Configuring an Auto Scaling Group to automatically add more EC2 instances when CPU utilization exceeds a certain threshold.
- **Lambda:** Lambda scales automatically and instantly. AWS manages the scaling based on the number of incoming requests. This makes Lambda ideal for applications with unpredictable or spiky traffic patterns.
  - **Example:** A Lambda function that processes user registrations. During peak hours, Lambda automatically scales to handle the increased load without any manual intervention.
- **Containers (ECS, EKS, Fargate):** Containers provide flexible scaling options. With ECS and EKS, you can scale your containers by adjusting the number of tasks or pods. With Fargate, AWS automatically scales the underlying infrastructure. This is suitable for applications that require more control over scaling than Lambda but less operational effort than EC2.
  - **Example:** Using ECS to scale your application based on CPU utilization or memory usage. You can configure ECS to automatically add more containers when the load increases.

Cost Considerations:

Cost is a crucial factor when choosing a compute service.

- **EC2:** EC2 is priced per hour or second of instance usage. You pay for the instances even when they are idle. EC2 is cost-effective for applications that run continuously and have consistent utilization.
  - **Example:** Running a web server 24/7 requires you to pay for the EC2 instance for the entire duration, even during periods of low traffic.
- **Lambda:** Lambda is priced per request and execution duration. You only pay when your function is running. Lambda is cost-effective for applications with infrequent or variable usage patterns.
  - **Example:** Using Lambda to process images only when they are uploaded to an S3 bucket. You only pay for the execution time of the Lambda function, making it cost-effective for infrequent uploads.
- **Containers (ECS, EKS, Fargate):** Containers costs depend on the underlying resources used. With ECS and EKS, you pay for the EC2 instances that run your containers. With Fargate, you pay per vCPU and memory used by your containers. Containers can be cost-effective for applications that can be efficiently packed into containers and scaled based on demand.

- Example: Using Fargate to run a microservices architecture. Fargate allows you to pay only for the resources used by your containers, making it more cost-effective than running dedicated EC2 instances for each microservice.

Chapter 6 Core Building Blocks of AWS Architecture- Storage Solutions: S3, EBS, EFS, and Glacier Explained

- **Object Storage (S3):** Highly scalable, durable storage for unstructured data; ideal for static assets, backups, and data lakes.

- **Block Storage (EBS):** Persistent block-level storage volumes for EC2 instances; suitable for databases, operating systems, and applications requiring direct access.

- **File Storage (EFS):** Shared file system for Linux-based EC2 instances; simplifies file sharing and collaboration across multiple instances.

- **Archival Storage (Glacier/Glacier Deep Archive):** Low-cost storage for infrequently accessed data; optimized for long-term archiving and data retention.

- **Choosing the Right Storage:** Select storage based on access frequency, performance needs, cost considerations, and data lifecycle requirements.

Object Storage (S3): In Detail

Object Storage, specifically Amazon S3 (Simple Storage Service), provides a way to store data as objects. Think of it like having a vast warehouse where you can store anything from photos and videos to documents and backups. Unlike traditional file systems that organize data in folders, S3 stores data as individual objects within "buckets." These buckets are like top-level folders, but they offer much more scalability and flexibility.

Highly Scalable, Durable Storage for Unstructured Data:

S3 is designed to handle massive amounts of data. You can store virtually unlimited amounts of data without worrying about running out of space. The system automatically scales to accommodate your storage needs.

Durability is also a core feature. S3 is engineered to provide extremely high data durability, meaning your data is highly unlikely to be lost or corrupted. Amazon guarantees a 99.999999999% durability for S3 objects. This is achieved through data redundancy, where multiple copies of your data are stored across different facilities. If one facility experiences a failure, your data remains accessible.

S3 is particularly well-suited for *unstructured data*. Unstructured data doesn't have a predefined format or organization. Examples include:

- **Images:** Photos for a website, medical imaging files.
- **Videos:** Streaming content, security camera footage.
- **Documents:** PDFs, Word documents, text files.
- **Log Files:** Application logs, server logs.
- **Backups:** Database backups, system images.

Ideal for Static Assets, Backups, and Data Lakes:

S3's characteristics make it an excellent choice for several use cases:

- **Static Assets:** Websites often use static assets like images, CSS files, and JavaScript files. Storing these assets in S3 allows you to serve them directly to users, reducing the load on your web servers and improving website performance.

  For example, imagine a website with many product images. Instead of storing these images on the web server, you can store them in an S3 bucket. When a user visits a product page, the website retrieves the image directly from S3, resulting in faster loading times.

  ```
  <img src="https://your-bucket-name.s3.amazonaws.com/images/product1.jpg" alt="Product 1">
  ```

  In this example, the `src` attribute of the `img` tag points directly to the image stored in the S3 bucket.

- **Backups:** S3 provides a reliable and cost-effective way to store backups of your data. You can create automated backup processes that regularly copy your data to S3, protecting you from data loss in case of hardware failure or other disasters.

  Many backup tools and services integrate directly with S3, making it easy to create and manage backups.

  You can also use the AWS CLI to upload your files/folders to S3 bucket

  ```
  aws s3 cp /path/to/your/local/folder s3://your-bucket-name/backup/ --recursive
  ```

  This command copies the entire folder to the bucket under the prefix `backup`.

- **Data Lakes:** A data lake is a centralized repository for storing large volumes of structured, semi-structured, and unstructured data. S3 is often used as the foundation for data lakes due to its scalability, durability, and cost-effectiveness.

  You can ingest data from various sources into S3 and then use analytics tools to analyze and gain insights from the data. For example, a company might ingest customer data from CRM systems, website logs, and social media feeds into an S3 data lake. They can then use tools like Amazon Athena or Amazon EMR to query and analyze this data to understand customer behavior and trends.

  A basic sketch to illustrate a Data Lake using S3:

  ```
  [Data Sources] --> [Ingestion Layer] --> [S3 Data Lake] --> [Analytics/Processing] --> [Ins
  ```

  Where:

  - **Data Sources:** Various systems and applications generating data (e.g., CRM, Web Logs, IoT devices).
  - **Ingestion Layer:** Tools and processes to move data into the data lake (e.g., AWS Glue, custom scripts).
  - **S3 Data Lake:** The central repository in S3.
  - **Analytics/Processing:** Tools to analyze and transform the data (e.g., Amazon Athena, EMR).
  - **Insights/Reports:** Visualizations and dashboards for business users.

Block Storage (EBS)

Persistent block-level storage volumes for EC2 instances: Elastic Block Storage (EBS) provides block-level storage volumes that you can use with EC2 instances. Think of EBS as a virtual hard drive that you attach to your computer (your EC2 instance). Unlike instance storage, which is temporary and disappears when you stop or terminate your instance, EBS volumes persist even after the EC2 instance is stopped or terminated. This persistence is critical for data that you need to keep long-term.

Suitable for databases, operating systems, and applications requiring direct access: Because EBS provides direct access to raw block storage, it's well-suited for a variety of workloads:

- **Databases:** Databases like MySQL, PostgreSQL, and Oracle benefit from the low-latency, high-throughput EBS volumes, particularly when configured with Provisioned IOPS for predictable performance.
- **Operating Systems:** When you launch an EC2 instance, the root volume where the operating system is installed is often an EBS volume. This allows you to stop and restart your instance without losing the OS or other system files.
- **Applications:** Applications that require direct access to block storage for reading and writing data, such as file systems, enterprise applications, and custom applications, are excellent candidates for EBS.

To illustrate how an EBS volume is used in practice, consider the following scenario:

1. You launch an EC2 instance.
2. You create an EBS volume of a specific size and type (e.g., General Purpose SSD (gp2)).
3. You attach the EBS volume to your EC2 instance. The volume appears as a block device within the instance's operating system (e.g., /dev/xvdf in Linux).
4. You format the block device with a file system (e.g., ext4, XFS).
5. You mount the file system to a directory (e.g., /data).
6. Your application can now read and write data directly to the /data directory, which is backed by the EBS volume.

Here's a simplified representation:

```
+--------------------+     +--------------------+     +--------------------+
| EC2 Instance       | --> | Network Connection | --> | EBS Volume         |
| (e.g., Linux Server)|     |                    |     | (Persistent Storage)|
+--------------------+     +--------------------+     +--------------------+
         |
         | Mount Point (/data)
         |
+--------------------+
| Application        |
| (Reads/Writes data)|
+--------------------+
```

This diagram shows how the application reads and writes data to a mount point on the EC2 instance, which is ultimately backed by the EBS volume through a network connection.

Example with Code (Linux):

```
# 1. Attach the EBS volume /dev/xvdf (hypothetical device name after attaching)

# 2. Format the volume with ext4 filesystem (only do this the first time)
sudo mkfs -t ext4 /dev/xvdf

# 3. Create a mount point
sudo mkdir /data

# 4. Mount the volume to the mount point
sudo mount /dev/xvdf /data

# 5. Verify the volume is mounted
df -h /data
```

```
# Your application can now read/write to /data
```

This bash script demonstrates the basic steps of attaching an EBS volume to a Linux EC2 instance, formatting it, and mounting it. Remember to replace `/dev/xvdf` with the actual device name assigned to your EBS volume.

In summary, EBS provides a reliable, persistent, and high-performance block storage solution for EC2 instances, making it a fundamental component for many cloud-based applications.

File Storage (EFS): Simplified File Sharing for Linux Systems

This section dives into Amazon Elastic File System (EFS), a file storage service offered by AWS. EFS is specifically designed to work with Linux-based EC2 instances, making it easy to share files and collaborate across multiple virtual servers.

Shared file system for Linux-based EC2 instances: EFS is essentially a network file system that can be mounted on multiple EC2 instances concurrently. This means that several EC2 instances can access and modify the same files simultaneously, which is crucial for applications that require shared storage. Think of it like a shared folder on a local network, but hosted in the cloud.

Simplifies file sharing and collaboration across multiple instances: Traditional methods of file sharing between servers often involve complex setups or transferring files back and forth. EFS eliminates this complexity. By mounting an EFS file system on multiple EC2 instances, you create a centralized location for files that all instances can access as if it were a local drive. This greatly simplifies collaboration and data management.

Example Scenarios:

- *Web Server Farms:* Imagine you have multiple web servers serving content to users. Instead of duplicating website files on each server, you can store the website files on EFS and mount the file system on each web server. This ensures that all web servers are serving the same content and simplifies updates. A diagram is provided here.

```
+-----------------+    +-----------------+    +-----------------+
| EC2 Web Server 1 |   | EC2 Web Server 2 |   | EC2 Web Server 3 |
| Mount Point: /var/www/html | Mount Point: /var/www/html | Mount Point: /var/www/html |
+-----------------+    +-----------------+    +-----------------+
         |                      |                     |
   +--------------------+--------------------+--------------------+
                        |
                        |
            +----------------------------+
            |      EFS File System        |
            | (Shared files in /var/www/html) |
            +----------------------------+
```

- *Content Management Systems (CMS):* If you are running a CMS like WordPress on multiple EC2 instances, EFS can be used to store media files and plugins. This way, any changes made to the media library or plugins are immediately reflected across all instances.
- *Data Analytics:* You can use EFS to share data files among multiple EC2 instances running data analytics tasks. This allows different instances to work on the same data set without having to copy the data to each instance individually.

Example Mounting Procedure (Simplified)

While the actual procedure involves AWS CLI or the AWS console, the concept is simple:

1. Create an EFS file system in your AWS account.

2. Mount the EFS file system to a mount point on each EC2 instance (e.g., `/mnt/efs`). This establishes a connection between the EC2 instance and the EFS file system.

From the EC2 instance's perspective, the mount point will appear as a regular directory on the file system. Any files placed in that directory are automatically stored in the EFS file system and accessible from other EC2 instances that have also mounted the same file system. *Code Example (Conceptual)*

```
#On EC2 Instance:
sudo mount -t efs <efs-file-system-id>:/ /mnt/efs
#now anything you put into /mnt/efs is in the EFS file system
```

Key Benefits:

- *Scalability:* EFS automatically scales its storage capacity as you add or remove files, so you don't have to worry about provisioning storage in advance.
- *Availability and Durability:* EFS is designed to be highly available and durable, meaning that your files are protected from data loss.
- *Pay-as-you-go pricing:* You only pay for the storage you actually use.
- *Integration with AWS Services:* EFS integrates seamlessly with other AWS services like EC2, ECS, and Lambda.

In conclusion, EFS provides a simple and efficient way to share files between Linux-based EC2 instances, making it an ideal solution for a variety of applications that require shared storage and collaboration.

Archival Storage (Glacier/Glacier Deep Archive)

Archival storage, specifically using services like Amazon Glacier and Glacier Deep Archive, is designed for data that isn't accessed very often. Think of it like a digital time capsule for information you need to keep but don't need to look at regularly.

Low-Cost Storage for Infrequently Accessed Data: The primary purpose of Glacier and Glacier Deep Archive is to provide a very inexpensive way to store data. The trade-off for this low cost is that retrieving your data takes longer compared to other storage options like S3 or EBS. It's a good choice when cost savings are more important than immediate access.

- **Example:** Imagine a company that scans and stores invoices for tax purposes. They legally need to keep these records for seven years. After the initial year, the chances of needing to access a specific invoice are very low. Storing these invoices in Glacier makes sense because they are rarely accessed, saving a significant amount of money compared to storing them in standard storage.

Optimized for Long-Term Archiving and Data Retention: Glacier is designed for storing data for months, years, or even decades. It's suitable for regulatory compliance, digital preservation, and long-term backups.

- **Example:** A hospital might use Glacier to archive patient medical records after a certain number of years. Even though these records are rarely needed, they must be retained for legal and historical purposes. Similarly, a research institution could archive raw data from long-term experiments.

Understanding the Trade-offs: Retrieval Time

The key factor differentiating Glacier from other storage options is its retrieval time. Accessing data stored in Glacier is not instantaneous. You have to initiate a retrieval request, and it can take several hours (Glacier) or even longer (Glacier Deep Archive) to get your data.

- **Glacier Retrieval:** Offers different retrieval options, ranging from expedited (costly) to standard (several hours).
- **Glacier Deep Archive Retrieval:** Offers the lowest storage cost but the longest retrieval times, typically taking 12-48 hours.

Illustrative Sketch:

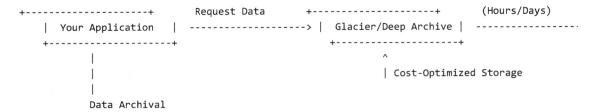

Programming Example (AWS CLI):

While you don't directly interact with Glacier like a regular file system, you use tools and APIs to manage and retrieve data. Here's a simplified AWS CLI example showing how to initiate a retrieval request (note: replace placeholders with your actual values):

```
aws glacier initiate-job \
    --account-id - \
    --vault-name my-vault \
    --job-parameters '{"Type": "archive-retrieval", "ArchiveId": "YOUR_ARCHIVE_ID", "Description
    --region YOUR_AWS_REGION
```

- `account-id`: Your AWS account ID. Use "-" for the current account.
- `vault-name`: The name of the Glacier vault where your data is stored.
- `ArchiveId`: The unique ID of the specific file/archive you want to retrieve.
- `Tier`: Specifies the retrieval speed (e.g., "Standard", "Expedited", "Bulk"). This affects the retrieval cost and time.

When to Choose Glacier/Glacier Deep Archive:

- **Data that is rarely accessed:** If you access your data only a few times a year, Glacier is a good choice.
- **Data where immediate access is not critical:** If you can wait several hours or even a day to retrieve your data, Glacier is a good fit.
- **Long-term data retention:** If you need to keep data for many years for compliance or archival purposes, Glacier is a cost-effective solution.
- **Large volumes of data:** The cost savings become more significant as the amount of data you're archiving increases.

Choosing the Right Storage

Selecting the correct type of storage depends on several factors, including how often you need to access the data, how quickly you need to access it (performance), how much you're willing to spend (cost), and how long you need to keep the data (data lifecycle). Let's examine each of these considerations:

1. Access Frequency:

How often will you need to retrieve the data? This is crucial. If you need data constantly, like for a running application, you need faster storage. If you rarely need it, you can opt for cheaper, slower options.

- **Frequent Access:** If you are using the data daily or even hourly, consider Block Storage (EBS), File Storage (EFS), or Object Storage (S3). These options are designed for quick retrieval. Imagine a database that powers a website; it needs to access information constantly.

- **Infrequent Access:** If you only need the data once a month, once a year, or even less, then Archival Storage (Glacier/Glacier Deep Archive) is a better choice. This is perfect for backups that you hope you never need to use.

2. Performance Needs:

How quickly do you need to access the data? This refers to latency and throughput. Latency is the time it takes to retrieve a single piece of data. Throughput is the amount of data you can retrieve over a period of time.

- **High Performance:** Block Storage (EBS) generally provides the best performance because it's directly attached to your server and behaves like a hard drive. This is crucial for databases or applications requiring very fast read and write speeds.

- **Medium Performance:** File Storage (EFS) offers good performance and is suitable for shared file systems where multiple servers need to access the same files. It's a balance between speed and shared access. Object Storage (S3) also fits here for web serving and general purpose needs

- **Low Performance:** Archival Storage (Glacier/Glacier Deep Archive) is the slowest but most cost-effective option. It's designed for data that you don't need to access quickly. Retrieving data from Glacier can take hours.

3. Cost Considerations:

Storage costs vary significantly depending on the type of storage.

- **Most Expensive (per GB):** Block Storage (EBS) tends to be the most expensive due to its high performance. You pay for the storage whether you use it or not.

- **Mid-Range:** File Storage (EFS) and Object Storage (S3) offer a balance between cost and performance. You generally pay for the amount of storage you use and the amount of data you transfer.

- **Least Expensive:** Archival Storage (Glacier/Glacier Deep Archive) is the cheapest option for long-term storage. However, you also pay a fee for retrieving the data.

4. Data Lifecycle Requirements:

How long do you need to keep the data? And how will you manage it over time?

- **Short-Term:** If you only need the data for a few days or weeks, you might consider using Block Storage (EBS) for temporary processing and then deleting it.

- **Medium-Term:** For data that you need to keep for a few months or years, Object Storage (S3) or File Storage (EFS) is a good choice.

- **Long-Term:** If you need to keep the data for years or decades (for compliance or archival purposes), Archival Storage (Glacier/Glacier Deep Archive) is the most cost-effective solution.

Putting It All Together:

Consideration	Block Storage (EBS)	File Storage (EFS)	Object Storage (S3)	Archival Storage (Glacier)
Access Frequency	Frequent	Frequent	Frequent/Infrequent	Infrequent
Performance	High	Medium	Medium	Low
Cost (per GB)	High	Medium	Medium	Low
Data Lifecycle	Short/Medium	Medium	Medium/Long	Long

Example Scenarios:

- **Scenario 1: Web Application**

  - You have a website with lots of images and videos. You also have a database storing user information.
  - *Images/Videos:* Store these in Object Storage (S3). They are accessed frequently by website visitors, and S3 is designed to serve this type of content efficiently.
  - *Database:* Store the database on Block Storage (EBS) attached to an EC2 instance. The database needs fast access to data for quick website response times.

- **Scenario 2: Data Backup**

- You need to back up your important files regularly.
- *Initial Backups:* You might use Object Storage (S3) for recent backups that you might need to restore quickly.
- *Archival Backups:* Move older backups to Archival Storage (Glacier/Glacier Deep Archive) to save money. These backups are less likely to be needed but must be retained for compliance.

- **Scenario 3: Shared Project Files**

  - A team of researchers needs to collaborate on a set of files.
  - *Shared Files:* Use File Storage (EFS) to create a shared file system that all team members can access from their EC2 instances. This simplifies collaboration and ensures everyone is working with the same versions of the files.

By carefully considering access frequency, performance needs, cost, and data lifecycle, you can choose the right storage option for your specific requirements.

Chapter 7 Core Building Blocks of AWS Architecture- Databases on AWS: RDS, DynamoDB, and NoSQL Alternatives

Here are 5 bullet points outlining the concept of Databases on AWS in the context of system design, suitable for a single slide:

- **Relational Database Service (RDS):** Managed service supporting SQL databases (MySQL, PostgreSQL, SQL Server, etc.) for transactional workloads.

- **DynamoDB:** Fully managed NoSQL database offering extreme scalability and low latency for high-traffic applications.

- **NoSQL Alternatives:** Exploring other NoSQL options like DocumentDB, Cassandra for specific data models and performance needs.

- **Database Selection Criteria:** Evaluating data volume, velocity, variety, and application requirements to choose the optimal database.

- **Scalability and Resilience:** Designing database architectures for horizontal scaling, replication, and automated failover on AWS.

Relational Database Service (RDS)

The Relational Database Service (RDS) is a managed service provided by AWS. Think of it as a way to use popular SQL databases without having to worry about the underlying hardware and operating system. AWS handles the installation, patching, backups, and other administrative tasks, allowing you to focus on building your application.

Supporting SQL Databases:

RDS supports several well-known SQL database engines, including:

- **MySQL:** A widely used open-source database, popular for web applications.
- **PostgreSQL:** Another powerful open-source database known for its standards compliance and advanced features.
- **SQL Server:** A commercial database developed by Microsoft, often used in enterprise environments.
- **MariaDB:** A community-developed fork of MySQL, also open-source.
- **Oracle:** A robust and widely adopted commercial database management system.

Example:

Imagine you are building a simple e-commerce website. You need a database to store information about products, customers, and orders. You could choose MySQL or PostgreSQL as your database engine within RDS.

For Transactional Workloads:

RDS is particularly well-suited for transactional workloads. These are applications that require consistent and reliable data storage and retrieval, where multiple operations must succeed or fail together. Common examples include banking systems, e-commerce platforms, and inventory management systems.

Example:

In our e-commerce example, placing an order involves multiple steps: updating inventory, recording the order details, and processing the payment. RDS ensures that all these steps happen correctly, or none at all, maintaining data integrity.

A Simple Analogy

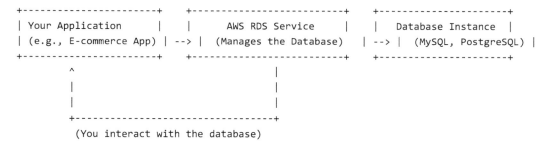

```
+----------------------+    +--------------------------+    +----------------------+
| Your Application     |    |     AWS RDS Service      |    |  Database Instance   |
| (e.g., E-commerce App) | --> |  (Manages the Database)  | --> |  (MySQL, PostgreSQL) |
+----------------------+    +--------------------------+    +----------------------+
          ^                              |
          |                              |
          |                              |
          +------------------------------+
        (You interact with the database)
```

You interact with RDS service and AWS RDS manage your database.

DynamoDB

DynamoDB is a fully managed NoSQL database service offered by AWS. This means AWS handles all the operational aspects, such as provisioning, patching, and scaling. The key features of DynamoDB are its extreme scalability and low latency, making it ideal for high-traffic applications.

Extreme Scalability:

DynamoDB can automatically scale to handle virtually any amount of data and traffic. You don't need to manually provision or manage servers. As your application grows, DynamoDB seamlessly adapts to meet the increased demand.

Low Latency:

DynamoDB is designed for very fast read and write operations. It can deliver single-digit millisecond latency even at a massive scale. This is crucial for applications that require real-time performance.

Example:

Consider a social media application with millions of users. DynamoDB can store user profiles, posts, and connections, and it can handle the massive read and write operations generated by user activity with low latency.

For High-Traffic Applications:

DynamoDB is an excellent choice for applications with high volumes of traffic, such as gaming platforms, ad tech, and IoT (Internet of Things) applications. These applications often require fast and reliable data access, and DynamoDB can provide the necessary performance.

Key-Value and Document Data Model:

DynamoDB primarily uses a key-value and document data model. This means you store data as items, where each item has a unique key, and the item's attributes are stored as a document (typically in JSON format). This allows for flexible and schema-less data storage.

Example:

In our social media example, a user profile could be stored as a DynamoDB item with the user ID as the key. The item's attributes could include the user's name, email address, and profile picture, stored as a JSON document.

Why DynamoDB?

- **Automatic Scaling:** Handles traffic spikes without manual intervention.
- **Fast Performance:** Single-digit millisecond latency.
- **Fully Managed:** No operational overhead.

A Diagram Showing Scalability

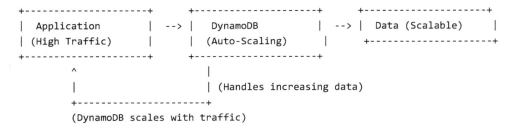

```
+--------------------+        +--------------------+        +--------------------+
| Application        | -->  | DynamoDB           | -->  | Data (Scalable)    |
| (High Traffic)     |        | (Auto-Scaling)     |        +--------------------+
+--------------------+        +--------------------+
         ^                              |
         |                              | (Handles increasing data)
         +--------------------+
       (DynamoDB scales with traffic)
```

As traffic increases, dynamoDB scales and handles it.

NoSQL Alternatives

Beyond DynamoDB, AWS offers other NoSQL database options. Each of these is designed for specific data models and performance requirements.

DocumentDB:

DocumentDB is a fully managed document database service that is compatible with MongoDB. It's designed for applications that use JSON-like documents for data storage.

- **Use Case:** Content management systems, catalog management, and mobile gaming.
- **Data Model:** Stores data as JSON documents, allowing for nested structures and flexible schemas.

Example:

Imagine you are building a content management system (CMS) for a website. You can use DocumentDB to store articles, blog posts, and other content as JSON documents. Each document can have different fields and structures, allowing for flexibility in content creation.

Cassandra:

Cassandra is a distributed NoSQL database designed for high availability and scalability. It's a good choice for applications that require continuous uptime and the ability to handle large volumes of data.

- **Use Case:** Time-series data, sensor data, and social media analytics.
- **Data Model:** Uses a wide-column store, which is well-suited for handling structured and semi-structured data.

Example:

Suppose you are building a system to collect and analyze sensor data from IoT devices. You can use Cassandra to store the sensor data, and its distributed architecture ensures that the system remains available even if some nodes fail.

When to Consider Alternatives:

- **Specific Data Models:** If your application requires a specific data model (e.g., graph data), you might choose a database like Neptune, which is designed for graph-based data.
- **Performance Needs:** Some NoSQL databases are optimized for specific types of queries or data access patterns. Consider your application's performance requirements when choosing a database.
- **Existing Expertise:** If you have existing expertise with a particular NoSQL database (e.g., MongoDB), you might choose a compatible service like DocumentDB.

Diagram showing Alternatives

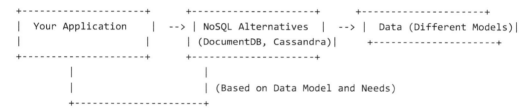

Your application data structure and application needs will decide from the NoSQL Alternatives, which one to choose.

Database Selection Criteria

Choosing the right database for your application is a critical decision. Several factors should be considered, including data volume, velocity, variety, and specific application requirements.

Data Volume:

- **Definition:** The amount of data that your application will store.
- **Considerations:**
  - **Small Data Volume:** RDS might be sufficient.
  - **Large Data Volume:** DynamoDB or Cassandra might be more appropriate due to their scalability.

Data Velocity:

- **Definition:** The rate at which data is generated and processed.
- **Considerations:**
  - **High Data Velocity:** DynamoDB or Cassandra can handle high write throughput.
  - **Low Data Velocity:** RDS might be adequate.

Data Variety:

- **Definition:** The different types of data that your application will store (e.g., structured, semi-structured, unstructured).
- **Considerations:**
    - **Structured Data:** RDS is a good choice.
    - **Semi-Structured or Unstructured Data:** NoSQL databases like DocumentDB or DynamoDB are more flexible.

Application Requirements:

- **Transactions:** If your application requires ACID transactions, RDS is a better choice.
- **Latency:** If your application needs low latency, DynamoDB is a strong contender.
- **Scalability:** For applications that need to scale rapidly, DynamoDB or Cassandra are excellent options.
- **Query Patterns:** Consider the types of queries your application will perform. Some databases are better suited for specific query patterns.
- **Consistency:** Evaluate the consistency requirements of your application. Some NoSQL databases offer eventual consistency, while others provide strong consistency.

Example:

Let's say you are building a real-time analytics dashboard that needs to process a continuous stream of data from various sources. In this case, you would need a database that can handle high data velocity, such as Cassandra. If, instead, you're building an accounting system that needs to guarantee data consistency, RDS would be a better choice.

Decision Diagram:

```
+-------------------------+
| Evaluate Data:          |
| Volume, Velocity, Variety|
+-------------------------+
            |
            v
+-------------------------+
| Consider Application:   |
| Requirements (Transactions,|
| Latency, Scalability)   |
+-------------------------+
            |
            v
+-------------------------+
| Choose Optimal Database |
| (RDS, DynamoDB, NoSQL)  |
+-------------------------+
```

Based on data volume and velocity and your application requirement and latency it will help you to select the right database for your applications.

Scalability and Resilience

Designing database architectures for scalability and resilience is crucial for ensuring that your application can handle increased traffic and remain available in the event of failures.

Horizontal Scaling:

- **Definition:** Adding more machines to your database cluster to handle increased load.
- **How it Works:** Both RDS and DynamoDB support horizontal scaling. In RDS, you can use read replicas to distribute read traffic. In DynamoDB, the service automatically scales based on demand.

- **Benefits:** Improves performance and availability.

Replication:

- **Definition:** Creating multiple copies of your data and distributing them across different locations.
- **How it Works:** RDS supports replication through read replicas and multi-AZ deployments. DynamoDB automatically replicates data across multiple availability zones.
- **Benefits:** Provides data redundancy and protects against data loss.

Automated Failover:

- **Definition:** Automatically switching to a backup database instance in the event of a failure.
- **How it Works:** RDS offers Multi-AZ deployments, which automatically fail over to a standby instance in a different Availability Zone if the primary instance fails. DynamoDB is inherently resilient and automatically handles failures.
- **Benefits:** Minimizes downtime and ensures continuous availability.

Example:

Suppose you have an e-commerce website that experiences a surge in traffic during the holiday season. By using read replicas in RDS, you can distribute the read traffic across multiple database instances, preventing the primary instance from being overloaded. If the primary instance fails, the system automatically fails over to a standby instance, ensuring that the website remains available.

Availability Zones (AZs):

It's important to utilize multiple Availability Zones (AZs) to increase the resilience of your database. AZs are distinct locations within an AWS region that are designed to be isolated from failures in other AZs.

Diagram: Redundancy Using Multiple Availability Zones

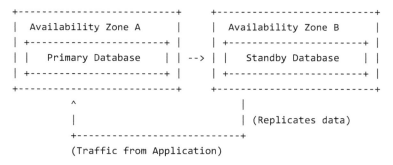

```
+--------------------------+      +--------------------------+
| Availability Zone A      |      | Availability Zone B      |
| +----------------------+ |      | +----------------------+ |
| |   Primary Database   | | -->  | |   Standby Database   | |
| +----------------------+ |      | +----------------------+ |
+--------------------------+      +--------------------------+
            ^                                |
            |                                | (Replicates data)
            +--------------------------+
            (Traffic from Application)
```

If Zone A fails, traffic automatically shifts to zone B, minimising downtime.

DynamoDB: Fully Managed NoSQL Database

DynamoDB is a fully managed NoSQL database service offered by AWS. Think of it as a highly scalable and very fast digital filing cabinet, but instead of physical files, you are storing data. Because it's "fully managed," AWS handles tasks like server setup, patching, and backups, so you can focus on using your data. DynamoDB excels when you need extreme scalability and low latency, particularly for applications with high traffic.

Let's break down what that means:

- **NoSQL:** Unlike traditional relational databases (like MySQL or PostgreSQL) that use tables with rows and columns, DynamoDB uses a different approach. It's a "NoSQL" or "not only SQL" database. Think of it more like storing collections of documents.

- **Fully Managed:** You don't have to worry about the underlying infrastructure. AWS takes care of server maintenance, software updates, scaling, and other administrative tasks. This significantly reduces operational overhead.

- **Extreme Scalability:** DynamoDB can handle massive amounts of data and traffic. If your application suddenly experiences a surge in users, DynamoDB can automatically scale up to meet the increased demand without you having to manually adjust anything.

- **Low Latency:** Low latency means quick response times. DynamoDB is designed to retrieve data very quickly, even under heavy load. This is crucial for applications where speed is paramount.

Understanding the Data Model

DynamoDB uses a key-value and document data model. That means you access data by providing a key. You can think of it like a dictionary where you look up a word (the key) to find its definition (the value).

- **Tables:** These are similar to tables in relational databases, but with more flexibility.
- **Items:** Each item is like a row in a relational database table. It's a collection of attributes.
- **Attributes:** These are the individual data elements within an item. They're like columns in a relational database.

Example:

Imagine you are building an e-commerce application and want to store product information in DynamoDB. A table named `Products` could store each product as an item.

An item (representing a single product) might look like this in JSON format:

```
{
  "ProductID": "12345",
  "ProductName": "Awesome T-Shirt",
  "Description": "A comfortable cotton t-shirt.",
  "Price": 25.99,
  "Category": "Apparel",
  "Inventory": 100
}
```

In this example:

- `ProductID` is the primary key (used to uniquely identify the product).
- `ProductName`, `Description`, `Price`, `Category`, and `Inventory` are attributes containing information about the product.

Accessing Data (Code Example)

Here's a simplified Python code snippet using the `boto3` library (AWS SDK for Python) to retrieve the product with `ProductID` "12345":

```
import boto3

# Configure the DynamoDB client
dynamodb = boto3.resource('dynamodb', region_name='your_aws_region') # Replace 'your_aws_region'
table = dynamodb.Table('Products')

# Get the item with ProductID "12345"
response = table.get_item(Key={'ProductID': '12345'})

# Print the item (if found)
if 'Item' in response:
    product = response['Item']
```

```
    print(product)
else:
    print("Product not found.")
```

Explanation:

1. `import boto3`: Imports the AWS SDK for Python.
2. `dynamodb = boto3.resource(...)`: Creates a DynamoDB resource object, specifying your AWS region. *Important: Replace 'your_aws_region' with your actual AWS region (e.g., 'us-west-2').*
3. `table = dynamodb.Table('Products')`: Gets a reference to the 'Products' table.
4. `response = table.get_item(Key={'ProductID': '12345'})`: Retrieves the item with the primary key `ProductID` equal to "12345".
5. The `if 'Item' in response:` block checks if the item was found and, if so, prints the product details.

Use Cases for DynamoDB

DynamoDB is well-suited for a variety of use cases, including:

- **Session Management:** Storing user session data for web applications. Because of its speed and scalability, DynamoDB can handle large numbers of concurrent users.
- **Gaming:** Storing player profiles, game state, and leaderboard information. Games require fast read and write operations, which DynamoDB provides.
- **E-commerce:** Storing product catalogs, shopping carts, and order information. DynamoDB can handle the fluctuating traffic patterns common in e-commerce.
- **Mobile Applications:** Storing user data, application settings, and other mobile app data.

Important Considerations

- **Data Modeling:** Careful data modeling is crucial for DynamoDB to ensure optimal performance. You need to consider how you will access your data and design your tables and keys accordingly.
- **Cost:** DynamoDB pricing is based on consumed read and write capacity, as well as data storage. It's important to understand the pricing model to optimize your costs.

In summary, DynamoDB provides a powerful and scalable solution for applications that require a NoSQL database with high performance and minimal operational overhead. Its "fully managed" nature lets developers focus on building their applications, not managing databases.

NoSQL Alternatives

Beyond DynamoDB, AWS offers a variety of NoSQL databases, each suited for particular data models and performance requirements. Choosing the right alternative depends heavily on the specific needs of your application.

Exploring other NoSQL options like DocumentDB, Cassandra for specific data models and performance needs.

Let's explore some prominent NoSQL alternatives and their ideal use cases:

- **DocumentDB:** DocumentDB is a NoSQL document database service that supports MongoDB workloads. It's designed to give you the performance, scalability, and availability you need when working with JSON-like documents.

    - **Data Model:** Stores data as JSON-like documents with flexible schemas. Each document can have different fields.

    - **Use Cases:** Content management systems, product catalogs, user profiles, and applications where flexible and evolving data structures are common.

    - **Example:** Consider an application that manages blog posts. Each blog post can be stored as a document, with fields for title, content, author, tags, and publication date. The structure of these documents can evolve over time without requiring schema migrations.

```
{
    "_id": "post123",
    "title": "Understanding DocumentDB",
    "content": "This post explains DocumentDB...",
    "author": "John Doe",
    "tags": ["aws", "nosql", "documentdb"],
    "publication_date": "2024-01-01"
}
```

- **Cassandra:** Apache Cassandra is a wide-column NoSQL database known for its high availability and scalability. AWS offers a managed Cassandra service.

  - **Data Model:** Stores data in tables with rows and columns, but with a flexible schema. Data is partitioned across multiple nodes for scalability and fault tolerance.

  - **Use Cases:** Time-series data, social media feeds, IoT data, and applications requiring high write throughput and availability.

  - **Example:** Imagine an application tracking sensor data from multiple devices. Each sensor reading can be stored as a row in a Cassandra table, with columns for sensor ID, timestamp, and the sensor value. Cassandra's distributed architecture can handle the high volume of data generated by these sensors.

    ```
    CREATE TABLE sensor_data (
        sensor_id text,
        timestamp timestamp,
        value double,
        PRIMARY KEY (sensor_id, timestamp)
    ) WITH CLUSTERING ORDER BY (timestamp DESC);
    ```

- **Graph Databases (Neptune):** Graph databases excel when relationships between data points are paramount. Amazon Neptune is a fully managed graph database service.

  - **Data Model:** Stores data as nodes (vertices) and relationships (edges).
  - **Use Cases:** Social networks, recommendation engines, knowledge graphs, fraud detection, and applications where relationships between data are critical.
  - **Example:** Consider a social network. Users can be represented as nodes, and friendships can be represented as edges. A graph database can efficiently answer queries like "Find all friends of a friend" or "Find users with similar interests."

- **Key-Value Stores:** These are the simplest NoSQL databases, offering basic key-value storage.

  - **Data Model:** Data is stored as a simple key-value pair.
  - **Use Cases:** Caching, session management, storing user preferences, and other simple data storage needs.
  - **Example:** Consider a session management system for a web application. Each session can be stored as a key-value pair, with the session ID as the key and the session data as the value.

Database Selection Criteria:

Different NoSQL databases are built with unique architectures which makes them suitable for particular types of workloads, and each of them are tailored for specific use cases.

Evaluating data volume, velocity, variety, and application requirements to choose the optimal database.

- **Data Volume:** The amount of data you need to store. Some NoSQL databases are designed for massive datasets, while others are better suited for smaller datasets.

- **Data Velocity:** The rate at which data is ingested and processed. Some NoSQL databases are optimized for high write throughput, while others are optimized for read performance.
- **Data Variety:** The structure and complexity of your data. Some NoSQL databases are better suited for structured data, while others are better suited for unstructured or semi-structured data.
- **Application Requirements:** The specific needs of your application, such as latency requirements, consistency requirements, and availability requirements.

In general, consider the following:

- **Document Databases (DocumentDB):** Good for flexible schemas, content management, and evolving data.
- **Wide-Column Stores (Cassandra):** Good for high write throughput, time-series data, and high availability.
- **Graph Databases (Neptune):** Good for relationship-heavy data, social networks, and recommendation engines.

Scalability and Resilience:

Designing database architectures for horizontal scaling, replication, and automated failover on AWS.

NoSQL databases are inherently designed for scalability and resilience. However, you need to architect your database properly to take full advantage of these capabilities.

- **Horizontal Scaling:** The ability to add more nodes to your database cluster to increase capacity. This is a key advantage of NoSQL databases over traditional relational databases.
- **Replication:** Creating multiple copies of your data across different nodes or availability zones. This ensures data durability and availability in the event of a failure.
- **Automated Failover:** The ability to automatically switch to a replica of your database in the event of a failure. This minimizes downtime and ensures business continuity.

On AWS, these features are typically managed by the database service itself. For example, DynamoDB automatically handles replication and failover. For Cassandra, you would configure replication factors to determine how many copies of your data are stored. DocumentDB also provides automated failover capabilities.

A simple sketch showing horizontal scaling:

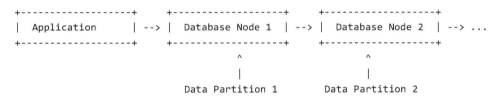

```
+-------------------+     +-------------------+     +-------------------+
|    Application    | --> |  Database Node 1  | --> |  Database Node 2  | --> ...
+-------------------+     +-------------------+     +-------------------+
                                   ^                         ^
                                   |                         |
                            Data Partition 1          Data Partition 2
```

This sketch shows how an application interacts with multiple database nodes, each storing a partition of the data. This allows the database to scale horizontally to handle increasing data volumes and traffic.

Choosing the right NoSQL database depends on a careful evaluation of your specific needs. AWS provides a rich ecosystem of NoSQL options, each with its own strengths and weaknesses. Understanding these alternatives and how to architect them for scalability and resilience is critical for building robust and performant applications.

Database Selection Criteria

Choosing the right database is crucial for the success of any application. The ideal database depends on factors such as the amount of data you expect to store, how fast you need to access it, the different types of data you are working with, and the specific requirements of your application. Let's break down these key criteria in detail:

1. Evaluating Data Volume

Data volume refers to the amount of data your application will handle. This includes both the data you initially store and the data you expect to accumulate over time. The database you choose should be capable of storing and managing this volume efficiently.

- **Small to Medium Datasets:** For applications with relatively small datasets (a few gigabytes to a few terabytes), traditional Relational Database Management Systems (RDBMS) like MySQL, PostgreSQL, or SQL Server (available through AWS RDS) are often suitable. These databases offer strong consistency, ACID (Atomicity, Consistency, Isolation, Durability) properties, and mature tooling.

- **Large Datasets:** Applications dealing with petabytes or even exabytes of data, or those anticipating rapid data growth, often benefit from NoSQL databases like DynamoDB or Cassandra. These databases are designed for horizontal scalability, allowing you to add more machines to handle increasing data volumes.

2. Evaluating Data Velocity

Data velocity refers to the rate at which data is being generated and processed. Some applications require real-time or near real-time data ingestion and analysis.

- **Low to Moderate Velocity:** For applications where data is generated at a moderate pace (e.g., a few transactions per second), RDBMS databases are generally sufficient. They can handle a reasonable transaction rate while maintaining data consistency.

- **High Velocity:** For applications with extremely high data ingestion rates (e.g., millions of events per second), such as real-time analytics or IoT applications, NoSQL databases like DynamoDB or Cassandra are better choices. Their distributed architecture allows them to handle a much higher write throughput.

3. Evaluating Data Variety

Data variety refers to the different types of data your application needs to store and process.

- **Structured Data:** If your data is highly structured (e.g., rows and columns), an RDBMS is a natural fit. RDBMS databases excel at managing data with a predefined schema and enforcing relationships between data elements. Example: A banking application where customer data, account information, and transaction details are stored in well-defined tables.

```
-- Example SQL Table Structure
CREATE TABLE Customers (
    CustomerID INT PRIMARY KEY,
    FirstName VARCHAR(255),
    LastName VARCHAR(255),
    Email VARCHAR(255)
);
```

- **Semi-structured or Unstructured Data:** If your data is semi-structured (e.g., JSON, XML) or unstructured (e.g., text, images, videos), NoSQL databases like DocumentDB are often a better choice. These databases are more flexible and can accommodate evolving data structures. Example: A content management system (CMS) where articles, images, and videos are stored with varying metadata.

```
// Example JSON Document in DocumentDB
{
    "articleId": "12345",
    "title": "My Amazing Article",
    "content": "This is the content of my article.",
    "author": "John Doe",
    "tags": ["technology", "programming"]
}
```

4. Evaluating Application Requirements

Beyond the data itself, the specific requirements of your application play a significant role in database selection.

- **ACID Transactions:** If your application requires strong consistency and ACID properties (Atomicity, Consistency, Isolation, Durability) – where data integrity is paramount – an RDBMS is typically the best option. Examples include financial transactions, order processing, and inventory management.

- **High Availability and Scalability:** If your application requires high availability and the ability to scale horizontally to handle increasing load, a NoSQL database designed for distributed systems is more suitable. Examples include social media platforms, online gaming, and large-scale e-commerce sites.

- **Specific Data Models:** Some applications may benefit from specific data models offered by NoSQL databases. For example, graph databases are well-suited for applications that need to analyze relationships between data elements, such as social networks or recommendation engines.

Example Scenario:

Suppose you are building an e-commerce application. You'll likely need to store customer data, product information, orders, and payment details.

- **Customer data:** Customer data (name, address, email) is structured and requires strong consistency. **RDS (e.g., PostgreSQL) is a good choice.**

- **Product catalog:** Product information (name, description, price, images) can be semi-structured and might evolve over time. **DocumentDB or DynamoDB could be suitable.**

- **Orders:** Orders require ACID transactions to ensure that payments are processed correctly and inventory is updated accurately. **RDS (e.g., MySQL) is a strong contender.**

- **Website activity:** The website needs to track every user click, view, and transaction. **DynamoDB is likely the best fit.**

Sketch Example:

A simple sketch might illustrate this concept.

```
+----------------------+      +-----------------------+
|   RDBMS (e.g., RDS)  | -->  | Structured Data       |
| ACID Transactions    |      | (Customer, Orders)    |
+----------------------+      +-----------------------+
         ^                              |
         |                              |
         | Data Integrity              |
         |                              |
+----------------------+      +-----------------------+
|  NoSQL (e.g., DynamoDB) | --> | Semi/Unstructured Data|
| Scalability, Velocity   |     | (Product Catalog, Logs)|
+----------------------+      +-----------------------+
```

This sketch visualizes how different databases fit different data types and application needs. RDBMS handles structured data that requires integrity and ACID transactions, while NoSQL database is suitable for semi-structured data that requires scalability and velocity.

By carefully evaluating these criteria – data volume, velocity, variety, and application requirements – you can make an informed decision about the optimal database for your specific use case.

Scalability and Resilience: Designing Robust Database Architectures on AWS

When building applications on AWS, ensuring your databases can handle increasing workloads and remain available during unexpected events is paramount. Scalability and resilience are not just features; they are fundamental requirements for any system designed for long-term success.

Scalability: The ability of your database to handle a growing amount of data and user traffic is what we mean by scalability. AWS offers several strategies to scale your databases both vertically and horizontally.

- **Vertical Scaling (Scaling Up):** This involves increasing the resources of a single database instance. For example, you might upgrade the CPU, memory, or storage of an Amazon RDS instance. This is often simpler to implement initially but has limitations as you can only scale up to the maximum capacity of an instance type.

  Example: Imagine you're running a small e-commerce website on a single RDS MySQL instance. As your website gains popularity and handles more transactions, you notice performance degradation. To improve performance, you could upgrade the instance type from `db.t3.small` to `db.m5.large`, providing more CPU and memory.

  Sketch: A single server icon labelled "RDS Instance - Small" with an arrow pointing to another server icon labelled "RDS Instance - Large (Upgraded CPU/Memory)".

- **Horizontal Scaling (Scaling Out):** This involves distributing your data and workload across multiple database instances. This offers greater scalability and resilience compared to vertical scaling. With horizontal scaling, we can achieve more fault tolerance if one instance fails. Some common techniques for horizontal scaling include:

  - **Read Replicas (RDS):** Create multiple read-only copies of your database. Read Replicas offload read traffic from the primary database instance, improving performance and availability.

    Example: Continuing with the e-commerce website, you can create several read replicas in different AWS Availability Zones. The application directs all read queries (e.g., product catalog searches) to the read replicas, reducing the load on the primary database instance responsible for writes (e.g., order placement).

    Sketch: A central server icon labelled "RDS Primary Instance (Write)" with arrows pointing to three server icons labelled "RDS Read Replica" located in different regions.

    ```
    -- Example application logic for routing read queries to read replicas
    if (query_type == "read") {
        connection = get_read_replica_connection();
    } else {
        connection = get_primary_instance_connection();
    }
    ```

  - **Sharding (DynamoDB, Custom Implementations):** Divide your data into smaller, more manageable chunks (shards) and distribute them across multiple database instances. This is particularly useful for NoSQL databases like DynamoDB or can be implemented in relational databases with custom logic.
    Example: For a large social media application using DynamoDB, you could shard user data based on user ID ranges. Users with IDs from 0-9999 would be stored on shard 1, 10000-19999 on shard 2, and so on. DynamoDB automatically handles sharding and rebalancing, making it a suitable choice for this scenario.

    Sketch: A large database icon split into three smaller database icons labelled "Shard 1", "Shard 2", and "Shard 3", showing data being distributed.

Resilience: Resilience refers to your database's ability to withstand failures and continue operating with minimal downtime. AWS provides several features to enhance database resilience:

- **Multi-AZ Deployments (RDS):** Run your database in multiple Availability Zones (AZs). In case of a failure in one AZ, AWS automatically fails over to the standby instance in another AZ, ensuring minimal downtime.

  Example: When configuring your RDS instance, you can enable the Multi-AZ option. AWS will create a synchronous replica of your database in a different AZ. If the primary instance fails due to hardware issues or network outages, AWS automatically promotes the standby replica to be the new primary instance.

Sketch: Two server icons labelled "RDS Primary Instance (AZ1)" and "RDS Standby Instance (AZ2)" connected with a sync symbol (double arrow circle) showing synchronization, indicating data replication across availability zones.

- **Backup and Restore:** Regularly back up your database to Amazon S3. In case of data loss or corruption, you can quickly restore your database to a previous point in time.

  Example: Set up automated daily backups for your RDS instance. Amazon RDS stores these backups in S3. If a developer accidentally deletes critical data, you can restore the database to the point before the deletion, minimizing data loss.

  ```
  # Example AWS CLI command for restoring RDS instance
  aws rds restore-db-instance-from-db-snapshot \
      --db-instance-identifier my-restored-db \
      --db-snapshot-identifier my-daily-backup
  ```

- **Disaster Recovery (DR):** Implement a comprehensive DR strategy that includes replicating your database to a different AWS Region. In case of a regional outage, you can fail over to the replicated database in the other Region.

  Example: You can use AWS Database Migration Service (DMS) or native database replication features to replicate data from your primary RDS instance in us-east-1 to a standby RDS instance in us-west-2. Regularly test your failover process to ensure a smooth transition in case of a disaster.

  Sketch: Two cloud icons labelled "AWS Region 1" and "AWS Region 2". Each region has a RDS instance. An arrow connects Region 1 RDS to Region 2 RDS, showing data replication for disaster recovery.

Database Selection and Optimal Choice

The optimal choice of database directly impacts scalability and resilience. Choosing a managed NoSQL database like DynamoDB for high-throughput applications needing extreme scalability and low latency, will allow developers to focus on application logic instead of the underlying infrastructure.

Relational Database (RDS): Ideal for applications where you want transactional consistency, but horizontal scaling can be more complex compared to NoSQL databases.

NoSQL (DynamoDB): Ideal for use-cases where extreme scalability and low-latency is needed. Built in features to handle sharding, failover and multi-region replication.

By combining these scalability and resilience strategies with appropriate database selection based on your application's unique requirements, you can build robust and high-performing database architectures on AWS. This approach ensures your applications can handle increasing workloads while minimizing downtime and data loss.

Chapter 8 Core Building Blocks of AWS Architecture-Networking and Security: VPC, IAM, and Best Practices

Here are 5 bullet points outlining the core building blocks of AWS networking and security (VPC, IAM) for system design:

- **Virtual Private Cloud (VPC):** Foundation for isolated network environments.

  - Subnets: Segregate resources into public/private tiers.
  - Route Tables: Control traffic flow within VPC and to internet.

- **Identity and Access Management (IAM):** Securely control access to AWS resources.

  - IAM Roles: Grant permissions to EC2 instances and services.
  - Least Privilege: Grant only necessary permissions.

- **Network Security Groups (NSGs):** Instance-level firewalls, controlling inbound/outbound traffic.

- **Security Best Practices:** Essential for robust and secure architectures.

  - Principle of Least Privilege: Limit access to only what is needed.
  - Regular Security Audits: Proactively identify vulnerabilities.

- **VPC Peering/Transit Gateway:** Connect multiple VPCs for inter-VPC communication.

Virtual Private Cloud (VPC)

Foundation for isolated network environments: A Virtual Private Cloud (VPC) serves as the bedrock for building your network infrastructure within the AWS cloud. Think of it as your own logically isolated data center within AWS. It allows you to define a virtual network where you can launch AWS resources like EC2 instances, databases (RDS), and load balancers, giving you complete control over your networking environment.

Analogy: Imagine you're building a house. The VPC is like buying a plot of land on which you will construct your home. You define the boundaries of your property and decide how everything within it is organized.

Why is this important? Without a VPC, your resources would be placed in the default AWS network, which lacks the control and isolation you typically need for production environments. VPCs provide security, customization, and a clear separation of your resources from other AWS users.

Subnets: Segregate resources into public/private tiers: Within your VPC, you create subnets. Subnets are subdivisions of your VPC's IP address range, allowing you to further organize and isolate your resources.

Sketch:

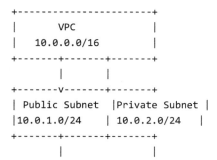

```
+-----------------------+
|      VPC              |
|   10.0.0.0/16         |
+-------+-------+-------+
        |       |
+-------v-------+-------+
| Public Subnet |Private Subnet |
|10.0.1.0/24    | 10.0.2.0/24   |
+-------+-------+-------+
        |               |
```

```
+-------v-------+-------+
| EC2 Instance | RDS Instance|
+---------------+-------+
| Internet      |              |
+---------------+---------------+
```

Public Subnets: Resources in a public subnet can be directly accessed from the internet. Typically, you'd place resources like web servers or load balancers in a public subnet. To enable internet access, you must attach an Internet Gateway to your VPC.

Private Subnets: Resources in a private subnet cannot be directly accessed from the internet. These subnets are generally used for resources like databases or application servers, which should not be exposed directly to the public internet. Resources in a private subnet can access the internet through Network Address Translation (NAT) Gateway or NAT Instance in a public subnet.

Example:

- You might place your web servers in a public subnet so they can handle incoming web traffic.
- You might put your database server in a private subnet to protect it from direct access from the outside world.

Route Tables: Control traffic flow within VPC and to internet: Route tables are used to define the paths that network traffic takes within your VPC and to external networks like the internet. Every subnet is associated with a route table, and the route table contains rules (routes) that determine where network traffic is directed.

Explanation: A route table contains a list of routes. Each route specifies a destination (a range of IP addresses) and a target (where the traffic should be sent).

- **Local Route:** A default route exists in every route table that allows communication between subnets within the same VPC. This route typically has a destination of your VPC's CIDR block (e.g., 10.0.0.0/16) and a target of "local".

- **Internet Gateway Route:** To enable a subnet to access the internet, you create a route that sends traffic destined for the internet (0.0.0.0/0) to an Internet Gateway.

- **NAT Gateway Route:** To enable instances in a private subnet to access the internet without being directly exposed, you create a route that sends traffic destined for the internet (0.0.0.0/0) to a NAT Gateway located in a public subnet.

Example of Route Table Configuration (Conceptual):

Let's say your VPC has a CIDR block of 10.0.0.0/16.

Public Subnet Route Table:

| Destination | Target | | :------------- | :----------------- | | 10.0.0.0/16 | local | | 0.0.0.0/0 | Internet Gateway |

Private Subnet Route Table:

| Destination | Target | | :------------- | :----------------- | | 10.0.0.0/16 | local | | 0.0.0.0/0 | NAT Gateway (e.g., nat-xxxxxxxxxxxxxxxxx) |

Code Example (AWS CLI - showing how to associate a Route Table with a Subnet): (This assumes you have the Route Table ID and Subnet ID)

```
aws ec2 associate-route-table --subnet-id subnet-0abcdef1234567890 --route-table-id rtb-0fedcba9
```

In summary: VPCs are the fundamental building block for creating isolated and controlled networks within AWS. Subnets allow you to segment your network further, and route tables govern how traffic flows both within your VPC and to the outside world. Together, these components provide a secure and flexible networking foundation for your applications.

Subnets: Segregate Resources into Public/Private Tiers

Subnets are like dividing your house (your VPC) into different rooms. Each room (subnet) can have a specific purpose and level of access to the outside world. In AWS, subnets are subdivisions of your VPC's IP address range where you can place your AWS resources, such as EC2 instances or databases. You carve out smaller networks (subnets) from the bigger network (VPC).

Imagine your VPC is a large plot of land (e.g., using the IP address range 10.0.0.0/16). You could divide this land into smaller plots:

- **Subnet A:** 10.0.1.0/24
- **Subnet B:** 10.0.2.0/24
- **Subnet C:** 10.0.3.0/24

Each of these represents a subnet. The /24 indicates the size of the subnet (how many IP addresses are available within it).

Public Subnets: These subnets are exposed to the internet via an Internet Gateway. Resources placed in public subnets can directly communicate with the outside world. This is where you might place your web servers, load balancers, or other components that need to be publicly accessible.

Private Subnets: These subnets are isolated from the internet. Resources placed in private subnets cannot directly communicate with the internet. They can still access the internet, but this is typically done through a Network Address Translation (NAT) Gateway or NAT Instance, which allows them to initiate outbound traffic while preventing inbound traffic initiated from the internet. You might place your database servers, application servers, or other sensitive components in private subnets.

Why Use Subnets?

- **Security:** By segregating your resources into public and private subnets, you can isolate your more sensitive resources from direct internet exposure. Public subnets are designed to communicate with public. Private subnets are designed to communicate with internal network, preventing external access.
- **Organization:** Subnets help you organize your resources logically based on their function and security requirements. For example, all web-facing components can be grouped into a public subnet, while backend databases reside in a private subnet.
- **Control:** You can apply different network access control rules (Network ACLs and Security Groups) to each subnet, further controlling the flow of traffic in and out.

Example:

Imagine you are building a web application.

1. You create a VPC with the address range 10.0.0.0/16.
2. You create a public subnet (10.0.1.0/24) for your web servers. These servers need to be accessible to users on the internet.
3. You create a private subnet (10.0.2.0/24) for your database server. The database server should *not* be directly accessible from the internet.
4. You configure a NAT Gateway in the public subnet. The EC2 instance in the private subnet can use this to access the internet for updates, without being publicly exposed.
5. You create a Route Table and associate to route internet traffic to your webserver through the Internet Gateway.

Sketch:

```
Internet
   |
Internet Gateway
   |
```

```
Public Subnet (10.0.1.0/24) - Web Servers
    |
NAT Gateway
    |
Private Subnet (10.0.2.0/24) - Database Server
```

Configuration (Conceptual AWS CLI Example):

While creating actual subnets requires a deeper dive, here's a conceptual example showing how you might think about defining subnets:

```
#Pseudo code

#Create the VPC

# Create a public subnet
aws ec2 create-subnet --vpc-id vpc-xxxxxxxx --cidr-block 10.0.1.0/24 --availability-zone us-east

# Create a private subnet
aws ec2 create-subnet --vpc-id vpc-xxxxxxxx --cidr-block 10.0.2.0/24 --availability-zone us-east

# Associate a route table to your subnet
aws ec2 associate-route-table --subnet-id subnet-xxxx --route-table-id rtb-xxxx
```

This illustrates the fundamental concept of carving out smaller, isolated networks within your VPC, improving security and organization.

In essence, subnets provide a way to logically partition your network infrastructure within AWS, mirroring how you might structure networks in a traditional on-premises environment, but with the added flexibility and scalability of the cloud.

Route Tables: Directing Traffic Within Your Virtual Network

Route tables are fundamental to how traffic is directed within your Virtual Private Cloud (VPC) and to external networks like the internet. Think of a route table as a roadmap for your network. Each route table contains a set of rules, called routes, that determine where network traffic is directed. Without route tables, your VPC would be like a city with roads but no traffic signs – chaos would ensue!

Core Functionality:

The primary function of a route table is to determine the next hop for a given packet based on its destination IP address. When a resource within your VPC, like an EC2 instance, needs to send traffic, the VPC's routing mechanism consults the route table associated with the subnet the instance resides in. It then finds the route that best matches the destination IP address of the packet and forwards the traffic accordingly.

Components of a Route:

Each route in a route table consists of two main components:

- **Destination:** This specifies the destination IP address range (in CIDR notation) to which the route applies. For example, `10.0.0.0/16` represents all IP addresses within the `10.0.0.0` to `10.0.255.255` range. A destination of `0.0.0.0/0` represents *all* IP addresses not covered by any other more specific route, and is commonly used to route traffic to the internet.
- **Target:** This specifies where the traffic should be sent. The target could be an internet gateway, a virtual private gateway, a NAT gateway, a VPC peering connection, a network interface, or even another instance within your VPC.

Example Scenario:

Let's say you have a VPC with the CIDR block `10.0.0.0/16`. You've created two subnets:

- Subnet A: `10.0.1.0/24` (Public Subnet)
- Subnet B: `10.0.2.0/24` (Private Subnet)

You want instances in Subnet A to be able to access the internet, but instances in Subnet B should not.

Here's how you would configure the route tables:

1. **Public Subnet Route Table (Associated with Subnet A):**

   | Destination | Target | |---------------|----------------------|| `10.0.0.0/16` | `local` | | `0.0.0.0/0` | `igw-xxxxxxxxxxxxxxxxx` |

   - The first route (`10.0.0.0/16` to `local`) ensures that traffic within the VPC stays within the VPC. `local` is an implicit target that always exists and represents routing within the VPC's CIDR block.
   - The second route (`0.0.0.0/0` to `igw-xxxxxxxxxxxxxxxx`) sends all traffic destined for the internet (any IP address not within the VPC) to an Internet Gateway (IGW). The `igw-xxxxxxxxxxxxxxxx` is the ID of the internet gateway attached to your VPC.

2. **Private Subnet Route Table (Associated with Subnet B):**

   | Destination | Target | |---------------|-----------|| `10.0.0.0/16` | `local` |

   - This route table *only* contains the route for traffic within the VPC. There is no route to an Internet Gateway. Instances in this subnet can communicate with each other and with resources in the public subnet, but they cannot directly access the internet.

Sketch Representation:

Here's a simple sketch to visualize this:

```
+---------------------+     +---------------------+
|    Subnet A         |     |    Subnet B         |
|  (10.0.1.0/24)      |     |  (10.0.2.0/24)      |
+---------+-----------+     +---------+-----------+
          |                           |
          |  Route Table A    |    |  Route Table B    |
          |  10.0.0.0/16 -> local|    |  10.0.0.0/16 -> local|
          |  0.0.0.0/0  -> IGW |    |                     |
          |                   |    |                     |
      +---------+-----------+     +---------+-----------+
          |                           |
          |  Internet Gateway |
          |  (Allows outbound |
          |   internet access) |
      +---------------------+
```

Code Example (AWS CLI):

While you can't create "code" for route tables in the traditional programming sense, you can use the AWS Command Line Interface (CLI) to manage them. Here's an example of how you might create a route in a route table to an internet gateway:

```
aws ec2 create-route --route-table-id rtb-xxxxxxxxxxxxxxxx --destination-cidr-block 0.0.0.0/0
```

- `rtb-xxxxxxxxxxxxxxxx`: Replace with the actual ID of your route table.
- `igw-yyyyyyyyyyyyyyyyy`: Replace with the actual ID of your internet gateway.

Important Considerations:

- **Explicit vs. Implicit Association:** Each subnet *must* be associated with a route table. If you don't explicitly associate a subnet with a route table, it is automatically associated with the VPC's *main* route table. The main route table typically only contains the local route.
- **Route Precedence:** If multiple routes match a destination IP address, the *most specific* route takes precedence. For example, a route with a destination of `10.0.1.0/24` will take precedence over a route with a destination of `10.0.0.0/16` for traffic destined to `10.0.1.5`.
- **Route Propagation:** Route propagation is a feature that allows you to automatically add routes to your route tables from your virtual private gateway (VGW). This is useful when you are connecting your VPC to your on-premises network using AWS Site-to-Site VPN.

In summary, Route Tables are the control center for directing network traffic within your VPC. Understanding how to configure and manage them is crucial for designing secure and functional AWS environments. They define the pathways your network traffic takes, dictating whether resources can communicate internally, access the internet, or connect to other networks.

Identity and Access Management (IAM)

IAM is your gatekeeper to AWS resources. It's how you control *who* can do *what* within your AWS environment. Think of it like the security system for your house: you decide who gets a key and what rooms they can access. Without IAM, anyone could potentially access and modify your resources, leading to security breaches and data loss.

IAM Roles: Granting Permissions to EC2 Instances and Services

Instead of directly assigning access keys to applications running on EC2 instances or other AWS services, you use IAM Roles. An IAM role is like a job description for an entity. It defines what permissions that entity has.

Imagine you have an application running on an EC2 instance that needs to write data to an S3 bucket. You wouldn't want to hardcode AWS credentials directly into your application code, as that presents a huge security risk. Instead, you create an IAM role with permissions to write to that specific S3 bucket. Then, you associate that role with your EC2 instance. The application running on the instance can then assume the role and securely access the S3 bucket without needing explicit access keys.

```
//Example of a role with S3 write permission to my-example-bucket
 {
   "Version": "2012-10-17",
   "Statement": [
   {
   "Effect": "Allow",
   "Action": "s3:PutObject",
   "Resource": "arn:aws:s3:::my-example-bucket/"
   }
   ]
 }
```

In this example, JSON code represents an IAM policy granting permissions to upload objects (`s3:PutObject`) to an S3 bucket named "my-example-bucket."

Sketch IAM role on EC2 instance accessing s3

```
+--------------------+      +--------------------+      +----------------------+
| EC2 Instance       |----->| IAM Role           |----->| S3 Bucket            |
| (Application running)|    | (Permissions to S3) |      | (Data Storage)       |
+--------------------+      +--------------------+      +----------------------+
         |                           |
         |                           |
```

```
                       |Assumes Role          |
                       |                      |
                       +----------------------+
```

Least Privilege: Grant Only Necessary Permissions

The principle of least privilege is a cornerstone of security. It means granting users and services only the *minimum* permissions they need to perform their tasks, and nothing more. It's like giving someone a key that only opens the front door, instead of giving them the master key to the entire building.

For instance, if a user only needs to read data from a DynamoDB table, you should grant them dynamodb:GetItem and dynamodb:Query permissions, but *not* dynamodb:UpdateItem or dynamodb:DeleteItem. This way, even if their account is compromised, the attacker's impact is limited.

Giving more permissions than necessary opens up security vulnerabilities. Following the least privilege principle minimizes the "attack surface," making it harder for attackers to exploit your system.

Sketch Showing least privilege

```
+------------------+        +---------------------+
| User/Application |------->| IAM Policy          |
| (Needs access)   |        | (Limited Permissions)|
+------------------+        +---------------------+
        ^
        | Only the needed permissions.
        |
        +---------------------+
        | AWS Resources       |
        | (DynamoDB, S3, etc.)|
        +---------------------+
```

IAM Roles: Securely Granting Permissions in AWS

IAM Roles are a cornerstone of secure access management within the AWS ecosystem. They provide a mechanism to grant permissions to AWS resources, allowing them to perform actions on your behalf without needing to hardcode or embed credentials. This is especially critical for applications running on EC2 instances or utilizing other AWS services. Think of an IAM role as a temporary security badge that a service or instance can use to access resources.

- **IAM Roles: Grant permissions to EC2 instances and services.**

    At its core, an IAM role is an identity that an AWS service or instance *assumes*. Instead of directly associating IAM user credentials (like access keys and secret keys) with an EC2 instance, you assign the instance an IAM role. This role defines what the instance is allowed to do within your AWS environment.

    Consider an EC2 instance hosting a web application that needs to store log files in an S3 bucket. Instead of giving the instance the long-term credentials of an IAM user, you create an IAM role that grants s3:PutObject permission to the specific S3 bucket. The EC2 instance assumes this role, allowing it to upload logs without ever needing to know or store any permanent security credentials.

```
# Example scenario: EC2 instance writing logs to S3

+---------------------+    assumes   +---------------------+   has permission  +---------------·
|  EC2 Instance       | ---------->  |   IAM Role          |----------------->  |  S3 Bucket
| (Web Application)   |              | (s3:PutObject)      |                   | (Log Storage)
+---------------------+              +---------------------+                   +-------------·
```

This approach has several advantages:

```
Enhanced Security: Eliminates the risk of hardcoding or storing credentials on instances.  If ar
    Simplified Management:  Managing permissions becomes centralized. Changing the role's policy
    Temporary Credentials: The instance receives temporary credentials when it assumes the role.
```

- **Least Privilege: Grant only necessary permissions.**

  Following the principle of least privilege is essential when defining IAM roles. This means granting only the *minimum* permissions required for the instance or service to perform its intended task. Avoid granting overly broad or permissive access. If an EC2 instance only needs to read data from a DynamoDB table, the IAM role should only include dynamodb:GetItem and dynamodb:Query (if needed) permissions for that specific table – no more, no less.

  Here's a simple example of an IAM policy that adheres to the principle of least privilege:

  ```json
  {
    "Version": "2012-10-17",
    "Statement": [
      {
        "Effect": "Allow",
        "Action": [
          "s3:GetObject"
        ],
        "Resource": "arn:aws:s3:::my-example-bucket/my-data.txt"
      }
    ]
  }
  ```

  This policy allows the role to *only* retrieve (s3:GetObject) the object my-data.txt from the my-example-bucket S3 bucket. It cannot list buckets, upload objects, or perform any other action on S3.

  By consistently applying the principle of least privilege, you can significantly reduce the potential blast radius of a security incident. If an instance with a tightly scoped IAM role is compromised, the attacker's ability to access and manipulate other resources in your AWS environment is severely limited.

  In summary, IAM Roles are a fundamental mechanism for secure and controlled access management in AWS. Using them effectively, combined with the principle of least privilege, is crucial for building robust and secure cloud applications. They facilitate granting temporary access to resources, simplify access management, and minimize the risk of credential exposure.

Least Privilege

The Principle of Least Privilege is a core security practice, especially vital in cloud environments like AWS. It dictates that every user, service, or system should have only the minimum necessary access rights to perform its intended task. Nothing more.

Why is it Important?

Imagine a scenario where an application on an EC2 instance requires access to an S3 bucket to read configuration files. Applying the Principle of Least Privilege means granting *only* read access to that *specific* S3 bucket. It should *not* have permission to delete objects, list other buckets, or access other AWS services. If that EC2 instance is compromised by malicious code, the attacker's scope of action is drastically limited. They can only read the configuration files – they cannot cause broader damage to your AWS environment.

How it Works in Practice:

- **IAM Policies:** IAM Policies are the primary mechanism for implementing Least Privilege in AWS. Policies are JSON documents that define permissions. You attach these policies to IAM Users, IAM Groups, or IAM Roles.

  Here's a simple example of an IAM policy that grants read-only access to a specific S3 bucket:

```
{
    "Version": "2012-10-17",
    "Statement": [
        {
            "Effect": "Allow",
            "Action": [
                "s3:GetObject",
                "s3:ListBucket"
            ],
            "Resource": [
                "arn:aws:s3:::your-bucket-name",
                "arn:aws:s3:::your-bucket-name/"
            ]
        }
    ]
}
```

  In this policy:

  - `"Effect": "Allow"` indicates that the policy grants permission.
  - `"Action"` specifies the permitted S3 actions: `"s3:GetObject"` (read objects) and `"s3:ListBucket"` (list the bucket's contents).
  - `"Resource"` defines the scope of the permission – in this case, the S3 bucket named `your-bucket-name` and all its objects.

- **IAM Roles:** IAM Roles are used to grant permissions to AWS services like EC2 instances, Lambda functions, etc. Instead of directly embedding credentials into your application code (which is a major security risk), you assign an IAM Role to the service. The service then assumes that role and obtains temporary AWS credentials. These credentials are automatically rotated, further enhancing security. Using the above IAM Policy, you'd attach the IAM Role to the service, ensuring it only can do what the policy specifies.

- **Analyzing Access Needs:** Carefully analyze the actual permissions required by each component of your system. Avoid the temptation to grant broad, unrestricted access (e.g., "AdministratorAccess"). For instance, If a Lambda function is only required to write log information, assign access only to CloudWatch Logs service.

- **Regular Audits:** Periodically review your IAM policies and roles to ensure they still adhere to the Principle of Least Privilege. As your application evolves, its access requirements may change. Remove any unnecessary permissions to minimize the attack surface.

- **Granular Permissions:** AWS offers a wide range of service-specific actions that you can use in IAM policies. Take advantage of these granular permissions to precisely control access to individual resources and operations. For example, instead of granting general DynamoDB access, you can grant permission only to perform `GetItem` operations on a specific table.

Example Scenario: Web Application

Consider a web application running on EC2 instances that needs to access a database (e.g., RDS) and store images in an S3 bucket.

1. **EC2 Instance Role:** The EC2 instances should have an IAM Role with permissions to:

- Read configuration data from a specific S3 bucket (as shown in the previous IAM policy example).
- Connect to the RDS database using specific database credentials (stored securely, not directly embedded in the code). Note: IAM Roles are *not* directly used for database authentication. However, the role *could* grant permission to fetch database credentials from AWS Secrets Manager.
- Write logs to CloudWatch Logs.

2. **Web Application Code:** The application code should *never* contain AWS credentials directly. Instead, it should use the AWS SDK to assume the IAM Role associated with the EC2 instance.

By following the Principle of Least Privilege, you minimize the potential damage from security breaches, reduce the risk of accidental data exposure, and improve the overall security posture of your AWS environment.

Chapter 9 Core Building Blocks of AWS Architecture-Serverless vs. Traditional Architectures: When to Use What

- **Serverless Architectures:**

  - **Benefits:** Cost-effective for unpredictable workloads; simplified operations; automatic scaling and high availability.

- **Traditional (EC2-based) Architectures:**

  - **Benefits:** Greater control over the environment; suitable for applications requiring specific OS or software dependencies.

- **Scaling Considerations:**

  - Serverless scales automatically, Traditional requires manual or auto scaling policies configuration.

- **Operational Overhead:**

  - Serverless reduces operational burden. Traditional requires managing servers and infrastructure.

- **Choosing the Right Approach:**

  - Consider workload characteristics, required control, operational effort, and cost when selecting between serverless and traditional architectures.

Serverless Architectures

Benefits:

Serverless architectures offer several key advantages, primarily centered around cost efficiency, operational simplicity, and built-in scalability and availability.

- **Cost-effective for unpredictable workloads:** With serverless, you only pay for the actual compute time your code consumes. Think of it like paying for electricity – you only pay for what you use. This is particularly beneficial for applications with fluctuating or unpredictable traffic patterns.

Consider an image processing application. It might experience peak usage during certain times of the day or after a marketing campaign. With a traditional server-based approach, you'd need to provision enough servers to handle the peak load, even if those servers are idle most of the time, incurring unnecessary costs. With serverless, the function automatically scales up to handle the demand, and you only pay for the actual processing time.

```python
# Example: AWS Lambda function (Python) - Simple image thumbnail generator
import boto3
import os
from PIL import Image
import io

s3 = boto3.client('s3')

def lambda_handler(event, context):
    bucket = event['Records'][0]['s3']['bucket']['name']
    key = event['Records'][0]['s3']['object']['key']
    download_path = '/tmp/{}{}'.format(uuid.uuid4(), key) # use uuid to generate unique nam
    upload_path = '/tmp/thumbnail-{}'.format(key)

    s3.download_file(bucket, key, download_path)

    try:
        image = Image.open(download_path)
        image.thumbnail((128, 128))  # Create a 128x128 thumbnail
        buffer = io.BytesIO()
        image.save(buffer, "JPEG")
        buffer.seek(0)
        s3.upload_fileobj(buffer, bucket, 'thumbnails/thumbnail-' + key, ExtraArgs={'Conten
    except Exception as e:
        print(e)
        print('Error creating thumbnail')
        raise e


#Sketch:

#   [S3 Bucket (Original Images)] -->  [Lambda Function (Thumbnail Generator)] --> [S3 Buck
#      ^                                                                              ^
#      |                                                                              |
#   Event Trigger (Image Upload)                                     Result (Thumbnail Image)
```

In this example, the Lambda function is triggered when an image is uploaded to an S3 bucket. The function downloads the image, creates a thumbnail, and uploads the thumbnail back to another location in S3. You only pay for the Lambda execution time and S3 storage, eliminating the need to manage a server continuously.

- **Simplified Operations:** Serverless computing abstracts away the complexities of server provisioning, patching, and management. Developers can focus on writing code and building applications without worrying about the underlying infrastructure. This reduces operational overhead and allows teams to move faster.

  Instead of manually configuring servers, operating systems, and network settings, developers deploy functions directly. The cloud provider handles all the infrastructure management aspects, allowing developers to concentrate solely on the application logic. Updates, security patches, and scaling are all managed automatically by the cloud provider.

  This simplification can dramatically decrease the time-to-market for new features and applications. It also frees up valuable engineering resources that can be directed toward innovation and development.

- **Automatic Scaling and High Availability:** Serverless platforms automatically scale resources to meet demand. You don't need to manually configure auto-scaling policies or worry about server capacity. The platform handles scaling automatically, ensuring your application can handle peak loads without performance degradation.

  Consider an API endpoint built using a serverless framework. As traffic to the API increases, the serverless platform automatically provisions more instances of the function to handle the load. When traffic decreases, the platform scales down, releasing resources and saving costs.

  Furthermore, serverless platforms are inherently highly available. The cloud provider distributes the functions across multiple availability zones, ensuring that the application remains available even if one availability zone experiences an outage. This built-in high availability eliminates the need to configure complex failover mechanisms.

  ```
  #Sketch:

  #  [User Requests] --> [API Gateway] --> [Serverless Function (e.g., AWS Lambda)] --> [Data
  #       |                    |
  #       V                    V
  #    Automatic         Automatic Scaling and
  #  Load Balancing        High Availability
  ```

  In this scenario, the API Gateway acts as the entry point for user requests. The gateway routes requests to the serverless function, which processes the request and interacts with other services. The serverless platform automatically handles scaling and ensures high availability, providing a resilient and scalable API endpoint.
  Scaling Considerations:

Serverless architectures excel at automatic scaling. Unlike traditional architectures where you need to define and configure auto-scaling policies, serverless platforms automatically adjust resources to meet demand. This means your application can handle sudden spikes in traffic without requiring any manual intervention. The scaling is typically fine-grained, scaling at the function level, and instantaneous, provisioning new instances as needed within milliseconds.

Operational Overhead:

Serverless significantly reduces operational overhead. You no longer have to manage servers, apply patches, monitor infrastructure, or worry about capacity planning. The cloud provider takes care of these tasks, freeing up your team to focus on building and improving your application. This can lead to faster development cycles, reduced operational costs, and increased agility. You shift from managing infrastructure to managing code.

Benefits: Serverless vs. Traditional Architectures

Let's explore the advantages of both serverless and traditional (EC2-based) architectures to help you understand when each approach is most suitable.

Serverless Architectures: Benefits in Detail

Serverless architectures offer distinct benefits, especially for applications with specific workload patterns and operational requirements. Here's a detailed look:

- **Cost-effective for unpredictable workloads:** The primary cost advantage of serverless comes from its pay-per-use model. You only pay for the compute time your code actually consumes.

  - **Explanation:** In a traditional server-based model, you provision servers and pay for them even when they are idle. This is inefficient if your application has unpredictable traffic patterns – periods of high activity followed by periods of inactivity. Serverless eliminates this waste.

  - **Example:** Imagine you're building an image resizing service. During peak hours, you might process thousands of images. Overnight, the service sees almost no traffic. With serverless, you only pay for the few seconds of compute time used to resize those images overnight. With a traditional server, you'd be paying for the server's uptime *regardless* of how much it's used.

  - **Code Example (AWS Lambda, Python):**

```python
import boto3
from PIL import Image
import io

s3 = boto3.client('s3')

def lambda_handler(event, context):
    bucket = event['Records'][0]['s3']['bucket']['name']
    key = event['Records'][0]['s3']['object']['key']

    image_object = s3.get_object(Bucket=bucket, Key=key)
    image_data = image_object['Body'].read()

    image = Image.open(io.BytesIO(image_data))
    image.thumbnail((128, 128)) # Resize

    buffer = io.BytesIO()
    image.save(buffer, "JPEG")
    buffer.seek(0)

    s3.put_object(Bucket=bucket, Key='resized/' + key, Body=buffer)
    return {
        'statusCode': 200,
        'body': 'Image Resized'
    }
```

    This Lambda function resizes images uploaded to an S3 bucket. You pay only for the execution time of this function each time an image is uploaded.

- **Simplified operations:** Serverless drastically reduces the operational burden on your team.

  - **Explanation:** With serverless, you don't need to worry about patching operating systems, managing servers, or configuring networking. The cloud provider handles these tasks for you. This frees up your team to focus on writing and deploying code.

  - **Example:** Instead of spending time configuring load balancers and auto-scaling groups, you can simply deploy your serverless function and let the cloud provider handle the scaling and availability. This allows developers to focus on feature development rather than infrastructure management.

- **Sketch:**

```
+--------------------+      +--------------------+      +--------------------+
| Developer Code     | -->  | Serverless Platform| -->  | Underlying         |
| (Focus on Business |      | (Provider Managed: |      | Infrastructure     |
|  Logic)            |      |  Scaling, Patching)|      | (Abstracted Away)  |
+--------------------+      +--------------------+      +--------------------+
```

- **Automatic scaling and high availability:** Serverless platforms automatically scale your application based on demand and provide built-in high availability.

  - **Explanation:** When demand increases, the serverless platform automatically provisions more resources to handle the load. When demand decreases, the platform scales down the resources. This ensures your application can handle unexpected traffic spikes without manual intervention. Furthermore, serverless platforms are inherently highly available, with automatic failover and redundancy built in.

  - **Example:** If your e-commerce website experiences a sudden surge in traffic during a flash sale, the serverless functions powering your product catalog and checkout process will automatically scale to handle the increased load, ensuring a smooth experience for your customers. You don't need to pre-provision resources or configure complex scaling policies.

  - **Conceptual Diagram:**

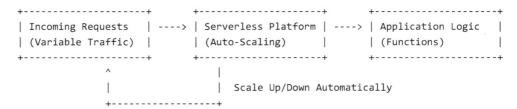

```
+--------------------+        +--------------------+        +--------------------+
| Incoming Requests  | ---->  | Serverless Platform| ---->  | Application Logic  |
| (Variable Traffic) |        | (Auto-Scaling)     |        | (Functions)        |
+--------------------+        +--------------------+        +--------------------+
          ^                            |
          |                            |   Scale Up/Down Automatically
     +------------------+
```

Traditional (EC2-based) Architectures: Benefits in Detail

While serverless offers many advantages, traditional EC2-based architectures also have their place, particularly when you need fine-grained control over the environment.

- **Greater control over the environment:** EC2 instances provide complete control over the operating system, installed software, and networking configuration.

  - **Explanation:** With EC2, you can customize the environment to meet the specific requirements of your application. This is important if you need to install custom libraries, configure specific system settings, or run applications that are not compatible with the serverless environment.

  - **Example:** If you need to run a legacy application that relies on a specific version of a library or requires a particular operating system kernel, an EC2 instance gives you the flexibility to create the exact environment needed. Serverless environments might have limitations on the operating system or available libraries.

- **Suitable for applications requiring specific OS or software dependencies:** Certain applications might have dependencies that are difficult or impossible to satisfy in a serverless environment.

  - **Explanation:** Some applications require direct access to hardware resources or specific low-level system calls that are not available in serverless environments. In such cases, EC2 instances are a better choice.

  - **Example:** Applications that require specialized hardware acceleration (e.g., GPUs for machine learning) or custom device drivers are often better suited for EC2 instances, where you have full control over the underlying hardware and software stack.

- ○ **Diagram:**

```
+--------------------+
| EC2 Instance       |
| (Full OS Control)  |
|--------------------|
| OS                 |
| Libraries          |
| System Settings    |
| Hardware Access    |
+--------------------+
```

Traditional (EC2-based) Architectures

Benefits:

Traditional architectures, often built using services like Amazon EC2 (Elastic Compute Cloud), offer a distinct set of advantages, particularly when compared to serverless options. The key benefit centers around **greater control over the environment**. With EC2 instances, you have direct access to the operating system (OS), the file system, and the entire software stack. This control enables deep customization and configuration tailored to the precise requirements of your application.

For instance, you might need to use a specific version of a database, a legacy library not easily compatible with serverless functions, or a custom kernel module. In such cases, the level of control provided by EC2 is invaluable. Serverless environments, while convenient, abstract away many of these underlying details, limiting customization options.

Another significant advantage is that EC2-based architectures are **suitable for applications requiring specific OS or software dependencies.** Some applications might be built on operating systems other than Linux, such as Windows Server, or might depend on software that necessitates a full-fledged server environment. EC2 provides the flexibility to run these applications without significant modification.

Consider a scenario where you have an application that uses a proprietary software package licensed for a specific OS. Migrating such an application to a serverless environment could involve significant effort and cost due to re-licensing or re-architecting the application. EC2 provides a more straightforward path, allowing you to run the application as-is on a virtual machine.

Example:

Imagine you need to run a financial modeling application that depends on a Windows-specific library. You can launch a Windows Server EC2 instance and install the application and library on it. This setup provides the necessary environment for the application to function correctly without requiring code changes or extensive refactoring.

Scaling Considerations:

While serverless architectures boast automatic scaling, traditional EC2-based architectures necessitate more hands-on approach. Scaling in EC2 involves configuring **manual or auto-scaling policies.**

- **Manual Scaling:** This approach requires you to monitor the load on your EC2 instances and manually add or remove instances based on demand. This method is suitable for applications with predictable traffic patterns.

- **Auto Scaling:** Auto Scaling automates the process by dynamically adjusting the number of EC2 instances based on predefined metrics like CPU utilization or network traffic. You define policies that specify when to launch or terminate instances.

    ○ **Example:** You can set up an auto-scaling group that maintains a minimum of 2 and a maximum of 10 EC2 instances. The group monitors the average CPU utilization of the instances, and if it exceeds 70%, it automatically launches a new instance. Conversely, if the utilization drops below 30%, it terminates an instance.

Code example (AWS CLI for setting up Auto Scaling):

While the AWS console is commonly used to create an auto-scaling group, here's a simplified illustration of some of the AWS CLI commands involved to define a launch configuration and autoscaling group.

```
# Create a Launch Configuration (specifies the instance type, AMI, etc.)
aws autoscaling create-launch-configuration \
    --launch-configuration-name my-launch-config \
    --image-id ami-0abcdef1234567890 \
    --instance-type t2.micro \
    --security-groups sg-0123456789abcdef0


# Create an Auto Scaling Group
aws autoscaling create-auto-scaling-group \
    --auto-scaling-group-name my-auto-scaling-group \
    --launch-configuration-name my-launch-config \
    --min-size 2 \
    --max-size 10 \
    --desired-capacity 2 \
    --vpc-zone-identifier subnet-0abcdef1234567890 \
    --health-check-type EC2 \
    --health-check-grace-period 300
```

Operational Overhead:

EC2-based architectures involve a higher degree of **operational burden** compared to serverless. This is because you are responsible for **managing servers and infrastructure.** This includes tasks such as:

- **Operating System Patching:** Regularly updating the OS with security patches.
- **Software Updates:** Maintaining and updating installed software.
- **Server Configuration:** Configuring and optimizing server settings.
- **Monitoring:** Monitoring server health, resource utilization, and performance.
- **Troubleshooting:** Diagnosing and resolving server-related issues.
- **Security:** Ensuring the security of the server environment.

This level of responsibility can require a dedicated operations team or significant time investment, particularly for complex applications. While tools like configuration management systems (e.g., Ansible, Chef, Puppet) can help automate some of these tasks, they still require initial setup and ongoing maintenance.

Sketch:

A simple sketch illustrates the difference in operational overhead:

```
Serverless:  [Application Code] --> Cloud Provider (Handles Scaling, OS, etc.)

    Traditional: [Application Code] --> [OS] --> [Server Hardware] (You Manage OS & Server)
```

The sketch highlights that with serverless, the cloud provider manages the underlying infrastructure, while with traditional architectures, you are responsible for managing the OS and server hardware.

Scaling Considerations

Scaling is a critical aspect of any application architecture. It refers to the ability of your system to handle increasing amounts of traffic or data. When comparing serverless and traditional (EC2-based) architectures, their scaling characteristics differ significantly.

Serverless scales automatically:

Serverless architectures are designed to scale automatically. This means that the underlying platform (like AWS Lambda or Azure Functions) automatically adjusts the resources allocated to your application based on the incoming demand. You don't need to manually configure or manage scaling policies. This "auto-scaling" is a key benefit, particularly for applications with unpredictable workloads.

Example: Imagine you have a photo processing application built using AWS Lambda. During off-peak hours, only a few users are uploading photos. Lambda automatically scales down the number of function instances, minimizing costs. When a popular social media campaign drives a surge in photo uploads, Lambda automatically scales up the number of function instances to handle the increased load without any manual intervention from you.

Traditional requires manual or auto scaling policies configuration:

In contrast, traditional architectures based on EC2 instances require you to explicitly configure scaling policies. You need to define rules that determine when to add or remove instances based on metrics like CPU utilization, network traffic, or queue length. This configuration can be done manually or through auto-scaling services provided by cloud providers (like AWS Auto Scaling).

Example: Let's say you have an e-commerce website running on EC2 instances. You might configure an auto-scaling group to add more instances when the average CPU utilization across your existing instances exceeds 70% for a certain period. Conversely, you might configure it to remove instances when the CPU utilization drops below 30%.

```
# Example of AWS Auto Scaling policy (simplified)
resource "aws_autoscaling_policy" "scale_up" {
  name                   = "scale_up_policy"
  scaling_adjustment     = 1  # Add one instance
  adjustment_type        = "ChangeInCapacity"
  cooldown               = 300
  autoscaling_group_name = "your-autoscaling-group-name"
}
```

Explanation: This code snippet (simplified for illustration) shows how you might define an auto-scaling policy in AWS. It specifies that one more EC2 instance should be added when the policy is triggered, which would be based on a CloudWatch alarm (not shown here) monitoring CPU utilization or other metrics.

Sketch to illustrate Scaling Considerations

```
Serverless:
    [Traffic Surge] --> [Platform (e.g., Lambda)] --> [Automatic Scaling of Function Instances]

Traditional (EC2):
    [Traffic Surge] --> [Monitoring (e.g., CPU Utilization)] --> [Auto Scaling Group] --> [Add/Re
```

Explanation of Sketch: The sketch shows visually how serverless automatically scales, while traditional EC2 requires pre-configured policies to manage scaling. The left side represent serverless and right side is EC2.

Operational Overhead

Serverless architectures and traditional (EC2-based) architectures differ significantly in the operational overhead they impose. Operational overhead refers to the effort and resources required to manage and maintain the underlying infrastructure and applications. Let's explore these differences in detail.

Serverless reduces operational burden.

Serverless computing, by design, abstracts away the need to manage servers. This means you don't need to provision, configure, patch, or maintain any servers. The cloud provider handles all of that for you. This drastically reduces the operational burden on your team.

- **Example:** Consider deploying a simple API endpoint. In a serverless environment (using AWS Lambda, for instance), you would upload your code, configure a trigger (like an HTTP request), and the service automatically scales and manages the execution environment. You don't need to worry about the underlying operating system, web server, or any other infrastructure components.

  A simplified illustration:

```
[Client Request] --> [API Gateway] --> [Lambda Function (your code)] --> [Response]
                                        ^
                                        |
                         (Managed by Cloud Provider)
```

  The cloud provider maintains the entire infra on behalf of you.

  In contrast, in traditional architecture, you'd have to manage your entire infrastructure.

Traditional requires managing servers and infrastructure.

With traditional EC2-based architectures, you are responsible for managing the entire server infrastructure. This includes tasks such as:

- **Provisioning servers:** Selecting the right instance types, configuring storage, and setting up networking.

- **Operating system maintenance:** Patching, updating, and securing the operating system.

- **Software installation and configuration:** Installing and configuring web servers, databases, and other necessary software.

- **Monitoring and troubleshooting:** Monitoring server health, identifying and resolving performance issues, and troubleshooting errors.

- **Scaling:** Manually or automatically scaling the number of servers to handle changes in traffic.

- **High Availability:** Managing Redundancy of the servers to ensure the system will be up and running.

- **Example:** If you want to deploy a web application on an EC2 instance, you would need to:

  1. Launch an EC2 instance.
  2. Install a web server (like Apache or Nginx).
  3. Configure the web server.
  4. Deploy your application code.
  5. Monitor the server's CPU, memory, and disk usage.
  6. Set up scaling policies to automatically add or remove instances based on traffic.
  7. Ensure that the OS are patched or not from any security breach.

  A simplified illustration:

```
[Client Request] --> [Load Balancer] --> [EC2 Instance 1 (Your Web Server)]
                                          ^
                                          |
                                          [EC2 Instance 2 (Your Web Server)]
                                          ^
                                          |
                                   (Managed by You)
```

In this scenario, you are entirely responsible for maintaining the servers.

Impact on Development Teams:

The reduced operational overhead of serverless architectures allows development teams to focus more on building and improving applications, rather than spending time on infrastructure management. This can lead to faster development cycles, increased productivity, and reduced operational costs.

Choosing the Right Approach

Selecting between serverless and traditional (EC2-based) architectures involves carefully evaluating several factors to determine which best aligns with your application's needs and constraints. The primary considerations are workload characteristics, required control, operational effort, and cost. Each of these plays a crucial role in making an informed decision.

Workload Characteristics

The nature of your workload is a significant factor. Workloads can be predictable or unpredictable. Serverless architectures shine when dealing with unpredictable workloads, meaning workloads that have spikes in traffic or are event-driven.

For example, consider an image processing application. Users upload images sporadically, and each upload triggers processing. Serverless functions can scale instantly to handle these bursts without any pre-configured infrastructure. The functions execute only when an image is uploaded, saving costs during idle periods.

```python
# Example: AWS Lambda function triggered by S3 upload (Python)
import boto3

def lambda_handler(event, context):
    bucket = event['Records'][0]['s3']['bucket']['name']
    key = event['Records'][0]['s3']['object']['key']
    print(f"Processing image {key} from bucket {bucket}")
    # Image processing logic here
    return {
        'statusCode': 200,
        'body': 'Image processed successfully!'
    }
```

In contrast, if you have a continuously running application with a consistent load, a traditional EC2-based architecture might be more suitable. This is particularly true if you have a fixed capacity that you can optimize and fully utilize.

Required Control

Traditional architectures offer greater control over the environment. This control extends to the operating system, software dependencies, and security configurations.

Some applications require very specific operating system versions, custom kernels, or particular software libraries.

For example, a legacy application might be dependent on an older version of a specific operating system library. Migrating such an application to a serverless environment might require significant code refactoring or be altogether impractical. In these scenarios, running the application on EC2 instances provides the necessary control and compatibility.

```
+------------------------+      +------------------------+
| EC2 Instance           |      | Serverless Function    |
|------------------------|      |------------------------|
| Full OS Control        |      | Limited OS Access      |
```

```
|  Custom Software       |      |  Predefined Runtime     |
|  Direct Network Config |      |  Managed Networking     |
+------------------------+      +------------------------+
```

Serverless environments, on the other hand, provide a managed runtime with limited control over the underlying infrastructure. While this simplifies operations, it can be a constraint for applications with specific dependencies.

Operational Effort

Serverless architectures significantly reduce operational overhead. You don't need to worry about patching servers, managing operating systems, or provisioning infrastructure. The cloud provider handles these tasks.

Consider a web application. With a serverless approach, you can deploy the application's backend logic as serverless functions and use a managed database service. You are free from the routine tasks of server maintenance and patching, allowing you to focus more on feature development and business logic.

Traditional architectures require you to manage servers, configure networks, and handle operating system updates. This demands skilled personnel and consumes valuable time and resources.

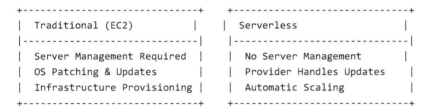

```
+------------------------------+      +------------------------------+
|  Traditional (EC2)           |      |  Serverless                  |
|------------------------------|      |------------------------------|
|  Server Management Required  |      |   No Server Management       |
|  OS Patching & Updates       |      |   Provider Handles Updates   |
|  Infrastructure Provisioning |      |   Automatic Scaling          |
+------------------------------+      +------------------------------+
```

Cost

Cost is a vital consideration. Serverless architectures are often cost-effective for unpredictable workloads because you only pay for the actual compute time consumed. When no requests are being processed, you incur minimal costs.

However, for consistently high workloads, traditional EC2-based architectures might be more cost-efficient. Reserving EC2 instances or utilizing spot instances can provide significant cost savings compared to the continuous execution of serverless functions.

For example, a video transcoding service might be implemented using either approach.

- **Serverless:** Each video transcoding job triggers a serverless function. Costs are directly proportional to the number of videos transcoded. Ideal for occasional or infrequent transcoding tasks.
- **EC2:** A cluster of EC2 instances continuously transcodes videos. Suitable for high-volume, continuous transcoding requirements.

```
+---------------------------------------+      +-----------------------------------------+
|  Serverless                           |      |  Traditional (EC2)                      |
|---------------------------------------|      |-----------------------------------------|
|  Pay-per-Execution                    |      |   Fixed Cost (Instance Hours)           |
|  Cost-Effective for Unpredictable Loads |    |   Cost-Effective for High, Steady Loads |
+---------------------------------------+      +-----------------------------------------+
```

To accurately assess costs, estimate the expected compute time, memory usage, and number of invocations for serverless functions. Compare these with the cost of running EC2 instances with comparable resources.

Chapter 10 Designing Scalable and Resilient Architectures-High Availability and Fault Tolerance on AWS

Here are 5 concise bullet points explaining High Availability and Fault Tolerance on AWS for your book:

- **Understanding Availability & Fault Tolerance:**

  - High Availability (HA): Minimizing downtime through redundancy.
  - Fault Tolerance: System continues operating despite component failures.

- **Leveraging AWS Global Infrastructure:**

  - Regions: Geographically isolated locations for redundancy.
  - Availability Zones (AZs): Distinct data centers within a Region.

- **Designing for Redundancy:**

  - Load Balancing: Distributing traffic across multiple instances (ELB).
  - Auto Scaling: Automatically adjusting resources based on demand.

- **Data Replication & Backup:**

  - Replication: Synchronizing data across multiple AZs/Regions.
  - Backup & Restore: Regularly backing up data for disaster recovery (S3).

- **Monitoring & Automation:**

  - CloudWatch: Monitoring application and infrastructure health.
  - Automated Failover: Automatically switching traffic to healthy instances.

Understanding Availability & Fault Tolerance

This section dives into two crucial concepts for building robust applications on AWS: High Availability and Fault Tolerance. While related, they address different aspects of system reliability.

High Availability (HA): Minimizing downtime through redundancy.

High Availability focuses on ensuring your application remains accessible to users with minimal interruption. It's achieved by building redundancy into your system. Redundancy means having multiple instances or components of your application running so that if one fails, another can immediately take over. The goal of HA is to minimize *downtime*, the period when your application is unavailable. Think of it like having a backup generator for your house. If the main power goes out, the generator kicks in, keeping the lights on.

Consider a simple web application. Without high availability, you might have a single web server. If that server crashes, your application is down. With high availability, you might have two or more web servers behind a *load balancer*. The load balancer distributes traffic among the servers. If one server fails, the load balancer automatically directs traffic to the remaining healthy servers, and your application remains online.

A very rudimentary Python code example, though not directly deployable on AWS without additional setup, illustrates the principle:

```python
# A simplified conceptual example, NOT production code.

import time
import random

class WebServer:
    def __init__(self, id):
        self.id = id
        self.is_healthy = True

    def process_request(self, request):
        if self.is_healthy:
            print(f"Server {self.id}: Processing request - {request}")
            # Simulate a random chance of failure.  A real server
            # would have proper health checks and error handling.
            if random.random() < 0.1:
                self.is_healthy = False
                print(f"Server {self.id}: FAILING!")
            return f"Server {self.id}: Response"
        else:
            print(f"Server {self.id}: Refusing request - Unhealthy")
            return None  # Indicate failure to process

class LoadBalancer:
    def __init__(self, servers):
        self.servers = servers
        self.current_server_index = 0

    def get_next_server(self):
        # Simple round-robin. A real load balancer is far more sophisticated.
        while True:
            server = self.servers[self.current_server_index]
            self.current_server_index = (self.current_server_index + 1) % len(self.servers)
            if server.is_healthy:
                return server
            print("Server unhealthy, trying next...")
            time.sleep(0.1) # Avoid tight loop

    def handle_request(self, request):
        server = self.get_next_server()
        if server:
            response = server.process_request(request)
            return response
        else:
            print("All servers are down!")
            return "Error: Service Unavailable"


# Example Usage
server1 = WebServer("A")
server2 = WebServer("B")
```

```
load_balancer = LoadBalancer([server1, server2])

for i in range(10):
    result = load_balancer.handle_request(f"Request {i}")
    print(f"Request {i} result: {result}")
    time.sleep(0.5)
```

This code provides a basic illustration. A real load balancer in AWS handles much more complex routing, health checks, and fault detection. This redundancy is key to achieving high availability.

Fault Tolerance: System continues operating despite component failures.

Fault Tolerance takes redundancy a step further. While high availability minimizes downtime, fault tolerance aims for *continuous operation* even in the face of failures. A fault-tolerant system is designed to automatically recover from failures without any noticeable impact on users. It anticipates and handles potential faults so the overall system remains functional.

Imagine a mission-critical system like a flight control system. It *cannot* afford any downtime. Fault tolerance is built into such systems with redundant hardware, software, and power sources. If one component fails, another instantly takes over, and the flight continues uninterrupted.

The difference between HA and Fault Tolerance: Consider the example with the web servers and the load balancer. If one server fails in an HA setup, there might be a brief period where the load balancer detects the failure and re-routes traffic. This is a short period of downtime, even if it's just a few seconds. In a fault-tolerant system, that switchover would ideally happen instantaneously and seamlessly, without any detectable downtime.

Visual Sketch:

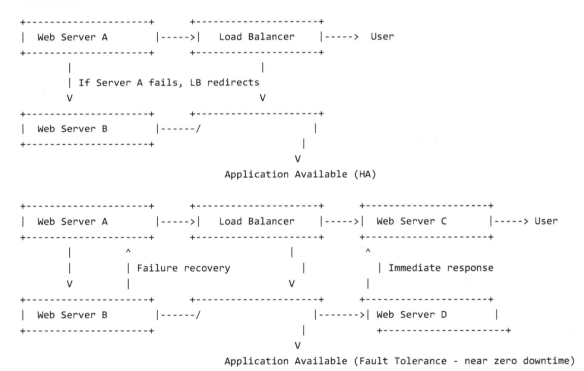

The first sketch demonstrates basic HA: A failure leads to redirection and eventual continued service. The second sketch depicts a more resilient fault-tolerant system with replicated servers handling load during failures. The core distinction lies in the immediacy and lack of detectable service interruption in the second scenario.

In practice, achieving true fault tolerance is complex and expensive. You need thorough testing, sophisticated monitoring, and automated recovery mechanisms. However, for critical applications, it is an essential investment. On AWS, both High Availability and Fault Tolerance are essential design considerations to deliver resilient and reliable services.

Leveraging AWS Global Infrastructure

AWS provides a global infrastructure to build highly available and fault-tolerant applications. This infrastructure is built around the concepts of Regions and Availability Zones (AZs). Understanding these concepts is crucial for designing resilient systems.

Regions: Geographically Isolated Locations for Redundancy

An AWS Region is a geographically separate and independent location. Each Region is designed to be completely isolated from other Regions. This isolation helps ensure that a failure in one Region does not impact other Regions. Each AWS Region contains multiple, physically separated Availability Zones.

Think of Regions as different cities or states. If something happens in one city (e.g., a power outage), it doesn't affect the other cities. This is how AWS Regions work. Each Region has its own independent power, cooling, and networking infrastructure.

Example: Let's say you're building a web application for customers in the United States. You could deploy your application across multiple AWS Regions, such as us-east-1 (Northern Virginia) and us-west-2 (Oregon). If one Region experiences an issue, your application can continue serving customers from the other Region. This setup significantly improves availability.

This geographic distribution of Regions allows you to locate your applications and data closer to your customers, reducing latency and improving performance. It also helps you comply with data sovereignty regulations, which may require you to store data in specific geographic locations.

Here's a simple sketch to visualize this:

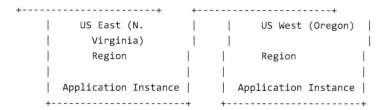

Availability Zones (AZs): Distinct Data Centers Within a Region

An Availability Zone (AZ) is one or more discrete data centers with redundant power, networking, and connectivity in an AWS Region. AZs provide fault tolerance within a Region. They are physically separated from each other, so a single event is unlikely to affect all AZs within a Region.

Each AZ is designed to be isolated from failures in other AZs. For instance, they are connected via low-latency, high-bandwidth networking. Deploying your application across multiple AZs provides high availability and fault tolerance within the Region.

Think of AZs as different buildings within the same city, but on different power grids. If one building loses power, the others are still operational.

Example: Within the us-east-1 Region, there are multiple AZs (e.g., us-east-1a, us-east-1b, us-east-1c). You can deploy your application instances across these AZs. If one AZ fails, the instances in the other AZs will continue to operate, ensuring your application remains available.

You can use a load balancer (covered in later sections) to distribute traffic across these instances. This helps to evenly distribute the load and automatically route traffic away from unhealthy instances.

Here's a sketch:

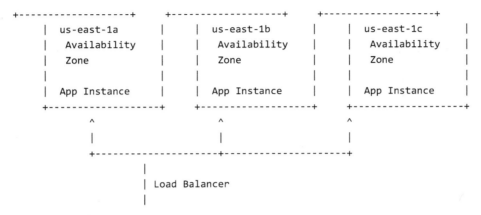

In summary, leveraging the AWS Global Infrastructure allows you to build applications that are highly available, fault-tolerant, and performant. By strategically using Regions and Availability Zones, you can minimize downtime and ensure your applications can withstand various types of failures.

Regions

Regions are a fundamental component of the AWS global infrastructure. They represent geographically isolated locations around the world where AWS operates data centers. Each Region is designed to be completely independent of other Regions, offering users the ability to deploy applications and store data in multiple geographic locations. This is critical for achieving high availability, disaster recovery, and compliance with local regulations.

Geographically Isolated Locations for Redundancy:

Think of AWS Regions like different cities spread across the globe. For instance, you might have a Region in the United States (e.g., us-east-1, located in Northern Virginia), another in Europe (e.g., eu-west-1, located in Ireland), and another in Asia (e.g., ap-southeast-1, located in Singapore). Each of these locations operates independently.

The key benefit of this geographic isolation is redundancy. If a major event (natural disaster, power outage, etc.) affects one Region, your applications and data in other Regions remain unaffected and continue to operate. This dramatically reduces the risk of widespread service disruption.

Imagine you are running an e-commerce website. You can deploy your application across multiple Regions. If one Region goes down, your website can still serve customers from other Regions, ensuring business continuity.

Example Scenario:

Let's say you have customers in both the United States and Europe. You could deploy your application in the us-east-1 Region for your US customers and the eu-west-1 Region for your European customers. This improves latency for your users in each region and provides redundancy in case of a regional outage.

Sketch illustrating Region Isolation:

```
+--------------------+      +--------------------+      +--------------------+
|      US Region     |      |      EU Region     |      |     Asia Region    |
|     (us-east-1)    |      |     (eu-west-1)    |      |   (ap-southeast-1) |
|                    |      |                    |      |                    |
|    [Application 1] |      |    [Application 2] |      |    [Application 3] |
|    [Database 1]    |      |    [Database 2]    |      |    [Database 3]    |
```

```
+--------------------+    +--------------------+    +--------------------+
|                    |    |                    |    |                    |
|   Independent      |    |   Independent      |    |   Independent      |
|   Infrastructure   |    |   Infrastructure   |    |   Infrastructure   |
|                    |    |                    |    |                    |
+--------------------+----+--------------------+----+--------------------+
```

```
(Each Region operates independently, providing redundancy)
```

The sketch above shows how three different regions operate independently. An outage in the US Region does not affect the EU or Asia regions, and vice versa.

Code Example (AWS CLI - Listing Available Regions):

While there's no *code* involved in defining a Region *itself*, you interact with Regions using the AWS CLI, SDKs, or the AWS Management Console. Here's how to list available AWS Regions using the AWS CLI:

```
aws ec2 describe-regions
```

This command will output a JSON document listing all available AWS Regions and associated information.

Example JSON output snippet:

```
{
    "Regions": [
        {
            "Endpoint": "ec2.us-east-1.amazonaws.com",
            "RegionName": "us-east-1"
        },
        {
            "Endpoint": "ec2.us-east-2.amazonaws.com",
            "RegionName": "us-east-2"
        },
        // ... more Regions
    ]
}
```

This output shows the `RegionName` (e.g., `us-east-1`) and the associated `Endpoint` used to access services within that Region. You specify the Region in your CLI commands or SDK configurations to tell AWS where you want to deploy or manage your resources. For example, to create an EC2 instance in the `us-west-2` Region:

```
aws ec2 run-instances --image-id ami-xxxxxxxx --instance-type t2.micro --region us-west-2
```

Note: Replace `ami-xxxxxxxx` with a valid AMI ID for the `us-west-2` Region.

By explicitly specifying the `--region` parameter, you ensure that the instance is launched in the desired geographic location. Failing to specify the region will result in AWS using the configured default region, which might not be the intended behavior for a resilient and globally distributed application.

Availability Zones (AZs)

Availability Zones are distinct data centers within an AWS Region. To understand this, picture a city (the Region) with several independent buildings (the Availability Zones).

Geographic Isolation:

Each Availability Zone is located in a separate geographic location from others within the same Region. This separation is designed to protect against localized failures like power outages, floods, or other disasters. If one

Availability Zone goes down, the others in the Region remain operational.

Example:

Imagine a Region called "US-East-1" (located in Northern Virginia, USA). Within this Region, you might have Availability Zones named "us-east-1a", "us-east-1b", "us-east-1c", etc. Each of these AZs is a physically separate data center, likely several kilometers apart.

Illustration:

```
Region (e.g., US-East-1)
    +-----------------------+
    | +-------+ +-------+ +-------+
    | | AZ a | | AZ b | | AZ c |  (Physically separated data centers)
    | +-------+ +-------+ +-------+
    +-----------------------+
```

Purpose:

The primary purpose of Availability Zones is to provide high availability and fault tolerance for your applications. By deploying your application across multiple Availability Zones, you can ensure that your application remains available even if one AZ experiences an outage.

Configuration:

When you launch resources on AWS, such as EC2 instances (virtual servers) or databases, you can choose which Availability Zone to place them in. Distributing these resources across multiple AZs is a key strategy for building resilient applications.

Code Example (AWS CLI):

```
# Launching an EC2 instance in us-east-1a
aws ec2 run-instances \
    --image-id ami-xxxxxxxxxxxxxxxxx \ # Replace with your AMI ID
    --instance-type t2.micro \
    --count 1 \
    --subnet-id subnet-xxxxxxxxxxxxx \ # Replace with your subnet ID
    --availability-zone us-east-1a

# Launching another EC2 instance in us-east-1b
aws ec2 run-instances \
    --image-id ami-xxxxxxxxxxxxxxxxx \ # Replace with your AMI ID
    --instance-type t2.micro \
    --count 1 \
    --subnet-id subnet-yyyyyyyyyyyyy \ # Replace with your subnet ID
    --availability-zone us-east-1b
```

Explanation: The code shows the command-line code in which an EC2 instance in a specified zone is launched. The --availability-zone parameter lets you specify the AZ in which the instance should be created. Ensure both instances are launched inside different subnets (as specified in subnet-id) to avoid conflicts, but keep the subnets inside the same region for low latency.

Benefits of Using Multiple AZs:

- **Increased Availability:** If one AZ fails, your application can continue running in the other AZs.
- **Reduced Downtime:** Failover to a healthy AZ can be automated, minimizing downtime.
- **Improved Fault Tolerance:** Your application is more resilient to failures.

Network Connectivity:

Availability Zones within a Region are connected by high-bandwidth, low-latency network connections. This allows for synchronous data replication and fast failover between AZs. The low latency is critical for applications that require real-time data consistency.

Summary

In essence, Availability Zones offer a way to isolate your applications from single points of failure. Distributing your resources across multiple AZs is a fundamental best practice for building highly available and fault-tolerant applications on AWS. Think of them as your building blocks for creating resilient architectures.

Designing for Redundancy

Designing for redundancy is a crucial aspect of building highly available and fault-tolerant applications on AWS. Redundancy ensures that your application remains operational even if one or more components fail. This section will explore two key AWS services that help achieve redundancy: Load Balancing and Auto Scaling.

Load Balancing: Distributing Traffic Across Multiple Instances (ELB)

Load balancing distributes incoming network traffic across multiple instances of your application. This prevents any single instance from being overwhelmed and ensures that traffic is directed to healthy instances. AWS offers Elastic Load Balancing (ELB) which comes in several types: Application Load Balancer (ALB), Network Load Balancer (NLB), and Classic Load Balancer (CLB). ALB is best for HTTP/HTTPS traffic, while NLB is suitable for TCP/UDP traffic, and CLB is the previous generation load balancer and less commonly used for new applications.

Imagine you have a web application running on three EC2 instances. Without a load balancer, users would need to know the specific address of each instance, and if one instance fails, those users would be unable to access the application. With a load balancer, users connect to a single entry point (the load balancer's address), and the load balancer intelligently routes traffic to the available instances.

Here's a basic sketch of how load balancing works:

```
[User] --> [ELB (Single Point of Entry)]
              |
              +--> [EC2 Instance 1]
              |
              +--> [EC2 Instance 2]
              |
              +--> [EC2 Instance 3]
```

In this diagram, the user interacts with the Elastic Load Balancer (ELB). The ELB then distributes the incoming requests to one of the available EC2 instances.

Example: Configuring an Application Load Balancer (ALB)

While the exact steps for configuring a load balancer are best performed via the AWS Management Console or AWS CLI, this code snippet demonstrates setting up the *target group* in Python, which is a core part of the process by defining *where* the traffic should be directed.

```
import boto3

# Create an ELB client
elb_client = boto3.client('elbv2', region_name='us-west-2')

# Create a target group
```

```
response = elb_client.create_target_group(
    Name='my-target-group',
    Protocol='HTTP',
    Port=80,
    VpcId='vpc-xxxxxxxxxxxxxxxxx', # Replace with your VPC ID
    HealthCheckProtocol='HTTP',
    HealthCheckPath='/healthcheck',  # Assuming you have a /healthcheck endpoint
    Matcher={
        'HttpCode': '200' # Expecting HTTP 200 response for healthy instances
    },
    TargetType='instance'
)

target_group_arn = response['TargetGroups'][0]['TargetGroupArn']

print(f"Target Group ARN: {target_group_arn}")

# Next steps would involve:
# 1. Creating an ALB
# 2. Creating a listener to forward traffic to the target group
# 3. Registering EC2 instances with the target group.
```

This Python code sets up a target group which informs the load balancer where to forward traffic. The target group uses HTTP protocol on port 80 inside a specified Virtual Private Cloud(VPC). Crucially, it defines a health check using /healthcheck endpoint to confirm the instance is healthy and responsive to the traffic. Without a health check, the load balancer might blindly forward traffic to an unhealthy instance.

Auto Scaling: Automatically Adjusting Resources Based on Demand

Auto Scaling automatically adjusts the number of EC2 instances running your application based on demand. This ensures that you have enough resources to handle peak traffic while minimizing costs during periods of low traffic. Auto Scaling works in conjunction with Load Balancing to maintain the health and performance of your application. If an instance fails or becomes unhealthy, Auto Scaling can automatically replace it with a new instance.

Imagine you have an e-commerce website that experiences a surge in traffic during Black Friday. Without Auto Scaling, you would need to manually provision additional servers to handle the increased load, which can be time-consuming and potentially lead to downtime. With Auto Scaling, the system automatically scales up the number of instances to meet the demand, and then scales down when the traffic subsides.

Here's a simplified representation:

```
[User Traffic] --> [ELB] --> [Auto Scaling Group] --> [EC2 Instances (Number Varies)]
                                      ^
                                      |
                              [CloudWatch Metrics (CPU Utilization, etc.)]
```

In this sketch, user traffic comes through the Elastic Load Balancer (ELB), which distributes it to the instances in the Auto Scaling Group. The Auto Scaling Group uses CloudWatch metrics (like CPU utilization) to determine when to launch or terminate EC2 instances, automatically adjusting the number of running instances to match the demand.

Example: Configuring an Auto Scaling Group (ASG)

Similarly, you can configure Auto Scaling groups with code. This example uses Python and the boto3 library to show the parameters:

```python
import boto3

# Create an Auto Scaling client
autoscaling_client = boto3.client('autoscaling', region_name='us-west-2')

# Launch Configuration (Defines the EC2 instance type and AMI)
launch_configuration_name = 'my-launch-configuration'
image_id = 'ami-xxxxxxxxxxxxxxxxx' # Replace with your AMI ID
instance_type = 't2.micro'

response = autoscaling_client.create_launch_configuration(
    LaunchConfigurationName=launch_configuration_name,
    ImageId=image_id,
    InstanceType=instance_type,
    SecurityGroups=['sg-xxxxxxxxxxxxxxxxx'], #Replace with your Security Group ID
    KeyName='your-key-pair' # Replace with your Key Pair name
)
print(f"Created Launch Configuration: {launch_configuration_name}")

# Auto Scaling Group
auto_scaling_group_name = 'my-auto-scaling-group'
min_size = 1
max_size = 3
desired_capacity = 1

response = autoscaling_client.create_auto_scaling_group(
    AutoScalingGroupName=auto_scaling_group_name,
    LaunchConfigurationName=launch_configuration_name,
    MinSize=min_size,
    MaxSize=max_size,
    DesiredCapacity=desired_capacity,
    VPCZoneIdentifier='subnet-xxxxxxxxxxxxx,subnet-yyyyyyyyyyyyy', # Replace with your Subnet I[
    LoadBalancerNames=['my-load-balancer'], # Optional: Associate with your load balancer
    HealthCheckType='ELB', #Important to use ELB as Health Check Type if you want to use ELB's I
    HealthCheckGracePeriod=300  #Time for the new instance to start service before ASG starts he
)

print(f"Created Auto Scaling Group: {auto_scaling_group_name}")
```

This code first creates a *launch configuration*, that defines the template for new EC2 instances created in the Auto Scaling group including the image ID, instance type, security groups and key pair. Then it creates the Auto Scaling Group, specifying the minimum, maximum, and desired number of instances and associating with the defined subnets inside VPC. It's set up to use ELB health checks, replacing instances if the load balancer determines them to be unhealthy. The `HealthCheckGracePeriod` provides a buffer time so the ASG don't kill instances right away since start up time for instances varies. By associating an Auto Scaling Group with an Elastic Load Balancer, you can ensure that traffic is only routed to healthy instances and that new instances are automatically added to the load balancer as they are launched.

By combining Load Balancing and Auto Scaling, you can create a highly resilient and scalable application infrastructure on AWS. Load Balancing distributes traffic across multiple instances, while Auto Scaling ensures that you have the right number of instances to handle the current demand. This combination provides both high availability and fault tolerance, ensuring that your application remains operational even in the face of component failures or traffic spikes.

Data Replication & Backup

This section focuses on how to protect your data on AWS through replication and backups. Data loss can be catastrophic for any application, so understanding these concepts is critical for building robust and resilient systems.

Replication: Synchronizing data across multiple AZs/Regions.

Replication is the process of copying your data from one location to another, ensuring that you have multiple identical copies. This is crucial for both high availability and disaster recovery. On AWS, replication typically happens across Availability Zones (AZs) within a Region, or even across different Regions entirely.

- **Within a Region (Across AZs):** This approach provides high availability. If one AZ experiences an outage, your application can continue to function using the replicated data in another AZ. This is faster and simpler to implement compared to cross-region replication.

  - *Example:* Imagine you have a database running in us-east-1a. You can configure replication to another AZ, us-east-1b. If us-east-1a becomes unavailable, your application automatically switches to using the database in us-east-1b.

```
+-----------------+        +-----------------+
|   us-east-1a    |        |   us-east-1b    |
|-----------------|        |-----------------|
|   Database      | <----  |   Database      |  (Replicated)
+-----------------+        +-----------------+
```

- **Across Regions:** This offers disaster recovery. If an entire region experiences an outage (rare, but possible), your application can failover to a different region where a copy of your data exists. This strategy is more complex and has higher latency, but provides greater protection against catastrophic failures.

  - *Example:* Consider an application primarily running in the us-east-1 region. You could replicate your data to us-west-2. In the event of a major issue affecting all AZs in us-east-1, your application can be brought online in us-west-2 using the replicated data.

```
+-----------------+        +-----------------+
|   us-east-1     |        |   us-west-2     |
|-----------------|        |-----------------|
|   Database      | <----  |   Database      |  (Replicated)
+-----------------+        +-----------------+
```

Example Code Snippet (Conceptual - Database Replication)

```
# Pseudo-code demonstrating database replication configuration
def configure_replication(source_db, destination_db):
    """
    Configures replication from a source database to a destination database.
    This is a simplified example and would require specific database client libraries.
    """
    try:
        # Connect to the source database
        source_conn = connect_to_database(source_db)

        # Connect to the destination database
        destination_conn = connect_to_database(destination_db)

        # Start replication process (implementation depends on the database)
        start_replication(source_conn, destination_conn)
```

```
        print(f"Replication configured from {source_db} to {destination_db}")

    except Exception as e:
        print(f"Error configuring replication: {e}")
```

Backup & Restore: Regularly backing up data for disaster recovery (S3).

Backup and restore is the process of creating copies of your data at specific points in time (backups) and then being able to restore that data to a previous state. AWS offers S3 (Simple Storage Service) as a reliable and cost-effective solution for storing backups. Backups, unlike replication are are not continuously synchronized. This typically means your recovery point (point where your data is restored from) is at a specific point in time.

- **Regular Backups:** Implement a backup schedule that meets your application's Recovery Point Objective (RPO). RPO defines the maximum acceptable amount of data loss (in terms of time). For example, if your RPO is 1 hour, you need to back up your data at least every hour.

- **Backup Storage (S3):** S3 offers high durability and availability, making it an ideal place to store your backups. It also offers different storage classes (Standard, Intelligent-Tiering, Glacier, etc.) allowing you to optimize costs based on how frequently you need to access the backups.

    - *Example:* You might back up your database every night at midnight and store the backup in S3. You might also store daily transaction logs in S3 to enable point-in-time recovery within a day.

- **Disaster Recovery:** In the event of a disaster, you can restore your data from the backups stored in S3 to a new environment. This could involve creating new instances, restoring the database from the backup, and configuring the application to use the restored data. The amount of time to do all this from point of diaster, is called Recovery Time Objective (RTO).

Example Code Snippet (Conceptual - S3 Backup)

```python
import boto3  # AWS SDK for Python

def backup_database_to_s3(database_name, s3_bucket, backup_file_name):
    """
    Backs up a database and uploads the backup to S3.
    This is a simplified example and would require specific database backup commands.
    """
    try:
        # Create an S3 client
        s3_client = boto3.client('s3')

        # Execute the database backup command (replace with your specific command)
        backup_command = f"pg_dump {database_name} > {backup_file_name}"  # Example for Postgres
        os.system(backup_command)

        # Upload the backup file to S3
        s3_client.upload_file(backup_file_name, s3_bucket, backup_file_name)

        print(f"Backup of {database_name} uploaded to s3://{s3_bucket}/{backup_file_name}")

    except Exception as e:
        print(f"Error backing up database: {e}")
```

In summary, data replication ensures continuous availability by keeping multiple synchronized copies of your data. Backup and restore procedures provide a safety net for disaster recovery, allowing you to recover data from specific points in time. Both strategies are essential for building resilient and reliable applications on AWS.

Chapter 11 Designing Scalable and Resilient Architectures-Scaling Strategies: Auto Scaling, Load Balancing, and Multi-Region Deployments

- **Auto Scaling:** Dynamically adjust compute capacity based on demand to maintain performance and cost-efficiency.

- **Load Balancing:** Distribute incoming traffic across multiple instances to prevent overload and ensure high availability.

- **Multi-Region Deployments:** Replicate application and data across multiple AWS regions for fault tolerance and disaster recovery.

- **Scaling Strategies:** Implement horizontal scaling using EC2 Auto Scaling groups, leveraging instance types optimized for workload.

- **Resilience:** Design for failure by incorporating redundancy, health checks, and automated failover mechanisms across regions.

Auto Scaling: Dynamic Resource Management

Auto Scaling is a fundamental concept in cloud computing, especially within environments like Amazon Web Services (AWS). Its core purpose is to dynamically adjust the amount of computing resources—such as servers—allocated to your application, based on the actual demand placed upon it. The goal is twofold: maintain consistent application performance and optimize cost-efficiency.

Imagine your application is a popular online store. During a regular weekday, you might only need a few servers to handle the traffic. However, during a weekend sale or holiday promotion, traffic can surge dramatically. Without Auto Scaling, you'd have two choices, both undesirable:

1. **Under-provisioning:** If you only provision the servers needed for regular weekday traffic, your website will likely become slow or even crash under the increased load during peak times, leading to frustrated customers and lost sales.

2. **Over-provisioning:** If you provision enough servers to handle the peak traffic, most of those servers will be idle during off-peak times, wasting money and resources.

Auto Scaling eliminates this dilemma. It automatically adds more servers when demand increases (scaling out) and removes them when demand decreases (scaling in). This dynamic adjustment ensures that you always have just the right amount of compute capacity to meet the current needs of your application.

Key Benefits:

- **Consistent Performance:** By automatically scaling resources, Auto Scaling ensures your application remains responsive and performs well, even during unexpected traffic spikes.

- **Cost Optimization:** You only pay for the resources you actually use. When demand is low, Auto Scaling removes unnecessary servers, reducing your cloud computing costs.

Practical Examples:

Consider a web application running on AWS using EC2 instances (virtual servers). You can configure an Auto Scaling group to automatically launch new EC2 instances when CPU utilization exceeds a certain threshold (e.g., 70%). Conversely, when CPU utilization drops below another threshold (e.g., 30%), Auto Scaling can terminate unused instances.

Example Scenario:

Let's say you have a simple web server that handles incoming HTTP requests. Each request consumes a certain amount of CPU resources on your server. You can configure Auto Scaling to monitor the CPU usage of your server instances.

Time	Traffic Level	CPU Usage	Auto Scaling Action	Number of Instances
9:00 AM	Low	20%	None	2
12:00 PM	Medium	60%	None	2
6:00 PM	High	85%	Launch new instance	3
9:00 PM	Medium	50%	None	3
2:00 AM	Very Low	15%	Terminate one instance	2

In this scenario, Auto Scaling automatically adjusts the number of instances based on the CPU usage, ensuring that your application remains responsive while optimizing costs.

Sketch Representation:

Imagine a line representing the desired level of application performance (e.g., response time).

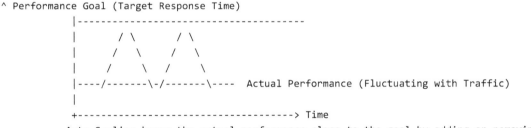

```
^ Performance Goal (Target Response Time)
        |--------------------------------------
        |      / \         / \
        |     /   \      /    \
        |    /     \   /       \
        |----/-------\-/--------\----  Actual Performance (Fluctuating with Traffic)
        |
        +------------------------------------> Time
          Auto Scaling keeps the actual performance close to the goal by adding or removing res
```

In this conceptual sketch, when the 'Actual Performance' line dips *below* the 'Performance Goal' (due to increased traffic), Auto Scaling *adds* resources to bring the performance back up. Conversely, when the 'Actual Performance' line is *above* the 'Performance Goal' (due to low traffic), Auto Scaling *removes* resources to optimize costs.

Load Balancing: Distributing the Workload

Load balancing is a crucial technique for managing and distributing incoming network traffic across multiple servers or instances. Its primary goal is to prevent any single server from becoming overloaded, which can lead to slow response times or even system failures. By distributing the workload evenly, load balancing ensures high availability, improved performance, and a better user experience.

To understand the concept, visualize a busy restaurant. If everyone tries to order from a single waiter, that waiter will be overwhelmed, and customers will experience long wait times. However, if there are multiple waiters, and customers are distributed among them, the service will be much faster and more efficient. Load balancing does the same thing for your applications and services.

Here's a breakdown of how load balancing works and its benefits:

- **Distribute incoming traffic:** The core function of load balancing is to distribute incoming client requests across multiple servers. Instead of sending all requests to a single server, the load balancer intelligently directs traffic to different servers based on predefined algorithms. This distribution prevents any single server from being overwhelmed, ensuring consistent performance.

```
Client --> Load Balancer --> Server 1
                      |
                      --> Server 2
                      |
                      --> Server 3
```

In the above sketch, the client's request is routed to one of the available servers (Server 1, Server 2, or Server 3) by the load balancer.

- **Prevent overload:** By distributing the load, load balancing prevents individual servers from becoming overloaded. Overloaded servers can experience slow response times, errors, or even complete failures. Load balancing ensures that each server handles a manageable amount of traffic, maintaining optimal performance.

Imagine multiple users simultaneously trying to access a website hosted on a single server. Without load balancing, the server might struggle to handle all the requests, resulting in slow loading times or errors for some users. With load balancing, the requests are distributed across multiple servers, ensuring a smooth experience for all users.

- **Ensure high availability:** Load balancing plays a vital role in ensuring high availability by distributing traffic across multiple servers. If one server fails, the load balancer automatically redirects traffic to the remaining healthy servers. This failover mechanism minimizes downtime and ensures that the application remains accessible to users.

```
Client --> Load Balancer --> Server 1 (Failed)
                      |
                      --> Server 2 (Active)
                      |
                      --> Server 3 (Active)
```

In this scenario, Server 1 has failed. The load balancer detects this failure and automatically redirects all traffic to Server 2 and Server 3, which are still active.

Example of using Load Balancing in AWS using Python boto3 SDK

```python
import boto3

# Create an Elastic Load Balancing client
elb_client = boto3.client('elbv2')

# Example: Create a load balancer
try:
    response = elb_client.create_load_balancer(
        Name='my-load-balancer',
        Subnets=[
            'subnet-xxxxxxxxxxxxxxxxx',  # Replace with your subnet IDs
            'subnet-yyyyyyyyyyyyyyyyy',
        ],
        SecurityGroups=[
            'sg-zzzzzzzzzzzzzzzzz',  # Replace with your security group ID
        ],
```

```python
        Scheme='internet-facing',  # or 'internal'
        Tags=[
            {
                'Key': 'Name',
                'Value': 'My Load Balancer'
            },
        ],
        Type='application'  # or 'network'
    )
    print("Load balancer created:", response['LoadBalancers'][0]['LoadBalancerArn'])
except Exception as e:
    print("Error creating load balancer:", e)


# Example: Create a target group
try:
    response = elb_client.create_target_group(
        Name='my-target-group',
        Protocol='HTTP',  # or 'HTTPS', 'TCP', 'TLS', 'UDP', 'TCP_UDP'
        Port=80,
        VpcId='vpc-0bb1c79de3EXAMPLE',  # Replace with your VPC ID
        HealthCheckProtocol='HTTP',
        HealthCheckPath='/',
        HealthCheckIntervalSeconds=30,
        HealthCheckTimeoutSeconds=5,
        HealthyThresholdCount=5,
        UnhealthyThresholdCount=2,
        Matcher={
            'HttpCode': '200'
        },
        TargetType='instance'  # or 'ip', 'lambda', 'alb'
    )
    print("Target group created:", response['TargetGroups'][0]['TargetGroupArn'])
    target_group_arn = response['TargetGroups'][0]['TargetGroupArn']
except Exception as e:
    print("Error creating target group:", e)

# Example: Register targets (EC2 instances) with the target group
try:
    response = elb_client.register_targets(
        TargetGroupArn=target_group_arn,
        Targets=[
            {
                'Id': 'i-0abcdefghijklmnop1',  # Replace with your instance IDs
                'Port': 80
            },
            {
                'Id': 'i-0abcdefghijklmnop2',
                'Port': 80
            },
        ]
    )
    print("Targets registered:", response)
except Exception as e:
```

```
        print("Error registering targets:", e)


# Example: Create a listener for the load balancer
try:
    load_balancer_arn = 'arn:aws:elasticloadbalancing:us-west-2:xxxxxxxxxxxx:loadbalancer/app/my
    response = elb_client.create_listener(
        LoadBalancerArn=load_balancer_arn,
        Protocol='HTTP',  # or 'HTTPS'
        Port=80,
        DefaultActions=[
            {
                'Type': 'forward',
                'TargetGroupArn': target_group_arn,
            },
        ]
    )
    print("Listener created:", response['Listeners'][0]['ListenerArn'])
except Exception as e:
    print("Error creating listener:", e)
```

Explanation:

1. **Import boto3:** This line imports the AWS SDK for Python.
2. **Create an ELB client:** This creates a client object that allows you to interact with the Elastic Load Balancing service.
3. **Create a load balancer:**
   - `Name`: A name for your load balancer.
   - `Subnets`: The subnets in which the load balancer will operate. These subnets should be in different Availability Zones for high availability.
   - `SecurityGroups`: The security groups associated with the load balancer.
   - `Scheme`: `internet-facing` makes the load balancer accessible from the internet. Use `internal` for internal applications.
   - `Tags`: Metadata you can assign to the load balancer.
   - `Type`: `application` for an Application Load Balancer (HTTP/HTTPS traffic), or `network` for a Network Load Balancer (TCP/UDP traffic).
4. **Create a target group:**
   - `Name`: A name for the target group.
   - `Protocol`: The protocol used to communicate with the targets (EC2 instances).
   - `Port`: The port on which the targets are listening.
   - `VpcId`: The ID of the VPC where your instances are located.
   - `HealthCheckProtocol`, `HealthCheckPath`, `HealthCheckIntervalSeconds`, `HealthCheckTimeoutSeconds`, `HealthyThresholdCount`, `UnhealthyThresholdCount`, `Matcher`: Configure health checks to determine if the targets are healthy.
   - `TargetType`: The type of target: `instance` for EC2 instances, `ip` for IP addresses, `lambda` for Lambda functions, or `alb` for other Application Load Balancers.
5. **Register targets:**
   - `TargetGroupArn`: The ARN of the target group.
   - `Targets`: A list of targets (EC2 instances) to register with the target group. Each target specifies the instance ID and the port.
6. **Create a listener:**
   - `LoadBalancerArn`: The ARN of the load balancer.
   - `Protocol`: The protocol used by the listener (e.g., HTTP or HTTPS).
   - `Port`: The port on which the listener listens for incoming traffic.

- ◦ `DefaultActions`: Specifies what the listener should do with incoming requests. In this case, it forwards them to the target group.

This example creates a basic Application Load Balancer that listens for HTTP traffic on port 80 and forwards it to a target group containing two EC2 instances. The load balancer health checks ensure that traffic is only sent to healthy instances.

Load balancing is an indispensable component of modern application architecture, enabling scalability, resilience, and optimal performance. Whether you're managing a small website or a large-scale enterprise application, understanding and implementing load balancing is crucial for ensuring a positive user experience.

Multi-Region Deployments

Multi-Region Deployments mean running your application and storing your data in more than one geographical location (AWS region). This is done to make your application more reliable and to protect against disasters.

Fault Tolerance: Think of fault tolerance like having a spare tire for your car. If one tire goes flat, you can switch to the spare and keep driving. In the context of cloud computing, if one AWS region experiences an issue, your application can automatically switch to another region and continue running without interruption. For example, if you are hosting your web application in `us-east-1` (Northern Virginia) and that region becomes unavailable, traffic can be automatically routed to `us-west-2` (Oregon) where an identical copy of your application is running.

Disaster Recovery: Disaster recovery is like having an emergency plan for your home. If a fire occurs, you know how to evacuate and where to go. Similarly, multi-region deployments act as a disaster recovery plan for your application. In the event of a large-scale outage affecting an entire AWS region (e.g., due to a natural disaster), your application can be recovered in another region with minimal data loss and downtime.

Consider an e-commerce application. Without multi-region deployment, if the primary region goes down, customers cannot access the website to make purchases, resulting in lost revenue and damaged reputation. With multi-region deployment, the application continues to serve customers from another region, ensuring business continuity.

Here's a simplified sketch representing a multi-region deployment:

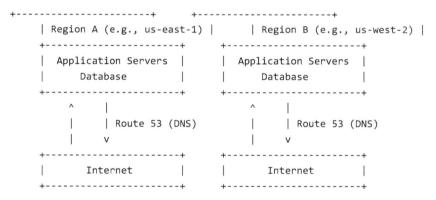

In this sketch, users access the application through the internet. Route 53, a DNS service, directs traffic to the active region. If Region A fails, Route 53 automatically redirects traffic to Region B. Application Servers running in each region serve the traffic and databases store the application data in respective regions.

Example code using AWS CLI to copy a snapshot of a database from one region to another to enable Multi-Region deployment:

```
aws ec2 copy-snapshot \
    --source-snapshot-id snap-xxxxxxxxxxxxxxxxx \
    --source-region us-east-1 \
```

```
    --region us-west-2 \
    --description "Copy of snapshot from us-east-1"
```

This command copies a snapshot (snap-xxxxxxxxxxxxxxxxx) from us-east-1 to us-west-2. This snapshot can then be used to restore the database in the secondary region.

Scaling Strategies

This section delves into how to strategically increase or decrease your application's resources to handle varying levels of demand. The goal is to maintain optimal performance without overspending on unused capacity. We will focus on horizontal scaling using EC2 Auto Scaling groups, leveraging instance types optimized for your specific workload.

Horizontal Scaling with EC2 Auto Scaling Groups:

Horizontal scaling involves adding more instances (virtual servers) to your application environment. EC2 Auto Scaling groups automate this process. Think of it like adding more lanes to a highway during rush hour – more lanes (instances) handle more traffic (user requests).

Mechanism:

1. *Define a Launch Template:* This template specifies the configuration of your EC2 instances (operating system, application code, etc.). It's like creating a blueprint for your servers.

2. *Create an Auto Scaling Group:* This group manages the number of EC2 instances running. You define minimum, maximum, and desired capacity.

3. *Set Scaling Policies:* These policies define when to add or remove instances. Common triggers include CPU utilization, network traffic, or custom metrics.

```
# Example (Conceptual): Define Auto Scaling Group parameters
min_size = 2  # Minimum number of instances
max_size = 10 # Maximum number of instances
desired_capacity = 4 # Start with 4 instances
instance_type = "t3.medium" # Instance type (CPU and memory)
ami_id = "ami-xxxxxxxxxxxxxxxxx" # Amazon Machine Image ID

#Scaling policy
target_cpu_utilization = 70 # Scale up if CPU exceeds 70%
```

Sketch to Illustrate:

```
+--------------------+      +--------------------+      +--------------------+
| EC2 Instance (t3.medium) | <-> | EC2 Instance (t3.medium) | <-> | EC2 Instance (t3.medium) | .
+--------------------+      +--------------------+      +--------------------+
    ^      ^      ^
    |      |      | Controlled by Auto Scaling Group (min_size, max_size, scaling policies)
    |      |      |
+--------------------+
|    Load Balancer   | Distributes traffic evenly across instances
+--------------------+
```

In above example, A load balancer is responsible for distributing incoming traffic efficiently among the available EC2 instances. This distribution ensures that no single instance is overwhelmed, contributing to the overall stability and responsiveness of the application.

Leveraging Instance Types Optimized for Workload:

EC2 offers a wide variety of instance types, each optimized for different workloads. Choosing the right instance type is crucial for performance and cost-effectiveness.

- *Compute-optimized (C-family):* Ideal for CPU-intensive tasks like batch processing, media transcoding, and high-performance computing.

- *Memory-optimized (R-family):* Suitable for memory-intensive applications like in-memory databases (e.g., Redis, Memcached), data analytics, and scientific computing.

- *Storage-optimized (I-family):* Designed for applications that require high-speed, low-latency access to large datasets, such as NoSQL databases (e.g., Cassandra, MongoDB) and data warehousing.

- *GPU instances (P and G families):* Best for machine learning, deep learning, and graphics-intensive applications.

Example Scenario:

Suppose you're running a video encoding application. Encoding video requires a lot of CPU power. Instead of using general-purpose instances, you would choose compute-optimized instances (like `c5.xlarge`) to significantly reduce encoding time and cost. Conversely, a large in-memory database would benefit from memory-optimized instances (like `r5.2xlarge`).

```
# Example (Conceptual): Selecting an instance type
workload_type = "video_encoding"

if workload_type == "video_encoding":
    instance_type = "c5.xlarge" # Compute Optimized
elif workload_type == "in_memory_database":
    instance_type = "r5.2xlarge" # Memory Optimized
else:
    instance_type = "t3.medium" # General Purpose

print(f"Recommended instance type: {instance_type}")
```

By carefully selecting instance types that match your workload requirements, you can achieve significant performance gains and cost savings. Auto Scaling groups allow you to seamlessly switch between instance types as your application evolves.

Resilience

Design for failure by incorporating redundancy, health checks, and automated failover mechanisms across regions.

Resilience in the cloud isn't about preventing failures; it's about gracefully handling them when they inevitably occur. It means building your application so that it can withstand disruptions and continue to function, even if some components fail. Think of it like designing a building to withstand an earthquake – you don't try to prevent the earthquake, but you build the structure strong enough to survive it.

This involves three key elements: redundancy, health checks, and automated failover mechanisms.

Redundancy

Redundancy means having multiple copies of critical components. If one component fails, another can take over. Imagine a car with two brake systems. If one fails, the other provides the needed redundancy to ensure continued operation.

In a cloud environment, this could mean having multiple instances of your application running. If one instance becomes unavailable, the others can continue to serve traffic.

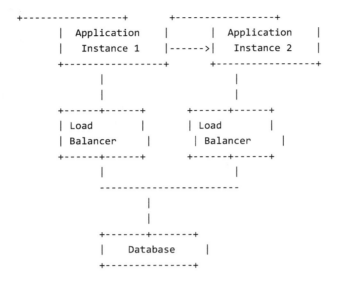

```
+-----------------+          +-----------------+
|  Application    |          |  Application    |
|   Instance 1    |------->|    Instance 2    |
+-----------------+          +-----------------+
        |                            |
        |                            |
+------+------+             +------+------+
| Load         |            | Load         |
| Balancer     |            | Balancer     |
+------+------+             +------+------+
       |                           |
       ------------------------
              |
              |
       +-------+-------+
       |    Database    |
       +---------------+
```

In the above simplified sketch, you have two application instances behind load balancers. Both instances access the same database. If "Application Instance 1" fails, "Application Instance 2" takes over (after the Load Balancer detects the failure, which we'll discuss next). Crucially, the database *itself* might also need to be redundant (using database replication) for true resilience.

Health Checks

Health checks are automated processes that periodically verify the health of your application components. They act like a doctor checking a patient's vital signs. If a health check fails, it indicates that the component is unhealthy and needs to be addressed.

For example, a health check might send a simple HTTP request to your application and verify that it returns a 200 OK status code. If it doesn't, the health check considers the application instance unhealthy. Load balancers use health checks to determine which instances are healthy and can receive traffic. This prevents traffic from being routed to failing instances.

Here's a simplified Python example of a health check:

```python
import http.client

def check_health(host, path):
    conn = http.client.HTTPConnection(host)
    try:
        conn.request("GET", path)
        response = conn.getresponse()
        if response.status == 200:
            print("Service is healthy")
            return True
        else:
            print(f"Service is unhealthy: Status code {response.status}")
            return False
    except Exception as e:
        print(f"Service is unhealthy: {e}")
        return False
    finally:
        conn.close()
```

```
# Example usage
check_health("your-application.com", "/health") #The "/health" is just a example. Create enpoint
```

This simple script connects to a web server and requests a specific path ("/health" in this example). A healthy server will respond with a 200 OK status. Any other response (or an error) indicates a problem. This is a rudimentary example; real-world health checks might involve more complex logic and checks (e.g., database connectivity).

Automated Failover Mechanisms Across Regions

Failover mechanisms are automated processes that switch traffic from a failed component to a healthy one. This minimizes downtime and ensures continuous service availability.

One particularly powerful form of failover is *regional failover*. This means replicating your application and data across multiple AWS regions (e.g., us-east-1 and us-west-2). If one entire region becomes unavailable (due to a major disaster, for example), traffic can be automatically routed to another region.

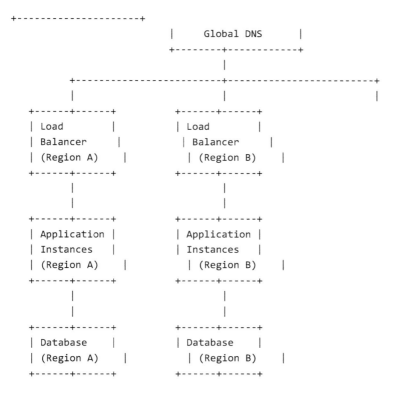

This sketch illustrates a multi-region deployment. A global DNS service (like AWS Route 53) is configured to route traffic to load balancers in different regions. The application and database are replicated across both regions. If Region A fails, the global DNS automatically redirects traffic to the Load Balancer in Region B, ensuring continuous availability. Achieving this requires careful planning of data replication and application state management.

Chapter 12 Designing Scalable and Resilient Architectures-Event-Driven Architecture with AWS Lambda and SNS/SQS

Here are 5 bullet points outlining Event-Driven Architecture with AWS Lambda and SNS/SQS for "System Design on AWS":

- **Decoupling Services:**

    - Enables independent scaling and fault isolation by decoupling services through asynchronous events.

- **Event Producers & Consumers:**

    - Producers emit events; consumers react without direct dependencies.

- **AWS SNS for Fanout:**

    - SNS publishes messages to multiple SQS queues for parallel processing by Lambda functions.

- **AWS SQS for Buffering:**

    - SQS queues buffer events, handling traffic spikes and ensuring reliable delivery to Lambda.

- **Lambda for Event Processing:**

    - Lambda functions triggered by SNS/SQS process events, scaling automatically based on demand.

Decoupling Services: Event-Driven Architecture on AWS

Decoupling services is a core principle of building resilient and scalable systems, especially within the AWS cloud. In an Event-Driven Architecture (EDA), this decoupling is achieved by allowing services to communicate through asynchronous events rather than direct, synchronous calls. This results in independent scaling and fault isolation.

Independent Scaling

Consider two services: an *Order Service* and an *Inventory Service*. In a tightly coupled system, when an order is placed, the *Order Service* might directly call the *Inventory Service* to check stock and reserve items. If the *Inventory Service* is overloaded or experiences a spike in requests, it can slow down or even crash, directly impacting the *Order Service*.

In a decoupled, event-driven system, the *Order Service* emits an "Order Placed" event. The *Inventory Service*, subscribed to this event, reacts to it by checking stock. If the *Inventory Service* becomes overloaded, the event is simply queued (handled by AWS SQS, as we'll see later). The *Order Service* doesn't have to wait for the *Inventory Service* to respond; it can continue processing other orders. The *Inventory Service* processes the events from the queue at its own pace. This allows each service to scale independently based on its individual needs.

```python
# Example: Order Service (Python) emitting an event using boto3 (AWS SDK)

import boto3
import json

sns = boto3.client('sns') #or SQS base on your use case
```

```python
def place_order(order_details):
    # ... (Order processing logic) ...

    message = {
        'event_type': 'OrderPlaced',
        'order_id': order_details['order_id'],
        'customer_id': order_details['customer_id'],
        'items': order_details['items']
    }

    sns.publish(
        TopicArn='arn:aws:sns:your-region:your-account-id:OrderEventsTopic',
        Message=json.dumps(message)
    )

    return { 'status': 'Order Placed' }

# Example: Inventory Service (Python) processing the event (using Lambda triggered by SQS)

def lambda_handler(event, context):
    for record in event['Records']:
        message = json.loads(record['body'])
        if message['event_type'] == 'OrderPlaced':
            order_id = message['order_id']
            items = message['items']
            # ... (Inventory check and reservation logic) ...
            print(f"Inventory updated for order: {order_id}")
    return { 'status': 'Inventory Updated' }
```

This example shows that the *Order Service* does not depend on the *Inventory Service*'s availability. It simply publishes a message. The *Inventory Service*, implemented as a Lambda function triggered by SQS, consumes this message and updates the inventory.

Fault Isolation

Fault isolation is another key benefit. If the *Inventory Service* fails in the tightly coupled example, the *Order Service* is directly impacted. In a decoupled system, a failure in the *Inventory Service* does not immediately bring down the *Order Service*.

Events related to inventory updates will still be queued in SQS. The *Order Service* continues to accept orders, queueing events. When the *Inventory Service* recovers (or a new instance is spun up), it can process the backlog of events.

Sketch Illustrating Decoupling

A simple sketch can illustrate this:

```
+-------------------+       +---------------------+
|   Order Service   |----->|   Inventory Service |  (Tight Coupling - Direct Call)
+-------------------+       +---------------------+
    (Slowdown!)              (Fails / Overloaded)


+-------------------+       +-------+       +---------------------+
|   Order Service   |----->|  SNS  |----->|   Inventory Service |  (Decoupled - Events)
```

```
+-------------------+     +-------+     +---------------------+
    (Publishes)         (Fanout)      (Subscribes & Reacts)
```

The first diagram shows the problem with tight coupling: a direct dependency that creates a single point of failure. The second diagram illustrates the decoupled system: the *Order Service* publishes to SNS, which then delivers events to subscribers, including the *Inventory Service*. This intermediary layer (SNS) provides the decoupling. SQS would likely sit between SNS and the Inventory Service in practice, but the high-level decoupling concept is shown.

Event Producers & Consumers

In an Event-Driven Architecture (EDA), services don't directly call or rely on each other. Instead, they communicate through events. Think of it like this: one service *announces* something happened (the event), and other services *listen* for those announcements and react if they're interested. The service that announces is the *event producer*, and the service that listens and reacts is the *event consumer*. This eliminates tight coupling.

- **Producers emit events; consumers react without direct dependencies.**

    Event producers are responsible for generating events when a significant change in state occurs or a specific action takes place within their domain. They don't need to know who will consume the event or how it will be processed. The sole responsibility of the producer is to publish the event to a central event bus or message queue. Consumers, on the other hand, subscribe to specific events or patterns of events. When a matching event is published, the consumer receives a notification and can then process the event data accordingly. The consumer operates independently of the producer, meaning that changes to the producer don't necessarily require changes to the consumer, and vice versa.

    Let's solidify that with an example. Imagine an e-commerce system. When a user places an order (producer), it emits an "OrderCreated" event. The inventory service (consumer) subscribes to "OrderCreated" events and reacts by decreasing the stock count of the ordered items. Another service, a shipping service (another consumer), also subscribes to "OrderCreated" events and prepares the shipment.

    Producer ------> Event Bus (SNS/SQS) ------> Consumer 1 (Inventory) |
    | ----> Consumer 2 (Shipping) **Example Scenario:** E-commerce Order System

    Producer (Order Service):

    The order service is responsible for creating and managing customer orders. When a new order is placed, the order service emits an `OrderCreated` event.

```python
import boto3
import json

sns = boto3.client('sns')
topic_arn = 'arn:aws:sns:YOUR_REGION:YOUR_ACCOUNT_ID:OrderEvents' # Replace with your SNS t

def create_order(order_details):
    # ... (Order creation logic here) ...
    order_id = 123  # Example order ID

    event = {
        'order_id': order_id,
        'user_id': order_details['user_id'],
        'items': order_details['items'],
        'total_amount': order_details['total_amount']
    }

    sns.publish(
```

```
            TopicArn=topic_arn,
            Message=json.dumps(event),
            MessageStructure='string'
        )
        print(f"OrderCreated event published for order ID: {order_id}")

# Example usage
order_data = {
    'user_id': 'user123',
    'items': ['productA', 'productB'],
    'total_amount': 100
}

create_order(order_data)
```

In this Python example:

- We use boto3, the AWS SDK for Python, to interact with SNS. You'll need to install it (`pip install boto3`) and configure your AWS credentials.
- `topic_arn` is the ARN (Amazon Resource Name) of your SNS topic. You'll find this in the AWS console.
- `create_order` simulates the order creation process. After an order is created, it constructs an OrderCreated event as a Python dictionary.
- `sns.publish` sends the event to the SNS topic. The message is serialized as JSON.

Consumer (Inventory Service):

The inventory service listens for OrderCreated events and updates the stock levels. It subscribes an SQS queue to the SNS topic where OrderCreated events are published.

```
import boto3
import json

sqs = boto3.client('sqs')
queue_url = 'YOUR_SQS_QUEUE_URL'  # Replace with your SQS queue URL

def process_order_event(event):
    order_id = event['order_id']
    items = event['items']

    # Simulate decreasing inventory
    for item in items:
        print(f"Decreasing inventory for item: {item} (order ID: {order_id})")
        # ... (Update inventory database here) ...

while True:
    response = sqs.receive_message(
        QueueUrl=queue_url,
        MaxNumberOfMessages=1,
        WaitTimeSeconds=20  # Long polling
    )

    messages = response.get('Messages', [])

    for message in messages:
```

```
    try:
        body = json.loads(message['Body'])
        # SNS sends a message with a "Message" field containing the actual event
        event = json.loads(body['Message'])
        process_order_event(event)

        # Delete the message from the queue to prevent reprocessing
        sqs.delete_message(
            QueueUrl=queue_url,
            ReceiptHandle=message['ReceiptHandle']
        )
        print(f"Processed and deleted message: {message['MessageId']}")

    except Exception as e:
        print(f"Error processing message: {e}")
```

In this Python example:

- We use boto3 to interact with SQS.
- queue_url is the URL of your SQS queue. You'll find this in the AWS console. This queue should be subscribed to the SNS topic that the Order Service publishes to.
- process_order_event simulates updating the inventory. It extracts the order details from the event and uses them to decrement stock levels. In a real system, this would involve updating a database.
- sqs.receive_message retrieves messages from the queue. WaitTimeSeconds=20 enables long polling, which reduces costs by waiting for messages to arrive rather than constantly polling the queue.
- The code then parses the message body (which is a JSON string containing an SNS message), extracts the actual event from the "Message" field, and calls process_order_event.
- Crucially, sqs.delete_message removes the message from the queue after it has been processed successfully. This prevents the same order from being processed multiple times if the consumer crashes before deleting the message.

Consumer (Shipping Service):

Similarly, the shipping service also subscribes to the same SNS topic via a different SQS queue.

```
import boto3
import json

sqs = boto3.client('sqs')
queue_url = 'YOUR_SHIPPING_SQS_QUEUE_URL' #Shipping Queue

def process_order_event(event):
    order_id = event['order_id']
    items = event['items']
    user_id = event['user_id']

    # Simulate shipping processing
    print(f"Shipping processing for order ID: {order_id}")

    # Shipping Logic
    # Get User Address

    print("User Address Retrieved Sucessfully, Order dispatched to User")
```

```
while True:
    response = sqs.receive_message(
        QueueUrl=queue_url,
        MaxNumberOfMessages=1,
        WaitTimeSeconds=20  # Long polling
    )

    messages = response.get('Messages', [])

    for message in messages:
        try:
            body = json.loads(message['Body'])
            # SNS sends a message with a "Message" field containing the actual event
            event = json.loads(body['Message'])
            process_order_event(event)

            # Delete the message from the queue to prevent reprocessing
            sqs.delete_message(
                QueueUrl=queue_url,
                ReceiptHandle=message['ReceiptHandle']
            )
            print(f"Processed and deleted message: {message['MessageId']}")

        except Exception as e:
            print(f"Error processing message: {e}")
```

Important considerations:

- **Error Handling:** Robust error handling is critical. Consumers should catch exceptions, log errors, and potentially retry processing messages. Dead-letter queues (DLQs) can be used to store messages that cannot be processed after multiple attempts.
- **Idempotency:** Consumers should ideally be idempotent, meaning that processing the same event multiple times has the same effect as processing it once. This is important to handle situations where a message might be delivered more than once (at-least-once delivery). Use order_id or some sort of tracking to make it idempotent.
- **Security:** Secure your SNS topics and SQS queues to prevent unauthorized access. Use IAM roles to grant permissions to your Lambda functions.
- **Monitoring:** Monitor your SNS topics, SQS queues, and Lambda functions to detect and resolve issues quickly. CloudWatch provides metrics and logging capabilities.
- **At-least-once delivery:** SNS and SQS provide at-least-once delivery. This means that a message might be delivered more than once, but it will not be lost. Your consumers must be designed to handle duplicate messages (idempotency).
- **Ordering (FIFO queues):** If the order of events is important, use SQS FIFO (First-In-First-Out) queues. However, FIFO queues have lower throughput than standard queues.

By embracing event producers and consumers, systems become more flexible, resilient, and scalable, allowing individual components to evolve independently while maintaining seamless communication and data flow. This architecture is particularly well-suited for complex and distributed applications in cloud environments.

AWS SNS for Fanout

AWS Simple Notification Service (SNS) plays a crucial role in event-driven architectures, particularly when you need to distribute events to multiple subscribers concurrently. This pattern is known as "fanout," where a single event triggers multiple independent actions.

- **AWS SNS for Fanout:**

  - SNS publishes messages to multiple SQS queues for parallel processing by Lambda functions.

SNS simplifies the process of sending messages to a large number of recipients. Instead of directly invoking each service or application, your application sends a single message to an SNS topic. SNS then takes responsibility for delivering that message to all subscribed endpoints. These endpoints are typically SQS queues, which in turn trigger Lambda functions.

Consider a scenario where a user uploads a photo to your application. This single event might need to trigger several actions:

1. **Thumbnail generation:** Create smaller versions of the image.
2. **Image analysis:** Analyze the image for content (e.g., objects, faces).
3. **Metadata extraction:** Extract information like date, location, and camera settings.
4. **Data backup:** Backup the image on a remote server.

Without SNS, your application would need to directly invoke each of these services, creating tight coupling and increasing complexity. With SNS, your application simply publishes a "photo uploaded" event to an SNS topic. Each of the services listed above subscribes to that topic via an SQS queue, and they independently process the event.

Here's a simplified representation of the SNS fanout pattern:

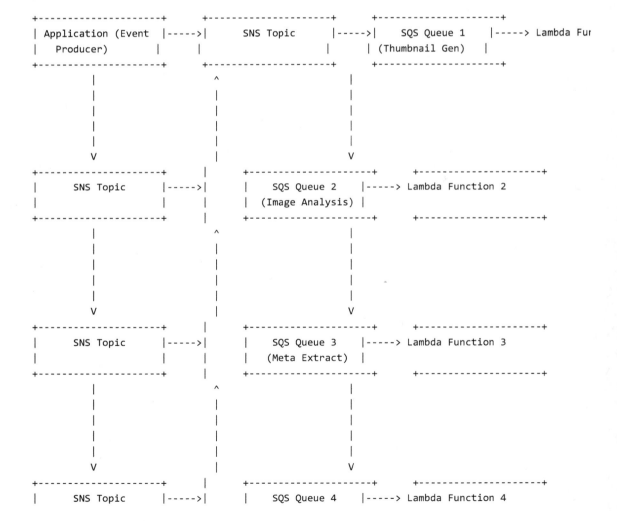

```
|                     |     |     |     |   (Data Backup)   |
+---------------------+     |     +---------------------+     +---------------------+
```

Let's illustrate with some simplified Python-like pseudocode:

Event Producer (e.g., your application):

```
import boto3
import json

sns_client = boto3.client('sns', region_name='your_aws_region') # us-east-1

def publish_photo_event(photo_url, user_id):
    message = {
        'photo_url': photo_url,
        'user_id': user_id
    }
    sns_client.publish(
        TopicArn='arn:aws:sns:your_aws_region:your_account_id:photo_upload_topic', # ARN example
        Message=json.dumps(message),
        Subject='New Photo Uploaded'
    )


# Example usage
publish_photo_event('s3://your-bucket/photos/image1.jpg', 'user123')
```

In this example, publish_photo_event sends a JSON message to the SNS topic photo_upload_topic. This topic will then distribute the message to all its subscribers (SQS queues in this case).

SNS Topic Configuration:

You'll create an SNS topic, giving it a name like photo_upload_topic. You need the ARN (Amazon Resource Name) of this topic to configure the event producer and the SQS queue subscriptions.

SQS Queues and Lambda Functions (Consumers):

Each service (thumbnail generation, image analysis, etc.) would have its own SQS queue subscribed to the SNS topic. Each queue would then trigger a corresponding Lambda function.

SQS Subscription filter policy

```
{
  "user_id": ["user123", "user456"]
}
```

Lambda Function (Example: Thumbnail Generation):

```
import boto3
import json

def lambda_handler(event, context):
    message = json.loads(event['Records'][0]['body']) #event['Records'][0]['Sns']['Message']
    photo_url = message['photo_url']
    user_id = message['user_id']

    print(f"Generating thumbnail for: {photo_url}, User: {user_id}")
    # Code to download the image from S3, generate thumbnail, and store it
```

```
    return {
        'statusCode': 200,
        'body': json.dumps('Thumbnail generated!')
    }
```

This Lambda function receives the message from the SQS queue, extracts the photo URL and user ID, and then performs the thumbnail generation task. Similar Lambda functions would be created for image analysis, metadata extraction, and data backup, each triggered by its own SQS queue subscribed to the same SNS topic.

The key advantage here is **decoupling**. The application doesn't need to know about or directly interact with the thumbnail generation service, image analysis service, etc. It simply publishes an event, and SNS ensures that the appropriate services are notified. This makes your system more scalable, resilient, and easier to maintain. Adding a new image processing task only requires creating a new SQS queue, subscribing it to the SNS topic, and creating a Lambda function to process the messages. No changes are needed to the original application that uploads the photo.

AWS SQS for Buffering

The Role of Buffering in Event-Driven Architectures:

In an event-driven system, services communicate through asynchronous events. These events, which are indications of state change or requests for action, are published and consumed by various components. One of the biggest challenges in such systems is managing the flow of these events, especially during periods of high load. Buffering plays a crucial role in addressing this challenge by providing a temporary storage mechanism for events, decoupling event producers and consumers, and improving overall system resilience.

AWS SQS as a Buffer:

AWS Simple Queue Service (SQS) is a fully managed message queuing service that enables you to decouple and scale microservices, distributed systems, and serverless applications. In the context of event-driven architectures, SQS acts as a buffer between event producers and consumers (typically Lambda functions).

Handling Traffic Spikes:

One of the primary benefits of using SQS for buffering is its ability to handle traffic spikes. Imagine a scenario where a sudden surge of events is generated by an application, perhaps due to a flash sale on an e-commerce website. Without a buffer, Lambda functions consuming these events might be overwhelmed, leading to performance degradation or even system failure. SQS acts as a shock absorber, queuing the incoming events and allowing Lambda functions to process them at their own pace, ensuring that no events are lost and the system remains stable.

```
# Example scenario:

# Events generated during a flash sale are added to the SQS queue.
# Lambda functions process messages from the queue at a consistent rate.

# Sketch:
#
# [Event Producer] --> [SQS Queue (buffer)] --> [Lambda Function]
#  (High event rate)    (Smooths out the flow)    (Processes events efficiently)
#
```

Ensuring Reliable Delivery:

SQS also ensures reliable delivery of events. It guarantees that each message is delivered at least once (and in some configurations, exactly once) to a consumer. This is crucial in scenarios where event processing is critical, and losing events is unacceptable. SQS provides mechanisms for retrying failed message processing and for dead-letter queues (DLQs) to handle messages that cannot be processed after a certain number of attempts.

Example: Order Processing System

Consider an order processing system where placing an order generates an event. This event can be placed in an SQS queue. A Lambda function subscribed to this queue then processes the order, updates the inventory, and sends a confirmation email.

```python
import boto3

# Initialize SQS client
sqs = boto3.client('sqs')

queue_url = 'YOUR_QUEUE_URL' # Replace with your actual SQS queue URL

def send_order_event(order_data):
    """Sends an order event to the SQS queue."""
    response = sqs.send_message(
        QueueUrl=queue_url,
        MessageBody=str(order_data) # Serialize your order data to a string (e.g., JSON)
    )
    print(f"Message ID: {response['MessageId']}")

# Example usage:
order = {
    'order_id': '12345',
    'customer_id': '67890',
    'items': ['item1', 'item2']
}

send_order_event(order)
```

This example demonstrates how to send an order event to an SQS queue. The Lambda function would retrieve this message and process the order information.

```python
import boto3
import json

def lambda_handler(event, context):
    """Processes messages from the SQS queue."""
    for record in event['Records']:
        message_body = record['body']
        order_data = json.loads(message_body) # Deserialize the JSON string
        print(f"Processing order: {order_data['order_id']}")
        # Your order processing logic here...
        # update_inventory(order_data['items'])
        # send_confirmation_email(order_data['customer_id'])

        # Example: Delete message after processing
        sqs = boto3.client('sqs')
        queue_url = 'YOUR_QUEUE_URL'  # Replace with your actual SQS queue URL
        receipt_handle = record['receiptHandle']
        sqs.delete_message(
            QueueUrl=queue_url,
            ReceiptHandle=receipt_handle
        )
    return {
```

```
        'statusCode': 200,
        'body': 'Messages processed successfully'
    }
```

Benefits Summarized:

- **Decoupling:** Producers and consumers don't need to know about each other.
- **Scalability:** SQS can handle a large volume of events, scaling automatically as needed.
- **Reliability:** Guarantees message delivery and provides mechanisms for handling failures.
- **Resilience:** Protects against system failures by buffering events and allowing consumers to recover.

In conclusion, AWS SQS provides a robust and scalable buffering mechanism for event-driven architectures. By smoothing out traffic spikes and ensuring reliable delivery, SQS helps to build resilient and efficient systems on AWS.

Lambda for Event Processing

Lambda functions form the core of processing within an Event-Driven Architecture (EDA) built on AWS. They are the compute units triggered by events emanating from services like SNS and SQS. The following aspects are vital to understanding Lambda's role in EDA:

Lambda functions triggered by SNS/SQS process events, scaling automatically based on demand.

Lambda processes events which originate from SNS or SQS and they automatically scale based on the amount of incoming events. Let's break this down into simpler terms. When a message arrives in an SQS queue or an SNS topic, it can trigger a Lambda function. This trigger acts like a signal, telling Lambda, "Hey, there's something to do!". When more events arrive, more Lambda functions automatically start up to handle them. This automatic scaling is one of the biggest benefits of using Lambda. You don't have to worry about provisioning servers or managing capacity; AWS handles it all for you. This ensures your application can handle increased traffic without any manual intervention. Automatic Scaling is useful to quickly handle increase workload to avoid performance issues.

For instance, suppose you have an image processing application. Every time a user uploads an image, a message is sent to an SQS queue. A Lambda function is triggered by this message. This function might resize the image, add a watermark, and store it in an S3 bucket. If suddenly many users upload images at the same time, Lambda automatically scales up and starts many instances of your image processing function. This is all done without you needing to manually launch more servers.

Here's a simple example to illustrate:

Imagine a very basic system where SNS sends a message to Lambda to log an event to CloudWatch.

```python
# Lambda function code (Python)
import json
import boto3

def lambda_handler(event, context):
    """
    This function logs the event data to CloudWatch.
    """
    print("Received event:", json.dumps(event, indent=2))

    # Optionally, you can send the log to CloudWatch Logs
    # client = boto3.client('logs')
    # client.put_log_events(
    #     logGroupName='your-log-group',
    #     logStreamName='your-log-stream',
```

```
#       logEvents=[
#           {
#               'timestamp': int(round(time.time()  1000)),
#               'message': json.dumps(event)
#           },
#       ]
#   )

    return {
        'statusCode': 200,
        'body': json.dumps('Event logged successfully!')
    }
```

In this simplified example:

- The `lambda_handler` function is executed each time the Lambda is triggered from SNS.
- It receives the `event` data (the SNS message) and logs it to CloudWatch (using `print`, which automatically gets routed to CloudWatch Logs).
- You can see how this can be extend. For example, we can add more features to notify via sending email to a user.

Lambda for Event Processing:

```
graph LR
    A[SNS Topic] --> B(Lambda Function);
    B --> C{Process Event};
    C --> D[Output (e.g., S3, DynamoDB)];
    style A fill:#f9f,stroke:#333,stroke-width:2px
    style B fill:#ccf,stroke:#333,stroke-width:2px
    style C fill:#ccf,stroke:#333,stroke-width:2px
    style D fill:#f9f,stroke:#333,stroke-width:2px
```

The diagram describes a basic flow where an SNS topic triggers a Lambda function. The Lambda function processes this event, and the output can be, say, storing the data in a database (like DynamoDB) or a storage service (like S3).

Here are the important things to remember when using Lambda for event processing:

- **Stateless:** Lambda functions should be stateless. Each invocation is independent. This is fundamental for scaling and fault tolerance. Do not assume data persists between invocations.
- **Idempotency:** Ensure your Lambda functions are idempotent, especially when processing events from SQS. Due to the nature of distributed systems, the same message might be delivered more than once. Idempotency means that processing the same event multiple times has the same effect as processing it only once.
- **Error Handling:** Implement robust error handling. Use dead-letter queues (DLQs) with SQS to capture messages that fail processing. Implement retries with appropriate backoff strategies.
- **Concurrency Limits:** Be aware of AWS Lambda's concurrency limits. If your function invocations exceed the account's limit, they will be throttled. You can request an increase in the concurrency limit if necessary. Reserve concurrency for critical functions.

In summary, Lambda functions offer a powerful and scalable way to process events in a distributed system on AWS. When designed correctly, Lambda facilitates building highly resilient and performant event-driven architectures.

Chapter 13 Designing Scalable and Resilient Architectures-Microservices Design on AWS: API Gateway, ECS, and Service Mesh

- **Microservices Decomposition:** Breaking down monolithic applications into smaller, independent services for scalability and independent deployments.
- **API Gateway:** Centralized entry point for clients, handling routing, authentication, and rate limiting.
- **Elastic Container Service (ECS):** Orchestrating and scaling microservices within containers, leveraging EC2 or Fargate for compute.
- **Service Mesh (e.g., AWS App Mesh):** Managing service-to-service communication, observability, and security (TLS, traffic management).
- **Resilience through Redundancy:** Implementing multiple instances of microservices across Availability Zones for high availability and fault tolerance.

Microservices Decomposition

Microservices decomposition is the core process of taking a large, single application (often called a monolithic application) and breaking it down into smaller, independent, and manageable services. Think of it like dismantling a giant, complicated clock into its individual gears, springs, and levers. Each of these pieces (the microservices) can then function and be maintained separately.

Why Decompose?

Imagine you have a large e-commerce website. A monolithic architecture would mean that all functionalities – product catalog, user accounts, order processing, payment gateway – are all bundled into one single application. If you need to update the order processing module, you potentially need to redeploy the entire application, even if the other modules haven't changed.

Microservices decomposition addresses this problem. Each function (product catalog, user accounts, etc.) becomes its own service. This brings several key benefits:

- **Scalability:** You can scale individual services based on their specific needs. If the product catalog is experiencing heavy traffic, you can scale just that service without affecting other parts of the application.

- **Independent Deployments:** Each microservice can be deployed and updated independently. This means faster release cycles and less risk, as changes to one service don't require redeploying the entire application.

- **Technology Diversity:** Different microservices can be built using different technologies that are best suited for their specific tasks. One service might use Python, while another uses Java, without impacting each other.

- **Fault Isolation:** If one microservice fails, it doesn't necessarily bring down the entire application. Other microservices can continue to function normally.

How to Approach Decomposition

Decomposition is not a one-size-fits-all process. It requires careful planning and consideration of your application's specific needs. Here's a general approach:

1. **Identify Bounded Contexts:** Analyze your application and identify distinct functional areas or business domains. These areas represent natural boundaries for microservices. In our e-commerce example, product catalog, user accounts, and order processing are good candidates.

2. **Define Service Boundaries:** Determine the responsibilities of each microservice and how they will interact with each other. Clear service boundaries are crucial for independent development and deployment.

3. **Choose a Communication Style:** Microservices need to communicate with each other. Common communication styles include:

   o **Synchronous (REST):** One service directly calls another using HTTP requests.

   ```python
   # Python (example)
   import requests

   response = requests.get('http://user-service/users/123')
   user_data = response.json()
   print(user_data)
   ```

   Sketch:

   ```
   [Client] --> [API Gateway] --> [Microservice A] --> [Microservice B]
   ```

   o **Asynchronous (Message Queues):** Services communicate through a message queue (e.g., RabbitMQ, Kafka). One service publishes a message to the queue, and another service subscribes to the queue and processes the message.

   ```python
   # Python (example using a hypothetical message queue library)
   import message_queue

   message_queue.publish('order.created', {'order_id': 456})
   ```

   Sketch:

   ```
   [Microservice A] --> [Message Queue] --> [Microservice B]
   ```

4. **Data Management:** Decide how data will be managed across microservices. Each microservice typically has its own database, which ensures data isolation and independence.

   Sketch:

   ```
   [Microservice A] --[Database A]
   [Microservice B] --[Database B]
   [Microservice C] --[Database C]
   ```

5. **Implement and Deploy:** Develop and deploy each microservice independently. Use continuous integration and continuous deployment (CI/CD) pipelines to automate the process.

Challenges of Decomposition

While microservices offer significant benefits, they also introduce new challenges:

- **Increased Complexity:** Managing a distributed system of microservices is more complex than managing a monolithic application.

- **Network Latency:** Communication between microservices can introduce network latency, which can impact performance.

- **Distributed Transactions:** Ensuring data consistency across multiple microservices can be challenging.

- **Observability:** Monitoring and troubleshooting a distributed system requires robust observability tools and practices.

In Summary

Microservices decomposition is a powerful technique for building scalable, resilient, and maintainable applications. However, it requires careful planning, design, and implementation. By understanding the benefits, challenges, and best practices, you can successfully decompose your monolithic applications into a collection of manageable microservices.

API Gateway

The API Gateway serves as the central entry point for all client requests to your microservices architecture. Think of it as a gatekeeper, standing between the outside world and your internal services. It's responsible for handling incoming requests, routing them to the appropriate backend services, and returning the responses to the client.

Core Responsibilities:

- **Centralized Entry Point:** All external requests first go through the API Gateway, regardless of which microservice ultimately handles the request. This provides a single, well-defined interface for clients.
- **Routing:** The API Gateway examines the incoming request (e.g., the URL path, HTTP method) and determines which microservice should handle it. For instance, a request to `/users` might be routed to the `UserService`, while a request to `/products` is routed to the `ProductService`.
- **Authentication:** The API Gateway can handle user authentication and authorization. This ensures that only authenticated users with the correct permissions can access your microservices. This avoids implementing authentication logic in every single microservice, centralizing it for better security and maintainability.
- **Rate Limiting:** To protect your backend services from being overwhelmed by too many requests, the API Gateway can implement rate limiting. This restricts the number of requests a client can make within a specific time period.

Example Scenario:

Consider an e-commerce application with `UserService`, `ProductService`, and `OrderService`. Instead of clients directly calling these services, they interact with the API Gateway.

A client wanting to fetch product details makes a request to `/products/123` (where 123 is the product ID). The API Gateway recognizes the `/products` path and routes the request to the `ProductService`. The `ProductService` retrieves the product information and sends it back to the API Gateway. The API Gateway then relays the response to the client.

```
Client --> API Gateway --> ProductService --> API Gateway --> Client
                          (Returns Product Data)
```

Sketch:

```
+-------+      +-------------+      +----------------+      +-------------+      +-------+
|Client |----->| API Gateway |----->| ProductService |----->| API Gateway |----->| Client |
+-------+      +-------------+      +----------------+      +-------------+      +-------+
               |   Routing   |      | Data Fetch  |         |  Response  |
               |Authentication|     +----------------+       |   Relay    |
               | Rate Limiting|                             |            |
```

Code Example (Conceptual - Simplified):

While specific implementation depends on the technology (e.g., Kong, Apigee, AWS API Gateway), the logic is similar. This Python example is for illustrative purposes only and requires a framework like Flask or FastAPI to actually run.

```python
# Conceptual API Gateway Route Handler (Python)
def handle_request(request):
    path = request.path

    if path.startswith("/users"):
        # Forward request to UserService
        user_service_response = call_user_service(request)
        return user_service_response
    elif path.startswith("/products"):
        # Forward request to ProductService
        product_service_response = call_product_service(request)
        return product_service_response
    else:
        return "404 Not Found"

def call_user_service(request):
    # ... Logic to forward request to UserService and return the response
    # (e.g., using HTTP libraries like 'requests')
    return "UserService Response" # Placeholder

def call_product_service(request):
    # ... Logic to forward request to ProductService and return the response
    return "ProductService Response" # Placeholder
```

This simplified example demonstrates the basic routing logic. A real-world API Gateway would handle authentication, rate limiting, request transformation (if needed), and more.

Benefits of using an API Gateway:

- **Decoupling:** Clients are decoupled from the internal microservice architecture. Changes to the backend services don't necessarily require changes to the clients.
- **Security:** Centralized authentication and authorization provide a single point of enforcement.
- **Simplified Client Experience:** Clients interact with a single endpoint, simplifying their development and integration.
- **Improved Observability:** The API Gateway provides a central point for monitoring and logging requests and responses.
- **Traffic Management:** Rate limiting and other traffic management features help protect your backend services.

In essence, the API Gateway is a crucial component of a microservices architecture, enabling efficient, secure, and scalable access to your services.

Elastic Container Service (ECS): Orchestrating and Scaling Microservices

Elastic Container Service (ECS) plays a vital role in managing and scaling your microservices when they are packaged as containers. Think of ECS as a conductor of an orchestra. Instead of musicians, ECS manages containers, ensuring they are running smoothly and efficiently. It handles the complexities of deploying, scaling, and managing these containers, so you can focus on developing your applications.

What does ECS do?

- **Orchestration:** ECS orchestrates your containers, meaning it decides where they should run, starts them, and makes sure they stay running. It's like a traffic controller for your containers. It can deploy containers on different platforms like EC2 instances (your own virtual machines) or Fargate (serverless compute).
- **Scaling:** ECS automatically adjusts the number of containers running based on the demand for your application. If your application is getting a lot of traffic, ECS can automatically spin up more containers to

handle the load. This ensures your application remains responsive and available, even during peak usage. Think of it like adding more lanes to a highway during rush hour.

- **Management:** ECS provides tools and APIs to manage your containers, monitor their health, and update them. It simplifies many of the common tasks associated with running containerized applications.

ECS with EC2 and Fargate

ECS allows you to run your containers on two primary compute options: EC2 instances or Fargate. The choice depends on your specific needs and preferences.

- **EC2:** In this mode, you manage the underlying EC2 instances yourself. This provides more control over the infrastructure but requires more operational overhead, such as patching, scaling, and securing the virtual machines. You are responsible for the underlying hardware, but you have full control over the operating system and environment.

  Example: You might choose EC2 if you need specific hardware configurations or want to optimize costs by closely managing the instance sizes.

```
//Conceptual Sketch: EC2-based ECS


+---------------------+   +---------------------+
| EC2 Instance        |   | EC2 Instance        |
|---------------------|   |---------------------|
| Container 1         |   | Container 3         |
| Container 2         |   | Container 4         |
+---------------------+   +---------------------+
        ^                         ^
        |                         |
+-----------------------------+
| ECS Control Plane           |
| (Manages EC2 instances &    |
| containers)                 |
+-----------------------------+
```

- **Fargate:** This is a serverless compute option. With Fargate, you don't need to manage any EC2 instances. AWS handles the underlying infrastructure, allowing you to focus solely on deploying and managing your containers. Fargate automatically scales and manages the compute resources needed to run your containers.

  Example: If you want to minimize operational overhead and avoid managing infrastructure, Fargate is a good choice.

```
//Conceptual Sketch: Fargate-based ECS


+-------------------------------+   +-------------------------------+
| Fargate Container 1           |   | Fargate Container 2           |
| (Managed by AWS)              |   | (Managed by AWS)              |
+-------------------------------+   +-------------------------------+
        ^                                   ^
        |                                   |
+---------------------------------------------+
| ECS Control Plane                           |
| (Manages Fargate containers)                |
+---------------------------------------------+
```

Simple Code Example (Task Definition)

Here's a simplified example of an ECS Task Definition in JSON format. This tells ECS how to run your container.

```
{
  "family": "my-web-app",
  "containerDefinitions": [
    {
      "name": "my-web-container",
      "image": "your-dockerhub-id/your-web-app-image:latest",
      "portMappings": [
        {
          "containerPort": 80,
          "hostPort": 80
        }
      ],
      "memory": 512,
      "cpu": 256
    }
  ],
  "networkMode": "awsvpc",
  "requiresCompatibilities": [
    "FARGATE" , "EC2"
  ],
  "cpu": "256",
  "memory": "512",
  "executionRoleArn": "arn:aws:iam::123456789012:role/ecsTaskExecutionRole"
}
```

Explanation:

- family: A name to group related task definitions.
- containerDefinitions: Describes the containers that will run within the task.
  - image: The Docker image to use for the container.
  - portMappings: Maps container ports to host ports.
  - memory and cpu: Resource limits for the container.
- networkMode: Specifies the networking mode. awsvpc is recommended.
- requiresCompatibilities: Specifies whether Fargate or EC2 is used.
- executionRoleArn: The IAM role that the task will assume.

This JSON file defines a simple web application container, specifying the Docker image to use, the port mappings, and the resource requirements. ECS uses this information to launch and manage the container.

Benefits of Using ECS

- **Scalability:** Easily scale your applications based on demand.
- **High Availability:** Ensures your applications are always available by distributing them across multiple instances or Fargate containers.
- **Simplified Management:** Provides tools and APIs to simplify the management of containerized applications.
- **Cost-Effective:** Optimize costs by using EC2 or Fargate, depending on your needs.
- **Integration:** Integrates well with other AWS services, such as load balancers, databases, and monitoring tools.

In summary, ECS is a powerful tool for orchestrating and scaling microservices packaged as containers. Whether you choose EC2 or Fargate, ECS simplifies the deployment and management of your applications, allowing you to focus on delivering value to your users.

Service Mesh (e.g., AWS App Mesh)

Service meshes are a dedicated infrastructure layer for managing service-to-service communication. They handle concerns like observability, security (TLS), and traffic management, allowing developers to focus on writing business logic instead of dealing with complex networking issues. AWS App Mesh is an example of a service mesh implementation provided by Amazon Web Services.

Managing service-to-service communication:

In a microservices architecture, services frequently communicate with each other to fulfill requests. Without a service mesh, managing this communication can become complex. You'd need to implement retry logic, circuit breakers, and service discovery within each service. A service mesh abstracts these complexities. It intercepts all network communication between services, adding features like routing, load balancing, and service discovery uniformly across the application. Think of it as a smart network that understands your microservices and helps them communicate efficiently.

Illustration of Service-to-Service Communication with and without Service Mesh:

```
Without Service Mesh:

[Service A] --> [Network, Custom Code for Resilience] --> [Service B]
                                                             ^
                                                             |
[Service C] -------------------------------------------------|


With Service Mesh:

[Service A] --> [Service Mesh Proxy] --> [Service B]
                                           ^
                                           |
[Service C] --> [Service Mesh Proxy] ----|
```

In this simple visual, service A is communicating with B and Service C is communicating with B. Without Service Mesh (top part of the illustration), the developers needs to build the functionality to handle resilience and networking code. With Service Mesh(bottom part of illustration), the service proxy intercepts the network communication.

Observability:

Service meshes provide deep insights into the communication between services. They collect metrics like latency, traffic volume, and error rates, and provide these metrics in a centralized location. This observability is crucial for identifying performance bottlenecks, debugging issues, and understanding the overall health of your application.

For example, imagine you are seeing increased latency for user requests. With a service mesh, you can quickly pinpoint if a specific service is the cause of the increased latency by examining its metrics. You could see increased error rates for the database calls made by that particular service, helping you quickly find the root cause.

Consider the below simple metric code to represent the number of request

```python
# Sample Python code (Conceptual)

# Assuming you have a service mesh client library
import service_mesh_client as smc

# increment requests
smc.increment_counter("requests", service="my_service", endpoint="/api/data")
```

In this simple conceptual example, it shows it uses `service_mesh_client` to increment the counter each time the request happens.

Security (TLS):

Service meshes can enforce security policies across your microservices. A key feature is mutual TLS (mTLS), where each service authenticates the identity of the other service before establishing a connection. This prevents unauthorized services from accessing sensitive data or resources.

For example, you can configure your service mesh to require mTLS for all communication between your authentication service and your payment service. This ensures that only the authentication service can communicate with the payment service, preventing other services from potentially accessing payment information.

Consider the below example sketch

```
[Service A] <--(mTLS handshake)--> [Service Mesh Proxy] <--(mTLS handshake)--> [Service B]
```

The illustration shows the mutual TLS connection between each services.

Traffic Management:

Service meshes provide advanced traffic management capabilities, enabling features like canary deployments, A/B testing, and traffic shifting. With canary deployments, you can gradually roll out new versions of a service to a small subset of users before releasing it to everyone. This allows you to monitor the new version for errors and performance issues before impacting all users.

Consider you have a service `User-Service` and you want to deploy a new version which is v2 but you don't trust it. You can gradually roll out v2 for a subset of users, you can manage the traffic via service mesh.

```
80% Traffic -> User-Service v1
[Incoming Request] --> [Service Mesh]
                                        20% Traffic -> User-Service v2 (Canary)
```

This way the incoming requests are being controlled by service mesh and the traffic % are distributed to each user.

AWS App Mesh:

AWS App Mesh is a fully managed service mesh that makes it easy to monitor and control microservices running on AWS. It integrates with other AWS services like ECS, EKS, and EC2, providing a seamless experience for managing your microservices. App Mesh uses the Envoy proxy, which is a high-performance, open-source proxy designed for cloud-native applications.

To configure App Mesh, you would define resources like:

- **Mesh:** Represents your entire service mesh.
- **Virtual Service:** An abstraction over one or more actual services, providing a consistent endpoint for clients to access.
- **Virtual Node:** Represents a specific instance of a service, typically running within a container.
- **Virtual Router:** Routes traffic to different virtual nodes based on rules you define.
- **Route:** Specifies the rules for routing traffic to a virtual node.

You can define all those components using declarative configuration (e.g. using YAML files) and apply them using the AWS CLI or SDKs.

For example, the following YAML snippet shows setting up virtual service with service mesh

```
apiVersion: appmesh.k8s.aws/v1beta2
kind: VirtualService
metadata:
  name: userservice.example.com
  namespace: default
spec:
```

```
meshRef:
  name: appmesh-mesh
provider:
  virtualNode:
    virtualNodeRef:
      name: userservice-vn
```

This is a basic example of how the virtual service is created.

Resilience through Redundancy

Resilience through redundancy means building your systems so they can keep working even if some parts fail. In the context of microservices, this usually means running multiple copies of each microservice across different locations, typically Availability Zones (AZs).

Why is Redundancy Important?

Imagine a website that only has one server. If that server goes down, the entire website becomes unavailable. That's a single point of failure. Redundancy eliminates single points of failure. If one instance of a microservice fails (due to a software bug, a hardware problem, or even just routine maintenance), the other instances can continue to handle requests, ensuring your application remains available.

Implementing Redundancy with Microservices

With microservices, achieving redundancy often involves these key practices:

- **Multiple Instances:** Deploy multiple instances of each microservice. Instead of running just one "Order Processing" service, you might run three or more.
- **Availability Zones (AZs):** Distribute these instances across different Availability Zones. An Availability Zone is a physically separate data center within a region. This way, if one AZ experiences an outage (power failure, network issue, etc.), the other AZs, and therefore the other instances of your microservice, can continue functioning.

Let's illustrate this with a simple diagram:

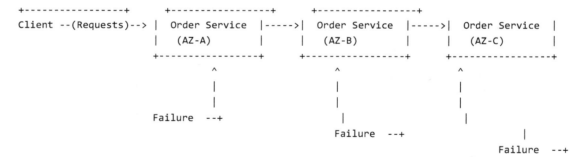

In this sketch, requests from a client are distributed across three instances of the Order Service, each running in a different Availability Zone (AZ-A, AZ-B, AZ-C). If one AZ fails, the client requests are automatically routed to the remaining healthy instances.

How Orchestration (ECS) Helps

Orchestration tools like Elastic Container Service (ECS) are crucial for managing this redundancy. ECS can automatically:

- **Deploy instances:** Spin up multiple copies of your microservices across AZs.
- **Monitor health:** Continuously check the health of each instance.
- **Replace failing instances:** If an instance fails, ECS can automatically start a new one in a healthy AZ.

- **Load balance traffic:** Distribute incoming requests evenly across the healthy instances.

Code Example (Conceptual)

While you wouldn't write code directly to implement AZ-level redundancy, you would configure your ECS service to achieve it. This is more configuration than coding:

```
// Example ECS Service Definition (Simplified)
{
  "serviceName": "OrderService",
  "desiredCount": 3, // Run three instances
  "launchType": "FARGATE", //Or EC2
  "networkConfiguration": {
    "awsvpcConfiguration": {
      "subnets": [
        "subnet-0123456789abcdef0", // Subnet in AZ-A
        "subnet-0fedcba9876543210", // Subnet in AZ-B
        "subnet-0abcdef1234567890"  // Subnet in AZ-C
      ],
      "assignPublicIp": "DISABLED"
    }
  },
  "loadBalancers": [
      {
          "targetGroupArn": "arn:aws:elasticloadbalancing:us-west-2:123456789012:targetgroup/r
          "containerName": "simple-app",
          "containerPort": 8080
      }
    ]
}
```

In this example:

- `desiredCount`: 3 tells ECS to run three instances of the Order Service.
- The `subnets` array specifies subnets in different Availability Zones. ECS will launch instances into these subnets, distributing them across the AZs.
- `loadBalancers` is configuring the loadbalancer which will distribute traffic to containers.

Service Mesh and Redundancy

Service meshes, like AWS App Mesh, further enhance redundancy. They provide:

- **Intelligent routing:** Route traffic away from unhealthy instances, even if they haven't fully failed yet.
- **Retry mechanisms:** If a request to one instance fails, the service mesh can automatically retry the request on another instance.
- **Circuit breaking:** If a particular instance consistently fails, the service mesh can temporarily stop sending traffic to it, preventing cascading failures.

Trade-offs

While redundancy is crucial, it's important to consider the trade-offs:

- **Cost:** Running multiple instances increases infrastructure costs.
- **Complexity:** Managing multiple instances requires more sophisticated deployment and monitoring strategies.
- **Data Consistency:** Ensuring data consistency across multiple instances requires careful consideration of database replication and consistency models (e.g., eventual consistency).

Despite these trade-offs, the increased availability and fault tolerance provided by redundancy are often essential for building reliable microservices applications. The costs associated with downtime typically outweigh the costs of implementing redundancy.

Chapter 14 Designing Scalable and Resilient Architectures-Hybrid and Multi-Cloud Strategies with AWS

Here are 5 bullet points outlining hybrid and multi-cloud strategies within system design on AWS:

- **Hybrid Cloud Architecture:**
  - Extending AWS infrastructure to on-premises environments to support legacy applications.
  - Using AWS Direct Connect or VPNs for secure, low-latency connectivity.
- **Multi-Cloud Deployment:**
  - Leveraging multiple cloud providers (AWS, Azure, GCP) for redundancy and vendor diversification.
  - Distributing workloads based on each provider's strengths (e.g., AI/ML on one, data warehousing on another).
- **Workload Portability:**
  - Containerization (Docker, Kubernetes) for easier application migration between clouds and on-prem.
  - Infrastructure as Code (IaC) tools (Terraform, CloudFormation) for consistent infrastructure provisioning.
- **Data Management:**
  - Implementing strategies for data replication and synchronization across environments.
  - Consider data governance and compliance requirements for hybrid and multi-cloud deployments.
- **Cost Optimization:**
  - Optimizing resource utilization in each environment to reduce overall cloud spending.
  - Monitoring and analyzing costs across all cloud providers to identify potential savings.

Hybrid Cloud Architecture

Hybrid cloud architecture represents a system design where you combine your existing on-premises infrastructure with the capabilities of a public cloud provider like AWS. This approach allows you to leverage the benefits of both environments, addressing specific needs and constraints. Think of it as having both your own private data center and renting resources from AWS, making them work together seamlessly.

Extending AWS infrastructure to on-premises environments to support legacy applications.

Often, businesses have applications that are difficult or impossible to migrate directly to the cloud. These "legacy applications" might rely on older operating systems, specific hardware, or tight integration with other on-premises systems. Instead of rewriting these applications from scratch, a hybrid approach allows you to keep them running where they are while still taking advantage of AWS for other workloads or new development.

For example, a manufacturing company might have a critical machine control system running on a local server. It's not practical to move this system to the cloud because of latency requirements and the need for direct hardware control. However, the company can use AWS for data analytics, collecting data from the on-premises system and processing it in the cloud to gain insights into manufacturing efficiency.

```
#Conceptual Example (Illustrative, not executable)
on_prem_system.send_data(aws_analytics_endpoint, data)
```

This snippet represents data being sent from an on-premises system to AWS for analytics.

Using AWS Direct Connect or VPNs for secure, low-latency connectivity.

A crucial aspect of a hybrid cloud is establishing a reliable and secure connection between your on-premises environment and AWS. This is typically achieved using either AWS Direct Connect or Virtual Private Networks (VPNs).

- **AWS Direct Connect:** This creates a dedicated network connection between your data center and AWS. It offers lower latency, increased bandwidth, and more consistent network performance compared to internet-based connections. Think of it as a private highway directly to AWS, ensuring fast and reliable data transfer.

  ```
  [On-Premises Data Center] --(Dedicated Connection: AWS Direct Connect)--> [AWS Cloud]
  ```

- **VPNs (Virtual Private Networks):** A VPN uses the public internet to create an encrypted tunnel between your on-premises network and AWS. This is a more cost-effective option for smaller workloads or when dedicated bandwidth isn't required. Consider it as a secured passage through public road.

  ```
  [On-Premises Data Center] --(Encrypted Tunnel: VPN over Internet)--> [AWS Cloud]
  ```

  For example, you might configure an IPsec VPN using AWS's Virtual Private Gateway on the AWS side and a compatible VPN device on your on-premises network.

  ```
  #Conceptual Example (AWS CLI, simplified)
  aws ec2 create-vpn-connection --type ipsec.1 --customer-gateway-id cgw-xxxxxxxx --vpn-gatew
  ```

  This command creates a VPN connection between your on-premises network (represented by **cgw-xxxxxxxx**) and your AWS VPC (represented by **vgw-yyyyyyyy**). The actual configuration would involve setting up routing and security policies on both sides.

The choice between Direct Connect and VPN depends on your specific requirements for bandwidth, latency, security, and cost. Direct Connect is generally preferred for mission-critical applications requiring consistent performance, while VPNs are suitable for less demanding workloads or as a backup connection.

Extending AWS Infrastructure to On-Premises Environments to Support Legacy Applications

This section explores how to bridge the gap between the AWS cloud and your existing on-premises infrastructure, specifically focusing on scenarios where you need to support older, "legacy" applications. These applications might be difficult or impossible to move directly to the cloud without significant changes. This approach allows you to leverage the benefits of AWS while still maintaining your legacy systems where they are.

Understanding the Need

Imagine you have a critical application that runs your core business processes. It's been running for years, and while it works well, it was designed for an on-premises environment. Re-writing it for the cloud would be extremely expensive and time-consuming. However, you'd still like to take advantage of AWS services for things like storage, backup, or disaster recovery. Extending your AWS infrastructure to your on-premises environment makes this possible.

How it Works: A Practical View

The key is to create a network connection between your on-premises data center and your AWS environment. This allows your on-premises applications to communicate with AWS services as if they were part of the same network.

Think of it as building a bridge between two islands. Your on-premises environment is one island, AWS is the other. The bridge allows traffic (data) to flow freely between them.

Example:

Suppose you have an old inventory management system running on a server in your office. You want to back up its data to Amazon S3, AWS's object storage service. By extending your AWS infrastructure, the on-premises server can directly upload backup files to S3 without having to go through the public internet (if using Direct Connect).

Components Involved

Extending AWS infrastructure involves several key components:

1. **AWS Virtual Private Cloud (VPC):** Your private network within AWS. It's the foundation for your AWS resources.

2. **Networking:** The "bridge" that connects your on-premises environment to your AWS VPC. Two primary options exist: AWS Direct Connect and VPN.

3. **Security:** Implementing security measures to protect data as it moves between environments.

AWS Direct Connect:

AWS Direct Connect establishes a dedicated network connection between your on-premises network and AWS.

- **Benefits:**
  - Lower latency (faster data transfer).
  - More predictable network performance.
  - Potentially reduced network costs compared to internet-based connections.

- **Considerations:**
  - Requires a physical connection to an AWS Direct Connect location.
  - Involves a longer setup process than VPN.

AWS Direct Connect Sketch:

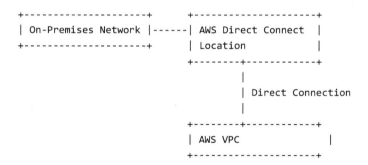

```
+---------------------+        +---------------------+
| On-Premises Network |------| AWS Direct Connect  |
+---------------------+        | Location            |
                               +--------+------------+
                                        |
                                        | Direct Connection
                                        |
                               +--------+------------+
                               | AWS VPC             |
                               +---------------------+
```

VPN (Virtual Private Network):

A VPN creates a secure, encrypted connection between your on-premises network and your AWS VPC over the internet.

- **Benefits:**
  - Faster to set up than Direct Connect.

- Lower initial cost.
  - Suitable for less bandwidth-intensive workloads.

- **Considerations:**

  - Relies on the public internet, so performance can be less predictable.
  - May have higher latency than Direct Connect.
  - Requires careful configuration to ensure security.

VPN Sketch:

```
+--------------------+        +--------------------+        +--------------------+
| On-Premises Network |------|   Internet          |------|  AWS VPC           |
+--------------------+        |   (VPN Tunnel)      |        +--------------------+
                              +--------------------+
```

Code Example (Illustrative - CloudFormation for Site-to-Site VPN):

While a full, working example is beyond the scope of this explanation, this snippet illustrates how Infrastructure as Code (IaC) could be used to define a Site-to-Site VPN connection using AWS CloudFormation. It should be noted that this configuration will require customization based on your on-premise environment.

```
Resources:
  VPNGateway:
    Type: AWS::EC2::VPNGateway
    Properties:
      Type: ipsec.1
      # Tags: ...

  CustomerGateway:
    Type: AWS::EC2::CustomerGateway
    Properties:
      BgpAsn: 65000 # Example ASN
      IpAddress: 203.0.113.25 # Example Public IP of your Customer Gateway
      Type: ipsec.1
      # Tags: ...

  VPNConnection:
    Type: AWS::EC2::VPNConnection
    Properties:
      Type: ipsec.1
      CustomerGatewayId: !Ref CustomerGateway
      VpnGatewayId: !Ref VPNGateway
      StaticRoutesOnly: true
      # Tags: ...

Outputs:
  VPNConnectionId:
    Description: The ID of the VPN Connection
    Value: !Ref VPNConnection
```

This CloudFormation template is a simplified example. A production-ready template would include more detailed configurations, security settings, and routing configurations. CloudFormation is one way to automate creating the needed connection.

When to use it:

- **Database Replication:** You want to replicate data from an on-premises database to an AWS database (e.g., using AWS Database Migration Service).
- **Disaster Recovery:** You want to use AWS as a backup and recovery site for your on-premises applications.
- **Hybrid Applications:** Some parts of your application run on-premises, while others run in AWS, requiring communication between the two.
- **Data Processing:** You have data generated on-premises that needs to be processed by AWS services like AWS Glue or Amazon EMR.

Security Considerations

Security is paramount. You need to ensure that data transmitted between your on-premises environment and AWS is protected.

- **Encryption:** Use strong encryption for data in transit (VPN, Direct Connect encryption).
- **Access Control:** Implement strict access control policies to limit who can access resources in both environments.
- **Monitoring:** Continuously monitor your hybrid environment for security threats.
- **Firewall Rules:** Properly configure firewall rules on both sides of the connection to restrict network traffic to only the needed ports and protocols.

Conclusion

Extending AWS infrastructure to on-premises environments is a valuable strategy for organizations that need to support legacy applications while leveraging the benefits of the cloud. Careful planning, secure network connections, and robust security measures are essential for a successful hybrid cloud deployment. The decision between AWS Direct Connect and VPN will depend on your specific requirements for bandwidth, latency, and cost.

Secure, Low-Latency Connectivity with AWS Direct Connect and VPNs

When extending your AWS infrastructure to on-premises environments for a hybrid cloud architecture, establishing a reliable and secure network connection is critical. AWS provides two primary services for this purpose: AWS Direct Connect and Virtual Private Networks (VPNs). Both offer distinct advantages, and the choice depends on your specific requirements for bandwidth, latency, security, and cost.

AWS Direct Connect

AWS Direct Connect establishes a dedicated network connection from your on-premises environment directly to AWS. Think of it as a private highway connecting your office or data center to the AWS cloud, bypassing the public internet.

Benefits:

- **Lower Latency:** Because data travels over a dedicated physical connection, latency (the time it takes for data to travel between locations) is significantly reduced compared to using the internet. This is crucial for applications that require near-real-time communication, such as high-frequency trading platforms or interactive gaming applications.
- **Increased Bandwidth:** Direct Connect offers various bandwidth options, ranging from 1 Gbps to 100 Gbps, providing ample capacity for transferring large datasets or supporting bandwidth-intensive applications.
- **Consistent Network Performance:** The dedicated connection ensures consistent network performance, minimizing unpredictable fluctuations that can occur with internet-based connections. This is vital for applications that demand stable and reliable network conditions.
- **Enhanced Security:** By bypassing the public internet, Direct Connect reduces the risk of exposure to cyber threats. Data transmitted over the dedicated connection is more secure than data transmitted over the internet.
- **Cost Savings:** For organizations with substantial data transfer needs, Direct Connect can be more cost-effective than using the internet, especially when considering data egress charges (the cost of transferring data out of AWS).

How it Works (Sketch):

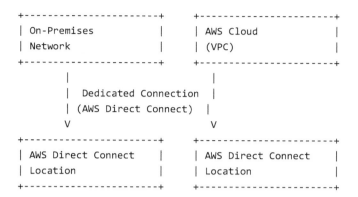

The sketch represents your on-premises network connecting to an AWS VPC via an AWS Direct Connect connection. A physical cable runs from your location to an AWS Direct Connect location. This connection is then configured to route traffic between your network and your AWS resources.

Configuration Example (Simplified):

While the actual configuration involves working with AWS Direct Connect partners and configuring routers, here's a conceptual example using a hypothetical command-line interface:

```
# On-Premises Router Configuration
interface GigabitEthernet0/0
  ip address 192.168.1.1 255.255.255.0
  # Configure BGP (Border Gateway Protocol) to advertise routes to AWS

# AWS Router Configuration (Conceptual)
interface DirectConnectInterface
  ip address 10.0.0.1 255.255.255.0
  # Configure BGP to learn routes from on-premises
```

Considerations:

- **Location:** Direct Connect requires you to connect to an AWS Direct Connect location, which may necessitate physical colocation or working with a network provider.
- **Cost:** There are costs associated with port fees, data transfer, and potentially colocation charges.
- **Complexity:** Setting up Direct Connect involves more complexity than VPNs, requiring coordination with AWS and potentially network providers.

Virtual Private Networks (VPNs)

A VPN creates a secure, encrypted connection between your on-premises environment and your AWS Virtual Private Cloud (VPC) over the internet. Think of it as a secure tunnel through the public internet.

Benefits:

- **Cost-Effective:** VPNs are generally more cost-effective than Direct Connect, especially for lower bandwidth requirements or temporary connections.
- **Easy to Set Up:** AWS provides tools and wizards to simplify the creation and configuration of VPN connections.
- **Flexibility:** VPNs can be quickly established and terminated, offering flexibility for dynamic or short-term hybrid cloud scenarios.
- **Security:** VPNs use strong encryption protocols to protect data transmitted between your on-premises environment and AWS.

How it Works (Sketch):

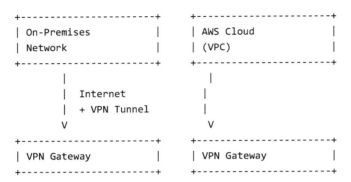

The sketch illustrates your on-premises network connecting to an AWS VPC via a VPN connection over the internet. The VPN Gateway on both sides encrypts and decrypts traffic, ensuring secure communication.

Configuration Example (Simplified):

AWS provides a managed VPN service. The basic process involves:

1. **Creating a Virtual Private Gateway (VGW) in your VPC:** This is the AWS side of the VPN connection.

2. **Creating a Customer Gateway (CGW):** This represents your on-premises VPN device. You'll need to provide the public IP address of your VPN device.

3. **Creating a VPN Connection:** You link the VGW and CGW, specifying the routing options (static or dynamic).

4. **Configuring your On-Premises VPN Device:** You'll need to configure your VPN device with the settings provided by AWS (IPsec parameters, pre-shared key, etc.).

While the specific configuration steps vary depending on your VPN device, here's a conceptual example of the IPsec configuration on your on-premises router:

```
# Sample On-Premises VPN Router Configuration (Conceptual)
crypto isakmp policy 10
 encr aes 256
 hash sha256
 authentication pre-share
 group 14

crypto isakmp key YOUR_PRE_SHARED_KEY address AWS_VPN_GATEWAY_PUBLIC_IP

crypto ipsec transform-set ESP-AES256-SHA256 esp-aes 256 esp-sha256-hmac
 mode tunnel

crypto map VPN-MAP 10 ipsec-isakmp
 set peer AWS_VPN_GATEWAY_PUBLIC_IP
 set transform-set ESP-AES256-SHA256
 match address VPN_TRAFFIC_ACL

access-list VPN_TRAFFIC_ACL permit ip 192.168.1.0 0.0.0.255 10.0.0.0 0.0.255.255
```

Important considerations with code above *Replace YOUR_PRE_SHARED_KEY with the actual pre-shared key provided by AWS when you create the VPN connection. Replace AWS_VPN_GATEWAY_PUBLIC_IP with the public*

IP address of the AWS VPN Gateway. Replace VPN_TRAFFIC_ACL with an access list that defines the traffic you want to encrypt. This is a simplified example and the specific commands may vary depending on your router.

Considerations:

- **Latency:** VPN latency is affected by the internet connection and can be higher and less predictable than Direct Connect.
- **Bandwidth:** VPN bandwidth is limited by your internet connection and the VPN device's capabilities.
- **Security:** While VPNs provide secure encryption, they are still subject to the vulnerabilities of the public internet.
- **Maintenance:** You are responsible for managing and maintaining your on-premises VPN device.

Choosing Between Direct Connect and VPN

Feature	AWS Direct Connect	VPN
Latency	Lower	Higher
Bandwidth	Higher	Lower
Security	Higher	Good (with strong encryption)
Cost	Higher (for initial setup)	Lower
Complexity	Higher	Lower
Best Use Cases	High bandwidth, low latency applications	Temporary connections, cost-sensitive scenarios
Example Applications	Database replication, high-performance computing, real-time applications	Development/testing, infrequent data transfers

In summary, Direct Connect is ideal for organizations that require high bandwidth, low latency, and consistent network performance. VPNs are a more cost-effective and flexible option for organizations with lower bandwidth requirements or temporary hybrid cloud needs. Careful analysis of your application requirements, security needs, and budget is essential to make the right choice. You can even use both, creating a VPN as a backup for a Direct Connect connection.

Multi-Cloud Deployment

Multi-cloud deployment involves using services from multiple cloud providers such as AWS, Azure, and Google Cloud Platform (GCP). This strategy aims to achieve redundancy and avoid being locked into a single vendor. It also allows you to leverage the unique strengths of each provider for different workloads.

Leveraging Multiple Cloud Providers:

The core idea behind multi-cloud deployment is to spread your applications and data across different cloud platforms. Instead of relying solely on AWS, you might also use Azure and GCP. This approach can be driven by several factors:

- **Redundancy:** If one cloud provider experiences an outage, your application can continue running on another provider, ensuring high availability.
- **Vendor Diversification:** Reduces dependency on a single provider, mitigating risks associated with pricing changes, service limitations, or platform-specific issues.
- **Compliance:** Different cloud providers may offer specific compliance certifications or data residency options that align better with certain regulatory requirements.
- **Geographic Distribution:** Distribute your application across different geographic locations using multiple cloud providers that may offer local edge locations.
- **Avoiding Vendor Lock-in:** By diversifying across multiple providers, you reduce the risk of being locked into a single ecosystem, giving you more flexibility in terms of pricing, technology choices, and service offerings.

Example:

Imagine you have a web application. Instead of hosting everything on AWS, you could host the front-end on AWS, the database on Azure, and use GCP for machine learning tasks. If AWS has an outage, the front-end might be affected, but your database and AI components remain operational on other platforms.

Distributing Workloads Based on Provider Strengths:

Each cloud provider has its own set of strengths and weaknesses. A multi-cloud strategy allows you to choose the best platform for each specific workload. For example:

- **AWS:** AWS has a broad range of services and a mature ecosystem, making it suitable for general-purpose computing, storage, and networking. It's a good all-rounder choice.
- **Azure:** Azure integrates well with Microsoft products and services, making it a strong choice for organizations already using Windows Server, .NET, or SQL Server. Also it has strong suite of services.
- **GCP:** GCP is known for its strengths in data analytics, machine learning, and containerization (Kubernetes). Services like BigQuery and TensorFlow are highly regarded.

Example:

Let's say you need to implement a machine learning model. GCP's TensorFlow and Vertex AI might be a better fit than the machine learning services offered by AWS or Azure. On the other hand, if you need to run a large-scale .NET application, Azure might be the more logical choice. If you have an exisiting legacy application that can be directly integrated with AWS cloud service, than AWS is more suitable.

Sketch: Here's how the multi-cloud deployment concept is visualized :

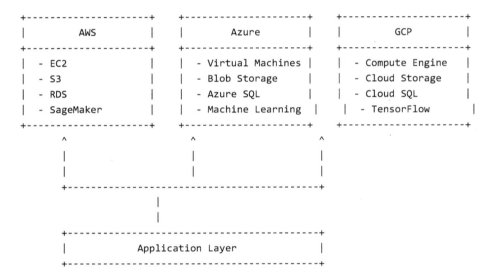

In this sketch, each cloud provider is represented as a separate entity (AWS, Azure, GCP), each offering its own set of services. The application layer sits on top, utilizing these services from different providers based on specific requirements. The arrows indicate that the application layer interacts with and leverages services from each cloud provider.

Multi-Cloud Deployment: Redundancy and Vendor Diversification

This section explores the strategy of using multiple cloud providers – specifically, AWS (Amazon Web Services), Azure (Microsoft Azure), and GCP (Google Cloud Platform) – to achieve redundancy and vendor diversification.

What it Means

Leveraging multiple cloud providers means distributing your applications and data across different cloud platforms instead of relying solely on one. The core idea is to avoid "putting all your eggs in one basket." This approach mitigates risks associated with service outages, vendor lock-in, and regional disasters. It also allows you to take advantage of the unique strengths and pricing models offered by each provider.

Why is it important? Imagine a scenario where a single cloud provider experiences a major outage. If all your systems are hosted on that provider, your entire business could be severely impacted. By distributing your workloads across multiple clouds, you ensure that even if one provider experiences issues, your critical applications can continue to run on another platform. Vendor diversification protects you against potential price increases or changes in service offerings from a single provider. It also gives you more leverage when negotiating contracts and ensures you're always getting the best value for your cloud investments.

Redundancy

Redundancy ensures high availability and business continuity. By replicating your applications and data across multiple cloud providers, you can automatically failover to a different cloud in case of an outage or disaster.

Example: Consider a critical e-commerce application. You could deploy the application's frontend on AWS, the backend on Azure, and the database on GCP. If AWS experiences an outage, the application can seamlessly switch to using a backup frontend instance on Azure or GCP, ensuring minimal downtime for your customers.

Vendor Diversification

Vendor diversification reduces your dependence on a single cloud provider. This gives you greater flexibility, control, and negotiating power.

Example:

Suppose you're running a data analytics platform. You could use AWS for data storage (e.g., S3), Azure for machine learning (e.g., Azure Machine Learning), and GCP for data warehousing (e.g., BigQuery). This allows you to leverage the best-of-breed services from each provider and avoid being locked into a single ecosystem. If, for instance, Azure increases its machine learning pricing, you have the option of migrating your workloads to another provider without disrupting your entire platform.

A Simple Illustration of Multi-Cloud Architecture

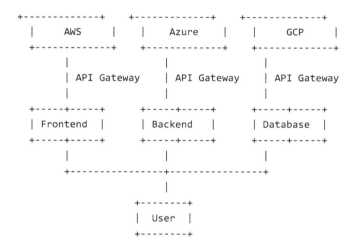

In this simplified sketch:

- Users interact with the application through a common interface (API Gateway).
- The frontend, backend, and database components are distributed across AWS, Azure, and GCP.
- This approach provides redundancy and allows you to leverage the specific strengths of each cloud provider.

Challenges and Considerations

While multi-cloud deployment offers significant benefits, it also introduces complexity. Managing multiple cloud environments requires expertise in different platforms, tools, and processes. Security, networking, and data management can also be more challenging in a multi-cloud environment. Careful planning, robust automation, and strong governance are essential for successful multi-cloud adoption.

Distributing Workloads Based on Each Provider's Strengths

The core idea behind distributing workloads based on each provider's strengths is to strategically place different parts of your application across different cloud providers like AWS, Azure, and GCP. The goal is to exploit the unique advantages each cloud offers, optimizing performance, cost, and specific technological needs. Think of it as assembling a team where each member (cloud provider) brings a special skill to the table.

Understanding Provider Specializations

Cloud providers have evolved with different strengths. Instead of using only one, this strategy intelligently chooses the best platform for each workload. Here are a few examples:

- **AWS (Amazon Web Services):** Well-established with a broad suite of services. Known for its maturity, extensive marketplace, and strong infrastructure-as-a-service (IaaS) offerings. AWS is very good at global scale and has a lot of different services.

- **Azure (Microsoft Azure):** Tightly integrated with Microsoft ecosystems (Windows Server, .NET). Excelled in hybrid cloud solutions and enterprise-focused services. A good place to run Windows related solutions.

- **GCP (Google Cloud Platform):** Strong in data analytics, machine learning (AI/ML), and container orchestration (Kubernetes). GCP is the leader in innovating cloud solutions.

Practical Examples of Workload Distribution

Let's make it clearer with real-world scenarios:

1. **AI/ML Workloads:** Imagine you have a machine-learning application. GCP offers advanced services like TensorFlow and TPUs (Tensor Processing Units) optimized for AI training. It might make sense to run your ML training tasks on GCP and then deploy the trained model to AWS for serving predictions to your users due to AWS's broader reach and integration with other services.

```
# Example (Conceptual - Using a framework like TensorFlow on GCP)
import tensorflow as tf

# Build a neural network model
model = tf.keras.models.Sequential([
  tf.keras.layers.Dense(64, activation='relu', input_shape=(784,)),
  tf.keras.layers.Dense(10, activation='softmax')
])

# Compile the model
model.compile(optimizer='adam',
              loss='categorical_crossentropy',
              metrics=['accuracy'])

# Train the model on GCP's powerful infrastructure
model.fit(x_train, y_train, epochs=2)

#Save model
model.save('my_model')
```

Once the model is trained and saved, the model file can be copied and deployed to AWS using AWS Sagemaker for example.

2. **Data Warehousing:** Consider a scenario where you need to store and analyze massive datasets. AWS offers Redshift, a powerful data warehouse service. However, GCP's BigQuery might be a better option if you already leverage other Google services and prefer its serverless architecture and cost model.

```
-- Example (Simple SQL query on BigQuery - GCP)
SELECT
```

```
  customer_id,
  SUM(order_total) AS total_spent
FROM
  `your-project.your_dataset.orders`
GROUP BY
  customer_id
ORDER BY
  total_spent DESC
LIMIT 10;
```

This query can be run on BigQuery in GCP and data can be shared in AWS also.

3. **Enterprise Applications:** If your organization heavily relies on Microsoft technologies like .NET and Windows Server, Azure becomes a natural choice for hosting those applications. You can run these legacy systems on Azure, and then connect to new cloud services that might be running on AWS or GCP.

4. **Redundancy and Disaster Recovery:** Spreading your applications across multiple clouds drastically improves resilience. If one cloud experiences an outage, your application can continue running on another. This dramatically improves your system's uptime and availability.

```
|----------------AWS Region A----------------|        |----------------Azure Region B--------
|                                            |        |
| Web App (Primary) <---> Database (Primary) |        | Web App (Secondary) <---> Database (
|                                            |        |
|---------Replication-------->                        |------> |---------Replication-------->
```

Sketch Illustration

Imagine this simple visual:

```
[Cloud A: AWS]  ----  [Cloud B: Azure] ----  [Cloud C: GCP]
|              |       |            |         |               |
Web Server     | Data  | AI/ML      |
               | Warehouse |        |
```

This very simple sketch illustrates how various components are spread between different cloud providers. Web Server sits on AWS, Data Warehouse sits on Azure and AI/ML sits on GCP. Each component is best at each cloud providers.

Chapter 15 Performance Optimization and Cost Efficiency-Optimizing AWS Costs: Best Practices and Cost-Aware Design

- **Right Sizing Resources:**

  - Choose the optimal instance types and storage classes based on workload requirements to avoid over-provisioning.

- **Leveraging AWS Cost Explorer:**

  - Utilize Cost Explorer to analyze spending patterns and identify cost optimization opportunities.

- **Implementing Auto Scaling:**

  - Dynamically adjust resources based on demand to optimize costs during peak and off-peak periods.

- **Utilizing Reserved Instances (RIs) and Savings Plans:**

  - Commit to consistent usage for significant discounts on compute resources.

- **Data Lifecycle Management:**

  - Employ cost-effective storage tiers (S3 Glacier, etc.) for infrequently accessed data.

Right Sizing Resources

Choosing the right size of your resources in the cloud, like on AWS, is like picking the right tool for a job. If you use a tool that's too big, you waste energy and money. If it's too small, you can't get the job done efficiently. Right sizing is about finding the sweet spot. We should follow the below points.

Choose the optimal instance types and storage classes based on workload requirements to avoid over-provisioning.

This means carefully selecting the type of computer (instance) and storage that you rent from AWS, based on what your application actually needs. Over-provisioning is when you rent more computer power or storage than you're really using. This costs extra money for no reason.

Let's consider a simple example. Suppose you're running a small website that doesn't get a lot of traffic. You could choose a very large, powerful server instance with lots of memory and processing power. But if your website only uses a small fraction of that capacity, you're essentially paying for resources you aren't using.

Instead, you could choose a smaller, less expensive instance that better matches your website's actual needs. AWS offers many different instance types, each with different amounts of CPU, memory, and storage. By carefully analyzing your workload's requirements, you can choose the instance type that provides the necessary performance at the lowest possible cost.

Similarly, AWS offers different storage classes for storing your data. For example, S3 Standard is designed for frequently accessed data, while S3 Glacier is designed for infrequently accessed data that you can archive. If you store infrequently accessed data in S3 Standard, you're paying a higher price than if you stored it in S3 Glacier.

Choosing the right instance type is crucial. It's like selecting the appropriate size of truck for a delivery. You would not select a semi truck for a small box. You would instead choose a pickup truck. Similarly storage classes are important for data management to avoid overpaying.

```
Workload Requirement --> Optimal Instance Type --> Storage Class
    High CPU usage, large memory --> High-performance instance (e.g., memory-optimized, compute

    Infrequent access, archival --> Low-cost instance (e.g., burstable instance) --> Low speed,
```

A sketch to illustrate this concept:

```
+--------------------+      +--------------------+
|    Small Website   | ---> |   Small Instance   |
```

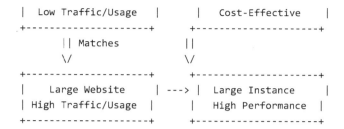

```
|  Low Traffic/Usage  |       |    Cost-Effective   |
 +--------------------+       +--------------------+
         || Matches          ||
         \/                  \/
 +--------------------+       +--------------------+
 |    Large Website    | ---> |    Large Instance   |
 |  High Traffic/Usage |      |   High Performance  |
 +--------------------+       +--------------------+
```

Leveraging AWS Cost Explorer

AWS Cost Explorer is a powerful tool provided by Amazon Web Services (AWS) that helps you understand and analyze your AWS spending. Think of it as your personal AWS spending detective. It allows you to visualize your costs, identify trends, and pinpoint areas where you can optimize your spending.

- **Utilize Cost Explorer to analyze spending patterns and identify cost optimization opportunities.**

Let's break this down further:

1. Analyzing Spending Patterns:

Cost Explorer allows you to visualize your AWS spending over time. You can see how much you're spending on different services (like EC2, S3, Lambda), different AWS Regions, different accounts within your organization, and even based on tags you've applied to your resources. It shows all costs that you have over time.

Imagine you're running a web application. You can use Cost Explorer to see how much you spent on EC2 instances (your servers) in the last month, how much you spent on S3 (your storage) and how much you spent on RDS (your database). You can view this month-by-month, week-by-week, or even day-by-day. With all these costs details, you can understand the costing trend.

2. Identifying Cost Optimization Opportunities:

By analyzing your spending patterns, Cost Explorer can help you identify areas where you're potentially overspending. For example:

- **Idle Resources:** Are you paying for EC2 instances that are running but not doing anything? Cost Explorer can help you spot these.
- **Underutilized Resources:** Are you using a large EC2 instance when a smaller one would suffice? Cost Explorer can help you identify instances with low CPU utilization.
- **Expensive Services:** Is one particular service unexpectedly expensive? Cost Explorer can help you drill down and understand why.
- **Region-Based Costs:** Maybe running your workload in one Region is significantly more expensive than another (due to different pricing). Cost Explorer can help you compare costs across Regions.

Cost Explorer provides pre-built reports and the ability to create custom reports to answer specific questions about your AWS spending.

Let's say you notice a spike in your EC2 costs. You can use Cost Explorer to filter by EC2 and then further filter by instance type to see which instances are contributing the most to the increased costs. Then you can dig into those instances to see if they are appropriately sized for the workload they are running. If you understand the cost that you have, you can decide to re-architecturing, such as serverless functions or cost effective regions.

Example Scenario:

Suppose you discover that your S3 costs are higher than expected. Using Cost Explorer, you can filter your spending by the S3 service and then break down the costs by storage class (e.g., Standard, Intelligent-Tiering, Glacier). You might find that you're storing a large amount of infrequently accessed data in the Standard storage class, which is more expensive than Glacier. This gives you a direct opportunity to move this data to Glacier and reduce your storage costs.

Cost Explorer Reports:

Cost Explorer provides several predefined reports.

- **Costs by Service:** This report shows you the cost of each AWS service you are using.
- **Costs by Region:** This report shows you the cost of each AWS Region.
- **Costs by Linked Account:** This report shows you the cost of each AWS Account within your organization.
- **RI Utilization:** This report shows you how well you are utilizing your Reserved Instances.
- **RI Coverage:** This report shows how much of your eligible instance usage is covered by Reserved Instances.

You can customize all of these reports by adding filters (to focus on specific resources or tags), changing the time range, and grouping the data in different ways.

Tips for Effective Use of Cost Explorer:

- **Enable Cost Allocation Tags:** Tag your AWS resources (EC2 instances, S3 buckets, etc.) with meaningful tags. Cost Explorer can then use these tags to break down your costs and give you a much more granular view of your spending. Example tags might be `Environment: Production/Staging/Development`, `Application: WebApp/BatchProcessing`, or `Owner: JohnDoe/JaneSmith`.
- **Regularly Review Reports:** Make it a habit to review Cost Explorer reports regularly (e.g., weekly or monthly). This will help you stay on top of your AWS spending and identify potential cost optimization opportunities early on.
- **Set Up Budgets and Alerts:** AWS Budgets allows you to set budgets for your AWS spending and receive alerts when you exceed those budgets. This is a proactive way to manage your costs.
- **Integrate with Other Tools:** Cost Explorer can be integrated with other AWS services and third-party tools to provide even more insights into your spending.

By effectively using AWS Cost Explorer, you can gain a clear understanding of your AWS spending, identify cost optimization opportunities, and ensure that you're getting the most value out of your AWS investment.

Implementing Auto Scaling

Auto Scaling dynamically adjusts your cloud resources based on the real-time demand of your applications. This means that you automatically increase the number of resources when demand is high and decrease them when demand is low. This approach avoids over-provisioning, saving you money during off-peak periods and ensuring your application can handle peak loads.

Here's a breakdown of the key concepts:

Dynamically Adjust Resources:

Instead of having a fixed number of servers or other resources running all the time, Auto Scaling lets you change the number of resources in response to changes in demand. Think of it like this: Imagine you have a lemonade stand. On a hot day, you need more people to serve customers. Auto Scaling is like automatically adding more lemonade pitchers and helpers when the line gets long, and then reducing them when the rush is over.

Optimize Costs During Peak and Off-Peak Periods:

The main benefit of Auto Scaling is cost optimization. During peak periods, your application can handle the load without performance issues because Auto Scaling adds more resources. However, during off-peak periods, Auto Scaling removes unnecessary resources, reducing your cloud spending.

Here's a simple sketch to illustrate this:

Load

^

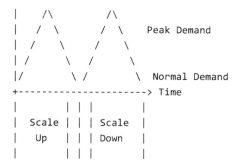

```
|   /\         /\
|  / \        /  \     Peak Demand
| /   \      /    \
|/     \    /      \
|/      \  /        \  Normal Demand
+-------------------------> Time
|        | | |        |
| Scale  | | | Scale  |
|  Up    | | | Down   |
|        | | |        |
```

In the sketch above, you can see how Auto Scaling responds to changes in load. When demand is high (peaks), resources are added ("Scale Up"). When demand decreases, resources are removed ("Scale Down").

Example:

Imagine you have a web application running on AWS. You can use Auto Scaling to automatically launch more EC2 instances (virtual servers) when the CPU utilization of your existing instances exceeds a certain threshold (e.g., 70%). Conversely, Auto Scaling can terminate instances when CPU utilization drops below a certain threshold (e.g., 30%).

Let's consider a simplified AWS CloudFormation template snippet to set up a basic Auto Scaling Group (ASG):

```yaml
Resources:
  MyASG:
    Type: AWS::AutoScaling::AutoScalingGroup
    Properties:
      LaunchConfigurationName: !Ref MyLaunchConfig
      MinSize: '1'
      MaxSize: '3'
      DesiredCapacity: '1'
      AvailabilityZones: !GetAZs ''
      TargetGroupARNs:
        - !Ref MyTargetGroup

  MyLaunchConfig:
    Type: AWS::AutoScaling::LaunchConfiguration
    Properties:
      ImageId: ami-xxxxxxxxxxxxxxxxx # Replace with a valid AMI ID
      InstanceType: t2.micro
      SecurityGroups:
        - !Ref MySecurityGroup

  MyTargetGroup:
    Type: AWS::ElasticLoadBalancingV2::TargetGroup
    Properties:
      Port: 80
      Protocol: HTTP
      VpcId: vpc-xxxxxxxxxxxxxxxxx # Replace with your VPC ID

  MySecurityGroup:
    Type: AWS::EC2::SecurityGroup
    Properties:
      GroupDescription: Allow HTTP traffic
      VpcId: vpc-xxxxxxxxxxxxxxxxx  # Replace with your VPC ID
```

```
SecurityGroupIngress:
  - IpProtocol: tcp
    FromPort: 80
    ToPort: 80
    CidrIp: 0.0.0.0/0
```

In this example:

- `MyASG`: Defines the Auto Scaling Group. `MinSize` sets the minimum number of instances, `MaxSize` sets the maximum, and `DesiredCapacity` sets the initial number of instances.
- `MyLaunchConfig`: Defines the template for launching new instances. It specifies the AMI (Amazon Machine Image), instance type, and security groups.
- `MyTargetGroup`: Associates the Auto Scaling Group with a load balancer, so traffic is distributed among the instances.
- `MySecurityGroup`: Allows HTTP traffic to the instances.

This example demonstrates how Auto Scaling can be set up to automatically manage the number of EC2 instances based on demand. The `TargetGroupARNs` allows for the integration with a load balancer, distributing incoming traffic effectively. When the load increases beyond the capacity of the initial `DesiredCapacity`, new instances will be launched up to the `MaxSize`, and conversely, instances will be terminated when load decreases and falls below a certain threshold, based on defined scaling policies (which are not explicitly shown here for brevity but are a crucial part of Auto Scaling configuration).

Utilizing Reserved Instances (RIs) and Savings Plans

Committing to consistent usage is key to unlocking significant discounts on your Amazon Web Services (AWS) compute resources. Reserved Instances (RIs) and Savings Plans are purchasing options that offer lower prices compared to On-Demand instances, in exchange for a commitment to a specific usage level over a period of time, typically one or three years. Consider them bulk discounts for your continuous cloud needs.

Reserved Instances (RIs): The Commitment to Specificity

Reserved Instances offer a discount on EC2 instance usage in exchange for a commitment to a specific instance configuration for a specified period (1 or 3 years). This configuration includes:

- **Instance Type:** (e.g., `m5.large`, `c5.xlarge`) The specific type of virtual machine.
- **Region:** (e.g., `us-east-1`, `eu-west-1`) The AWS region where the instance runs.
- **Availability Zone (Optional):** (e.g., `us-east-1a`, `us-east-1b`) A specific data center within the region. Specifying an Availability Zone provides the greatest savings potential but also the least flexibility.
- **Operating System:** (e.g., Linux, Windows) The operating system running on the instance.
- **Tenancy:** (Dedicated or Shared) Dedicated tenancy ensures your instance runs on dedicated hardware.
- **Instance size:** The instance size such as large or xlarge.

There are three RI offering types:

- **Standard RIs:** Provide the most significant discount (up to 75% off On-Demand pricing). They are ideal for steady-state workloads with predictable usage. Standard RIs can be sold in the AWS Marketplace if they are no longer needed.
- **Convertible RIs:** Offer a lower discount than Standard RIs (typically up to 54% off On-Demand pricing) but provide the flexibility to change the instance type, operating system, or tenancy during the reservation term. This flexibility comes at the cost of a lower discount.
- **Scheduled RIs:** Available to launch within the time windows you reserve. This option allows you to match your capacity reservation to a predictable recurring schedule that only requires a fraction of a day, a week, or a month.

Here's a simple analogy: Imagine you always buy the same brand of coffee every week. A Standard RI is like buying a year's supply of that coffee upfront at a heavily discounted price. A Convertible RI is like buying a year's supply of coffee with the option to switch to a different blend mid-year, but at a slightly smaller discount.

Savings Plans: The Commitment to Spend

Savings Plans offer significant cost savings (up to 72% compared to On-Demand prices) in exchange for a commitment to a consistent amount of usage, measured in dollars per hour, for a 1- or 3-year term. Savings Plans are more flexible than RIs because they automatically apply to any EC2 instance, AWS Lambda function, or AWS Fargate usage, regardless of instance type, region, or operating system. They come in two types:

- **Compute Savings Plans:** Automatically apply to EC2 instance usage regardless of region, instance size, operating system, or tenancy, as well as AWS Lambda and AWS Fargate usage. This plan offers the most flexibility.
- **EC2 Instance Savings Plans:** Apply to EC2 instance usage within a region. This plan allows you to change the instance family, size, operating system, and tenancy of your instances while still benefiting from the savings.

Think of Savings Plans as committing to spend a certain amount of money on cloud resources each month for a year, and in return, AWS gives you a discount on those resources. The resources you use don't have to be the same every month, as long as you're spending up to your committed amount.

Example Scenario and Code (Illustrative):

Let's say you have a web application running on two `m5.large` EC2 instances in `us-east-1`, running Linux, 24/7. You anticipate this usage to continue for the next year.

1. **Calculating RI Savings:** Research the cost of an `m5.large` Linux instance in `us-east-1`. Then, compare the On-Demand price to the Standard RI price for a 1-year term. The savings can be significant (e.g., 40-70%).

2. **Calculating Savings Plan Savings:** Analyze your current monthly spending on EC2, Lambda, and Fargate. Determine the dollar amount per hour you're consistently spending. Purchase a Compute Savings Plan for that hourly amount. Any usage up to that committed amount will be billed at the Savings Plan rate, while any usage beyond that will be billed at the On-Demand rate.

Code Snippet (AWS CLI - illustrative, not executable directly):

```
# Example: Describe Reserved Instances (replace with your actual filters)
aws ec2 describe-reserved-instances --filters "Name=instance-type,Values=m5.large" "Name=availak

# Example: Purchase a Savings Plan (replace with your actual parameters)
aws savingsplans create-savings-plan --savings-plan-offering-id <your_offering_id> --commitment
```

Sketches for Conceptual Understanding:

Let's use simple diagrams to clarify the concepts:

Reserved Instances:

```
[Instance Type: m5.large] --(Locked In)--> [Region: us-east-1] --(Locked In)--> [OS: Linux] --(I
```

This sketch represents how RIs lock you into specific attributes to give you a discounted price.

Savings Plans:

```
[Commitment: $X/hour] --(Flexible Usage)--> [EC2, Lambda, Fargate] --(Savings Plan Rate)--> [Sav
[Excess Usage] --------------------------> [On-Demand Rate]
```

This sketch illustrates the hourly commitment of Savings Plans and their application to various compute services, with the possibility of exceeding the committed amount at On-Demand rates.

Important Considerations:

- **Utilization:** Ensure you are fully utilizing your RIs and Savings Plans. Underutilization negates the cost benefits. AWS provides tools and reports to monitor utilization.
- **Capacity Planning:** Accurately forecast your capacity needs to avoid over- or under-committing.
- **Flexibility vs. Savings:** Choose the right balance between flexibility (Convertible RIs, Savings Plans) and savings (Standard RIs) based on your workload characteristics.
- **Continuous Monitoring:** Regularly review your RI and Savings Plan usage and adjust your strategy as your needs evolve.
- **AWS Cost Explorer:** Use the AWS Cost Explorer to forecast, purchase and monitor the Savings Plans.

By strategically utilizing Reserved Instances and Savings Plans, you can significantly reduce your AWS compute costs while maintaining the performance and reliability of your applications. The key is to carefully analyze your usage patterns, choose the right purchasing option, and continuously monitor your utilization.

Data Lifecycle Management

Data Lifecycle Management (DLM) is about managing your data effectively throughout its lifespan, from the moment it's created to the moment it's no longer needed and can be archived or deleted. The goal is to ensure data is stored in the most cost-effective way possible, based on how frequently it's accessed.

Employ cost-effective storage tiers (S3 Glacier, etc.) for infrequently accessed data.

This means using different storage options based on how often you need to access your data. Think of it like organizing your closet: items you use every day are within easy reach, while seasonal clothes are stored in a less accessible place. In the cloud, this translates to different storage classes with varying costs and retrieval times.

Let's focus on Amazon S3 (Simple Storage Service) as an example. S3 offers several storage classes, each designed for different access patterns.

- **S3 Standard:** This is the default and most expensive option. It's suitable for frequently accessed data, like images for a website or data used in real-time applications.
- **S3 Standard-IA (Infrequent Access):** This is a lower-cost option for data that is accessed less frequently but still needs to be available when needed. Examples include backups and older log files. It's cheaper than S3 Standard for storage but incurs retrieval costs when the data is accessed.
- **S3 One Zone-IA:** Similar to S3 Standard-IA but stores data in a single availability zone instead of multiple. This makes it cheaper but less resilient in the event of an availability zone outage. Suitable for easily reproducible data.
- **S3 Glacier Instant Retrieval:** This storage class offers low-cost storage for data that is rarely accessed but requires near-instant retrieval times. It is suitable for archives where occasional access is needed without long delays.
- **S3 Glacier Flexible Retrieval (formerly S3 Glacier):** Designed for archival purposes. Data retrieval can take several hours (typically 3-5 hours). It is a very low-cost option for data you rarely, if ever, need to access.
- **S3 Glacier Deep Archive:** The cheapest storage option, intended for long-term archival where retrieval times of 12 hours or more are acceptable. Great for compliance archiving where data must be kept for many years but rarely accessed.
- **S3 Intelligent-Tiering:** This storage class automatically moves data between frequent, infrequent, and archive access tiers based on your access patterns, optimizing cost and performance.

Why is this important?

Without DLM, you might end up storing all your data in S3 Standard, even if much of it is rarely accessed. This means you're paying a premium for storage you don't need. By implementing DLM and moving infrequently accessed data to lower-cost storage tiers like S3 Glacier, you can significantly reduce your storage costs.

How to implement Data Lifecycle Management with AWS S3:

You can use S3 Lifecycle policies to automate the movement of data between storage classes. Here's how it works conceptually:

1. **Define Rules:** You create rules that specify when data should be transitioned to a different storage class or deleted.
2. **Apply to Objects:** These rules can be applied to specific objects based on prefixes (folders) or object tags.
3. **Automation:** S3 automatically applies these rules to your objects, moving them to the appropriate storage class based on their age or access patterns.

Example AWS CLI command for creating a lifecycle rule (Conceptual Example):

```
aws s3api put-bucket-lifecycle-configuration \
    --bucket your-bucket-name \
    --lifecycle-configuration '{
        "Rules": [
            {
                "ID": "MoveToGlacier",
                "Prefix": "logs/",
                "Status": "Enabled",
                "Transitions": [
                    {
                        "Date": "2024-12-31T00:00:00.0Z",
                        "StorageClass": "GLACIER"
                    }
                ],
                "NoncurrentVersionTransitions": [
                    {
                        "NoncurrentDays": 90,
                        "StorageClass": "GLACIER"
                    }
                ],
                "Expiration": {
                    "Days": 365
                }
            }
        ]
    }'
```

In this conceptual example:

- your-bucket-name should be replaced with the name of your S3 bucket.
- logs/ is the prefix (folder) where the rule applies.
- Status: "Enabled" activates the rule.
- Transitions: defines the transition to Glacier storage on 2024-12-31T00:00:00.0Z.
- NoncurrentVersionTransitions: If versioning is enabled, transitions older (non-current) versions of the object to GLACIER.
- Expiration : Object will be automatically deleted after 365 days.

Conceptual Sketch:

```
+--------------------+        +--------------------+        +--------------------+
|    S3 Standard     | --->   |   S3 Standard-IA   | --->   |    S3 Glacier      |
|  Frequent Access   |        |  Infrequent Access |        |      Archive       |
|     High Cost      |        |     Lower Cost     |        |    Lowest Cost     |
|   Fast Retrieval   |        |  Slower Retrieval  |        |  Slowest Retrieval |
+--------------------+        +--------------------+        +--------------------+
```

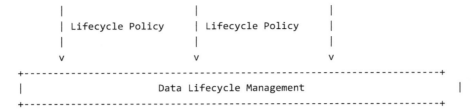

```
    |                   |                   |
| Lifecycle Policy | Lifecycle Policy |                   |
    |                   |                   |
    v                   v                   v
+----------------------------------------------------------------------+
|                    Data Lifecycle Management                         |
+----------------------------------------------------------------------+
```

The sketch illustrates the transition of data from a higher-cost, frequently accessed storage tier (S3 Standard) to lower-cost, infrequently accessed tiers (S3 Standard-IA and S3 Glacier) over time, governed by lifecycle policies.

Key Considerations:

- **Data Access Patterns:** Understanding how frequently your data is accessed is crucial for choosing the right storage tiers.
- **Retrieval Costs:** Be aware of the retrieval costs associated with lower-cost storage tiers, as accessing data from these tiers can incur additional charges.
- **Compliance Requirements:** Some data may need to be stored for a specific duration due to regulatory requirements. DLM policies should align with these requirements.
- **Monitoring:** Regularly monitor your storage costs and access patterns to ensure your DLM policies are effective and optimized.
- **Automation is Key:** Manual management of data lifecycle can be cumbersome and error-prone. Automating the process with lifecycle policies is essential for scalability and efficiency.

In summary, Data Lifecycle Management is a crucial practice for optimizing storage costs in the cloud. By understanding your data access patterns and utilizing cost-effective storage tiers, you can significantly reduce your storage expenses while ensuring your data is stored appropriately based on its usage.

Chapter 16 Performance Optimization and Cost Efficiency-Monitoring and Observability with CloudWatch and X-Ray

- **CloudWatch Monitoring:** Collect metrics, logs, and events for insights into application and infrastructure performance.
- **X-Ray Tracing:** Trace user requests across distributed services to identify bottlenecks and latency issues.
- **Performance Optimization:** Utilize CloudWatch and X-Ray data to pinpoint areas for code improvements, resource allocation adjustments, and architectural refinements.
- **Cost Efficiency:** Optimize resource utilization based on monitoring data to reduce unnecessary spending on underutilized services.
- **Proactive Observability:** Implement alerts and dashboards to proactively identify and address performance degradation or cost anomalies.

CloudWatch Monitoring

CloudWatch Monitoring focuses on gathering information about your applications and the underlying infrastructure they run on. This information comes in three main forms: metrics, logs, and events. By collecting and analyzing these, you gain insights into how well your applications are performing and whether your infrastructure is behaving as expected.

Metrics:

Metrics are numerical data points that represent the performance of your resources over time. Think of them as measurements of key performance indicators (KPIs).

- **Example:** CPU utilization of an EC2 instance (a virtual server), the number of requests an API receives, or the amount of free disk space on a database server.

CloudWatch automatically collects some basic metrics for services like EC2 instances. You can also define and collect your own custom metrics.

- **Custom Metric Example:** Imagine you have an e-commerce application. You could create a custom metric to track the number of successful transactions per minute. This metric could alert you to issues if the number drops unexpectedly.

Code Example (using the AWS SDK for Python, boto3):

```python
import boto3
import datetime

cloudwatch = boto3.client('cloudwatch')

def put_transaction_metric(transactions):
    cloudwatch.put_metric_data(
        Namespace='MyECommerceApp',
        MetricData=[
            {
                'MetricName': 'SuccessfulTransactions',
                'Timestamp': datetime.datetime.now(),
                'Unit': 'Count',
                'Value': transactions
            },
        ]
    )

# Example usage: Let's say you had 10 successful transactions this minute
put_transaction_metric(10)
```

This code snippet demonstrates how to send a custom metric, `SuccessfulTransactions`, to CloudWatch. You specify the metric name, timestamp, unit, and value. The `Namespace` helps organize your metrics.

Logs:

Logs are records of events that occur within your applications and systems. They provide detailed information about what happened, when it happened, and often, why it happened.

- **Example:** Application logs that record errors, warnings, and informational messages; system logs that track system events; or access logs that record who accessed your web server and when.

CloudWatch Logs allows you to collect, monitor, and store these logs. You can then search and filter the logs to troubleshoot issues or analyze trends.

- **Log Example:** Suppose your application throws an exception. The log might contain a stack trace that pinpoint the exact line of code causing the error.

  ```
  2024-10-27 10:00:00 ERROR: Exception occurred in process_payment: ValueError: Invalid card
  Stacktrace:
  File "app.py", line 50, in process_payment
      validate_card(card_number)
  File "app.py", line 60, in validate_card
      raise ValueError("Invalid card number")
  ```

  CloudWatch Logs can collect these error messages.

Events:

Events indicate changes in the state of your AWS resources. They can signal various occurrences, such as an EC2 instance starting or stopping, a new object being created in an S3 bucket, or a scheduled task running.

- **Example:** An event might be triggered when an Auto Scaling group scales up to add more instances, or when a security group rule is modified.

CloudWatch Events (now part of EventBridge) allows you to react to these events in near real-time. You can set up rules that trigger actions based on specific events.

- **Event Example:** When a new EC2 instance is launched, an event can trigger a Lambda function to automatically install necessary software on the instance.

Visual Representation (Sketch):

Imagine three containers labeled "Metrics," "Logs," and "Events." Arrows point from your AWS resources (like EC2 instances, databases, etc.) into these containers. A larger container labeled "CloudWatch" surrounds all three. An arrow points from "CloudWatch" to a "Dashboard" and an "Alerts" system.

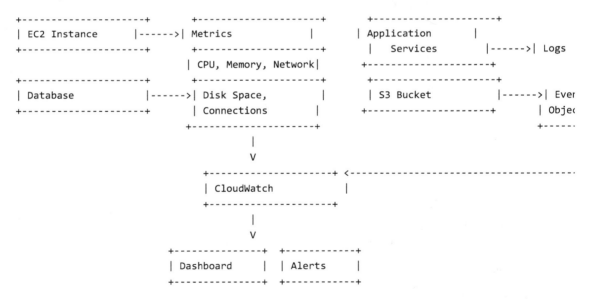

This sketch visualizes how resources feed data into CloudWatch, which then enables dashboards for monitoring and alerts for proactive notifications.

X-Ray Tracing: In Detail

X-Ray Tracing is a powerful tool for understanding how user requests travel through a complex application, especially those built with microservices or distributed architectures. It helps pinpoint performance bottlenecks and latency issues that can negatively impact the user experience. Think of it as a detective that follows a request as it moves from service to service, collecting clues along the way.

Trace user requests across distributed services to identify bottlenecks and latency issues.

Imagine a user placing an order on an e-commerce website. The request might first hit a front-end service, then an authentication service, followed by an inventory service, a payment processing service, and finally, an order fulfillment service. Each of these services could be running on different servers, potentially in different geographic locations. If the user experiences a delay, it's crucial to understand *where* that delay is occurring. X-Ray tracing allows you to visualize this entire journey.

X-Ray works by assigning a unique ID to each request as it enters the application. This ID, along with timing information and metadata, is passed along to each service that handles the request. X-Ray then collects this data and assembles it into a visual trace, showing the path the request took and the time spent in each service.

```
User Request --> Front-End Service --> Authentication Service --> Inventory Service --> Payment
```

Example with Code:

While a full example requires several deployed services, we can simulate a simplified tracing setup. Assume we have two microservices: `ServiceA` and `ServiceB`. `ServiceA` calls `ServiceB`. We'll show how to add basic X-Ray tracing to these services using a hypothetical SDK (actual implementation varies based on language and cloud provider).

ServiceA:

```python
# Assume you have an X-Ray SDK initialized
import xray_sdk

@xray_sdk.trace('ServiceA_Handler')  # Annotation starts a segment
def handle_request():
    # ServiceA Logic
    print("Service A processing...")
    response = call_service_b()  # Call ServiceB
    print("Service A done.")
    return response

@xray_sdk.trace('Call_ServiceB') # Annotation starts a subsegment
def call_service_b():
    print("Calling Service B")
    # ... Code to actually make the HTTP call to Service B ...
    response = "Service B's response" #replace with service B response after api call
    return response
```

ServiceB:

```python
import xray_sdk

@xray_sdk.trace('ServiceB_Handler')
def handle_request():
    print("Service B processing request.")
    # ... Service B Logic ...
    print("Service B done.")
    return "Processing complete"
```

In this simplified example, `@xray_sdk.trace` acts as a placeholder. The real SDK would automatically:

1. Create a *segment* when `ServiceA_Handler` is called, representing the entire operation within ServiceA.

2. Create a *subsegment* when `Call_ServiceB` is called, nested within the `ServiceA` segment. This represents the work done specifically to call ServiceB.
3. Propagate the tracing information (trace ID) to ServiceB (typically via HTTP headers).
4. In ServiceB, create a segment for the `ServiceB_Handler`.
5. Capture timing information (start and end times) for each segment and subsegment.
6. Send this data to the X-Ray service for aggregation and visualization.

The `handle_request` in service B would function as follows:

```
import xray_sdk

@xray_sdk.trace('ServiceB_Handler')
def handle_request():
    print("Service B processing request.")
    # ... Service B Logic ...
    print("Service B done.")
    return "Processing complete"
```

The X-Ray console would then display a trace showing:

- The overall time spent handling the request.
- The time spent in `ServiceA_Handler`.
- The time spent in `Call_ServiceB`.
- The time spent in `ServiceB_Handler`.

If `ServiceB_Handler` was slow, this would be immediately apparent in the trace, highlighting it as a potential bottleneck.

Benefits Summarized:

- **Visualizing the Request Flow:** See exactly how requests move through your services.
- **Identifying Bottlenecks:** Quickly pinpoint services causing latency.
- **Understanding Dependencies:** Discover dependencies between services.
- **Troubleshooting Errors:** Trace errors to their source within a distributed system.

In conclusion, X-Ray Tracing is an essential tool for maintaining the performance and stability of complex, distributed applications. It gives developers the visibility they need to understand and optimize the entire request lifecycle.

Performance Optimization

Performance optimization is about making your applications and infrastructure run faster and more efficiently. It's like tuning a car engine to get more power and better gas mileage. In the context of cloud computing, especially when using services like AWS, it means using tools like CloudWatch and X-Ray to find areas where improvements can be made. This leads to better user experiences, reduced costs, and a more stable system.

The goal is to take the data gathered from CloudWatch and X-Ray and use it to make informed decisions about improving your code, adjusting resource allocation, and refining your overall system architecture.

Utilize CloudWatch and X-Ray data to pinpoint areas for code improvements, resource allocation adjustments, and architectural refinements.

This is the core of performance optimization. CloudWatch provides metrics, logs, and events related to your application and infrastructure. X-Ray traces user requests as they move through different services, helping you identify bottlenecks and latency issues.

Let's break this down with an example:

Suppose your application is a simple e-commerce website built on AWS using services like API Gateway, Lambda, and DynamoDB.

- **CloudWatch Example:** You might notice, through CloudWatch metrics, that your Lambda function's average execution time has increased significantly over the past week. This could indicate a problem within the function's code or resource constraints.

- **X-Ray Example:** Using X-Ray, you can trace a specific user request and see that the Lambda function is indeed the slowest part of the process. Within the trace, you might find that a particular database query within the Lambda function is taking an unusually long time.

```python
# Example Lambda function (Python) causing a bottleneck
import boto3
import time

dynamodb = boto3.resource('dynamodb')
table = dynamodb.Table('Products')

def lambda_handler(event, context):
    start_time = time.time() # To measure execution time

    product_id = event['product_id'] # Sample product ID

    # Problematic database query
    response = table.get_item(Key={'product_id': product_id})

    end_time = time.time()
    execution_time = end_time - start_time
    print(f"Database query execution time: {execution_time} seconds")

    item = response.get('Item')
    return {
        'statusCode': 200,
        'body': item
    }
```

In this simplified example, `time.time()` functions demonstrate measuring execution time. CloudWatch Logs would capture the output of the `print` statement, highlighting the duration of the database query. X-Ray would visually represent this function as a segment in the request trace, clearly showing it as the source of the bottleneck.

Based on this information:

1. **Code Improvements:** You might optimize the database query (perhaps by adding an index to the `product_id` column or restructuring the query).

2. **Resource Allocation Adjustments:** You might increase the memory allocated to the Lambda function if it's running out of resources.

3. **Architectural Refinements:** You might consider caching frequently accessed product data to reduce the number of database queries.

These actions directly translate into a more responsive application and a better experience for users.

Cost Efficiency:

Optimizing performance often leads to cost savings. When your applications run efficiently, they use fewer resources, which translates to lower cloud bills. Think of it as improving the fuel efficiency of a car – you can travel the same distance with less fuel.

By reducing the execution time of Lambda functions, you not only improve performance but also reduce the cost associated with function invocations. Likewise, right-sizing EC2 instances based on actual usage data ensures that you are not paying for unused capacity.

Optimize resource utilization based on monitoring data to reduce unnecessary spending on underutilized services.

This aspect emphasizes the financial benefits of performance optimization. Using CloudWatch, you can identify underutilized resources.

For example:

- **EC2 Instances:** CloudWatch can show you the CPU utilization of your EC2 instances. If an instance consistently runs at a low CPU utilization (e.g., below 10%), it indicates that the instance is oversized for its workload. You can then downsize the instance to a smaller, less expensive instance type.

```
+-----------------+     +-----------------+
|  Oversized EC2  | ->  | Rightsized EC2  |
|  (High Cost)    |     |  (Lower Cost)   |
|  Low Utilization|     |  Optimal Usage  |
+-----------------+     +-----------------+
```

- **EBS Volumes:** Similarly, if you have EBS volumes with consistently low I/O utilization, you might be able to switch to a less expensive volume type.

- **Auto Scaling Groups:** By analyzing CloudWatch metrics, you can adjust the scaling policies of your Auto Scaling Groups to ensure that you only have the necessary number of instances running at any given time.

By continuously monitoring and optimizing resource utilization, you can significantly reduce your cloud spending without sacrificing performance.

Proactive Observability:

Proactive observability is about setting up alerts and dashboards that notify you *before* problems impact your users. It's like having a check engine light in your car that alerts you to potential issues before they cause a breakdown.

Implement alerts and dashboards to proactively identify and address performance degradation or cost anomalies.

This involves creating proactive monitoring solutions using CloudWatch alarms and dashboards.

For example:

- **CloudWatch Alarms:** Set up alarms that trigger when specific metrics exceed certain thresholds. For instance, you could create an alarm that triggers when the average latency of your API Gateway exceeds 500 milliseconds.

```
+-----------------+     +-----------------+
| Metric Exceeds  | ->  |  CloudWatch     |
| Threshold       |     |  Alarm Triggered|
| (e.g., Latency) |     +-----------------+
|                 |             |
|                 |             V
|                 |     +-----------------+
|                 | ->  |  Notification   |
|                 |     |  (Email, SMS)   |
+-----------------+     +-----------------+
```

- **CloudWatch Dashboards:** Create dashboards that provide a visual overview of your system's performance. These dashboards should include key metrics such as CPU utilization, memory usage, latency, error rates, and cost data. This allows you to quickly identify and respond to performance degradation or cost anomalies.

By implementing proactive observability, you can identify and address issues before they impact your users, ensuring a stable and performant system.

Cost Efficiency

The goal of Cost Efficiency is to spend less money while still getting the performance and reliability you need from your applications and infrastructure. This is achieved by carefully watching how your resources are being used and making adjustments to avoid wasting money on things you don't need.

Optimize resource utilization based on monitoring data to reduce unnecessary spending on underutilized services.

To understand Cost Efficiency, you need to understand resource utilization. Resource utilization means how much of your available resources (like CPU, memory, storage) are actually being used. When resources are sitting idle, you are essentially paying for something you're not using.

Consider an example with an AWS EC2 instance (a virtual server). You might have an EC2 instance with a lot of processing power and memory, but if your application is only using 10% of that capacity most of the time, you're wasting money. Cost Efficiency involves finding those underutilized services and adjusting them.

Here's how you could use CloudWatch to monitor CPU utilization and determine if an instance is underutilized:

First, you need to gather the CPU utilization metrics.

```python
import boto3

cloudwatch = boto3.client('cloudwatch')

response = cloudwatch.get_metric_data(
    Namespace='AWS/EC2',
    MetricName='CPUUtilization',
    Dimensions=[
        {
            'Name': 'InstanceId',
            'Value': 'your-instance-id'  # Replace with your instance ID
        },
    ],
    StartTime=datetime.datetime.now() - datetime.timedelta(days=7),
    EndTime=datetime.datetime.now(),
    Period=3600,  # 1 hour
    Statistics=['Average'],
)

#print(response) # to view full resonse
# Process the data
for data_point in response['MetricDataResults'][0]['Values']:
    timestamp = data_point['Timestamp']
    utilization = data_point['Average']
    print(f"{timestamp}: {utilization}%")
```

If your average CPU utilization is consistently low (for example, below 20%), it might be a candidate for downsizing to a smaller, cheaper instance type.

Example Sketch:

Imagine a graph of CPU Utilization over time.

```
CPU Utilization (%)
^
|      _____
|     |        |
|     |        |
|     |        |
| ___ |        |___
|/                    \
+------------------> Time (Days)
0%
```

If the graph consistently stays low, it indicates underutilization.

You can also have some script which runs and identify such issue

```python
import boto3
import datetime

def check_cpu_utilization(instance_id):
    cloudwatch = boto3.client('cloudwatch')
    response = cloudwatch.get_metric_data(
        Namespace='AWS/EC2',
        MetricName='CPUUtilization',
        Dimensions=[
            {
                'Name': 'InstanceId',
                'Value': instance_id
            },
        ],
        StartTime=datetime.datetime.now() - datetime.timedelta(days=7),
        EndTime=datetime.datetime.now(),
        Period=86400,  # 1 day
        Statistics=['Average'],
    )

    total = 0
    count = 0
    for data_point in response['MetricDataResults'][0]['Values']:
        total = total + data_point['Average']
        count = count + 1
        #timestamp = data_point['Timestamp']
        #utilization = data_point['Average']
        #print(f"{timestamp}: {utilization}%")


    average_utilization = total / count
    #print(f"Average CPU Utilization for {instance_id}: {average_utilization}%")

    return average_utilization

def downsize_instance(instance_id):
```

```python
        # Perform the instance downsizing operation
        # This will depend on the specifics of your cloud provider (e.g., AWS, Azure, GCP)

        ec2 = boto3.client('ec2')
        instance_info = ec2.describe_instances(InstanceIds=[instance_id])

        current_instance_type = instance_info['Reservations'][0]['Instances'][0]['InstanceType']
        print(f"Current Instance Type: {current_instance_type}")


        #logic to select an instance from available instance
        new_instance_type = "t2.micro" # here implement logic from list of possible instances
        #new_instance_type = new_instance_type.get_new_instance(current_instance_type)
        print(f"New Instance Type Selected: {new_instance_type}")

        # Step 1: Stop the Instance
        ec2.stop_instances(InstanceIds=[instance_id])
        waiter = ec2.get_waiter('instance_stopped')
        waiter.wait(InstanceIds=[instance_id])
        print(f"Instance {instance_id} stopped")

        # Step 2: Change the Instance Type
        ec2.modify_instance_attribute(InstanceId=instance_id, Attribute='instanceType', Value=new_in
        print(f"Instance {instance_id} changed to instance type {new_instance_type}")

        # Step 3: Start the Instance
        ec2.start_instances(InstanceIds=[instance_id])
        print(f"Instance {instance_id} started")

        waiter = ec2.get_waiter('instance_running')
        waiter.wait(InstanceIds=[instance_id])
        print(f"Instance {instance_id} is running")

def main():
    instance_id = 'i-xxxxxxxxxxxxxxxxx'  # instance ID

    average_utilization = check_cpu_utilization(instance_id)

    print(f"Average CPU Utilization for {instance_id}: {average_utilization}%")

    if average_utilization < 20:
        print(f"CPU utilization is low, initiating downsizing for instance {instance_id}")
        downsize_instance(instance_id)
    else:
        print(f"CPU utilization for {instance_id} is within acceptable range")

if __name__ == "__main__":
    main()
```

This code provides a function named as check_cpu_utilization will check for utilization and downsize_instance will downsize it.

Key Takeaway:

- Monitoring helps identify underutilized resources.

- Adjusting resource allocation (e.g., downsizing instances) reduces costs.

By proactively monitoring and optimizing resource utilization, you can significantly reduce unnecessary spending and achieve greater Cost Efficiency.

Proactive Observability

Proactive Observability means setting up systems that watch your applications and infrastructure *before* problems actually impact users. Instead of waiting for someone to complain that something is slow or broken, you are actively looking for potential issues and fixing them early. This is achieved through setting up alerts and using dashboards.

Implement alerts... This means creating automatic notifications that trigger when certain performance metrics or cost metrics cross predefined thresholds. These alerts act like an early warning system. Think of it like a smoke detector in your house. It doesn't wait for a full-blown fire; it alerts you at the first sign of smoke, allowing you to address the problem before it becomes a disaster.

For example, you could set up an alert that triggers if the average response time of your web application exceeds 500 milliseconds for more than five minutes. This indicates a potential performance issue that needs investigation.

Here's an example of how you might configure a CloudWatch alarm using the AWS CLI:

```
aws cloudwatch put-metric-alarm \
    --alarm-name "HighResponseTimeAlarm" \
    --metric-name "Latency" \
    --namespace "MyApp" \
    --statistic "Average" \
    --period 60 \
    --evaluation-periods 5 \
    --threshold 0.5 \
    --comparison-operator GreaterThanThreshold \
    --alarm-actions arn:aws:sns:REGION:ACCOUNT_ID:MyTopic
```

In this example, "HighResponseTimeAlarm" is the name of your alarm. It watches the "Latency" metric in the "MyApp" namespace, calculates the average latency over 60-second periods, and checks if that average exceeds 0.5 seconds (500 milliseconds) for five consecutive periods. If it does, the alarm triggers, and an alert is sent to the SNS topic "MyTopic". Replace REGION and ACCOUNT_ID with your AWS region and account ID.

...and dashboards... Dashboards provide a visual overview of your system's health. Instead of manually checking individual metrics, you can see all the important information in one place. Dashboards consolidate key performance indicators (KPIs), resource utilization, and cost data into a single, easy-to-understand view.

Think of a car dashboard. It shows your speed, fuel level, engine temperature, and other critical information at a glance. Similarly, a well-designed observability dashboard gives you a clear picture of your application's and infrastructure's health.

A simple dashboard might show the following:

- CPU utilization of your servers
- Memory usage of your applications
- Database query latency
- Number of active users
- Error rates

By monitoring these metrics on a dashboard, you can quickly identify trends and anomalies that might indicate an upcoming problem.

...to proactively identify and address performance degradation or cost anomalies. This is the core of proactive observability. By using alerts and dashboards, you can spot potential problems before they impact your users or significantly increase your costs.

For example, imagine you see a gradual increase in database query latency on your dashboard. This might not trigger an immediate alert, but it's a sign that something is changing. By investigating this trend early, you might discover that a recent code change is causing more database queries than necessary. You can then fix the code and prevent a full-blown performance crisis.

Similarly, you might notice a sudden spike in the cost of a particular service on your cost dashboard. This could be due to a configuration error, a sudden increase in traffic, or even a security breach. By investigating this anomaly, you can identify the root cause and take corrective action, potentially saving your organization a significant amount of money.

In summary, Proactive Observability isn't just about monitoring; it's about actively using the information you gather to anticipate and prevent problems. It's a proactive approach to ensuring the reliability, performance, and cost-effectiveness of your systems.

Chapter 17 Performance Optimization and Cost Efficiency-Performance Tuning for AWS Workloads

Here are five bullet points outlining performance optimization and cost efficiency strategies for AWS workloads:

- **Right Sizing:**

    - Analyze workload resource consumption (CPU, memory, I/O).
    - Choose appropriate instance types matching requirements.

- **Caching Strategies:**

    - Implement caching layers (e.g., Amazon ElastiCache, CloudFront).
    - Reduce database load and improve response times.

- **Database Optimization:**

    - Use appropriate database types (RDS, DynamoDB).
    - Optimize queries, indexing, and data modeling.

- **Auto Scaling:**

    - Dynamically adjust resources based on demand.
    - Scale-in during low traffic periods to save costs.

- **Serverless Technologies:**

- Utilize AWS Lambda, API Gateway, and other serverless services.
- Pay-per-use model, eliminating idle resource costs.

Right Sizing

Right Sizing is about matching your AWS resources to the actual needs of your workloads. It involves understanding how much CPU, memory, and I/O your applications require and then selecting the appropriate instance types that meet those requirements without overspending.

- **Analyze workload resource consumption (CPU, memory, I/O).**

Before selecting an instance, understand the demands of your application. Is it CPU-intensive, memory-intensive, or does it heavily rely on input/output operations? Collect metrics on resource usage over time. AWS provides services like CloudWatch that can help track CPU utilization, memory usage, disk I/O, and network I/O. Examine historical data to identify peak and average usage patterns.

For example, you might find that your web application consistently uses 60% CPU during peak hours and only 10% during off-peak hours. Similarly, you might observe that your database server requires a large amount of memory to cache frequently accessed data, or that your data processing job spends a significant amount of time reading and writing data to disk.

Tools like `top` (on Linux) or Resource Monitor (on Windows) can be used within the instance itself for real-time monitoring. AWS CloudWatch is used for metrics collection and visualization at the AWS level.

```
# Example using boto3 (AWS SDK for Python) to retrieve CPU utilization metrics from CloudWatch
import boto3

cloudwatch = boto3.client('cloudwatch', region_name='us-east-1') # Replace with your region

response = cloudwatch.get_metric_data(
    Namespace='AWS/EC2',
    MetricName='CPUUtilization',
    Dimensions=[
        {
            'Name': 'InstanceId',
            'Value': 'i-xxxxxxxxxxxxxxxxx'  # Replace with your instance ID
        },
    ],
    StartTime=datetime.datetime(2024, 1, 1),
    EndTime=datetime.datetime.now(),
    Period=3600,  # 1 hour intervals
    Statistics=['Average'],
)

# Process the response to analyze CPU utilization
print(response)
```

- **Choose appropriate instance types matching requirements.**

Once you understand your workload's resource needs, select the appropriate instance types. AWS offers a wide variety of instance types optimized for different workloads. These are categorized into families like general-purpose (e.g., `m5`, `m6`), compute-optimized (e.g., `c5`, `c6`), memory-optimized (e.g., `r5`, `r6`), and storage-optimized (e.g., `i3`, `i4`). Within each family, instances come in various sizes with differing amounts of CPU, memory, and networking capacity.

For example, if your application is CPU-bound, consider a compute-optimized instance type like `c5.xlarge`. If it's memory-intensive, choose a memory-optimized instance like `r5.xlarge`. If your application requires high I/O throughput, explore storage-optimized instances like `i3.xlarge`.

- **Right Sizing Sketch**
  - Imagine three servers:
  - Server A: Over-provisioned (too much CPU, Memory than needs).
  - Server B: Right-Sized (Correct CPU, Memory to needs).
  - Server C: Under-provisioned (less CPU, Memory than needs).

Server A: Wasted Resources (Cost Inefficient) Server B: Optimal Performance and Cost. Server C: Potential Performance Bottlenecks

- **Right Sizing Example**
  - Old way: Start with largest resources.
  - New way: Measure resource utilization and find correct instance.
- **Benefits of Right Sizing**
  - Reduce cost
  - Improve Performance
  - Efficient resource use.

Analyze Workload Resource Consumption

Understanding how your applications use resources is the first and most important step in making sure they run efficiently and cost-effectively on AWS. Think of it as taking a detailed inventory of everything your application needs to operate smoothly. This involves carefully tracking and measuring the amount of CPU, memory, input/output (I/O), and network bandwidth your workload consumes.

CPU Utilization:

CPU utilization refers to the percentage of time the central processing unit (CPU) is actively processing instructions. High CPU utilization might indicate that your application is working hard, but consistently high CPU utilization (near 100%) could mean your instances are overloaded and need to be scaled up to prevent performance degradation. Low CPU utilization suggests that you are paying for more computing power than you need and could scale down to save money. Sketch:

```
+--------------------+
| CPU Utilization    |
+--------------------+
|  Low: Underutilized |
|  High: Overloaded   |
+--------------------+
```

Example *Consider you have an e-commerce website that experiences high traffic during business hours and low traffic during the night.*

1. Monitoring:
   - You continuously monitor the CPU utilization of the EC2 instances that host your website's backend.
2. Observation:
   - During peak hours (9 AM to 5 PM), the CPU utilization consistently remains above 80%, indicating a heavy workload.
   - During off-peak hours (10 PM to 6 AM), the CPU utilization drops to around 10-20%.
3. Analysis:
   - High CPU Utilization During Peak Hours:
     - The servers are working hard to handle incoming requests, process transactions, and serve content.
     - This high utilization may lead to slower response times and a poor user experience if not addressed.
   - Low CPU Utilization During Off-Peak Hours:

- The servers are mostly idle, consuming resources without significant workload.
- Maintaining the same number of instances during these hours is inefficient and costly.

4. Action:
  - Implement Auto Scaling:
    - Configure auto-scaling policies to automatically increase the number of instances during peak hours to handle the increased load.
    - Configure auto-scaling policies to automatically decrease the number of instances during off-peak hours to reduce unnecessary resource consumption.
  - Example Auto Scaling Policy (using AWS CLI):

```
aws autoscaling put-scaling-policy \
    --policy-name scale-out-policy \
    --auto-scaling-group-name my-asg \
    --scaling-adjustment 1 \
    --adjustment-type ChangeInCapacity \
    --cooldown 300

aws autoscaling put-scaling-policy \
    --policy-name scale-in-policy \
    --auto-scaling-group-name my-asg \
    --scaling-adjustment -1 \
    --adjustment-type ChangeInCapacity \
    --cooldown 300
```

  - These policies can be triggered by CloudWatch alarms monitoring CPU utilization.

Memory Utilization:

Memory utilization is the amount of RAM (random access memory) being used by your application. Running out of memory can lead to performance issues such as swapping (where the system uses hard drive space as memory), which is very slow. Monitoring memory usage helps you determine if your instances have enough RAM to handle the workload. Sketch:

```
+--------------------+
| Memory Utilization |
+--------------------+
|  Low: Wasted Memory |
|  High: Potential Swap|
+--------------------+
```

Example *Imagine you're running a data processing application on EC2 instances. You need to monitor memory utilization to ensure efficient operation.*

1. Monitoring:
   - Use tools like CloudWatch or third-party monitoring solutions to track the memory usage of your EC2 instances.
2. Observation:
   - You notice that memory utilization frequently exceeds 90%, and the system is using swap space.
3. Analysis:
   - High memory utilization and the use of swap space indicate that the instances are running out of physical memory.
   - This can cause performance degradation as the system relies on the slower disk storage for memory operations.
4. Action:
   - Increase Instance Size:

- Upgrade to an EC2 instance type with more RAM to accommodate the memory requirements of the data processing application.
- For example, upgrade from `t3.medium` to `t3.large`.
- Optimize Application Memory Usage:
  - Review the application code to identify and fix memory leaks.
  - Implement more efficient data structures and algorithms to reduce memory footprint.
- Implement Caching:
  - Use caching mechanisms to store frequently accessed data in memory, reducing the need to read from slower storage.

I/O (Input/Output) Operations:

I/O refers to the rate at which your application reads and writes data to storage (like disks or SSDs) or the network. High I/O can be a bottleneck, especially for database-heavy applications. Monitoring I/O helps you identify if your storage is performing optimally. Sketch:

```
+---------------------+
| I/O Utilization     |
+---------------------+
|  High: Bottleneck   |
|  Low: Underutilized |
+---------------------+
```

Example *Consider a scenario where you're running a database server on an EC2 instance in AWS. You need to monitor the I/O operations to ensure the database is performing efficiently.*

1. Monitoring:
   - Use CloudWatch or AWS Performance Insights to track I/O metrics such as disk read/write latency, disk I/O operations per second (IOPS), and throughput.
2. Observation:
   - You observe that the disk read/write latency is consistently high, and the database is slow to respond to queries.
3. Analysis:
   - High disk latency indicates that the storage is struggling to keep up with the demands of the database.
   - This could be due to insufficient IOPS, slow storage media, or inefficient database queries.
4. Action:
   - Upgrade Storage:
     - Switch to a faster storage option, such as Provisioned IOPS SSD (io1 or io2) volumes, to increase the number of I/O operations the storage can handle.
     - `aws ec2 modify-volume --volume-id vol-xxxxxxxxxxxxxxxxx --iops 1000`
   - Optimize Database Queries:
     - Analyze and optimize slow-running queries to reduce the number of read/write operations.
     - Use database indexing to speed up data retrieval.
   - Implement Caching:
     - Implement caching mechanisms to store frequently accessed data in memory, reducing the need to read from disk.

Network Bandwidth:

Network bandwidth measures the amount of data transferred in and out of your instances. High network usage can indicate that your application is transferring large files, streaming media, or experiencing a denial-of-service attack. Monitoring network bandwidth helps you identify potential bottlenecks and security issues. Sketch:

```
+---------------------+
| Network Bandwidth   |
```

```
+---------------------+
|  High: Congestion   |
|  Low: Underutilized |
+---------------------+
```

Example *Consider a scenario where you're running a web application that serves images and videos to users. You need to monitor the network bandwidth to ensure the application can handle the traffic efficiently.*

1. Monitoring:
    o Use CloudWatch or VPC Flow Logs to track network traffic metrics such as bytes in/out, packets in/out, and network interface utilization.
2. Observation:
    o You observe that network bandwidth usage spikes during peak hours, and users report slow loading times.
3. Analysis:
    o High network bandwidth usage during peak hours indicates that the application is struggling to handle the traffic.
    o This could be due to serving large files, inefficient data transfer protocols, or a large number of concurrent users.
4. Action:
    o Content Delivery Network (CDN):
        ▪ Implement a CDN like Amazon CloudFront to cache and deliver static assets (images, videos, CSS, JavaScript) from edge locations closer to the users.
        ▪ This reduces the load on the origin server and improves the user experience.
        ▪ Configure CloudFront:

        ```
        aws cloudfront create-distribution --distribution-config file://distribution.json
        ```

        Where `distribution.json` contains the configuration for your CloudFront distribution.

    o Optimize Images and Videos:
        ▪ Compress and optimize images and videos to reduce their file size and improve loading times.
        ▪ Use tools like ImageMagick or FFmpeg to optimize media files.
    o Load Balancing:
        ▪ Use a load balancer like Elastic Load Balancer (ELB) to distribute traffic across multiple instances, preventing any single instance from being overloaded.
    o Optimize Data Transfer Protocols:
        ▪ Use efficient data transfer protocols like HTTP/2 or QUIC to reduce overhead and improve transfer speeds.

By carefully analyzing these resources, you can gain valuable insights into your workload's behavior. This information enables you to make informed decisions about instance types, scaling strategies, and optimization techniques to improve performance and reduce costs.

Choose Appropriate Instance Types

Selecting the right Amazon EC2 instance type is a cornerstone of both performance optimization and cost efficiency in AWS. It involves carefully matching the characteristics of your workload to the specifications of the available instance types. Poor instance selection leads to either underutilization (paying for resources you don't need) or overutilization (suffering performance bottlenecks).

- **Analyze Workload Resource Consumption (CPU, Memory, I/O):**

Before choosing an instance, you need to deeply understand your application's demands. This means monitoring your application's usage of CPU, memory (RAM), disk I/O (reads and writes), and network I/O. AWS provides tools like CloudWatch metrics and the AWS Command Line Interface (CLI) to collect this data.

CPU: The percentage of processing power your application consumes. High CPU utilization (near 100%) suggests your application is CPU-bound and needs a more powerful instance with more CPU cores. **Memory:** The amount of RAM your application uses. Insufficient memory leads to swapping, which drastically slows down performance. **Disk I/O:** The rate at which your application reads from and writes to disk. High disk I/O can indicate a need for faster storage (e.g., SSD-backed instances) or optimized data access patterns. **Network I/O:** The volume of data your application sends and receives over the network. High network I/O suggests you need instances with higher network bandwidth.

Here's an example using the AWS CLI to get CPU utilization for an EC2 instance:

```
aws cloudwatch get-metric-statistics \
    --namespace AWS/EC2 \
    --metric-name CPUUtilization \
    --dimensions Name=InstanceId,Value=i-xxxxxxxxxxxxxxxxx \
    --start-time $(date -v-1d +%Y-%m-%dT%H:%M:%SZ) \
    --end-time $(date +%Y-%m-%dT%H:%M:%SZ) \
    --period 3600 \
    --statistics Average
```

This command retrieves the average CPU utilization for instance i-xxxxxxxxxxxxxxxxx over the past 24 hours, aggregated hourly. Analyze the result and similarly find memory , disk IO and network IO utization. Collect metrics for a representative period (e.g., a week or a month) to capture variations in workload demands.

- **Choose Appropriate Instance Types Matching Requirements:**

AWS offers a wide variety of EC2 instance types, categorized and optimized for different workloads. The key is to match the instance's capabilities to your application's needs.

Here's a breakdown of common instance families:

General Purpose (e.g., m5, m6i): Balanced compute, memory, and networking. Suitable for web servers, application servers, and small to medium databases.

Compute Optimized (e.g., c5, c6g): High performance processors. Ideal for compute-intensive applications like batch processing, video encoding, and high-performance computing (HPC).

Memory Optimized (e.g., r5, r6g): Large amounts of memory. Best for memory-intensive applications like in-memory databases (e.g., Redis, Memcached), data analytics, and scientific computing.

Storage Optimized (e.g., i3, i4i): High-speed, local storage. Well-suited for applications that require high I/O throughput and low latency, such as NoSQL databases (e.g., Cassandra), data warehousing, and large-scale data processing.

Accelerated Computing (e.g., p3, g4): Use hardware accelerators, such as GPUs, to accelerate specific workloads. Ideal for machine learning, graphics rendering, and video processing.

Illustration of EC2 Instance selection

```
+----------------------------------------------------------------+
|                  EC2 Instance Selection Process                |
+----------------------------------------------------------------+
| 1. Workload Analysis --> CPU, Memory, I/O Requirements         |
|   |                                                            |
|   V                                                            |
|   +------------------------------------------------------------+
|   | 2. Determine the Instance Family --> Based on Analysis     |
|   |   |                                                        |
|   |   V                                                        |
```

```
| |  +------------------------------------------------------------+
| |  | 3. Instance Type within Family --> Balance Cost & Performance |
| |  |  |
| |  |  V
| |  |  +------------------------------------------------------------+
| |  |  | 4. Test & Monitor Performance --> Iterate if needed        |
| |  |  +------------------------------------------------------------+
| |  +------------------------------------------------------------+
+------------------------------------------------------------+
```

When selecting a specific instance *within* a family, consider the trade-offs between vCPUs, memory, storage, and network performance, alongside the associated cost.

Example:

Suppose you are running a web application. After monitoring, you determine it's CPU-bound and requires at least 4 vCPUs and 8 GB of RAM.

1. You would select an instance from the *Compute Optimized* family (e.g., a `c5` or `c6g` instance).
2. Then, within that family, you would look for an instance type that meets or exceeds your CPU and memory requirements. A `c5.xlarge` (4 vCPUs, 8 GB RAM) might be a good starting point. However, depending on the specific I/O, you might still need to optimize storage or network.
3. After deploying the application on the `c5.xlarge` instance, continue to monitor its performance. If CPU utilization remains consistently high (e.g., above 80%), you may need to scale up to a larger instance type (e.g., `c5.2xlarge`). Conversely, if CPU utilization is consistently low (e.g., below 20%), you could save costs by scaling down to a smaller instance type (e.g., `c5.large`).

Choosing appropriate instance types is an iterative process. Regularly monitor your application's performance and adjust instance types as needed to optimize performance and control costs. Consider AWS Compute Optimizer as a potential tool for recommendations.

Caching Strategies

Caching is a technique used to store frequently accessed data in a temporary storage location, called a cache, for faster retrieval. In the context of AWS workloads, implementing effective caching strategies is crucial for both optimizing performance and reducing costs. Caching minimizes the need to repeatedly access slower, more expensive data sources like databases, thus improving application responsiveness and lowering infrastructure expenses.

Implement Caching Layers

The core of any caching strategy involves introducing caching layers into your application architecture. Two popular AWS services that facilitate this are Amazon ElastiCache and Amazon CloudFront.

- **Amazon ElastiCache:** This service provides fully managed, in-memory data stores that are compatible with popular caching engines like Redis and Memcached. ElastiCache sits between your application and your primary data store (e.g., a database). When your application needs data, it first checks the cache. If the data is present (a "cache hit"), it is retrieved quickly from ElastiCache. If the data is not present (a "cache miss"), the application retrieves it from the database, stores a copy in ElastiCache, and then returns it to the user. Subsequent requests for the same data can then be served directly from the cache.

  For example, suppose you have an e-commerce application that frequently retrieves product details. Instead of querying the database every time a user views a product, you can cache the product details in ElastiCache.

  Sketch:

```
[User Request] --> [Application] --> [ElastiCache (Check if data exists)]
                                        |
```

```
| Yes (Cache Hit) --> [Return Data]
|
| No (Cache Miss) --> [Database] --> [Return Data & S
```

Example Code (Python with Redis):

```python
import redis
import time

# Connect to Redis (ElastiCache)
redis_client = redis.Redis(host='your_elasticache_endpoint', port=6379, db=0)

def get_product_details(product_id):
    # Try to get data from cache
    cached_data = redis_client.get(f"product:{product_id}")

    if cached_data:
        print("Data retrieved from cache!")
        return cached_data.decode('utf-8')  # Decode from bytes
    else:
        print("Data not in cache. Fetching from database...")
        # Simulate fetching from database
        time.sleep(2)  # Simulate database latency
        product_details = f"Details for product ID {product_id} from database"

        # Store data in cache
        redis_client.set(f"product:{product_id}", product_details)
        redis_client.expire(f"product:{product_id}", 3600)  # Expire after 1 hour

        return product_details

# Example usage
product_id = 123
print(get_product_details(product_id))
print(get_product_details(product_id))  # Second request will be served from cache
```

In this code example, `redis_client.get` attempts to retrieve product details from the Redis cache (ElastiCache). If the data is found, it's returned. If not, the code simulates fetching from a database (with a delay), stores the fetched data in the cache with an expiration time of one hour, and then returns the data. The subsequent request from the cache will be served from cache with one hour.

- **Amazon CloudFront:** This is a Content Delivery Network (CDN) that caches static and dynamic content closer to your users. CloudFront caches content at edge locations around the world. When a user requests content, CloudFront serves it from the nearest edge location, reducing latency and improving the user experience.

  For example, if your application serves images, videos, or static website files, you can use CloudFront to cache these assets.

Sketch:

```
[User] --> [CloudFront Edge Location (Check if data exists)]
                |
                | Yes (Cache Hit) --> [Return Data]
                |
                | No (Cache Miss) --> [Origin (e.g., S3 Bucket)] --> [Return Data & Store in
```

Configuration Example (Conceptual):

1. Upload your static website files (HTML, CSS, JavaScript, images) to an S3 bucket.
2. Create a CloudFront distribution that points to your S3 bucket as the origin.
3. Configure cache behavior settings in CloudFront, such as Time To Live (TTL) for cached objects.
4. Update your DNS records to point your website's domain name to the CloudFront distribution.

Reduce Database Load and Improve Response Times

The primary benefit of implementing caching strategies is the significant reduction in database load. By serving frequently accessed data from the cache, you minimize the number of requests that reach the database. This reduction in load can translate to:

- **Lower database costs:** Fewer database requests can mean that you can use a smaller, less expensive database instance.

- **Improved database performance:** With fewer requests, the database can focus on serving more complex queries and transactions.

- **Faster response times:** Retrieving data from a cache is generally much faster than retrieving it from a database, resulting in a more responsive application.

  Consider an application that displays real-time stock prices. Instead of querying a database for every price update, you can cache the stock prices in ElastiCache and update the cache periodically. The application then retrieves the prices from the cache, providing near-instant updates to users without overwhelming the database. If the stock prices are stored in the cache for an extended period, such as an hour without expiry, the user experience would suffer because the user would not see the real time prices for any stock. In such cases, caching strategy and expiry time for the cache should be choosen accordingly. If user gets updated prices after every 5 minutes, for most of the applications that strategy should be fine.

Caching Strategies

Caching is like creating shortcuts for your data. Instead of always going to the original source (like a database), you store frequently accessed information in a faster, temporary location called a cache. This significantly speeds up response times and reduces the load on your backend systems.

Implement Caching Layers

To implement caching, you introduce intermediary layers that sit between your application and your data sources. These layers store copies of frequently requested data, so subsequent requests can be served directly from the cache, avoiding the slower trip to the original data source.

Think of it like this: Imagine you're a librarian. Instead of fetching a popular book from the main stacks every time someone asks for it, you keep a copy on a shelf right next to the checkout counter. This saves you time and effort.

AWS offers several services that can be used as caching layers:

- **Amazon ElastiCache:** This is a fully managed, in-memory data store service. It supports two popular caching engines:

  - **Memcached:** A simple, widely adopted memory object caching system. It's great for speeding up dynamic web applications by alleviating database load.
  - **Redis:** An advanced, in-memory data structure store that can be used as a cache, message broker, and database. It offers more features than Memcached, such as data persistence and more complex data structures.

- **Amazon CloudFront:** A content delivery network (CDN) that caches static and dynamic content closer to your users. This reduces latency and improves the user experience.

Example Scenario: Caching Database Query Results with ElastiCache (Redis)

Let's say you have a web application that frequently displays product information from a database. Without caching, every request for a product involves querying the database, which can be slow and resource-intensive.

Here's how you can use ElastiCache (Redis) to cache product information:

1. **Application Request:** User requests product information.
2. **Cache Check:** The application checks the Redis cache for the product data.
    - **Cache Hit:** If the data is in the cache (a "cache hit"), the application retrieves the data from the cache and displays it to the user.
    - **Cache Miss:** If the data is not in the cache (a "cache miss"), the application queries the database.
3. **Database Query:** The application retrieves the product data from the database.
4. **Cache Update:** The application stores the product data in the Redis cache with a specified time-to-live (TTL). This means the data will expire after a certain period and be refreshed from the database if needed.
5. **Display Data:** The application displays the product information to the user.

```python
import redis
import pymysql # Example library, other could be used

# Redis connection details
redis_host = "your_redis_host"
redis_port = 6379
redis_password = "your_redis_password"

# Database connection details
db_host = "your_db_host"
db_port = 3306
db_user = "your_db_user"
db_password = "your_db_password"
db_name = "your_db_name"

# Initialize Redis client
redis_client = redis.Redis(host=redis_host, port=redis_port, password=redis_password, decode_res

def get_product_info(product_id):
    """Retrieves product information, using cache if available."""

    # Try to get data from cache
    product_data = redis_client.get(f"product:{product_id}")

    if product_data:
        print("Data retrieved from cache!")
        # Cache data is stored as a string, may need to parse like json.loads if stored as JSON
        return eval(product_data) # Evaluate string as a python dict

    else:
        print("Data not in cache, retrieving from database...")
        # Connect to the database
        connection = pymysql.connect(host=db_host,port=db_port, user=db_user, password=db_passwo
        try:
            with connection.cursor() as cursor:
                sql = "SELECT  FROM products WHERE product_id = %s"
                cursor.execute(sql, (product_id,))
                result = cursor.fetchone()
```

```
            if result:
                # Convert the database result to a dictionary
                product_data = {
                    'product_id': result[0],
                    'product_name': result[1],
                    'description': result[2],
                    'price': float(result[3])
                }

                # Store data in cache with a TTL (e.g., 60 seconds)
                redis_client.set(f"product:{product_id}", str(product_data), ex=60) # Store
                return product_data
            else:
                return None
    finally:
        connection.close()

# Example usage
product_id = 123
product_info = get_product_info(product_id)

if product_info:
    print(f"Product Information: {product_info}")
else:
    print("Product not found.")
```

Explanation:

- The code first attempts to retrieve product information from the Redis cache using the product ID as the key.
- If the data is found in the cache, it's returned directly.
- If the data is not found (cache miss), the code connects to the database, retrieves the product information, stores it in the Redis cache with a TTL of 60 seconds, and then returns it.
- The next time the same product is requested within the 60-second TTL, the data will be retrieved from the cache, resulting in a much faster response.

This example demonstrates a simple but effective caching strategy using ElastiCache (Redis). You can adapt this approach to cache other types of data, such as API responses, rendered web pages, or frequently accessed configuration settings.

Reduce Database Load and Improve Response Times

The primary benefit of implementing caching layers is to reduce the load on your databases and improve response times for your applications. By serving requests from the cache instead of the database, you can significantly decrease the number of database queries, freeing up resources for other tasks.

Consider the following diagram that illustrates the flow of requests with and without caching:

Without Caching:

```
[User] --> [Application Server] --> [Database] --> [Application Server] --> [User]
                                        ^
                                        |
                                   (Each Request)
```

With Caching:

```
[User] --> [Application Server] --> [Cache] --> [Application Server] --> [User] (Cache Hit)
                                       ^
                                       |
                         [Database]-------+ (Cache Miss, Data Fetched and Cached)
```

As you can see, with caching, the database is only accessed when the data is not already in the cache (cache miss). Subsequent requests for the same data are served directly from the cache, resulting in faster response times and reduced database load. The trade-off is the added complexity of managing the cache and ensuring data consistency, but the performance benefits often outweigh these concerns.

Database Optimization

Database optimization is a critical aspect of building efficient and cost-effective applications on AWS. It involves selecting the right database for your workload, tuning database performance, and structuring your data for optimal access. Poor database design can lead to slow response times, increased infrastructure costs, and a frustrating user experience.

- **Use appropriate database types (RDS, DynamoDB).**

The first step in database optimization is selecting the appropriate database service for your application's needs. AWS offers a variety of managed database services, each with different strengths and weaknesses. Choosing the right one can significantly impact performance and cost.

Amazon Relational Database Service (RDS): RDS supports several relational database engines like MySQL, PostgreSQL, MariaDB, Oracle, and SQL Server. Relational databases are well-suited for applications that require strong consistency, complex transactions, and structured data.

Example Scenario: If you're migrating an existing on-premises application that uses MySQL to AWS, RDS for MySQL would be a natural choice. This allows you to leverage your existing knowledge and tools. Another use case is an e-commerce platform where transactional integrity for orders and inventory is critical.

Amazon DynamoDB: DynamoDB is a NoSQL database service that provides extremely fast and predictable performance at any scale. It's a key-value and document database, ideal for applications that require high throughput and low latency, and can tolerate eventual consistency.

Example Scenario: For a mobile gaming application that needs to store player profiles and game state data with very low latency, DynamoDB is an excellent choice. It can handle millions of requests per second with minimal delay. Another use case might be storing session data for a high-traffic website.

Illustrative Sketch:

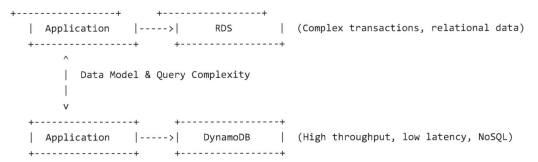

This sketch illustrates how the data model and query complexity influence the choice between RDS and DynamoDB.

- **Optimize queries, indexing, and data modeling.**

Once you've chosen the right database, the next step is to optimize how you interact with it. This involves tuning queries, creating appropriate indexes, and designing your data model efficiently.

Query Optimization: Poorly written queries can be a major bottleneck. Tools like EXPLAIN in MySQL or PostgreSQL can help you understand how the database executes your queries and identify areas for improvement.

Example:

Let's say you have a table called orders with columns like order_id, customer_id, and order_date.

A slow query:

```
SELECT  FROM orders WHERE customer_id = 123 AND order_date > '2023-01-01';
```

If you frequently query orders by customer_id and order_date, creating a composite index on these columns can significantly speed up the query.

Optimized query with index (in MySQL):

```
CREATE INDEX idx_customer_date ON orders (customer_id, order_date);

SELECT  FROM orders WHERE customer_id = 123 AND order_date > '2023-01-01';
```

Indexing: Indexes are special data structures that allow the database to quickly locate rows that match specific search criteria. However, adding too many indexes can slow down write operations, so it's important to strike a balance.

Example: Consider an e-commerce site where you frequently search for products by name. Creating an index on the product_name column would speed up these searches. However, adding an index to every column would slow down the process of adding new products or updating product information.

Data Modeling: A well-designed data model can make queries simpler, faster, and more efficient. In relational databases, normalization helps reduce redundancy and improve data integrity. In NoSQL databases like DynamoDB, denormalization can improve read performance by reducing the need for joins.

Example (DynamoDB): Suppose you need to store user profiles and their associated orders. Instead of storing orders in a separate table and performing joins, you could embed the order data directly within the user profile document in DynamoDB. This reduces the number of requests needed to retrieve user information and their orders, improving read performance.

Illustrative Sketch (Indexing):

```
Table:  Users (user_id, name, email, city)
   +-------+-------+---------------------+-------+
   | user_id | name  | email               | city  |
   +-------+-------+---------------------+-------+
   | 1       | Alice | alice@example.com   | NY    |
   | 2       | Bob   | bob@example.com     | LA    |
   | 3       | Carol | carol@example.com   | NY    |
   +-------+-------+---------------------+-------+

  Index on 'city':
  NY -> [1, 3]
  LA -> [2]

  Query:  SELECT  FROM Users WHERE city = 'NY';  (Index helps quickly find user_id 1 & 3)
```

This sketch visually demonstrates how an index on the city column speeds up queries that filter by city.

Chapter 18 Performance Optimization and Cost Efficiency-Caching Strategies: Using CloudFront, ElastiCache, and CDNs

- **Caching Overview:**

  - Improving performance and reducing costs by storing frequently accessed data closer to users.

- **CloudFront for Content Delivery:**

  - Global CDN caching static and dynamic content, optimizing delivery speed.

- **ElastiCache for Data Caching:**

  - In-memory data caching (Redis/Memcached) for databases and application layers.

- **Cache Invalidation Strategies:**

  - Implementing TTLs, versioning, and invalidation techniques to maintain data freshness.

- **Cost-Effective Caching:**

  - Balancing cache hit ratio, storage costs, and invalidation frequency for optimal ROI.

Caching Overview

This section introduces the fundamental concept of caching. At its core, caching is a technique designed to enhance performance and reduce costs in computer systems. This is achieved by storing frequently accessed data in a location that is faster and closer to the user or application that needs it.

Improving performance and reducing costs by storing frequently accessed data closer to users.

The primary goal of caching is twofold: to accelerate data retrieval and to minimize the resources required to access that data. Imagine a popular website that displays the current weather. Without caching, every time a user requests the weather, the website would have to fetch the data from an external weather service. This process involves network latency (the time it takes for the request to travel and the response to return) and processing overhead (the time it takes the server to prepare and send the data).

With caching, the website stores a copy of the weather data in a faster, more readily accessible location, such as the web server's memory or a dedicated caching server. When a user requests the weather, the website first checks the cache. If the data is present (a "cache hit"), the website can serve the data directly from the cache, bypassing the slower external service. This significantly reduces the response time and improves the user experience. If the data is not present (a "cache miss"), the website retrieves the data from the external service, serves it to the user, and *also* stores a copy in the cache for future requests.

To illustrate, consider a database query that retrieves a user's profile information. Without caching, each request for a user profile would require a database query. This can be slow and resource-intensive, especially if the database is under heavy load.

With caching, the first time a user profile is requested, the system retrieves the data from the database and stores it in the cache. Subsequent requests for the same user profile can be served directly from the cache, avoiding the database query altogether.

Here's a simplified Python example illustrating the concept:

```python
import time

# Simulate a slow data retrieval function (e.g., a database query)
def get_data_from_source(key):
    print(f"Fetching data for key: {key} from slow source...")
    time.sleep(2)  # Simulate delay
    data = f"Data for {key}"
    return data

# Simple cache implementation using a dictionary
cache = {}

def get_data(key):
    if key in cache:
        print(f"Fetching data for key: {key} from cache...")
        return cache[key]
    else:
        data = get_data_from_source(key)
        cache[key] = data
        return data

# Example usage:
print(get_data("user123"))  # First request - fetches from slow source
print(get_data("user123"))  # Second request - fetches from cache
print(get_data("user456"))  # Third request - fetches from slow source
print(get_data("user123"))  # Fourth request - fetches from cache
```

In this example, get_data_from_source simulates a slow operation like a database query. The get_data function first checks if the data is in the cache. If it is, it returns the cached data. Otherwise, it fetches the data from the slow source, stores it in the cache, and returns it. Running this code will show that the first request for "user123" takes longer because it fetches from the slow source, while subsequent requests are much faster because they retrieve the data from the cache.

Beyond performance, caching can significantly reduce costs. By reducing the load on backend systems like databases, caching can lower infrastructure costs. For example, fewer database servers may be needed to handle the same traffic volume if caching is effectively implemented. Additionally, by serving data closer to users, caching can reduce bandwidth costs.

Consider the following sketch to represent the caching concept:

```
+--------------------+      +--------------------+      +--------------------+
|    User/Client     | --> |       Cache        | --> |    Data Source     |
+--------------------+      +--------------------+      +--------------------+
        Request              | Cache Hit: Data    |      | (e.g., Database, API)|
        for Data             |  Returned Quickly  |      | Cache Miss: Fetch   |
                             | Cache Miss: Request | --> |   and Store Data    |
```

```
|  Data from Source  |      |                        |
+--------------------+      +------------------------+
```

This sketch shows the basic flow of a request: the user requests data, the cache is checked, and either the cached data is returned quickly, or the data is fetched from the original data source and stored in the cache for future use.

CloudFront for Content Delivery

CloudFront is a global Content Delivery Network (CDN) service. Its primary purpose is to speed up the delivery of web content—both static and dynamic—to users around the world. It achieves this by caching content at edge locations closer to users. Let's break down what this means and how it works.

Global CDN Caching:

The core function of CloudFront is caching. Instead of every user requesting content directly from your origin server (the server where your website or application is hosted), CloudFront stores copies of your content in multiple geographically distributed data centers called *edge locations*. When a user requests content, CloudFront delivers it from the nearest edge location, reducing latency (delay) and improving loading times.

Think of it like this: suppose your website's server is in New York. If someone in London visits your site, their browser would normally have to fetch the content all the way from New York. With CloudFront, a copy of your site's content is cached in an edge location in London. The user in London gets the content from the London edge location, which is much faster than going to New York.

Sketch to illustrate:

```
User (London) --> CloudFront Edge (London) --> Origin Server (New York)
      |
      ----------------------------------------/
      (Faster Delivery)
```

Static and Dynamic Content:

CloudFront can cache both *static* and *dynamic* content.

- **Static Content:** This includes files that don't change frequently, such as images (like .jpg, .png), stylesheets (.css), JavaScript files (.js), and HTML files. Because these files don't change often, CloudFront can cache them for extended periods, significantly reducing the load on your origin server.

- **Dynamic Content:** This refers to content that changes frequently based on user interactions or other factors. Examples include personalized recommendations, search results, and content generated in real-time. While caching dynamic content is more complex, CloudFront can still optimize its delivery. CloudFront can cache the response from API endpoints that generate dynamic content, using techniques like setting appropriate Cache-Control headers to define how long the content should be cached. CloudFront can also use its edge compute functions (Lambda@Edge or CloudFront Functions) to personalize content at the edge, further optimizing delivery.

Optimizing Delivery Speed:

CloudFront optimizes delivery speed in several ways:

1. **Low Latency:** By serving content from edge locations closer to users, CloudFront reduces network latency, which is the delay caused by transmitting data over long distances.

2. **Geographic Proximity:** CloudFront has a vast network of edge locations around the world. Requests are automatically routed to the nearest available edge location, further minimizing latency.

3. **Persistent Connections:** CloudFront uses persistent connections (keep-alive connections) to reduce the overhead of establishing new connections for each request. This improves performance, especially for

websites that require multiple requests to load.

4. **SSL/TLS Encryption:** CloudFront supports SSL/TLS encryption to secure data transmitted between users and edge locations. It can handle SSL/TLS termination at the edge, reducing the load on the origin server.

5. **Compression:** CloudFront can compress content before delivering it to users, reducing the amount of data that needs to be transmitted over the network.

Example Scenario:

Consider an e-commerce website with users worldwide. The website hosts product images, CSS stylesheets, and JavaScript files. Without CloudFront, users in different regions would experience varying loading times, depending on their distance from the origin server.

By using CloudFront, the e-commerce website can cache these static assets at edge locations around the world. When a user visits the website, the assets are delivered from the nearest edge location, resulting in faster loading times and a better user experience.

Additionally, the website can configure CloudFront to cache responses from its API endpoints that provide product recommendations. This reduces the load on the backend servers and improves the responsiveness of the website.

Configuration Example (Conceptual):

While a direct code example isn't applicable for CloudFront configuration (it's more about setup in the AWS console or using infrastructure-as-code tools), you can conceptually think of setting caching behaviors like this:

```
# Conceptual CloudFront Configuration (Not actual code)

distribution = CloudFrontDistribution(
    origin_server = "my-website.example.com",  # Your origin server
    cache_behaviors = [
        {
            "path_pattern": "/images/",  # Cache all images
            "ttl": 3600,  # Cache for 1 hour
            "allowed_methods": ["GET", "HEAD"]
        },
        {
            "path_pattern": "/css/",  # Cache CSS files
            "ttl": 86400,  # Cache for 1 day
            "allowed_methods": ["GET", "HEAD"]
        },
        {
            "path_pattern": "/api/recommendations", # API endpoint for recommendations
            "ttl": 60, # Cache for 60 seconds (dynamic content)
            "allowed_methods": ["GET"]
        }
    ]
)
```

This conceptual configuration demonstrates how you might define caching rules for different types of content. /images/ and /css/ are cached for longer durations (1 hour and 1 day, respectively) because they are static assets. /api/recommendations is cached for a shorter duration (60 seconds) because it is dynamic content that changes more frequently. The allowed_methods specify which HTTP methods (e.g., GET, HEAD) are allowed for cached requests.

In summary, CloudFront provides a robust and scalable solution for delivering content globally with low latency and high transfer speeds, improving the overall user experience and reducing the load on your origin infrastructure.

By understanding how CloudFront caches static and dynamic content, you can optimize your website or application for performance and cost-effectiveness.

ElastiCache for Data Caching

This section focuses on how ElastiCache helps improve application performance by serving as an in-memory data cache. It addresses common problems related to database load and application latency.

In-memory data caching (Redis/Memcached) for databases and application layers:

ElastiCache is a service that makes it easy to set up, manage, and scale distributed in-memory data cache environments in the cloud. Think of it as a temporary, super-fast storage area for frequently accessed data. It supports two popular open-source caching engines: Redis and Memcached. This strategic placement reduces the load on your primary databases and speeds up application response times.

Imagine you have a website that displays frequently changing product prices. Without a cache, every page request would require a query to your database, which can be slow and resource-intensive.

```
[User Request] --> [Application] --> [Database] --> [Application] --> [User Response] (Slow!)
```

With ElastiCache, the application first checks if the price is in the cache. If it is (a "cache hit"), the application retrieves the price directly from ElastiCache, bypassing the database. Only if the price is not in the cache (a "cache miss") does the application query the database, and then store the price in the cache for future requests.

```
[Cache Hit] --> [Application] --> [User Response] (Fast!)
[User Request] -->/
                   [Cache Miss]--> [Database] --> [Application] --> [Cache]
```

This significantly reduces the load on the database and dramatically improves response times. ElastiCache serves as an intermediary layer.

Redis vs. Memcached:

- **Redis:** Offers more advanced features such as data persistence (saving data to disk), complex data structures (lists, sets, hashes), and pub/sub messaging. It's suitable for scenarios where you need more than just simple key-value caching, such as session management or real-time analytics.

  For example, using Redis for session management allows you to store user session data in memory, providing fast access and improving the user experience.

  ```python
  # Example using Python and Redis
  import redis

  # Connect to Redis
  redis_client = redis.Redis(host='your_redis_endpoint', port=6379, db=0)

  # Set a session value
  redis_client.set('user_id:123', 'session_data')

  # Retrieve a session value
  session_data = redis_client.get('user_id:123')

  print(session_data) # Output: b'session_data'
  ```

- **Memcached:** Simpler and generally faster for basic key-value caching. It excels at distributing load across multiple nodes, making it a good choice for caching static content or frequently accessed data that doesn't require advanced features.

For example, Memcached can be used to cache the results of database queries, reducing the load on your database server.

```python
# Example using Python and Memcached
import memcache

# Connect to Memcached
mc = memcache.Client(['127.0.0.1:11211'], debug=0)

# Set a value
mc.set("product_name:456", "Awesome Gadget")

# Get a value
product_name = mc.get("product_name:456")

print(product_name) # Output: b'Awesome Gadget'
```

Use Cases and Benefits:

- **Reduced Database Load:** By caching frequently accessed data, ElastiCache significantly reduces the number of requests to your database, freeing up resources and improving overall performance.
- **Improved Application Performance:** Retrieving data from memory is much faster than retrieving it from disk. This leads to faster response times and a better user experience.
- **Scalability:** ElastiCache can be scaled horizontally by adding more cache nodes to handle increased traffic and data volume.
- **Real-time Analytics:** ElastiCache (especially Redis) is suitable for real-time analytics applications, such as tracking user activity or monitoring system performance.
- **Session Management:** Storing user session data in ElastiCache allows for fast and reliable access, improving the user experience.
- **Leaderboards:** Redis' sorted sets are perfect for implementing leaderboards in gaming applications.
- **Caching API responses**: When integrating with other API's whose data changes infrequently, you can use elasticache to cache those responses.

In essence, ElastiCache acts as a high-speed data buffer between your application and your data store, optimizing performance and scalability. Choosing between Redis and Memcached depends on the specific needs of your application, with Redis offering more features and Memcached excelling in simplicity and speed.

Cache Invalidation Strategies

Maintaining data freshness in a cache is a crucial aspect of its effectiveness. If the data stored in the cache becomes outdated (stale), it can lead to incorrect information being served to users, negating the benefits of caching. Cache invalidation strategies are the techniques used to ensure that the cache contains up-to-date data, balancing performance gains with data accuracy. This section explores common strategies used in cache invalidation, including Time-To-Live (TTL), versioning, and invalidation techniques.

Time-To-Live (TTL)

TTL is a straightforward invalidation strategy where each cached item is assigned an expiration time. After this time elapses, the cache entry is considered stale and is either removed or refreshed from the origin server on the next request. TTL is simple to implement and is suitable for data that changes predictably.

Explanation:

Imagine a website caching the stock price of a particular company. The stock price fluctuates throughout the day. Setting a TTL of, say, 5 minutes, ensures that the cached price is refreshed every 5 minutes, minimizing the risk of displaying a significantly outdated price.

Example:

Consider a simplified example using Redis as the caching system, a popular choice for implementing caching in applications.

```
import redis
#Connection to redis server
redis_client = redis.StrictRedis(host='localhost', port=6379, db=0)


#Set Value with TTL
redis_client.setex('stock_price_ABC', 300, 150.25) #Key: stock_price_ABC, TTL: 300 seconds, Valu
#Get the value later
price = redis_client.get('stock_price_ABC')
print(price) #prints the value of the stock price, until the 300 seconds have passed.
```

Advantages of TTL:

- **Simplicity:** Easy to understand and implement.
- **Automatic Expiration:** Cache entries expire automatically without requiring explicit invalidation.

Disadvantages of TTL:

- **Stale Data Potential:** Data can still be stale until the TTL expires. The data is only checked and potentially updated when a request is made after the TTL has expired.
- **Determining Optimal TTL:** Selecting the appropriate TTL value can be challenging; too short and the cache is frequently refreshed, reducing its effectiveness; too long and stale data may be served.

Versioning

Versioning involves assigning a version number to cached data. When the original data changes, the version number is incremented. The cache stores data along with its version number. When a request is made, the cache checks if the version number of the cached data matches the current version number of the original data. If they match, the cached data is served. If they don't match, the cache invalidates the old data and fetches the latest version from the origin server.

Explanation:

Consider a scenario where you are caching the content of a blog post. Each time the blog post is updated, its version number is incremented. The cache stores the blog post content along with its version number. When a user requests the blog post, the cache checks if the version number of the cached content matches the latest version number of the blog post. If they match, the cached content is served. If not, the cache fetches the latest version from the database.

Example:

Consider using a database column called `version` that is updated every time the row is updated.

```
-- Example table structure
CREATE TABLE blog_posts (
    id INT PRIMARY KEY,
    title VARCHAR(255),
    content TEXT,
    version INT DEFAULT 1
);


-- Example update statement (assuming update to content)
UPDATE blog_posts
SET content = 'New Content', version = version + 1
WHERE id = 1;
```

In the application layer, you would read the `version` column and compare it to the cached version to decide if you need to refresh your cache.

Advantages of Versioning:

- **Data Consistency:** Ensures that the cached data is always consistent with the original data.
- **Precise Invalidation:** Invalidates cache entries only when the original data changes.

Disadvantages of Versioning:

- **Complexity:** Requires managing version numbers and checking them during cache lookups.
- **Increased Storage:** Stores version information along with cached data, leading to slightly increased storage requirements.

Invalidation Techniques

Invalidation techniques involve actively removing or marking cache entries as invalid when the original data changes. This can be done using various methods, such as:

- **Event-Based Invalidation:** The origin server sends an event (e.g., a message) to the cache when data changes, triggering invalidation.
- **Tag-Based Invalidation:** Assigning tags to cached entries, and invalidating all entries with a specific tag when the associated data changes.
- **URL-Based Invalidation:** Invalidate cache entries based on their URLs.

Explanation:

Event-Based Invalidation: For example, when an e-commerce system updates the price of a product, it sends a message to the caching system, which then invalidates the cached price of that product.

Tag-Based Invalidation: Imagine caching data related to a specific user. You can tag all cached entries related to that user with the user's ID. When the user's profile is updated, all cached entries with that user's ID tag are invalidated.

URL-Based Invalidation: Invalidate cache entries based on their URLs. You could use the URL of the product page as the cache key. If the product page URL is updated you invalidate the cache related to the product page URL.

Example (Event-Based with Redis Pub/Sub):

```
import redis

redis_client = redis.StrictRedis(host='localhost', port=6379, db=0)

def invalidate_cache(product_id):
    redis_client.delete(f'product:{product_id}')

# Subscribe to the 'product_updates' channel
pubsub = redis_client.pubsub()
pubsub.subscribe('product_updates')

# Simulate listening for events
for message in pubsub.listen():
    if message['type'] == 'message':
        product_id = message['data'].decode('utf-8')
        invalidate_cache(product_id)
        print(f'Invalidated cache for product: {product_id}')
```

```
# In another part of the application (e.g., when updating a product):
# redis_client.publish('product_updates', '123') # Invalidate product with ID 123
```

Advantages of Invalidation Techniques:

- **Immediate Invalidation:** Ensures that the cache is updated immediately when the original data changes.
- **Granular Control:** Allows for invalidating specific cache entries based on events, tags, or URLs.

Disadvantages of Invalidation Techniques:

- **Complexity:** Requires implementing mechanisms for detecting data changes and triggering invalidation.
- **Potential for Race Conditions:** If not implemented carefully, invalidation can lead to race conditions where stale data is served before the cache is updated.

Sketch explanation of invalidation strategies

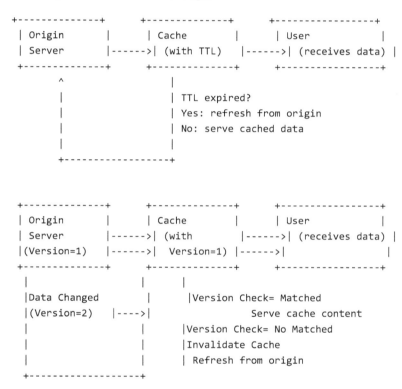

Choosing the Right Strategy

Selecting the appropriate cache invalidation strategy depends on the specific requirements of the application, including:

- **Data Change Frequency:** How often does the original data change? For frequently changing data, TTL or invalidation techniques may be more suitable. For less frequently changing data, versioning may be a better option.
- **Data Consistency Requirements:** How important is it to ensure that the cached data is always consistent with the original data? If data consistency is critical, versioning or invalidation techniques are preferred.
- **Complexity and Cost:** How complex is the implementation and maintenance of the strategy? Simpler strategies like TTL are easier to implement, while more complex strategies like invalidation techniques require more effort.
- **Resources and Cost:** Considering the resources and cost for each strategy, some of them may be cheaper and more expensive to implement.

By carefully considering these factors, you can choose the cache invalidation strategy that best balances performance, data accuracy, and cost for your application.

Cost-Effective Caching

Caching, while a powerful tool for improving performance, also introduces cost considerations. Achieving cost-effective caching involves carefully balancing several factors to maximize the return on investment (ROI). We need to consider the cache hit ratio, the cost of storage for the cache, and the frequency with which we need to update (invalidate) the cache's contents.

- **Balancing cache hit ratio, storage costs, and invalidation frequency for optimal ROI:**

The core of cost-effective caching is finding the sweet spot between how often the cache is useful (hit ratio), how much the cache costs to maintain (storage), and how often we need to refresh the data (invalidation). A high cache hit ratio means that requests are frequently served from the cache, reducing load on the origin server and improving response times. However, storing a large amount of data to achieve a high hit ratio can be expensive. Similarly, frequent invalidations ensure data freshness but can increase processing overhead and potentially negate the benefits of caching if the cache is constantly being updated.

To understand the trade-offs, let's consider a few scenarios.

Scenario 1: High Storage Cost, Low Invalidation:

Imagine you are caching product catalog data for an e-commerce website. The catalog doesn't change very often (e.g., new products are added weekly, but existing products are rarely updated). You decide to cache the entire catalog in memory using a service like Redis.

- **Benefit:** Very high cache hit ratio, leading to extremely fast product page load times for most users.
- **Cost:** Higher upfront cost for the Redis instance with enough memory to hold the entire catalog.
- **ROI Analysis:** If the increased sales due to faster page load times outweigh the cost of the Redis instance, this is a good strategy.

Scenario 2: Lower Storage Cost, Moderate Invalidation:

You're building an API that returns user profile information. The profile data changes occasionally as users update their information. Instead of caching everything, you decide to cache only the most frequently accessed profiles and set a Time-To-Live (TTL) of one hour.

- **Benefit:** Lower storage cost since you're not caching every profile. Moderate cache hit ratio, as popular profiles will be served from the cache.
- **Cost:** Need to handle cache misses (requests for profiles not in the cache) by fetching data from the database. Possible data staleness for up to one hour.
- **ROI Analysis:** This approach is cost-effective if the reduction in database load and improved response times for frequently accessed profiles outweighs the cost of handling cache misses and the risk of serving slightly stale data.

Scenario 3: Low Storage Cost, High Invalidation:

You are caching stock prices for a financial application. Stock prices change very frequently, so you implement a caching strategy with a very short TTL (e.g., 1 minute).

- **Benefit:** Low storage cost since you don't need to store data for long.
- **Cost:** Lower cache hit ratio, as the cache is constantly being invalidated. Higher processing overhead due to frequent cache updates.
- **ROI Analysis:** This is a viable strategy if the cost of accessing the real-time stock price feed is high, and even a short-lived cache can reduce the load on that feed.

Let's visualize these scenarios:

```
Scenario 1: High Storage, Low Invalidation
+--------------------+        Infrequent Updates     +--------------------+
|  Large Cache       |    ------------------------>   |  Origin Server     |
|  (High Hit Ratio)  |                                |  (Less Load)       |
+--------------------+                                +--------------------+

Scenario 2: Lower Storage, Moderate Invalidation
+--------------------+        Periodic Updates        +--------------------+
|  Smaller Cache     |    ------------------------>   |  Origin Server     |
|  (Moderate Hit Ratio)|                              |  (Moderate Load)   |
+--------------------+                                +--------------------+

Scenario 3: Low Storage, High Invalidation
+--------------------+        Frequent Updates        +--------------------+
|  Small Cache       |    ------------------------>   |  Origin Server     |
|  (Low Hit Ratio)   |                                |  (Higher Load)     |
+--------------------+                                +--------------------+
```

To make informed decisions about cost-effective caching, consider these practices:

1. **Monitor Cache Performance:** Use monitoring tools to track cache hit ratio, miss rates, and invalidation frequency. This data will help you understand how effectively your cache is performing.
2. **Right-Size Your Cache:** Avoid over-provisioning cache storage. Analyze your data access patterns and allocate only the necessary resources.
3. **Implement Smart Invalidation:** Use techniques like versioning or change notifications to invalidate only the data that has actually changed, rather than invalidating entire cache segments.
4. **Tiered Caching:** Implement multiple layers of caching (e.g., browser cache, CDN, in-memory cache) to optimize performance at different levels of the application architecture. This helps reduce costs by utilizing resources effectively.
5. **Cost-Aware Technology Choices:** Services like CloudFront and ElastiCache provide various pricing models. Evaluate the pricing implications of each choice with factors such as request volume, data transfer, and storage requirements.

Chapter 19 Advanced Use Cases and Real-World Scenarios-Big Data and Analytics on AWS: Redshift, EMR, and Athena

- **Big Data Challenges & AWS Solutions:** Overview of challenges and how AWS services address them for scalability and resilience.

- **Redshift Data Warehousing:**

- Scalable data warehouse for complex analytical queries; discusses use cases for reporting and business intelligence.

- **EMR for Data Processing:**

    - Using Elastic MapReduce for large-scale data processing with Hadoop and Spark; common ETL and machine learning workloads.

- **Athena for Serverless Querying:**

    - Ad-hoc querying of data in S3 using SQL; cost-effective analysis of data lakes without infrastructure management.

- **Real-World Examples:**

    - Architectural patterns for building data pipelines using Redshift, EMR, and Athena; considerations for data security and governance.

Big Data Challenges & AWS Solutions

This section explores the primary hurdles associated with handling big data and demonstrates how Amazon Web Services (AWS) provides solutions to overcome these challenges, ensuring scalability and resilience.

Overview of Challenges:

Big data presents a unique set of challenges due to its sheer volume, velocity, variety, and veracity. These "four V's" necessitate specialized infrastructure and techniques for effective processing and analysis.

- **Volume:** The sheer amount of data is often overwhelming. Traditional databases and processing methods struggle to handle datasets that can range from terabytes to petabytes.
    - *Challenge Example:* Imagine a social media company needing to store and analyze billions of user posts, images, and videos generated daily. A standard database server would quickly become overloaded.
- **Velocity:** The speed at which data is generated and needs to be processed is increasing. Real-time or near-real-time analysis is often required to derive timely insights.
    - *Challenge Example:* Consider a financial institution monitoring stock market data. They need to analyze incoming data streams in real-time to detect fraudulent transactions or identify trading opportunities.
- **Variety:** Data comes in various formats, including structured, semi-structured, and unstructured data. Integrating and analyzing these diverse data types is complex.
    - *Challenge Example:* A marketing company may need to combine structured customer data from a CRM with unstructured text data from social media posts and semi-structured data from web server logs to understand customer sentiment and behavior.
- **Veracity:** Data quality and accuracy can vary significantly. Noisy, inconsistent, or incomplete data can lead to incorrect analysis and flawed decision-making.
    - *Challenge Example:* An e-commerce company analyzing customer reviews may encounter spam, fake reviews, or reviews with incorrect ratings, which need to be filtered or corrected to obtain accurate insights.

How AWS Services Address These Challenges for Scalability and Resilience:

AWS offers a comprehensive suite of services designed to tackle these big data challenges, enabling scalable and resilient solutions.

- **Scalability:** AWS services are designed to scale horizontally, allowing you to increase resources as data volumes grow without significant downtime or performance degradation.
    - *AWS Solution Example:* Amazon S3 provides virtually unlimited storage for data lakes. You can store massive amounts of data without worrying about capacity limitations. Amazon EC2 allows you to spin

up virtual servers as needed to handle increased processing demands.

- **Resilience:** AWS services are built with redundancy and fault tolerance in mind, ensuring that your data pipelines remain operational even in the event of hardware failures or other disruptions.
  - *AWS Solution Example:* Amazon S3 replicates data across multiple availability zones, ensuring data durability and availability. Amazon EMR distributes processing across multiple nodes, so if one node fails, the job can continue without interruption.

Specific AWS Services and How They Help:

- **Amazon S3 (Simple Storage Service):** Serves as a scalable and durable data lake for storing massive amounts of data in various formats.
  - *Example Use Case:* Storing raw log files, sensor data, and media files.
  - *Code Snippet (Python with Boto3):*

```python
import boto3

s3 = boto3.resource('s3')
bucket_name = 'your-bucket-name'
file_path = 'path/to/your/file.txt'
key_name = 'file.txt'

try:
    s3.Bucket(bucket_name).upload_file(file_path, key_name)
    print(f"File {file_path} uploaded to s3://{bucket_name}/{key_name}")
except Exception as e:
    print(f"Error uploading file: {e}")
```

- **Amazon EC2 (Elastic Compute Cloud):** Provides scalable compute capacity in the cloud, allowing you to run various data processing and analytics workloads.
  - *Example Use Case:* Running custom data processing scripts, deploying machine learning models.
- **Amazon EMR (Elastic MapReduce):** A managed Hadoop and Spark service for processing large datasets using open-source frameworks.
  - *Example Use Case:* Performing ETL (Extract, Transform, Load) operations, running machine learning algorithms on large datasets.
  - *Sketch:*

```
+-----------------+        +-----------------+        +-----------------+
|  Input Data     | -->    |  EMR Cluster    | -->    |  Output Data    |
|  (e.g., S3)     |        |  (Hadoop/Spark) |        |  (e.g., S3/RDS) |
+-----------------+        +-----------------+        +-----------------+
```

- **Amazon Redshift:** A fully managed data warehouse service for running complex analytical queries on large datasets.
  - *Example Use Case:* Generating reports, performing business intelligence analysis.
- **Amazon Athena:** A serverless query service that allows you to analyze data stored in S3 using standard SQL.
  - *Example Use Case:* Ad-hoc querying of data lakes, exploring data without setting up infrastructure.
- **AWS Glue:** A fully managed ETL service that simplifies the process of preparing and loading data for analytics.
  - *Example Use Case:* Discovering data schemas, transforming data, and loading data into data warehouses.
- **Amazon Kinesis:** A platform for streaming data on AWS, enabling real-time data ingestion and processing.
  - *Example Use Case:* Collecting and processing real-time data from sensors, clickstreams, and social media feeds.

By leveraging these AWS services, organizations can build scalable, resilient, and cost-effective big data solutions that address the challenges of volume, velocity, variety, and veracity.

Redshift Data Warehousing

This section delves into Amazon Redshift, a powerful and scalable data warehouse service provided by AWS. We'll explore its capabilities for handling complex analytical queries and its applicability in various reporting and business intelligence scenarios.

Scalable data warehouse for complex analytical queries;

Redshift is designed from the ground up as a data warehouse, meaning it's specifically built for storing and analyzing large datasets to gain business insights. Unlike traditional databases optimized for transactional workloads (e.g., processing orders, updating customer information), Redshift excels at handling analytical queries that often involve aggregating, filtering, and joining massive amounts of data.

Think of a typical retail business. They might have sales data, customer data, product data, and marketing campaign data. Individually, these datasets are useful, but the *real* power comes from analyzing them together. For example, you might want to answer questions like:

- "What are the top-selling products in each region, broken down by customer demographics?"
- "How effective was our recent marketing campaign in driving sales of a particular product line?"
- "What's the correlation between customer loyalty program participation and average order value?"

Answering these kinds of questions requires complex queries that scan through vast amounts of historical data. Redshift's architecture is optimized for these types of workloads. It utilizes columnar storage, data compression, and massively parallel processing (MPP) to achieve high query performance at scale.

Columnar Storage:

Traditional databases often use row-based storage, where all the data for a single row is stored together. In contrast, Redshift uses columnar storage, where the data for each column is stored together. This is particularly advantageous for analytical queries because they often only need to access a subset of the columns in a table. Columnar storage allows Redshift to read only the necessary columns, significantly reducing I/O and improving query performance.

Data Compression:

Redshift automatically compresses data as it's loaded into the warehouse. This reduces the storage footprint and improves query performance by reducing the amount of data that needs to be read from disk. Redshift supports various compression encodings, and it can automatically choose the most appropriate encoding based on the data type and distribution.

Massively Parallel Processing (MPP):

Redshift is built on an MPP architecture, which means that data is distributed across multiple compute nodes, and queries are executed in parallel across these nodes. This allows Redshift to process very large datasets quickly and efficiently.

Here's a simplified sketch of how MPP works in Redshift:

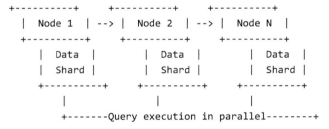

```
+----------+      +----------+      +----------+
|  Node 1  | -->  |  Node 2  | -->  |  Node N  |
+----------+      +----------+      +----------+
    | Data |          | Data |          | Data |
    | Shard|          | Shard|          | Shard|
    +----------+      +----------+      +----------+
        |                 |                 |
        +-------Query execution in parallel--------+
```

The query is distributed to each node, and each node processes its portion of the data in parallel. The results are then aggregated and returned to the user.

discusses use cases for reporting and business intelligence.

Redshift is particularly well-suited for reporting and business intelligence (BI) use cases. These applications typically involve generating reports, dashboards, and visualizations to help business users understand trends, identify opportunities, and make data-driven decisions.

Here are some common use cases:

- **Executive Dashboards:** Redshift can power dashboards that provide executives with a high-level overview of key performance indicators (KPIs). These dashboards can be updated in real-time to provide a current view of the business.

- **Sales Reporting:** Redshift can be used to generate detailed sales reports, analyzing sales performance by product, region, customer, and other dimensions.

- **Marketing Analytics:** Redshift can be used to analyze marketing campaign data, measuring the effectiveness of different campaigns and identifying opportunities for improvement.

- **Financial Reporting:** Redshift can be used to generate financial reports, such as balance sheets, income statements, and cash flow statements.

- **Customer Analytics:** Redshift can be used to analyze customer data, understanding customer behavior, identifying customer segments, and personalizing customer experiences.

To illustrate with code, consider a scenario where we want to find the top 5 customers by total spending in a hypothetical `sales` table. Here's how we might write that query in SQL for Redshift:

```
SELECT
    customer_id,
    SUM(sale_amount) AS total_spending
FROM
    sales
GROUP BY
    customer_id
ORDER BY
    total_spending DESC
LIMIT 5;
```

This is a simple example, but it demonstrates the kind of analytical queries that Redshift is designed to handle.

Example: Building a Simple BI Dashboard

Let's say you want to build a simple BI dashboard showing sales trends over time. You could use Redshift to query your sales data and then use a BI tool like Tableau or Power BI to visualize the results.

1. **Data Loading:** First, you'd load your sales data into a Redshift table. This could be done using tools like AWS Glue or AWS Data Pipeline.

2. **Querying Data:** Next, you'd write a SQL query to retrieve the sales data you need for your dashboard. For example:

```
SELECT
    DATE(sale_date) AS sale_day,
    SUM(sale_amount) AS total_sales
FROM
    sales
GROUP BY
    sale_day
```

```
ORDER BY
    sale_day;
```

3. **Connecting to BI Tool:** You'd then connect your BI tool to your Redshift cluster. This typically involves providing the connection details (e.g., hostname, port, database name, username, password) and the SQL query you want to execute.

4. **Visualization:** Finally, you'd use the BI tool to create visualizations based on the query results. For example, you could create a line chart showing total sales over time.

In summary, Redshift empowers organizations to unlock valuable insights from their data through its scalable architecture, optimized query performance, and seamless integration with popular BI tools. By leveraging Redshift's capabilities, businesses can gain a competitive edge by making more informed decisions based on data-driven insights.

EMR for Data Processing

This section delves into using Amazon Elastic MapReduce (EMR) for large-scale data processing. EMR allows you to efficiently process vast amounts of data using popular open-source frameworks like Hadoop and Spark. We'll cover common use cases, including Extract, Transform, Load (ETL) processes and machine learning workloads.

Using Elastic MapReduce for Large-Scale Data Processing with Hadoop and Spark

EMR simplifies the deployment, management, and scaling of distributed data processing frameworks. Instead of setting up and maintaining your own Hadoop or Spark cluster, EMR provides a managed service. This means AWS handles the underlying infrastructure, allowing you to focus on your data processing logic.

Hadoop and Spark are frameworks designed for parallel processing of large datasets. Hadoop uses a distributed file system (HDFS) and a programming model called MapReduce. Spark, on the other hand, performs in-memory processing, making it significantly faster than Hadoop for many workloads. EMR supports both of these frameworks, and others like Hive, Pig, and Presto, giving you the flexibility to choose the right tools for your specific needs.

Consider a scenario where you have web server logs stored in Amazon S3. These logs contain valuable information about user behavior, system performance, and potential security threats. The sheer volume of these logs makes it impractical to analyze them using traditional methods. EMR, combined with Hadoop or Spark, provides a scalable and cost-effective solution.

Sketch of basic Hadoop processing:

```
[Data in S3] -->  [EMR Cluster: Hadoop]  --> [Processed Data in S3/Redshift]
```

Sketch of basic Spark processing:

```
[Data in S3] -->  [EMR Cluster: Spark]  --> [Processed Data in S3/Redshift]
```

These sketches illustrate the general flow: data resides in a source (often S3), EMR processes it, and results are output to a destination, again frequently S3 or a data warehouse like Redshift.

Common ETL and Machine Learning Workloads

EMR is widely used for ETL (Extract, Transform, Load) and machine learning tasks. ETL involves extracting data from various sources, transforming it into a usable format, and loading it into a data warehouse or data lake for analysis. Machine learning tasks, such as training models or making predictions, often require processing massive amounts of data, which EMR can handle efficiently.

- **ETL Example:** Let's say you need to load data from several relational databases into a Redshift data warehouse. Your databases have sales and marketing data, and you need to consolidate this data for reporting purposes. You can use EMR with Spark to extract data from these databases, clean and transform it, and then load it into Redshift.

A simple Python script using Spark (via PySpark) could look like this to perform the ETL:

```python
from pyspark.sql import SparkSession

# Initialize Spark session
spark = SparkSession.builder.appName("ETLJob").getOrCreate()

# Load data from a database (example: PostgreSQL)
jdbc_url = "jdbc:postgresql://your_db_host:5432/your_db_name"
connection_properties = {
    "user": "your_username",
    "password": "your_password",
    "driver": "org.postgresql.Driver" # Ensure driver is available in Spark classpath
}

sales_data = spark.read.jdbc(url=jdbc_url, table="sales", properties=connection_properties)
marketing_data = spark.read.jdbc(url=jdbc_url, table="marketing", properties=connection_propert:


# Perform transformations (example: cleaning null values, joining data)
sales_data = sales_data.dropna() # remove rows with null values
combined_data = sales_data.join(marketing_data, sales_data.sales_id == marketing_data.marketing_

# Load the transformed data into Redshift
redshift_url = "jdbc:redshift://your_redshift_host:5439/your_redshift_db"
redshift_properties = {
    "user": "your_redshift_user",
    "password": "your_redshift_password",
    "driver": "com.amazon.redshift.jdbc42.Driver" # Redshift JDBC driver
}

combined_data.write.jdbc(url=redshift_url, table="combined_sales_marketing", mode="overwrite", ｐ

# Stop the Spark session
spark.stop()
```

Explanation:

1. **Initialize Spark:** Creates a SparkSession, the entry point to Spark functionality.
2. **Load Data:** Reads data from two PostgreSQL tables ("sales" and "marketing") using JDBC. You'd replace the placeholders with your actual database connection details. *Crucially, the appropriate JDBC driver JAR files need to be available to Spark on the EMR cluster.* This can be accomplished through bootstrap actions during cluster creation or by installing the driver on running instances.
3. **Transform Data:** Drops rows with null values and joins the two DataFrames based on a common ID. This is a simple example; real-world transformations can be far more complex.
4. **Load Data:** Writes the transformed data to a Redshift table. The mode="overwrite" will replace the table if it exists. Again, ensure the Redshift JDBC driver is available.
5. **Stop Spark:** Shuts down the Spark session.

- **Machine Learning Example:** Suppose you want to train a machine learning model to predict customer churn. You have customer data stored in S3, including demographics, purchase history, and website activity.

You can use EMR with Spark and the MLlib library (Spark's machine learning library) to train a model on this data.

Another Python example (using Spark MLlib):

```python
from pyspark.sql import SparkSession
from pyspark.ml.classification import LogisticRegression
from pyspark.ml.feature import VectorAssembler
from pyspark.ml import Pipeline

# Initialize Spark session
spark = SparkSession.builder.appName("ChurnPrediction").getOrCreate()

# Load data from S3 (example: CSV format)
data = spark.read.csv("s3://your-bucket/customer_data.csv", header=True, inferSchema=True)

# Prepare data for machine learning
# Combine feature columns into a single vector column
feature_cols = ["age", "purchase_count", "website_visits"] # Your features here
assembler = VectorAssembler(inputCols=feature_cols, outputCol="features")

# Logistic Regression model
lr = LogisticRegression(labelCol="churn", featuresCol="features")  # Assuming 'churn' is the tar

# Create a pipeline
pipeline = Pipeline(stages=[assembler, lr])

# Train the model
model = pipeline.fit(data)

# Make predictions
predictions = model.transform(data)

# Evaluate the model (example: print the accuracy)
evaluator = BinaryClassificationEvaluator(labelCol="churn")
accuracy = evaluator.evaluate(predictions)
print(f"Accuracy = {accuracy}")

# Save the model (optional)
model.save("s3://your-bucket/churn_model")

# Stop the Spark session
spark.stop()
```

Explanation:

1. **Initialize Spark:** As before, sets up the SparkSession.
2. **Load Data:** Reads customer data from a CSV file in S3. inferSchema=True attempts to automatically determine the data types of the columns.
3. **Prepare Data:** The VectorAssembler combines the feature columns (age, purchase_count, website_visits) into a single "features" column, which is required by many Spark MLlib algorithms.
4. **Logistic Regression:** Creates a Logistic Regression model, specifying that the "churn" column is the target variable (label) and "features" is the features column.
5. **Pipeline:** A pipeline chains together multiple transformers and estimators to automate the machine learning workflow.

6. **Train Model:** `pipeline.fit(data)` trains the model using the input data.
7. **Make Predictions:** `model.transform(data)` applies the trained model to the data to generate predictions.
8. **Evaluate Model:** The `BinaryClassificationEvaluator` is used to evaluate the model's performance. We calculate and print the accuracy.
9. **Save Model:** The trained model is saved to S3 for later use.

These are basic illustrations. Real-world machine learning pipelines often involve more complex feature engineering, model selection, hyperparameter tuning, and evaluation.

EMR simplifies these tasks by providing a pre-configured environment with the necessary tools and libraries. You can launch an EMR cluster with the desired configuration (e.g., the number of nodes, the type of instances) and then submit your Spark or Hadoop jobs to the cluster. EMR automatically manages the cluster resources, ensuring that your jobs run efficiently and reliably.

By leveraging EMR, organizations can unlock the value hidden within their massive datasets, enabling data-driven decision-making and accelerating innovation. The ability to process vast amounts of data with frameworks like Hadoop and Spark, combined with the managed services offered by EMR, makes it a crucial component of modern data processing architectures.

Athena for Serverless Querying

Athena offers a way to analyze data stored directly in Amazon S3 using standard SQL queries. It's called "serverless" because you don't need to manage any servers or infrastructure to run your queries. This makes it particularly useful for analyzing large datasets (data lakes) in a cost-effective and simple manner.

Ad-hoc querying of data in S3 using SQL:

Imagine you have a collection of log files stored in an S3 bucket. These files could be in formats like CSV, JSON, or Parquet. Traditionally, querying this data would require setting up a database or data warehouse. Athena allows you to bypass this. You simply point Athena to your S3 bucket, define the schema of your data, and start querying using SQL.

Let's say you have a CSV file named `user_activity.csv` in your S3 bucket (`s3://my-data-bucket/`). This file contains user activity data with columns like `user_id`, `timestamp`, and `action`. You can define a table in Athena that corresponds to this file:

```
CREATE EXTERNAL TABLE IF NOT EXISTS user_activity (
  user_id STRING,
  timestamp STRING,
  action STRING
)
ROW FORMAT DELIMITED
FIELDS TERMINATED BY ','
LINES TERMINATED BY '\n'
LOCATION 's3://my-data-bucket/';
```

- `CREATE EXTERNAL TABLE`: This SQL command creates a table definition in Athena. It doesn't move or copy the data; it only defines the structure for Athena to understand it.
- `IF NOT EXISTS`: This clause prevents an error if the table already exists.
- `user_activity`: This is the name of the table you are creating.
- `user_id STRING, timestamp STRING, action STRING`: These lines define the columns and their data types. `STRING` represents text data.
- `ROW FORMAT DELIMITED`: Specifies that the data is organized in rows with delimiters between fields.
- `FIELDS TERMINATED BY ','`: Indicates that commas separate the values within each row.
- `LINES TERMINATED BY '\n'`: Indicates that each row is separated by a newline character.
- `LOCATION 's3://my-data-bucket/'`: This is the crucial part. It tells Athena where to find the data (the S3 bucket path).

Once you've created the table, you can run SQL queries like:

```sql
SELECT action, COUNT() AS action_count
FROM user_activity
GROUP BY action
ORDER BY action_count DESC
LIMIT 10;
```

This query would count the occurrences of each `action` in the `user_activity` data and return the top 10 most frequent actions. You'll get results displayed directly in the Athena console without managing any servers.

Sketch to explain this:

```
+---------------------+      +-----------------------------------------------------------------
  | user_activity.csv  | --> | Athena: (SQL Engine)
  | (in S3)            |      |  - CREATE EXTERNAL TABLE (defines schema pointing to S3)
  | user_id,timestamp,action|  |  - SELECT action, COUNT() ... (processes data directly in S:
  | 123,2024-10-26,login|    |  - Returns Results: (action | action_count)
  | 456,2024-10-26,logout|   |
  +---------------------+      +-----------------------------------------------------------------
```

Cost-effective analysis of data lakes without infrastructure management:

The primary advantage of Athena is its cost-effectiveness. You only pay for the queries you run. There are no upfront costs or ongoing server maintenance fees. Athena charges based on the amount of data scanned by each query. Therefore, optimizing your data storage and query design is important to minimize costs.

For example, consider partitioning your data in S3. Partitioning means organizing your data into separate directories based on a specific column, like date. If you frequently query your data by date, partitioning can significantly reduce the amount of data Athena needs to scan, lowering your query costs.

Let's say you partition your `user_activity.csv` data by date, storing each day's data in a separate directory:

```
s3://my-data-bucket/date=2024-10-25/user_activity.csv
s3://my-data-bucket/date=2024-10-26/user_activity.csv
s3://my-data-bucket/date=2024-10-27/user_activity.csv
```

You would need to alter your table definition in Athena to recognize the partitions:

```sql
ALTER TABLE user_activity ADD PARTITION (date='2024-10-25') LOCATION 's3://my-data-bucket/date=:
ALTER TABLE user_activity ADD PARTITION (date='2024-10-26') LOCATION 's3://my-data-bucket/date=:
ALTER TABLE user_activity ADD PARTITION (date='2024-10-27') LOCATION 's3://my-data-bucket/date=:
```

Alternatively, for a large number of partitions, you can use the `MSCK REPAIR TABLE` command to automatically discover and add partitions:

```sql
MSCK REPAIR TABLE user_activity;
```

Now, if you want to query data for a specific date:

```sql
SELECT action, COUNT() AS action_count
FROM user_activity
WHERE date = '2024-10-26'
GROUP BY action
ORDER BY action_count DESC
LIMIT 10;
```

Athena will only scan the data in the `s3://my-data-bucket/date=2024-10-26/` directory, significantly reducing the amount of data processed and, therefore, your costs.

Sketch to explain the partitioning:

```
+------------------------------------------------------------------------------------+
| S3 Bucket (my-data-bucket)                                                         |
|   +-- date=2024-10-25/                                                             |
|   |   +-- user_activity.csv (data for 2024-10-25)                                  |
|   +-- date=2024-10-26/                                                             |
|   |   +-- user_activity.csv (data for 2024-10-26)                                  |
|   +-- date=2024-10-27/                                                             |
|   |   +-- user_activity.csv (data for 2024-10-27)                                  |
+------------------------------------------------------------------------------------+

  Athena Query:  SELECT ... WHERE date = '2024-10-26'  --> Scans only date=2024-10-26 directory
```

In summary, Athena empowers you to analyze data directly where it resides in S3, eliminating the need for complex infrastructure setup. The cost-effective, serverless nature, combined with the familiarity of SQL, makes it an ideal choice for ad-hoc querying and data lake analytics. By understanding data formats and partitioning strategies, you can optimize Athena for efficient and cost-effective data analysis.

Real-World Examples

This section delves into practical applications, showing how Redshift, EMR, and Athena can be combined to build robust data pipelines. We'll explore common architectural patterns and highlight considerations for data security and governance within these setups.

Architectural Patterns for Data Pipelines

Data pipelines involve extracting data from various sources, transforming it into a usable format, and loading it into a destination for analysis. AWS offers several services to facilitate these steps, and integrating Redshift, EMR, and Athena unlocks powerful analytical capabilities.

- **Example 1: ETL Pipeline for E-commerce Data**

  Consider an e-commerce business. They collect data from various sources like website activity logs, sales transactions, and customer profiles. Building a data pipeline using AWS can centralize and transform this data for analytical insights.

  1. **Data Ingestion:** Raw data is ingested into S3 buckets. S3 acts as a data lake, providing scalable and cost-effective storage.

  2. **Data Transformation (EMR):** EMR (Elastic MapReduce) is used to process the raw data. An Apache Spark cluster on EMR can perform ETL (Extract, Transform, Load) operations. For instance, it might clean and transform the raw website logs, aggregate sales data, and join it with customer profiles.

  Example : Spark Code Snippet

  ```
  from pyspark.sql import SparkSession
  from pyspark.sql.functions import col, to_date

  spark = SparkSession.builder.appName("EcommerceETL").getOrCreate()

  # Read raw sales data from S3
  sales_df = spark.read.csv("s3://your-data-bucket/sales_data.csv", header=True, inferSc|

  # Clean and transform the data
  cleaned_sales_df = sales_df.withColumn("order_date", to_date(col("order_timestamp"))) '
                            .drop("order_timestamp") \
  ```

```
                    .filter(col("order_amount") > 0)

        # Aggregate sales data by day
        daily_sales_df = cleaned_sales_df.groupBy("order_date").sum("order_amount")

        # Write transformed data to S3
        daily_sales_df.write.parquet("s3://your-transformed-data-bucket/daily_sales")

        spark.stop()
```

This Spark code snippet demonstrates reading data from S3, cleaning it (converting timestamp to date, removing orders with zero amount), aggregating sales by date, and then writing the transformed data back to S3 in Parquet format.

3. **Data Warehousing (Redshift):** The transformed data from EMR is loaded into Redshift, a fully managed data warehouse. Redshift is optimized for analytical queries.

4. **Data Analysis (Redshift & Athena):** Business analysts can use Redshift to run complex SQL queries for reporting. For ad-hoc analysis of the raw data in S3, Athena can be used. Athena allows querying the data lake directly using SQL without the need to load it into a database.

This entire process forms a data pipeline, taking raw data and making it available for analysis.

- **Example 2: Real-time Analytics for IoT Devices**

Imagine a company managing thousands of IoT devices that constantly send data. They need to analyze this data in real-time to detect anomalies and optimize performance.

1. **Data Ingestion:** IoT data streams into AWS Kinesis Data Streams.

2. **Real-time Processing (EMR):** An EMR cluster running Apache Spark Streaming consumes data from Kinesis. Spark Streaming processes the data in micro-batches, performing real-time aggregations and anomaly detection.

3. **Data Storage (S3):** Processed and raw data are stored in S3 for historical analysis and auditing.

4. **Interactive Querying (Athena):** Analysts can use Athena to explore historical IoT data in S3, identify trends, and troubleshoot issues.

5. **Dashboards (Redshift):** Aggregated metrics are loaded into Redshift, providing a historical perspective to view performance and to create dashboards.

Diagramatic Representation of Data Pipeline

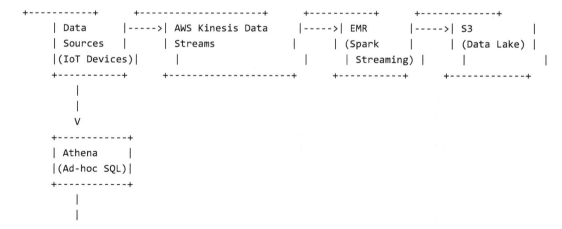

```
      V
+------------+
| Redshift   |
|(Dashboards)|
+------------+
```

Considerations for Data Security and Governance

Building data pipelines requires careful attention to security and governance.

- **Access Control:** Use IAM (Identity and Access Management) to control access to AWS resources. Grant the least privilege necessary to each user and service.
- **Encryption:** Encrypt data at rest (in S3 and Redshift) and in transit (using TLS).
- **Data Masking:** Mask sensitive data in Redshift to prevent unauthorized access.
- **Auditing:** Enable CloudTrail logging to track API calls and user activity.
- **Data Governance:** Establish clear data governance policies to ensure data quality, consistency, and compliance with regulations.
- **Compliance:** Adhere to relevant compliance standards (e.g., GDPR, HIPAA) when processing and storing data.
- **Data Catalog:** Use AWS Glue Data Catalog or other tools to maintain a central repository of metadata about your data assets.

By implementing these security and governance measures, you can build robust and reliable data pipelines that protect your data and meet regulatory requirements.

Chapter 20 Advanced Use Cases and Real-World Scenarios-AI/ML Workloads on AWS: SageMaker and AI Services

- **Scalable AI/ML Infrastructure:** Design patterns for handling large datasets and compute-intensive workloads.
- **SageMaker Pipelines:** Automating the ML lifecycle for repeatability and scalability.
- **Real-time Inference:** Architectures for low-latency predictions using SageMaker endpoints.
- **Serverless AI with AWS AI Services:** Integrating services like Rekognition, Comprehend, and Translate into serverless applications.
- **Cost Optimization:** Strategies for managing AI/ML costs using spot instances, reserved instances, and optimized algorithms.

Scalable AI/ML Infrastructure: Design Patterns for Handling Large Datasets and Compute-Intensive Workloads

Building AI/ML models often requires processing massive amounts of data and performing complex calculations. "Scalable AI/ML infrastructure" refers to the design and setup of your systems to handle these challenges efficiently. This means your infrastructure should be able to grow or shrink as needed, process large datasets quickly, and perform many computations without slowing down. It ensures that your AI/ML projects can handle increasing demands without performance bottlenecks.

Here, we'll explore key design patterns to manage large datasets and compute-intensive workloads effectively:

1. Distributed Data Storage:

The amount of data needed to train AI/ML models can be enormous. A single machine often cannot store or process this much data. A solution is "distributed data storage," which spreads the data across multiple machines. Each machine stores a portion of the data, and together they act as one large storage system.

Example:

Imagine you have a dataset of one trillion images. Storing this on a single hard drive is impractical. Instead, you can use a distributed file system like Hadoop Distributed File System (HDFS) or Amazon S3. HDFS, for example, splits the dataset into smaller blocks and stores these blocks across multiple machines in a cluster.

Diagram:

```
[Client] --> [NameNode (HDFS Master)]
             /  |  \
            /   |   \
  [DataNode 1] [DataNode 2] [DataNode 3]
  (Data Block 1) (Data Block 2) (Data Block 3)


  Each DataNode stores a fraction of the total dataset
```

In this sketch, the client interacts with the NameNode, which is the master node in HDFS. The NameNode manages the metadata of the distributed files. The actual data is stored in DataNodes, each holding a fraction of the total dataset.

2. Distributed Computing:

Even with data stored efficiently, processing it can take a long time if done on a single machine. "Distributed computing" involves splitting the computational tasks across multiple machines, allowing them to work in parallel. This drastically reduces the processing time.

Example:

Consider training a deep learning model on the trillion-image dataset. Instead of using one powerful machine, you can use a distributed computing framework like Apache Spark or TensorFlow Distributed Training. Spark, for instance, divides the training data into smaller chunks and distributes these chunks to multiple worker nodes. Each node trains the model on its chunk, and the results are aggregated to update the global model.

```
# Example using Apache Spark (Conceptual)

from pyspark import SparkContext

# Initialize Spark
sc = SparkContext("local", "ImageTraining")

# Load the data (assuming data is stored in a distributed file system)
data = sc.textFile("hdfs://namenode:9000/image_data")

# Map the data to perform image processing and feature extraction
```

```
features = data.map(extract_features)

# Train the model (simplified)
model = train_model(features)

# Save the model
model.save("hdfs://namenode:9000/trained_model")

sc.stop()
```

In this code sketch, Spark loads the data from a distributed file system (like HDFS), transforms it using the `extract_features` function, trains a model using the transformed data, and saves the trained model back to the distributed file system. This entire process is parallelized across the Spark cluster.

3. GPU Acceleration:

Graphics Processing Units (GPUs) are specialized processors designed for parallel computations. They are particularly effective for AI/ML tasks like deep learning, which involve many matrix operations. Using GPUs can significantly speed up training and inference.

Example:

Training a convolutional neural network (CNN) for image recognition can take days on a CPU. However, using a GPU can reduce this time to hours. Frameworks like TensorFlow and PyTorch are designed to leverage GPUs.

```
# Example using TensorFlow with GPU

import tensorflow as tf

# Check if GPU is available
if tf.config.list_physical_devices('GPU'):
    print('GPU is available')
else:
    print('GPU is NOT available')

# Define a simple model
model = tf.keras.models.Sequential([
    tf.keras.layers.Dense(10, activation='relu', input_shape=(10,)),
    tf.keras.layers.Dense(1)
])

# Compile the model
model.compile(optimizer='adam', loss='mse')

# Generate some dummy data
import numpy as np
x = np.random.rand(1000, 10)
y = np.random.rand(1000, 1)

# Train the model
model.fit(x, y, epochs=10)
```

This TensorFlow code checks for GPU availability and then trains a simple neural network. If a GPU is available, TensorFlow will automatically use it for the computations, accelerating the training process.

4. Containerization and Orchestration:

"Containerization" packages your AI/ML applications and their dependencies into lightweight, portable containers (e.g., using Docker). "Orchestration" manages these containers across multiple machines, automating deployment, scaling, and networking.

Example:

You can containerize your entire ML training pipeline, including the data preprocessing scripts, model code, and dependencies. Tools like Kubernetes can then be used to deploy and manage these containers across a cluster of machines. This makes it easier to scale your training jobs and ensure that they run consistently across different environments.

Diagram:

```
[Kubernetes Master]
      |
      --> [Node 1: Container 1 (Preprocessing), Container 2 (Training)]
      |
      --> [Node 2: Container 3 (Training), Container 4 (Evaluation)]
      |
      --> [Node 3: Container 5 (Monitoring)]

      Containers are orchestrated across multiple nodes
```

In this sketch, Kubernetes manages a cluster of nodes. Each node runs several containers, each responsible for a specific task (e.g., preprocessing, training, evaluation). Kubernetes ensures that the containers are deployed, scaled, and monitored automatically.

5. Auto-Scaling:

"Auto-scaling" automatically adjusts the number of computing resources based on the workload. This ensures that you have enough resources to handle peak loads while minimizing costs during periods of low activity.

Example:

During peak hours, when many users are making requests to your ML model, the auto-scaling system automatically adds more servers to handle the increased load. When the demand decreases, the system automatically removes servers, reducing costs.

Diagram:

```
[Load Balancer] --> [Server 1] [Server 2] [Server 3] ... [Server N]
```

Auto-scaling system monitors load and adjusts the number of servers (N) dynamically

In this sketch, a load balancer distributes incoming requests across a pool of servers. An auto-scaling system monitors the load on the servers and automatically adds or removes servers as needed.

By implementing these design patterns, you can build a scalable AI/ML infrastructure that can handle large datasets and compute-intensive workloads efficiently. This ensures that your AI/ML projects can scale to meet the demands of real-world applications.

SageMaker Pipelines: Automating the ML Lifecycle for Repeatability and Scalability

SageMaker Pipelines is a tool within Amazon SageMaker that helps you automate your machine learning (ML) workflow. Think of it as a way to create a clearly defined, repeatable process for building, training, evaluating, and deploying your ML models. This is particularly useful for projects where you need to update your models regularly or have a complex ML process involving multiple steps.

Why Use Pipelines?

The core idea behind SageMaker Pipelines is to move away from ad-hoc, manual execution of your ML tasks. Instead, you define a series of steps that are linked together, forming a pipeline. This pipeline can then be executed automatically, ensuring consistency and reducing errors. It also makes it easier to track and audit your ML workflow.

Key Benefits:

- **Repeatability:** Ensures consistent execution of your ML workflow, eliminating manual errors and variations. Each time you run the pipeline, it follows the exact same steps.
- **Scalability:** Handles large datasets and complex workflows efficiently. SageMaker Pipelines is built to scale with your needs.
- **Automation:** Automates the entire ML lifecycle, from data preparation to model deployment. This frees up your time to focus on other tasks.
- **Auditability:** Provides a clear record of each step in the pipeline, making it easier to track and debug issues. You can see exactly what happened at each stage of the model development process.
- **Collaboration:** Allows teams to collaborate on ML projects more effectively by providing a standardized and well-defined workflow. Everyone knows the steps and the expected inputs and outputs.

Understanding the Pipeline Structure

A SageMaker Pipeline consists of interconnected *steps*. Each step represents a specific task in the ML workflow. Common steps include:

- **Data Preparation:** Preparing data for training (e.g., cleaning, transforming, splitting).
- **Training:** Training the ML model on the prepared data.
- **Evaluation:** Evaluating the performance of the trained model.
- **Model Registration:** Registering the model in the SageMaker Model Registry.
- **Deployment:** Deploying the model to a SageMaker endpoint for real-time inference.

These steps are defined using SageMaker's Python SDK and connected to create a directed acyclic graph (DAG). The DAG defines the order in which the steps are executed and how data flows between them.

```
from sagemaker.pipeline import Pipeline
from sagemaker.processing import ProcessingInput, ProcessingOutput
from sagemaker.estimator import Estimator
from sagemaker.model_metrics import MetricsSource, ModelMetrics
from sagemaker.workflow.steps import ProcessingStep, TrainingStep, ModelStep
from sagemaker.workflow.parameters import ParameterString, ParameterInteger

# Example: Define a processing step
processing_input = ProcessingInput(
    source='/path/to/data',
    destination='/opt/ml/processing/input',
    input_name='input_data'
)

# Define a training step
estimator = Estimator(
    image_uri="your_training_image_uri",
    role="your_sagemaker_role",
    instance_count=1,
    instance_type="ml.m5.xlarge"
)
```

```
# Add training data
estimator.fit({'train': processing_input.destination})

# Define the pipeline
pipeline = Pipeline(
    name="your-pipeline-name",
    steps=[
        ProcessingStep(name="process_data", inputs=[processing_input]),
        TrainingStep(name="train_model", estimator=estimator)
    ]
)
```

Explanation

- **Pipeline**: Represents the overall pipeline structure. You give it a name and define the steps.
- **ProcessingStep**: Represents a data processing step. It takes input data, performs some transformations, and outputs the processed data.
- **TrainingStep**: Represents a model training step. It uses a SageMaker `Estimator` to train the model.
- **Estimator**: Configures the training job, including the image to use, the instance type, and the IAM role.

Data Flow and Dependencies

The data flows from one step to the next in the pipeline. For example, the output of the data preparation step might be used as the input to the training step. SageMaker Pipelines automatically manages these dependencies, ensuring that each step is executed only after its dependencies are met.

Example Scenario: Building a Simple ML Pipeline

Let's illustrate a basic example of a simplified ML pipeline that would prepare data and train a model.

1. **Data Preparation Step:** This step reads raw data, cleans it, transforms it, and splits it into training and validation sets. This involves creating the processing scripts and defining the input and output locations.

2. **Training Step:** This step takes the prepared training data and trains a machine learning model. The training script is executed within a SageMaker training job, and the resulting model artifacts are stored in S3.

3. **Execution:** SageMaker Pipelines will execute the steps automatically, handling dependencies. If the data preparation step fails, the training step won't start.

Parameters

Pipelines allow you to use parameters. Parameters let you define values that can be changed when you run the pipeline. This makes your pipelines more flexible and reusable.

```
from sagemaker.workflow.parameters import ParameterString

# Define parameters
processing_instance_type = ParameterString(
    name="ProcessingInstanceType",
    default_value="ml.m5.xlarge"
)

# Use the parameter in the processing step
processing_step = ProcessingStep(
    name="process_data",
    processor=processor,
    inputs=[processing_input],
    outputs=[processing_output],
```

```
        instance_type=processing_instance_type   # Use the parameter here
)
```

Benefits of Using Parameters:

- **Flexibility:** Modify pipeline behavior without changing the pipeline definition.
- **Reusability:** Use the same pipeline for different datasets or model configurations.
- **Experimentation:** Easily test different hyperparameter settings.

In Summary

SageMaker Pipelines provides a powerful framework for automating your ML workflows. By defining your ML process as a pipeline, you can improve consistency, scalability, and auditability, ultimately leading to faster and more reliable model development. Using parameters with pipelines will allows you to run same pipelines with minor configuration changes with out touching your codes. This tool significantly aids in managing complex ML projects and fostering collaboration among data science teams.

```
graph LR
    A[Raw Data] --> B(Data Preparation Step);
    B --> C(Training Step);
    C --> D(Model Evaluation Step);
    D --> E(Model Deployment Step);
    style A fill:#f9f,stroke:#333,stroke-width:2px
    style B fill:#ccf,stroke:#333,stroke-width:2px
    style C fill:#ccf,stroke:#333,stroke-width:2px
    style D fill:#ccf,stroke:#333,stroke-width:2px
    style E fill:#ccf,stroke:#333,stroke-width:2px
```

Real-time Inference

Real-time inference, in the context of machine learning, refers to the process of making predictions with trained models on new data as quickly as possible. These predictions are generated in response to immediate requests, enabling applications to react dynamically and intelligently. Imagine a self-driving car needing to instantly identify a pedestrian crossing the street, or a fraud detection system needing to flag a suspicious transaction as it happens – these are examples where real-time inference is crucial.

Architectures for Low-Latency Predictions Using SageMaker Endpoints

Achieving low latency in real-time inference requires careful consideration of the architecture used to deploy and serve the model. SageMaker endpoints provide a managed environment specifically designed for this purpose. Let's explore some key architectural patterns:

1. **Direct Invocation:** The simplest architecture involves a client application directly invoking a SageMaker endpoint via an API call. This is suitable for scenarios with moderate traffic and latency requirements.

```
import boto3
import json

# Replace with your endpoint name
ENDPOINT_NAME = 'your-endpoint-name'

client = boto3.client('sagemaker-runtime')

payload = {'features': [1.0, 2.0, 3.0]} # Example input data

response = client.invoke_endpoint(
    EndpointName=ENDPOINT_NAME,
```

```
        ContentType='application/json',
        Body=json.dumps(payload)
)

result = json.loads(response['Body'].read().decode())
print(result)
```

2. **Load Balancing:** For applications with high traffic volume, a load balancer is placed in front of multiple SageMaker endpoint instances. The load balancer distributes incoming requests across these instances, improving availability and reducing latency.

```
[Client] --> [Load Balancer] --> [SageMaker Endpoint Instance 1]
                             --> [SageMaker Endpoint Instance 2]
                             --> [SageMaker Endpoint Instance 3]
```

3. **Caching:** Caching frequently requested predictions can significantly reduce latency and endpoint load. A caching layer (e.g., Amazon ElastiCache or Redis) sits between the client application and the SageMaker endpoint. If a request can be served from the cache, the endpoint is bypassed.

```
[Client] --> [Cache] --> [SageMaker Endpoint]
```

4. **Asynchronous Inference (SageMaker Asynchronous Endpoints):** When low latency is important but not strictly *real-time* (e.g., a few seconds delay is acceptable), asynchronous inference can be used. Requests are placed in a queue (e.g., Amazon SQS), and SageMaker processes them separately. This is helpful for workloads where processing time fluctuates.

```
[Client] --> [Amazon SQS Queue] --> [SageMaker Endpoint] --> [Output to S3 or other storage
```

5. **Real-time inference on edge devices(AWS IoT Greengrass):** SageMaker can be integrated with AWS IoT Greengrass to deploy models on edge devices. This is beneficial when you need to make real-time predictions without relying on cloud connectivity, such as in remote locations or with devices that generate a large amount of data locally.

6. **Model Optimization:** The model itself significantly impacts latency. Techniques such as model quantization (reducing the precision of numerical values) and model pruning (removing unnecessary connections) can reduce model size and improve inference speed. SageMaker Neo can compile models for optimal performance on specific hardware platforms.

```
#example of model optimization
#using tensorflow lite for smaller model sizes and faster inference on edge devices
import tensorflow as tf

#Convert the model
converter = tf.lite.TFLiteConverter.from_saved_model(saved_model_dir) # path to the SavedMo
tflite_model = converter.convert()

# Save the model.
with open('model.tflite', 'wb') as f:
    f.write(tflite_model)
```

By carefully selecting and combining these architectural patterns, you can design real-time inference systems that meet the specific latency and throughput requirements of your applications.

Serverless AI with AWS AI Services

This section explores how to leverage AWS's pre-trained AI services within a serverless architecture. The combination allows you to build intelligent applications without managing any underlying infrastructure. You simply use the AI services through API calls, paying only for what you use.

Integrating services like Rekognition, Comprehend, and Translate into serverless applications.

AWS provides a suite of AI services like Rekognition (image and video analysis), Comprehend (natural language processing), and Translate (language translation). These services can be easily integrated into serverless applications built using AWS Lambda and other serverless components.

Think of a scenario where you're building a social media application. When a user uploads an image, you want to automatically tag it with relevant keywords and moderate potentially inappropriate content. Similarly, if a user posts text in one language, you might want to automatically translate it for other users. These tasks can be efficiently handled using AWS AI services in a serverless way.

The basic architecture involves a trigger, a Lambda function, and an AWS AI service. For example:

- **Trigger:** An image being uploaded to an S3 bucket.
- **Lambda Function:** A function written in Python, Node.js, or another supported language that gets triggered by the S3 event. This function receives the S3 event data (the location of the uploaded image), calls the Rekognition API to analyze the image, and then stores the analysis results (tags, moderation flags) in a database.
- **AWS AI Service:** Rekognition, which analyzes the image and returns information about the objects, faces, and potentially unsafe content.

The same concept applies to text analysis using Comprehend or translation using Translate. Instead of an image upload, the trigger could be a new message being posted to a message queue (like SQS), or a direct API call from a web application. The Lambda function would then call the appropriate AI service to process the text and store the results.

Here is a Python code example demonstrating how to use AWS Rekognition to detect labels in an image uploaded to an S3 bucket. This function uses boto3, the AWS SDK for Python.

```python
import boto3
import json

def lambda_handler(event, context):
    s3 = boto3.client('s3')
    rekognition = boto3.client('rekognition')

    bucket = event['Records'][0]['s3']['bucket']['name']
    key = event['Records'][0]['s3']['object']['key']

    try:
        response = rekognition.detect_labels(
            Image={'S3Object': {'Bucket': bucket, 'Name': key}},
            MaxLabels=10, # You can adjust the number of labels returned
            MinConfidence=70 # You can adjust the minimum confidence level
        )

        labels = response['Labels']

        # Here, you can do something with the labels, like storing them in a database
        # or sending them to another service for further processing.
        # For this example, let's just print them:

        print(json.dumps(labels)) # Convert the labels to a JSON string for easier readability.
```

```
        return {
            'statusCode': 200,
            'body': json.dumps('Image labels detected!')
        }

    except Exception as e:
        print(e)
        print('Error getting labels from Rekognition.')
        raise e
```

- **Explanation**

    1. **Import Libraries**: Import `boto3` to interact with AWS services and `json` for handling JSON data.

    2. **Lambda Handler**: The `lambda_handler` function is the entry point for the Lambda function. It takes `event` and `context` as arguments.

        - `event`: Contains data about the event that triggered the Lambda function (e.g., S3 event).
        - `context`: Provides information about the invocation, function, and execution environment.

    3. **Initialize AWS Clients**:

        - `s3 = boto3.client('s3')`: Creates an S3 client to interact with the S3 service.
        - `rekognition = boto3.client('rekognition')`: Creates a Rekognition client to interact with the Rekognition service.

    4. **Extract Bucket and Key**:

        - `bucket = event['Records'][0]['s3']['bucket']['name']`: Extracts the S3 bucket name from the event data.
        - `key = event['Records'][0]['s3']['object']['key']`: Extracts the S3 object key (file name) from the event data.

    5. **Detect Labels**:

        - `response = rekognition.detect_labels(...)`: Calls the `detect_labels` method of the Rekognition client.
            - `Image`: Specifies the image to analyze, in this case, an S3 object.
            - `S3Object`: Contains the bucket name and key of the image.
            - `MaxLabels`: The maximum number of labels to return (set to 10 in this example).
            - `MinConfidence`: The minimum confidence level for the labels (set to 70% in this example).

    6. **Process Labels**:

        - `labels = response['Labels']`: Extracts the detected labels from the response.
        - The code then prints the labels in JSON format for demonstration purposes. In a real-world scenario, you would likely store the labels in a database or use them to trigger other actions.

    7. **Error Handling**:

        - The `try...except` block catches any exceptions that might occur during the process.
        - If an error occurs, it prints the error message and raises the exception.

    8. **Return Response**:

        - The function returns a JSON response with a status code and a message indicating that the image labels were detected.

To use this example:

1. Create a Lambda function in the AWS console and upload this code.
2. Configure the Lambda function to be triggered by S3 events, specifically when an object is created in your desired S3 bucket.
3. Ensure that the Lambda function has the necessary IAM permissions to access S3 and Rekognition.

The key advantage here is the serverless nature of the setup. The entire process happens on demand, without the need to provision or manage any servers. This greatly simplifies deployment and scaling.

AWS AI Services: a high level diagram

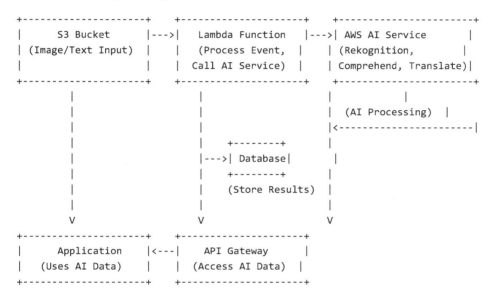

This diagram illustrates the data flow:

1. Data (image or text) is uploaded to an S3 bucket.
2. This triggers a Lambda function.
3. The Lambda function calls an AWS AI service (like Rekognition, Comprehend, or Translate) to process the data.
4. The AI service performs its analysis and returns the results to the Lambda function.
5. The Lambda function can then store these results in a database.
6. Finally, an application can retrieve and use the processed data through an API Gateway.

This setup combines the power of serverless computing with the intelligence of AWS AI services, enabling you to easily build and deploy AI-powered applications without the complexity of managing infrastructure.

Chapter 21 Advanced Use Cases and Real-World Scenarios-CI/CD Pipelines on AWS: Automating Deployments with CodePipeline

Here are five bullet points outlining CI/CD Pipelines on AWS with CodePipeline for "System Design on AWS":

- **Automated Deployment Strategy:** CI/CD pipelines using CodePipeline enhance deployment speed and consistency.

- **Infrastructure as Code (IaC) Integration:** Pipelines deploy infrastructure changes defined in CloudFormation or Terraform.

  - Ensures repeatable and version-controlled infrastructure provisioning.

- **Continuous Testing & Validation:** Integrating automated testing (unit, integration, security) in pipeline stages.

  - Improves application quality and reduces deployment risks.

- **Blue/Green Deployments:** CodePipeline facilitates zero-downtime deployments via blue/green strategies.

- **Rollback Mechanisms:** Implementing automated rollback strategies within the pipeline for failed deployments.

Automated Deployment Strategy

CI/CD pipelines using CodePipeline enhance deployment speed and consistency. This means that when developers make changes to the application code, the process of building, testing, and releasing that code is largely automated through AWS CodePipeline, making it faster and more reliable.

Speed:

- **Manual Process:** Traditionally, deployments involved multiple steps done manually, like copying files to servers, restarting services, and running database scripts. These are time-consuming and error-prone.
- **Automated with CodePipeline:** CodePipeline automates these steps. When a developer commits code, the pipeline automatically triggers, builds the application, runs tests, and deploys the code to the appropriate environments. This drastically reduces the time from code commit to deployment.
- **Example:** Imagine a developer fixes a bug. Without CodePipeline, it might take hours to deploy the fix. With CodePipeline, the fix could be live in production within minutes.

Consistency:

- **Manual Process:** Manual deployments are prone to human error. Different team members might follow slightly different procedures, leading to inconsistencies.
- **Automated with CodePipeline:** CodePipeline executes the same defined steps every time. This consistency ensures that the application is deployed in a predictable and repeatable manner, regardless of who initiates the deployment.
- **Example:** Consider a scenario where a database schema update is part of the deployment. In a manual process, the script might be executed differently on different servers, causing inconsistencies. With CodePipeline, the same script is executed in the same way every time, guaranteeing consistency.

The following simple example shows how deployment strategies can be configured with CodePipeline.

CodePipeline Example (Illustrative)

While the complete CodePipeline definition is complex and typically handled via CloudFormation or the AWS console, a simplified example clarifies the concept:

```json
{
  "pipeline": {
    "name": "MyWebAppPipeline",
    "stages": [
      {
        "name": "Source",
        "actions": [
          {
            "name": "GitHub",
            "actionTypeId": {
              "category": "Source",
              "owner": "AWS",
              "provider": "GitHub",
              "version": "1"
            },
            "configuration": {
              "Owner": "MyGitHubOrg",
              "Repo": "MyWebApp",
              "Branch": "main"
            },
            "outputArtifacts": [
              {
                "name": "SourceCode"
              }
            ]
          }
        ]
      },
      {
        "name": "Build",
        "actions": [
          {
            "name": "CodeBuild",
            "actionTypeId": {
              "category": "Build",
              "owner": "AWS",
              "provider": "CodeBuild",
              "version": "1"
            },
            "configuration": {
              "ProjectName": "MyWebAppBuildProject"
            },
            "inputArtifacts": [
              {
                "name": "SourceCode"
              }
            ],
            "outputArtifacts": [
              {
                "name": "BuiltCode"
              }
```

```
            ]
          }
        ]
      },
      {
        "name": "Deploy",
        "actions": [
          {
            "name": "ECSDeploy",
            "actionTypeId": {
              "category": "Deploy",
              "owner": "AWS",
              "provider": "ECS",
              "version": "1"
            },
            "configuration": {
              "ServiceName": "MyWebAppService",
              "ClusterName": "MyECSCluster"
            },
            "inputArtifacts": [
              {
                "name": "BuiltCode"
              }
            ]
          }
        ]
      }
    ],
    "artifactStore": {
      "type": "S3",
      "location": "my-codepipeline-bucket"
    },
    "roleArn": "arn:aws:iam::123456789012:role/AWS-CodePipeline-Service"
  }
}
```

This example illustrates a basic pipeline:

1. **Source Stage**: Fetches code from a GitHub repository.
2. **Build Stage**: Uses AWS CodeBuild to compile and package the application.
3. **Deploy Stage**: Deploys the built application to an Amazon ECS cluster.

Infrastructure as Code (IaC) Integration

Pipelines deploy infrastructure changes defined in CloudFormation or Terraform. This ensures repeatable and version-controlled infrastructure provisioning.

CloudFormation and Terraform:

- **What they are:** CloudFormation (AWS native) and Terraform (multi-cloud) are tools that allow you to define your infrastructure as code. Instead of manually creating servers, databases, and networks, you write code that describes the desired state of your infrastructure.
- **Example (CloudFormation):** A CloudFormation template might define an EC2 instance, an S3 bucket, and a security group, specifying their properties and configurations.

How CodePipeline Integrates:

- **Automated Infrastructure Updates:** CodePipeline can be configured to automatically deploy infrastructure changes defined in CloudFormation or Terraform templates. When you update your infrastructure code (e.g., change the instance type of an EC2 instance), committing the changes to your code repository triggers the pipeline.
- **Applying Changes:** The pipeline then uses CloudFormation or Terraform to apply these changes to your AWS environment, automatically creating, updating, or deleting resources as needed.

Repeatable and Version-Controlled Infrastructure Provisioning:

- **Repeatable:** Because the infrastructure is defined as code, you can create identical environments repeatedly. This is crucial for creating staging, testing, and production environments.

- **Version-Controlled:** The infrastructure code is stored in a version control system (e.g., Git). This means you can track changes to your infrastructure over time, roll back to previous versions if needed, and understand who made what changes and when.

- **Example:** Suppose you have an application that requires a specific version of the database. Using infrastructure as code, you define the database instance, version, and configurations in a CloudFormation template. When you need to create a new environment, the CodePipeline deploys the same template, ensuring the database is always provisioned with the correct version.

Continuous Testing & Validation

Integrating automated testing (unit, integration, security) in pipeline stages improves application quality and reduces deployment risks.

Types of Automated Tests:

- **Unit Tests:** Verify individual components of your application.
- **Integration Tests:** Ensure different parts of your application work together correctly.
- **Security Tests:** Identify vulnerabilities and security flaws.

How CodePipeline Integrates:

- **Test Stages:** CodePipeline allows you to define stages specifically for running automated tests. These stages can be configured to execute unit tests, integration tests, security tests, or any other type of automated test.
- **Example:** A CodePipeline might have a "Unit Test" stage that runs unit tests using a tool like JUnit. If any of the tests fail, the pipeline stops, preventing the deployment of faulty code.
- **Gate:** Test stages act as quality gates. Only code that passes all defined tests is allowed to proceed to the next stage in the pipeline.

Benefits:

- **Improved Application Quality:** Automated testing catches bugs and defects early in the development process.
- **Reduced Deployment Risks:** By ensuring code is thoroughly tested before deployment, you minimize the risk of deploying broken or vulnerable code to production.

Example (Illustrative):

Consider an example where a website should be scanned before deployment:

```
+-----------------+        +-----------------+        +-----------------+        +-----------------+
|  Source Stage   | -->    |   Build Stage   | -->    |   Test Stage    | -->    |  Deploy Stage   |
| (Get Code from  |        |  (Compile &     |        | (Run Unit Tests,|        | (Deploy to Prod)|
|    GitHub)      |        |  Package Code)  |        |  Security Scan) |        |                 |
+-----------------+        +-----------------+        +-----------------+        +-----------------+
        |                          |                      |         |                |                        |
```

```
      V                V                V         |          V                              V
  Success          Success          Success      |      Success
      \                \                \        |        /
  ------------------------------------------ |-----
                                               |
          Failure in Test Stage stops the pipeline
```

Blue/Green Deployments

CodePipeline facilitates zero-downtime deployments via blue/green strategies.

Blue/Green Deployment Explanation:

- **Two Environments:** You maintain two identical environments, "blue" and "green." Only one environment is live at any time, serving production traffic.
- **Deploy to Inactive Environment:** New code is deployed to the inactive environment (e.g., "green" if "blue" is live).
- **Testing:** After deployment, the new environment is thoroughly tested.
- **Switch Traffic:** Once satisfied, you switch traffic from the old environment ("blue") to the new environment ("green"). This switch can be done quickly and with minimal downtime.
- **Rollback:** If problems arise after the switch, you can quickly roll back by redirecting traffic back to the old environment ("blue").

How CodePipeline Facilitates Blue/Green Deployments:

- **Automated Environment Updates:** CodePipeline can be configured to automate the deployment to the inactive environment.
- **Traffic Switching:** While CodePipeline doesn't directly handle traffic switching, it can be integrated with services like Route 53 or load balancers to automate the traffic switch.
- **Example:** A CodePipeline could deploy new code to a "green" environment, run integration tests against it, and then trigger a Route 53 DNS update to redirect traffic from the "blue" environment to the "green" environment.

Benefits:

- **Zero Downtime:** Because traffic is switched rather than services restarted, users experience no downtime during deployments.
- **Reduced Risk:** The ability to quickly roll back to the previous environment minimizes the impact of deployment issues.

Rollback Mechanisms

Implementing automated rollback strategies within the pipeline for failed deployments.

Rollback Explanation:

- **Automated Response:** When a deployment fails (e.g., tests fail, health checks indicate problems), the pipeline automatically triggers a rollback to the previous working version of the application or infrastructure.
- **Minimize Impact:** Rollbacks aim to minimize the impact of failed deployments by quickly restoring the system to a known good state.

How CodePipeline Implements Rollback Strategies:

- **Conditional Logic:** CodePipeline can include conditional logic to detect deployment failures.
- **Rollback Actions:** Based on defined conditions and CloudFormation or Terraform, rollback actions can involve redeploying the previous version of the application, reverting infrastructure changes, or performing other corrective measures.

- **Example:** If a CloudFormation stack update fails, a CodePipeline can automatically trigger a rollback of the stack to the previous working version.

Benefits:

- **Fast Recovery:** Automated rollbacks allow for rapid recovery from failed deployments.
- **Reduced Downtime:** By quickly restoring the system to a working state, rollbacks minimize downtime and disruption.

CodePipeline Example of a Rollback Functionality

```json
{
    "pipeline": {
        "stages": [
            {
                "name": "Deploy",
                "actions": [
                    {
                        "name": "CloudFormationCreateOrUpdate",
                        "actionTypeId": {
                            "category": "Deploy",
                            "owner": "AWS",
                            "provider": "CloudFormation",
                            "version": "1"
                        },
                        "configuration": {
                            "ActionMode": "CREATE_UPDATE",
                            "Capabilities": "CAPABILITY_IAM",
                            "StackName": "MyWebAppStack",
                            "TemplatePath": "BuiltArtifact::template.yaml"
                        },
                        "runOrder": 1,
                        "inputArtifacts": [
                            {
                                "name": "BuiltArtifact"
                            }
                        ]
                    }
                ]
            }
        ]
    }
}
```

Explanation If the CloudFormation stack cannot be updated or creation fails, CloudFormation automatically tries to roll back to the previous working state and reverts the changes, the stack automatically rolls back to its last known good state.

By implementing automated deployment strategies, incorporating infrastructure as code, integrating continuous testing, and including blue/green deployments with rollback mechanisms, AWS CodePipeline enables faster, more reliable, and less risky software releases.

Infrastructure as Code (IaC) Integration

Infrastructure as Code (IaC) is a core practice for modern cloud deployments, especially when working with CI/CD pipelines on AWS using CodePipeline. It involves managing and provisioning your infrastructure through machine-readable definition files, rather than manual configuration. This approach brings several crucial advantages to your system design on AWS.

Pipelines deploy infrastructure changes defined in CloudFormation or Terraform.

Instead of manually clicking through the AWS Management Console to create or modify resources like EC2 instances, databases, or networking components, you define these resources in code. Two popular tools for achieving this on AWS are CloudFormation and Terraform.

- **CloudFormation:** This is AWS's native IaC service. You define your infrastructure in a JSON or YAML template, and CloudFormation provisions and manages those resources on AWS.
- **Terraform:** This is a third-party tool that supports multiple cloud providers, including AWS. You define your infrastructure using Terraform's HashiCorp Configuration Language (HCL), and Terraform manages the provisioning across those providers.

When integrating with CodePipeline, your infrastructure definitions (CloudFormation templates or Terraform configurations) are stored in a repository like AWS CodeCommit or GitHub. The pipeline is configured to automatically deploy these definitions whenever changes are pushed to the repository.

Example: CloudFormation Template Snippet

```
Resources:
  MyEC2Instance:
    Type: AWS::EC2::Instance
    Properties:
      ImageId: ami-xxxxxxxxxxxxxxxxx # Replace with your AMI ID
      InstanceType: t2.micro
      KeyName: MyKeyPair # Replace with your KeyPair name
```

This simple CloudFormation template defines an EC2 instance. It specifies the instance type, the AMI to use, and the key pair for SSH access. When this template is deployed through CodePipeline, CloudFormation will create the EC2 instance based on these parameters.

Example: Terraform Configuration Snippet

```
resource "aws_instance" "example" {
  ami           = "ami-xxxxxxxxxxxxxxxxx" # Replace with your AMI ID
  instance_type = "t2.micro"
  key_name      = "MyKeyPair" # Replace with your KeyPair name
}
```

This Terraform configuration achieves the same result as the CloudFormation template above: creating an EC2 instance. Both are representations of code.

Ensures repeatable and version-controlled infrastructure provisioning.

One of the most significant benefits of IaC is repeatability. By defining your infrastructure in code, you can consistently recreate the same environment multiple times. This is crucial for development, testing, and production environments. If you need a new environment for testing a feature, you can simply execute the same CloudFormation template or Terraform configuration, ensuring that the environment is identical to your production environment.

Version control is another key advantage. Because your infrastructure is defined in code, you can store it in a version control system like Git. This allows you to track changes to your infrastructure over time, revert to previous versions if necessary, and collaborate with other team members on infrastructure changes.

Sketch of Version Control with IaC

```
+--------------------+      +--------------------+      +--------------------+
| Developer A        |----->| Version Control    |----->| CodePipeline       |----->| AWS Env
| (Changes IaC)      |      | (Git: CodeCommit/GitHub)|  | (Deploys Changes) |----->| (Infr
+--------------------+      +--------------------+      +--------------------+

                                     ^
                                     |
+--------------------+      +--------------------+
| Developer B        |<-----| Version Control    |
| (Pulls/Pushes IaC) |      | (Git: CodeCommit/GitHub)|
+--------------------+      +--------------------+
```

This sketch illustrates how multiple developers can collaborate on infrastructure changes using a version control system. Changes are tracked, and CodePipeline ensures that those changes are automatically deployed to your AWS environment.

In essence, IaC integration into your CI/CD pipeline through tools like CloudFormation and Terraform brings consistency, reliability, and auditability to your infrastructure management process. This is paramount for effective system design on AWS, reducing errors, and accelerating the delivery of your applications.

Continuous Testing & Validation

Integrating automated testing (unit, integration, security) in pipeline stages. Improves application quality and reduces deployment risks.

Concept:

Continuous Testing & Validation is a critical component of CI/CD pipelines. It involves automatically executing various types of tests at different stages of the pipeline to ensure the application being deployed meets quality standards and doesn't introduce vulnerabilities. This proactive approach significantly reduces the risk of deploying faulty or insecure code to production environments.

Breaking down the types of testing:

- **Unit Tests:** These tests focus on individual components or functions of the application. The goal is to verify that each unit of code works as expected in isolation.

  - *Example:* Imagine you have a function that calculates the total price of items in a shopping cart. A unit test for this function would involve passing different sets of item prices and quantities to the function and asserting that it returns the correct total price.

  - *Code Example (Python):*

    ```python
    def calculate_total(price, quantity):
        return price  quantity

    def test_calculate_total():
        assert calculate_total(10, 2) == 20
        assert calculate_total(5.5, 3) == 16.5
        assert calculate_total(0, 10) == 0
    ```

- **Integration Tests:** These tests verify that different components or modules of the application work correctly together. They focus on the interactions between different parts of the system.

  - *Example:* Consider a web application that uses a database. An integration test would verify that the application can successfully connect to the database, retrieve data, and store data correctly.

  - *Sketch:*

```
[Web App Component] <--> [Database Component]
  | Integration Test  |
  --------------------->  Verify interaction
```

- **Security Tests:** These tests identify potential security vulnerabilities in the application. They can include static code analysis, dynamic application security testing (DAST), and vulnerability scanning.

  - *Example:* A security test might check for common vulnerabilities such as SQL injection, cross-site scripting (XSS), or insecure authentication mechanisms. A tool like OWASP ZAP could be integrated into the pipeline to perform dynamic scanning of the deployed application.
  - *Sketch:*

```
[Deployed Application] --> [OWASP ZAP]
            |Security Test|
            ---------------->Detecting vulnerabilities
```

Pipeline Integration:

These tests are integrated into different stages of the CodePipeline.

1. **Source Stage:** Not applicable to testing itself, but where code changes trigger the pipeline and subsequent tests.
2. **Build Stage:** Unit tests are commonly executed during the build stage. This allows for quick feedback on the code quality before proceeding to more complex tests.
3. **Test Stage:** Integration and security tests are typically executed in a dedicated test stage. This stage might involve deploying the application to a test environment and running automated tests against it.

Benefits:

- **Improved Application Quality:** By identifying and fixing defects early in the development cycle, continuous testing leads to higher-quality applications.
- **Reduced Deployment Risks:** Automated testing reduces the risk of deploying faulty code to production environments, minimizing potential disruptions.
- **Faster Feedback Loops:** Developers receive immediate feedback on their code changes, allowing them to fix issues quickly and efficiently.
- **Increased Confidence:** Continuous testing provides confidence in the application's reliability and security, enabling faster and more frequent deployments.

Configuration Example (Conceptual):

While specific configuration will depend on the testing tools and AWS services used, the following is a conceptual representation of how testing might be integrated:

```
# Simplified Pipeline Definition (Conceptual)

stages:
  - name: Build
    actions:
      - name: CompileAndUnitTest
        action_type_id: # ... appropriate for CodeBuild
        configuration:
          commands:
            - ./build.sh #compile the code
            - ./run_unit_tests.sh #execute unit tests
            - if [ $? -ne 0 ]; then exit 1; fi # Exit if tests fail

  - name: Test
```

```
actions:
  - name: DeployToTestEnv
    action_type_id: # ... appropriate deployment action
    configuration:
      # ... deploy configurations

  - name: RunIntegrationTests
    action_type_id: # ... appropriate for CodeBuild
    configuration:
      commands:
        - ./run_integration_tests.sh #execute integration tests
        - if [ $? -ne 0 ]; then exit 1; fi # Exit if tests fail

  - name: RunSecurityScan
    action_type_id: # ... appropriate for security scanning tool
    configuration:
      commands:
        - ./run_security_scan.sh # execute security scan
        - if [ $? -ne 0 ]; then exit 1; fi # Exit if tests fail
```

Conclusion:

Continuous Testing & Validation is not just about running tests; it's about building a culture of quality throughout the development process. By automating testing and integrating it into the CI/CD pipeline, teams can deliver higher-quality applications faster and with greater confidence. Failing tests should halt the pipeline, preventing faulty deployments. The exact configuration will depend on the specific tools and languages used in your project.

Blue/Green Deployments

CodePipeline can make "blue/green deployments" much easier to manage. Let's break down what that means and how it works.

What is Blue/Green Deployment?

Imagine you have two identical environments: one is "blue," and the other is "green." Only one of these environments is live and serving traffic to your users at any given time. Let's say "blue" is currently live.

Environment	Status	Traffic	Version
Blue	**Live**	100%	v1
Green	Idle (Staging)	0%	v1

When you want to deploy a new version of your application (let's call it v2), you deploy it to the "green" environment. The "green" environment becomes a staging environment. You perform all your testing and validation in this environment.

Environment	Status	Traffic	Version
Blue	Live	100%	v1
Green	**Staging**	0%	v2

Once you're confident that v2 is working correctly in the "green" environment, you switch the traffic so that it goes to the "green" environment instead of the "blue" environment. The "green" environment becomes live.

Environment	Status	Traffic	Version
Blue	Idle	0%	v1
Green	**Live**	100%	v2

Benefits of Blue/Green Deployment

- **Zero Downtime:** Because the new version is deployed and tested in a separate environment, there is no downtime when you switch traffic.

- **Reduced Risk:** If something goes wrong with the new version, you can quickly switch traffic back to the "blue" environment, which is still running the old version. This minimizes the impact on your users.
- **Simplified Rollbacks:** Rolling back is as simple as switching traffic back to the previous environment.

How CodePipeline Facilitates Blue/Green Deployments

CodePipeline can automate the entire blue/green deployment process. Here's a basic outline of how it would work:

1. **Source Stage:** CodePipeline detects a change in your source code repository (e.g., GitHub, CodeCommit).
2. **Build Stage:** CodePipeline builds your application and creates deployment artifacts.
3. **Deploy to Green Stage:** CodePipeline deploys the new version of your application to the "green" environment. This might involve deploying to a separate set of EC2 instances, containers, or a new environment in Elastic Beanstalk.
4. **Testing Stage:** CodePipeline runs automated tests against the "green" environment to ensure that the new version is working correctly.
5. **Switch Traffic Stage:** CodePipeline switches traffic from the "blue" environment to the "green" environment. This can be done using a load balancer (e.g., Elastic Load Balancing) or DNS changes.
6. **Monitoring Stage:** CodePipeline monitors the "green" environment to ensure that it is performing as expected.
7. **Idle Blue Stage**: Optionally CodePipeline can shut down or scale down the "blue" environment, if cost savings are needed.

Example: Using Elastic Beanstalk for Blue/Green Deployments

Elastic Beanstalk has built-in support for blue/green deployments. You can create two Elastic Beanstalk environments: one for "blue" and one for "green." CodePipeline can then be configured to deploy new versions of your application to the "green" environment and swap the environment URLs when you're ready to switch traffic.

Important Considerations

- **Database Migrations:** Blue/green deployments can be tricky when dealing with database migrations. You need to ensure that your database schema changes are backward-compatible so that both the "blue" and "green" environments can work with the same database.
- **Cost:** Maintaining two identical environments can be more expensive than a traditional deployment strategy. Consider the cost savings of reduced downtime and risk when evaluating blue/green deployments.

Code Example (CloudFormation Snippet)

This example shows how you might define an Elastic Load Balancer in CloudFormation to manage traffic switching in a blue/green deployment. Assume you have two Beanstalk environments named `BlueEnvironment` and `GreenEnvironment`.

```
Resources:
  MyLoadBalancer:
    Type: AWS::ElasticLoadBalancingV2::LoadBalancer
    Properties:
      Subnets: !Ref SubnetIds  # Replace with your Subnet IDs
      SecurityGroups: !Ref SecurityGroupIds # Replace with your Security Group IDs

  Listener:
    Type: AWS::ElasticLoadBalancingV2::Listener
    Properties:
      LoadBalancerArn: !Ref MyLoadBalancer
      Protocol: HTTP
      Port: 80
      DefaultActions:
        - Type: forward
```

```
        TargetGroupArn: !Ref BlueTargetGroup # Initial target group pointing to Blue

  BlueTargetGroup:
    Type: AWS::ElasticLoadBalancingV2::TargetGroup
    Properties:
      Port: 80
      Protocol: HTTP
      VpcId: !Ref VpcId  # Replace with your VPC ID
      Targets:
        - Id: !GetAtt BlueEnvironment.Instances.0  # Assuming a single instance for simplicity
          Port: 80

  GreenTargetGroup:
    Type: AWS::ElasticLoadBalancingV2::TargetGroup
    Properties:
      Port: 80
      Protocol: HTTP
      VpcId: !Ref VpcId  # Replace with your VPC ID
      Targets:
        - Id: !GetAtt GreenEnvironment.Instances.0  # Assuming a single instance for simplicity
          Port: 80
```

This CloudFormation template sets up a basic load balancer with two target groups: BlueTargetGroup and GreenTargetGroup. Initially, the listener forwards traffic to the BlueTargetGroup. To switch traffic to the green environment, you would update the Listener resource's DefaultActions to point to the GreenTargetGroup. CodePipeline can automate this update as part of its deployment process.

Sketch:

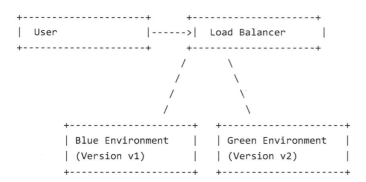

```
(Arrows indicate traffic flow.  During the switch, the LB target is changed)
```

Blue/green deployments are a powerful technique for reducing downtime and risk during deployments. CodePipeline can automate the process, making it easier to implement and manage. By automating the switch between environments, CodePipeline helps ensure your applications are always available and up-to-date.

Rollback Mechanisms

Implementing automated rollback strategies within the pipeline is crucial for mitigating risks associated with failed deployments. Rollback mechanisms allow you to quickly revert to a previously known stable state if a new deployment introduces errors or instability.

Why are Rollback Mechanisms Important?

Deployments are inherently risky. Even with thorough testing, unforeseen issues can arise in a production environment due to factors like unexpected traffic patterns, configuration inconsistencies, or integration problems with other services. Without a rollback mechanism, you're left scrambling to manually diagnose and fix the problem, potentially leading to significant downtime and user impact.

How Rollback Mechanisms Work in CodePipeline

The core principle of a rollback is to automatically revert to a previous, working version of your application or infrastructure. This usually involves the following steps:

1. **Detection of Failure:** The pipeline needs a way to determine if a deployment has failed. This can be achieved through automated tests, monitoring tools (like CloudWatch alarms), or manual approval gates.

2. **Triggering the Rollback:** Once a failure is detected, the pipeline initiates the rollback process. This might involve executing a set of predefined steps designed to undo the changes made by the failed deployment.

3. **Reverting to a Previous State:** The rollback process typically involves deploying a previously known good version of your application or infrastructure. This version might be stored in a repository like CodeCommit or S3.

4. **Verification:** After the rollback, the pipeline should perform automated tests to ensure that the system has successfully reverted to a stable state.

Example Scenarios and Implementation

Let's consider a few scenarios and how rollbacks can be implemented in CodePipeline:

- **Application Deployment (Blue/Green):** In a blue/green deployment, you have two identical environments: blue (the current production environment) and green (the new deployment environment). If the deployment to the green environment fails (e.g., automated tests fail after deployment), the rollback mechanism simply avoids switching traffic to the green environment and continues serving traffic from the blue environment. The failed green environment can then be investigated and fixed before attempting another deployment.

- **Infrastructure Changes (CloudFormation):** If you're using CloudFormation to manage your infrastructure, a failed CloudFormation stack update can lead to service disruptions. CodePipeline can be configured to automatically initiate a CloudFormation stack rollback if the update fails. This reverts the stack to its previous working state.

- **Database Migrations:** Database migrations are often a delicate operation. A rollback mechanism can involve reverting the database schema to its previous state and restoring data from a backup if a migration fails. Note that this scenario requires careful planning and execution to avoid data loss.

Implementation Example (Conceptual)

Here's a simplified, conceptual example of how a rollback mechanism could be implemented in a CodePipeline stage using AWS CLI commands within a Lambda function:

```
import boto3

def lambda_handler(event, context):
    codepipeline = boto3.client('codepipeline')
    cloudformation = boto3.client('cloudformation')

    pipeline_name = event['PipelineName']
    stack_name = 'MyWebAppStack' #Example name

    try:
        # Attempt to rollback the CloudFormation stack
```

```
        cloudformation.update_stack(
            StackName=stack_name,
            UsePreviousTemplate=True, # Use the previous template version
            Parameters=[
                {
                    'ParameterKey': 'EnvironmentType',
                    'ParameterValue': 'Production'
                }
            ],
            Capabilities=['CAPABILITY_IAM', 'CAPABILITY_NAMED_IAM', 'CAPABILITY_AUTO_EXPAND']
        )
        print(f"Rollback initiated for stack: {stack_name}")

    except Exception as e:
        print(f"Error initiating rollback: {e}")
        # Fail the CodePipeline stage
        codepipeline.put_job_failure_result(
            jobId=event['JobId'],
            failureDetails={
                'type': 'JobFailed',
                'message': f"Rollback failed: {e}"
            }
        )
        return

    # Mark the CodePipeline stage as successful (rollback initiated)
    codepipeline.put_job_success_result(jobId=event['JobId'])
    return
```

Explanation:

1. **boto3.client('codepipeline') and boto3.client('cloudformation'):** Create clients for interacting with CodePipeline and CloudFormation respectively.
2. **pipeline_name = event['PipelineName'] and stack_name = 'MyWebAppStack':** Get necessary details from the event passed to the Lambda function.
3. **cloudformation.update_stack(...):** This is the crucial part. The UsePreviousTemplate=True argument tells CloudFormation to revert to the previous working template.
4. **Exception Handling:** The try...except block handles potential errors during the rollback process. If the rollback fails, the CodePipeline stage is marked as failed, stopping the pipeline.
5. **Parameters:** Parameters array will let you pass the parameter needed for stack rollback.
6. **Capabilities** Capabilities values allows you to tell cloudformation that stack will be created with IAM roles.

Important Considerations:

- **Database Rollbacks:** Rolling back database changes can be extremely complex and may involve data loss. Carefully plan and test your database rollback strategy. Consider using techniques like shadow tables or transactional DDL to minimize the risk of data loss.
- **Stateful Applications:** For applications that maintain state (e.g., using databases or caches), rolling back may require additional steps to ensure data consistency.
- **Monitoring and Alerting:** Implement robust monitoring and alerting to detect failures quickly and trigger rollbacks automatically.
- **Testing:** Thoroughly test your rollback mechanisms to ensure they work as expected in various failure scenarios.
- **Considerations for other Resources** The rollback must be carefully considered based on the resources created.

Benefits of Automated Rollbacks:

- **Reduced Downtime:** Rollbacks can quickly restore service after a failed deployment, minimizing downtime.
- **Reduced Risk:** Automated rollbacks provide a safety net, allowing you to deploy changes with greater confidence.
- **Improved Reliability:** By quickly recovering from failures, rollbacks improve the overall reliability of your system.
- **Faster Time to Recovery:** Rollbacks automate the recovery process, reducing the time it takes to restore service.

By implementing robust rollback mechanisms within your CI/CD pipelines, you can significantly improve the stability and reliability of your applications and infrastructure on AWS.

Chapter 22 Advanced Use Cases and Real-World Scenarios-Security and Compliance: Meeting Regulatory Requirements

- **Compliance as Code:**

  - Automate security controls and compliance checks using AWS Config, CloudFormation, and custom scripts.

- **Data Residency & Sovereignty:**

  - Design architectures that ensure data stays within specific geographic regions using AWS Regions and services like S3 Object Lock.

- **Encryption Strategies:**

  - Implement comprehensive encryption at rest and in transit using KMS, CloudHSM, and TLS/SSL.

- **Identity and Access Management (IAM) Best Practices:**

  - Employ least privilege principle, role-based access control (RBAC), and multi-factor authentication (MFA) for enhanced security.

- **Audit Logging and Monitoring:**

  - Centralize logging with CloudWatch Logs and AWS CloudTrail for auditing and incident response, integrate with SIEM solutions.

Compliance as Code

Compliance as Code transforms security and regulatory compliance from a manual, often reactive process into an automated, proactive one. It involves defining compliance requirements as code, which can then be automatically checked and enforced. This approach significantly reduces the risk of human error, speeds up audit processes, and provides continuous visibility into the compliance posture of your infrastructure and applications.

Automate security controls and compliance checks using AWS Config, CloudFormation, and custom scripts.

This core aspect of Compliance as Code leverages the power of automation to ensure that your AWS environment adheres to your defined security and compliance standards. We accomplish this by using tools like AWS Config, CloudFormation, and custom scripts.

- **AWS Config:** Think of AWS Config as your environment's watchful eye. It continuously monitors the configuration of your AWS resources, comparing them against your desired state. For example, you might require that all S3 buckets are encrypted. AWS Config can detect any unencrypted buckets and flag them as non-compliant. You can even set it up to automatically remediate the issue.

  - *Example:* Suppose you need to ensure all your EC2 instances have a specific security group attached. You could define a Config rule that checks for this. If an instance is launched without the correct security group, AWS Config would highlight the violation, and you could configure it to automatically attach the missing security group.

- **CloudFormation:** CloudFormation allows you to define your infrastructure as code. You specify the resources you need (EC2 instances, databases, networks, etc.) and their configurations in a template. This ensures that your infrastructure is consistently deployed and configured according to your compliance requirements.

  - *Example:* Instead of manually creating an RDS database instance each time, you can create a CloudFormation template that defines the database's size, engine version, storage encryption, and backup settings. Every time you use this template, you're guaranteed to have a compliant database instance.

- **Custom Scripts:** While AWS Config and CloudFormation provide powerful built-in capabilities, sometimes you need more flexibility. Custom scripts allow you to perform specialized compliance checks and enforce specific policies that are not covered by the standard tools. These scripts can be written in languages like Python, Bash, or PowerShell, and can be triggered by AWS Lambda functions or other services.

  - *Example:* Let's say you have a requirement to regularly scan your EC2 instances for specific vulnerabilities. You can write a Python script that uses a vulnerability scanning tool, such as OpenVAS, to scan the instances. You can then schedule this script to run regularly using a Lambda function and store the results in a database for auditing purposes.

Code Example (Python Script for S3 Encryption Check):

```python
import boto3

def check_s3_encryption(bucket_name):
    """
    Checks if an S3 bucket has encryption enabled.
    """
    s3 = boto3.client('s3')
    try:
        encryption = s3.get_bucket_encryption(Bucket=bucket_name)
        if 'ServerSideEncryptionConfiguration' in encryption:
            return True
        else:
            return False
    except Exception as e:
```

```
        # Bucket may not have encryption configured
        return False

# Example usage
bucket_name = 'your-bucket-name'
if check_s3_encryption(bucket_name):
    print(f"Bucket {bucket_name} is encrypted.")
else:
    print(f"Bucket {bucket_name} is NOT encrypted.")
```

In essence, Compliance as Code allows you to encode your compliance requirements, creating a system where your infrastructure is constantly monitored and adjusted to meet those requirements. This leads to improved security, reduced risk, and more efficient compliance management.

Data Residency & Sovereignty

Data residency and data sovereignty are crucial considerations when designing and deploying applications in the cloud, especially when dealing with sensitive data or operating in regulated industries. They dictate where your data is physically stored and who has jurisdiction over it. AWS provides tools and services to help you meet these requirements.

Concept: Design architectures that ensure data stays within specific geographic regions using AWS Regions and services like S3 Object Lock.

Explanation:

Data residency refers to the physical location where your data is stored. Data sovereignty goes a step further, asserting that the data is subject to the laws and regulations of the country or region where it resides. Meeting these requirements often involves restricting data storage and processing to specific geographic locations.

AWS Regions for Geographic Control:

AWS Regions are geographically isolated locations around the world where AWS services are hosted. Each Region consists of multiple Availability Zones, which are physically separate data centers. By choosing the appropriate AWS Region, you can control where your data is stored and processed.

- **Example:** If your application needs to comply with European data protection laws like GDPR, you would choose an AWS Region located within Europe (e.g., Frankfurt, Ireland, London, Paris, Stockholm, or Milan).

S3 Object Lock for Data Retention and Compliance:

Amazon S3 Object Lock is a service that allows you to store objects using a Write Once Read Many (WORM) model. This means that once an object is locked, it cannot be deleted or modified for a specified retention period or indefinitely. This is useful for meeting regulatory and compliance requirements related to data retention.

- **Example:** To retain log files for auditing purposes, as mandated by industry regulations or government standards. You can create retention policies in S3 to retain objects/data for specific period of time.
- **Concept Sketch:** A visual representation of data residency with AWS Regions and S3 Object Lock might look like this:

```
+--------------------+      +--------------------+
|  AWS Region (Europe) |      |  AWS Region (USA)   |
|  Data Stored Here   |      |  Data Stored Here   |
|  (e.g., Frankfurt)  |      |  (e.g., US East)    |
+---------+---------+      +---------+---------+
          |                          |
          |  Data Residency          |
          |  Compliance with         |
```

```
     | European Laws      |
           v                    v
+---------------------+  +---------------------+
| S3 Bucket with      |  | S3 Bucket           |
| Object Lock Enabled |  |                     |
| (WORM Compliant)    |  |                     |
+---------------------+  +---------------------+

    [Data] --> [AWS Region] --> [S3 with Object Lock]
```

- **Code example:** To set Object Lock retention using AWS CLI:

```
aws s3api put-object-retention \
    --bucket my-example-bucket \
    --key my-image.jpg \
    --retention '{"Mode": "GOVERNANCE", "RetainUntilDate": "2025-01-01T00:00:00.000Z"}'
```

This command locks the object "my-image.jpg" in the "my-example-bucket" S3 bucket until January 1, 2025, in Governance mode, which requires special permissions to bypass.

Other AWS Services for Data Residency:

Several other AWS services can be configured to ensure data residency:

- **RDS and DynamoDB:** When using these database services, you specify the AWS Region where the data is stored.
- **CloudFront:** While CloudFront caches content globally, you can restrict the origin of the content to a specific AWS Region.
- **Snowball Edge/Snowcone:** For scenarios where data needs to be processed or stored in environments with limited or no network connectivity, Snowball Edge and Snowcone devices can be used. Data can then be transferred to a specific AWS Region later.

Considerations and Best Practices:

- **Data Replication and Backup:** When replicating or backing up data across regions for disaster recovery or other purposes, carefully consider the implications for data residency. Ensure that the replicated data also complies with the relevant regulations.
- **Data Processing:** Ensure that data processing activities also occur within the designated geographic region. For example, if you are using Lambda functions to process data, make sure the functions are deployed in the same region as the data.
- **Legal and Regulatory Compliance:** Consult with legal and compliance experts to fully understand the data residency and sovereignty requirements applicable to your business and industry.
- **Documentation:** Maintain clear documentation of your data residency and sovereignty strategy, including the AWS Regions used, the data stored in each region, and the controls implemented to ensure compliance.

By carefully selecting AWS Regions and utilizing services like S3 Object Lock, you can design architectures that meet your data residency and sovereignty requirements, enabling you to operate globally while complying with local regulations.

Encryption Strategies

This section focuses on how to protect your data using encryption, both when it's stored (at rest) and when it's being transmitted (in transit). We'll cover the tools and techniques you can use within AWS to achieve this.

Implement comprehensive encryption at rest and in transit using KMS, CloudHSM, and TLS/SSL.

Let's break this down. "Comprehensive" means we need a thorough approach, considering all aspects of data security. "Encryption at rest" refers to encrypting data when it's sitting on storage, like hard drives or databases.

"Encryption in transit" refers to encrypting data while it's moving between systems, like over the internet or within your AWS environment. The tools mentioned are KMS, CloudHSM, and TLS/SSL.

Encryption at Rest

Encryption at rest protects your data from unauthorized access if someone were to gain physical access to your storage devices or unauthorized access to your AWS account. Think of it like locking a safe where you keep your valuables.

- **Key Management Service (KMS):** AWS KMS is a managed service that makes it easy for you to create and control the encryption keys used to encrypt your data. It allows you to centrally manage keys, define usage policies, and audit key usage. KMS integrates with many other AWS services, making encryption straightforward.

  - **Example:** You can encrypt an S3 bucket using KMS. When you upload an object to the bucket, it is automatically encrypted using a key managed by KMS. When someone tries to download the object, S3 uses KMS to decrypt it on the fly, as long as the user has the necessary permissions.

    ```python
    # Example using boto3 (AWS SDK for Python) to create a KMS key
    import boto3

    kms_client = boto3.client('kms')

    response = kms_client.create_key(
        Description='My encryption key for S3 bucket',
        KeyUsage='ENCRYPT_DECRYPT',
        Origin='AWS_KMS'
    )

    key_id = response['KeyMetadata']['KeyId']
    print(f"KMS Key ID: {key_id}")
    #Store the key id securely and use it in s3 bucket policy and encryption
    ```

    Sketch:

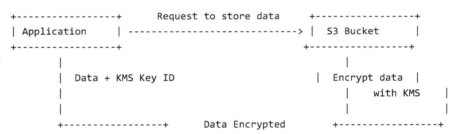

- **CloudHSM:** CloudHSM (Hardware Security Module) provides dedicated hardware appliances within AWS where you can generate and store your encryption keys. It gives you greater control over your keys compared to KMS, because the keys are stored in tamper-evident hardware. This is often used for compliance reasons or when you need the highest level of security and control.

  - **Example:** If your organization has strict regulatory requirements regarding key management (e.g., FIPS 140-2 Level 3 compliance), you might use CloudHSM. You can then integrate CloudHSM with databases like Oracle or SQL Server to encrypt data at rest.

    - Use cloudhsm with SDK like boto3, that will ask us to create a cluster, HSM instance, and security groups.

```
# Example of using boto3 to describe CloudHSM cluster
import boto3

cloudhsm_client = boto3.client('cloudhsmv2', region_name='your-region')

try:
    response = cloudhsm_client.describe_clusters(
        Filters={
            'clusterIds': ['your-cluster-id']
        }
    )
    print(response)

except Exception as e:
    print(f"Error describing cluster: {e}")
```

Sketch:

```
+-----------------+      Request to store data    +-----------------+
| Application     | ----------------------------> | Database Server |
+-----------------+                               +-----------------+
         |                                                  |
         | Data                                             | Encrypt data  |
         |                                                  |   with CloudHSM|
         |                                                  |               |
+-----------------+      Request Key              +-----------------+
|   CloudHSM      |<--------------------------------| Database Server |
+-----------------+                               +-----------------+
```

Encryption in Transit

Encryption in transit protects your data while it's being transmitted over a network. This prevents eavesdropping and ensures data integrity.

- **TLS/SSL:** TLS (Transport Layer Security) and its predecessor SSL (Secure Sockets Layer) are cryptographic protocols that provide secure communication over a network. You use TLS/SSL to encrypt the connection between a client (e.g., a web browser) and a server (e.g., a web server). This ensures that data transmitted between them is protected from eavesdropping.

    o **Example:** When you access a website using HTTPS, you are using TLS/SSL. The web server presents a digital certificate to your browser, which verifies the server's identity and establishes an encrypted connection. All data exchanged between your browser and the server is then encrypted.

    Sketch:

- **Implementation:** AWS Certificate Manager (ACM) lets you easily provision, manage, and deploy SSL/TLS certificates for use with AWS services like Elastic Load Balancing, Amazon CloudFront, and Amazon API Gateway. You can request a certificate from ACM or import a certificate that you obtained from a third-party certificate authority.

```python
#Example using boto3 to request a certificate with ACM
import boto3
acm_client = boto3.client('acm', region_name='your-region')

try:
    response = acm_client.request_certificate(
        DomainName='example.com',
        ValidationMethod='DNS',
        SubjectAlternativeNames=['www.example.com']
    )
    certificate_arn = response['CertificateArn']
    print(f"Certificate ARN: {certificate_arn}")

except Exception as e:
    print(f"Error requesting certificate: {e}")
```

Choosing the Right Encryption Strategy

The best encryption strategy depends on your specific security requirements, compliance obligations, and budget.

- **KMS** is a good choice for most use cases due to its ease of use and integration with other AWS services.
- **CloudHSM** is appropriate when you need dedicated hardware for key management and greater control over your keys.
- **TLS/SSL** is essential for securing communication over the internet and within your AWS environment.

By implementing comprehensive encryption strategies, you can significantly enhance the security of your data and protect it from unauthorized access and disclosure. Remember to regularly review and update your encryption practices to keep pace with evolving threats and best practices.

Identity and Access Management (IAM) Best Practices

IAM is crucial for controlling who can access your AWS resources and what they can do with them. Think of it as the gatekeeper to your cloud environment. Implementing IAM best practices significantly strengthens your security posture. This section dives into key IAM principles to keep your AWS resources safe.

Employ least privilege principle

The principle of least privilege means granting users only the minimum necessary permissions to perform their job. Don't give everyone administrative access! This limits the potential damage if an account is compromised. For example, if a developer only needs to read data from an S3 bucket, give them read-only access, not full S3 control.

Illustration:

Imagine a building with many rooms. Least privilege is like giving each person only the key to the rooms they need to access, rather than a master key to every room.

Code Example (IAM Policy):

```json
{
    "Version": "2012-10-17",
    "Statement": [
        {
            "Effect": "Allow",
```

```
            "Action": "s3:GetObject",
            "Resource": "arn:aws:s3:::your-bucket-name/"
        }
    ]
}
```

This policy allows a user to only get (read) objects from a specific S3 bucket. It doesn't allow them to list the bucket contents, upload files, or delete anything. If they need to list the bucket contents, a separate statement with `s3:ListBucket` action would be required.

Role-based access control (RBAC)

RBAC simplifies access management by assigning permissions to roles rather than individual users. Users are then assigned to these roles. When a user needs certain permissions, you assign them the appropriate role. This makes it easier to manage permissions across your organization. Changes to permissions are made at the role level, automatically affecting all users assigned to that role.

Illustration:

Think of roles like job titles. A "Database Administrator" role has permissions to manage databases. A "Developer" role has permissions to deploy code. Users are assigned to these roles based on their responsibilities.

Code Example (Creating an IAM Role with CloudFormation):

```
Resources:
  MyRole:
    Type: AWS::IAM::Role
    Properties:
      RoleName: MyWebAppRole
      AssumeRolePolicyDocument:
        Version: "2012-10-17"
        Statement:
          - Effect: Allow
            Principal:
              Service:
                - ec2.amazonaws.com
            Action: sts:AssumeRole
      Policies:
        - PolicyName: WebAppPolicy
          PolicyDocument:
            Version: "2012-10-17"
            Statement:
              - Effect: Allow
                Action:
                  - "s3:GetObject"
                Resource: "arn:aws:s3:::your-webapp-bucket/"
```

This CloudFormation snippet creates an IAM role that an EC2 instance can assume. The role is granted permissions to read objects from a specific S3 bucket.

Multi-factor authentication (MFA)

MFA adds an extra layer of security by requiring users to provide two or more authentication factors. Typically, this involves something they know (password) and something they have (a code from a mobile app or a hardware token). This makes it much harder for attackers to gain access to accounts, even if they have stolen the password. Enable MFA for all users, especially those with administrative privileges.

Illustration:

Imagine a safe that requires both a key *and* a combination to open. Even if someone gets the key, they still need the combination. MFA is like that combination lock.

There are three main ways to enable MFA on AWS:

1. **Virtual MFA:** Use an authenticator app (like Google Authenticator or Authy) on your smartphone.
2. **Hardware MFA:** Use a physical device that generates one-time passwords (like a YubiKey).
3. **U2F Security Key:** Use a USB security key.

Enabling MFA for a user is done directly in the IAM console for each user or programmatically through the AWS CLI or SDKs. There is no sample code applicable here; the setup is through the AWS IAM User interface.

Audit Logging and Monitoring

Centralized logging and monitoring are crucial for maintaining security, achieving compliance, and enabling effective incident response in cloud environments. AWS provides powerful tools such as CloudWatch Logs and AWS CloudTrail to achieve this. By centralizing logs and integrating them with Security Information and Event Management (SIEM) solutions, you can gain comprehensive visibility into your AWS infrastructure and applications.

Centralize logging with CloudWatch Logs and AWS CloudTrail for auditing and incident response:

- **CloudWatch Logs:** This service allows you to collect and monitor log data from various sources, including applications, operating systems, and AWS services. It enables you to store, analyze, and visualize log data, helping you identify potential security issues, troubleshoot application errors, and monitor performance.

  - **Example:** Suppose you have an application running on EC2 instances. You can configure the CloudWatch Agent on each instance to send application logs, system logs, and custom logs to CloudWatch Logs. Within CloudWatch Logs, you can create log groups for different applications or environments, making it easier to manage and analyze your log data.

  ```
  EC2 Instance -> CloudWatch Agent -> CloudWatch Logs
  ```

  - **Practical Example**: Configuring CloudWatch Agent on an EC2 instance:

    1. **Install the CloudWatch Agent**: Use the AWS CLI or Systems Manager to install the agent.

       ```
       sudo yum update -y
       sudo yum install -y amazon-cloudwatch-agent
       ```

    2. **Configure the Agent**: Create a configuration file (`/opt/aws/amazon-cloudwatch-agent/etc/amazon-cloudwatch-agent.json`) to specify which logs to collect.

       ```
       {
         "agent": {
           "metrics_collection_interval": 60,
           "run_as_user": "cwagent"
         },
         "logs": {
           "logs_collected": {
             "files": {
               "collect_list": [
                 {
                   "file_path": "/var/log/messages",
                   "log_group_name": "SystemLogs",
                   "log_stream_name": "{instance_id}"
       ```

```
            },
            {
              "file_path": "/var/log/httpd/access_log",
              "log_group_name": "HttpdAccessLogs",
              "log_stream_name": "{instance_id}"
            }
          ]
        }
      }
    }
}
```

3. **Start the Agent**: Use the following command to start the agent with your configuration.

```
sudo /opt/aws/amazon-cloudwatch-agent/bin/amazon-cloudwatch-agent-ctl -a fetch-con
```

- **AWS CloudTrail:** This service records API calls made within your AWS account and delivers log files to an S3 bucket. It captures information such as the identity of the caller, the time of the API call, the source IP address, and the request parameters. CloudTrail is essential for auditing, security monitoring, and compliance.

  - **Example:** If someone creates a new EC2 instance, modifies an IAM policy, or deletes an S3 bucket, CloudTrail will record these events. By analyzing CloudTrail logs, you can identify unauthorized activities, track changes to your infrastructure, and ensure compliance with regulatory requirements.

```
User/Application -> AWS API -> CloudTrail -> S3 Bucket
```

  - **Practical Example**: Configuring CloudTrail:

    1. **Enable CloudTrail**: Go to the CloudTrail service in the AWS Management Console.
    2. **Create a Trail**: Specify an S3 bucket where CloudTrail logs will be stored.
    3. **Configure Trail**: Choose to log all management events or specific events (e.g., data events for S3 buckets).

  Once enabled, CloudTrail automatically captures API activity and stores it in the specified S3 bucket. Here's an example CloudTrail event in JSON format:

```
{
  "eventVersion": "1.08",
  "userIdentity": {
    "type": "IAMUser",
    "principalId": "AIDACKCEVSQ6C2EXAMPLE",
    "arn": "arn:aws:iam::123456789012:user/Alice",
    "accountId": "123456789012",
    "accessKeyId": "AKIAIOSFODNN7EXAMPLE",
    "userName": "Alice"
  },
  "eventTime": "2024-01-26T12:00:00Z",
  "eventSource": "ec2.amazonaws.com",
  "eventName": "RunInstances",
  "awsRegion": "us-west-2",
  "sourceIPAddress": "203.0.113.0",
  "userAgent": "aws-cli/1.16.254 Python/2.7.16 Linux/4.14.133-113.105.amzn2.x86_64 bot(
  "requestParameters": {
    "instancesSet": {
      "items": [
        {
```

```
          "imageId": "ami-0abcdef1234567890",
          "minCount": 1,
          "maxCount": 1
        }
      ]
    },
    "launchSpecification": {
      "instanceType": "t2.micro",
      "placement": {
        "availabilityZone": "us-west-2a"
      },
      "securityGroupSet": {
        "items": [
          {
            "groupId": "sg-0abcdef1234567890"
          }
        ]
      },
      "subnetId": "subnet-0abcdef1234567890"
    }
  },
  "responseElements": {
    "instancesSet": {
      "items": [
        {
          "instanceId": "i-0abcdef1234567890"
        }
      ]
    }
  },
  "requestID": "12345678-1234-1234-1234-123456789012",
  "eventID": "12345678-1234-1234-1234-123456789012",
  "eventType": "AwsApiCall",
  "recipientAccountId": "123456789012"
}
```

Integrate with SIEM solutions:

- To effectively analyze and respond to security events, integrate CloudWatch Logs and CloudTrail with SIEM (Security Information and Event Management) solutions. SIEM solutions provide centralized dashboards, alerting capabilities, and advanced analytics to help you detect and respond to security threats in real-time.

  - **Example:** Splunk, QRadar, and Sumo Logic are popular SIEM solutions that can ingest log data from CloudWatch Logs and CloudTrail. By integrating these services, you can create custom alerts, perform threat hunting, and generate compliance reports.

```
CloudWatch Logs/CloudTrail -> SIEM (Splunk, QRadar, Sumo Logic) -> Security Dashboards & Al
```

  - **Practical Example**: Integrating CloudTrail with Splunk

    1. **Configure S3 Bucket for Splunk**: Ensure the S3 bucket containing CloudTrail logs is accessible by Splunk.

    2. **Install AWS Add-on for Splunk**: This add-on provides the necessary inputs and configurations for ingesting AWS data.

3. **Configure Input**: Create an S3 input in Splunk to read CloudTrail logs from the S3 bucket.

Here's a snippet from Splunk's `inputs.conf` file:

```
[aws:cloudtrail]
disabled = false
bucket_name = your-cloudtrail-bucket
interval = 300
sourcetype = aws:cloudtrail
index = main
```

4. **Analyze Logs**: Use Splunk's search language to analyze CloudTrail data, create dashboards, and set up alerts for specific events.

By following these guidelines, you can establish a robust audit logging and monitoring system in AWS, enhancing your security posture, ensuring compliance, and enabling rapid incident response.

Chapter 23 Advanced Use Cases and Real-World Scenarios-Disaster Recovery and Backup Strategies on AWS

- **Disaster Recovery (DR) Goals:**

  - RTO (Recovery Time Objective): Minimize downtime after a disaster.
  - RPO (Recovery Point Objective): Minimize data loss during a disaster.

- **Backup and Restore Strategies:** Implement regular data backups using services like S3, EBS snapshots, and RDS backups.

- **Multi-Region Active-Active:** Distribute applications across multiple AWS regions for continuous availability.

- **Pilot Light & Warm Standby:** Maintain a scaled-down environment or pre-configured infrastructure for faster recovery.

- **Testing and Automation:** Regularly test DR plans and automate failover procedures using services like CloudEndure DR.

Disaster Recovery (DR) Goals

Disaster Recovery (DR) goals are the core objectives you aim to achieve when preparing for and responding to a disaster. These goals define how quickly you need to recover and how much data loss you can tolerate. Two key metrics drive these goals: Recovery Time Objective (RTO) and Recovery Point Objective (RPO).

RTO (Recovery Time Objective): Minimize downtime after a disaster.

RTO represents the maximum acceptable time your application can be unavailable after a disaster. It's a measure of *how quickly* you need to get back up and running. A shorter RTO means less downtime, which is crucial for applications that require high availability.

Think of it this way: If your RTO is two hours, you must restore your application and make it accessible to users within two hours of a disaster occurring.

Example: An e-commerce website might have a very strict RTO (e.g., 15 minutes) because any downtime directly translates to lost sales. An internal reporting application, on the other hand, might have a more relaxed RTO (e.g., four hours) because the impact of downtime is less immediate.

To achieve a small RTO you can follow these steps:

1. **Identify Critical Application Components:** Identify components of an application that are crucial for the functionality of the overall application.

2. **Create a table:** After identifying all the components, create a table with components name, its importance on the application, dependencies of other components on it, and RTO of that component in minutes.

3. **Decide Technology:** Decide which AWS technologies or services will be used to recover it fast.

4. **Automate Recovery:** Automate the recovery mechanism by using Infrastructure as code.

5. **Continuous Drill and Improvement:** Perform disaster recovery drill frequently to test the recovery process.

RPO (Recovery Point Objective): Minimize data loss during a disaster.

RPO defines the maximum acceptable amount of data loss, measured in time. It specifies how far back in time you can go to recover your data. A shorter RPO means less data loss, which is vital for applications where data integrity is paramount.

Consider this: If your RPO is 15 minutes, you can only afford to lose a maximum of 15 minutes' worth of data in the event of a disaster. This means you must have backups or replication mechanisms in place that capture data changes at least every 15 minutes.

Example: A financial transaction processing system likely needs a very short RPO (e.g., a few seconds) to ensure that no financial transactions are lost. A less critical data archive might have a longer RPO (e.g., 24 hours) because the impact of data loss is less severe.

To achieve a small RPO you can follow these steps:

1. **Identify the Databases**: Identify databases that are being used in the application.
2. **Data Sensitiveness and backup requirment**: Now identify data sensitiveness and backup requirement of the database.
3. **Backup Schedule**: Create a backup schedule based on the database requirements.
4. **Use of right technology**: Use of right backup technology for the databases to store the backups.
5. **Regular monitoring**: Regular monitoring of backup health check to ensure the recoverablity.

RTO and RPO in Relation

RTO and RPO are often related, but not always perfectly correlated. They are linked as both are crucial aspects of DR planning that need to be addressed at the same time. You might achieve a fast RTO, but at the expense of a larger RPO (more data loss), or vice-versa. You should always aim to define both RTO and RPO to be low at the same time.

Illustrative Sketch

Here's a simple way to visualize these concepts, a timeline.

```
Time -->

[Disaster Strikes!]

|--------------------|----------------------|
RPO                  RTO
|--------------------|----------------------|
Data Lost            Downtime
|--------------------|----------------------|
Point of             Application
Last Backup           Restored
```

The segment labeled "RPO" represents the amount of data lost during a disaster which starts from the "Point of Last Backup". The Segment labeled "RTO" represents the application down time starting when Disaster stikes and when Application restores back.

Balancing RTO and RPO

Selecting the right RTO and RPO values involves a trade-off between cost and risk. Shorter RTOs and RPOs generally require more investment in infrastructure, redundancy, and automation. Therefore, it's essential to:

- **Assess the impact of downtime and data loss:** Quantify the financial and operational impact of both.
- **Determine business priorities:** Identify the most critical applications and data that require the fastest recovery and minimal data loss.
- **Evaluate the cost of different DR strategies:** Compare the cost of implementing solutions that meet different RTO and RPO targets.

By carefully considering these factors, you can establish DR goals that align with your business requirements and budget.

RTO (Recovery Time Objective)

The Recovery Time Objective (RTO) represents the target duration within which a business process *must* be restored after a disruption to avoid unacceptable consequences associated with a break in business continuity. In simpler terms, it's how long you can afford to be down after something goes wrong. Think of it as the deadline for getting your systems back up and running.

Understanding the Impact of RTO

A low RTO means you need to recover quickly, which usually requires more investment in sophisticated and automated recovery solutions. A high RTO indicates that the business can tolerate a longer outage, potentially allowing for simpler and less expensive recovery methods.

Consider an e-commerce website. If the website goes down, every minute of downtime translates to lost revenue. Therefore, an e-commerce business might have a very aggressive RTO (e.g., minutes or even seconds). On the other hand, an internal reporting system might have a more relaxed RTO (e.g., hours or days), as its downtime doesn't directly impact revenue generation.

Factors Influencing RTO

Several factors influence the RTO you choose:

- **Business Impact:** How critical is the application or system to the business? What are the financial and reputational consequences of downtime?

- **Cost:** Faster recovery often requires more expensive infrastructure and processes.

- **Complexity:** Complex systems may take longer to recover than simpler ones.

- **Regulatory Requirements:** Some industries have regulatory requirements for RTO.

Example Scenarios

Let's look at a few examples to illustrate the impact of RTO in different situations.

- **High-Frequency Trading Platform:** An RTO of *seconds* is crucial. Any longer, and the firm could miss critical trading opportunities and incur significant financial losses.

- **Hospital Patient Record System:** An RTO of *minutes* is essential. Doctors and nurses need immediate access to patient information to provide care.

- **Internal Email Server:** An RTO of *a few hours* might be acceptable. While email is important, a short delay in access won't critically impact most business operations.

- **Archived Data Storage:** An RTO of *a few days* is often acceptable. This data is not frequently accessed, so a longer recovery time is tolerable.

Strategies for Achieving RTO

Various DR strategies help you meet your RTO goals. Some common approaches include:

- **Multi-Region Active-Active:** Distributing applications across multiple AWS regions to achieve almost instantaneous failover. This is appropriate for extremely low RTO requirements.

- **Pilot Light:** Maintaining a minimal, always-on environment in a secondary region. When a disaster occurs, you quickly scale up this environment to handle production traffic.

- **Warm Standby:** Running a scaled-down but fully functional replica of your production environment in a secondary region. This allows for faster recovery than Pilot Light.

Testing Your RTO

It's crucial to *regularly test* your DR plans to ensure you can actually meet your RTO. Testing reveals any weaknesses in your recovery procedures and allows you to fine-tune them.

Code Example (Simulating RTO Impact)

While RTO is not directly represented in code, the *impact* of RTO can be simulated. This simple Python example models lost revenue based on downtime:

```
def calculate_lost_revenue(revenue_per_minute, downtime_minutes):
  """Calculates lost revenue due to downtime."""
  lost_revenue = revenue_per_minute  downtime_minutes
  return lost_revenue

# Example usage
revenue_per_minute = 1000  # Dollars
downtime_minutes = 60      # One hour of downtime

lost_revenue = calculate_lost_revenue(revenue_per_minute, downtime_minutes)
print(f"Lost revenue: ${lost_revenue}")
```

This code emphasizes the real-world impact of downtime, underlining the significance of a well-defined and achievable RTO. Reducing `downtime_minutes` by investing in robust DR mechanisms directly translates to reduced `lost_revenue`.

Sketch Example (Conceptual)

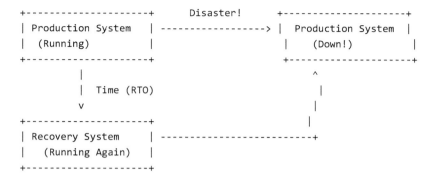

```
+--------------------+    Disaster!    +--------------------+
| Production System  | ----------------> | Production System  |
| (Running)          |                 |   (Down!)          |
+--------------------+                 +--------------------+
         |                                      ^
         |  Time (RTO)                          |
         v                                      |
+--------------------+                          |
| Recovery System    | -------------------------+
|  (Running Again)   |
+--------------------+
```

This simple sketch shows the sequence of events: the production system goes down, and the recovery system needs to be up and running within the defined RTO. The shorter the arrow representing "Time (RTO)", the better.

In summary, understanding and strategically planning for RTO is paramount for ensuring business continuity and minimizing the impact of unexpected disruptions. Regularly evaluate your RTO, test your recovery plans, and choose DR strategies that align with your business needs and budgetary constraints.

RPO (Recovery Point Objective)

RPO, or Recovery Point Objective, represents the *maximum acceptable amount of data loss*, measured in time. It defines how far back in time you might potentially have to go to recover your data in the event of a disaster. In simpler terms, it answers the question: "How much data are we willing to lose?"

To illustrate, consider a scenario: Imagine you have an e-commerce website. If your RPO is set to one hour, it means that in the worst-case scenario after a disaster, you could potentially lose up to one hour's worth of transactions. Conversely, if your RPO is 15 minutes, you're aiming to recover to a point where only the last 15 minutes of data are potentially unrecoverable.

The shorter the RPO, the more frequently you need to back up your data, and generally, the more complex and expensive your disaster recovery solution becomes. A very short RPO necessitates more frequent backups and potentially continuous data replication.

Consider a database: if your RPO is set to 1 hour, you might choose to perform transaction log backups every 15 minutes. In the event of a failure, you would restore the last full backup and then apply the transaction log backups up to the point just before the failure. The data loss would therefore be less than or equal to the RPO.

Here's a visual to help:

```
Time --------|--------|--------|--------|-------->
             ^        ^        ^        ^
        Backup 1 Backup 2 Backup 3 Backup 4

    RPO = Time between backups (e.g., 1 hour)
```

In this sketch, the arrows pointing up represent backups taken at regular intervals. The RPO is essentially the time between those backup points.

Let's put this into a code-related context. Assume you're writing a script to handle database backups:

```python
import time
import subprocess


def backup_database(database_name, backup_location):
    """
    Creates a database backup.
```

```
    Args:
      database_name: The name of the database to backup.
      backup_location: The location to store the backup.
    """
    timestamp = time.strftime("%Y%m%d-%H%M%S")
    backup_file = f"{backup_location}/{database_name}_{timestamp}.sql"

    try:
      # Replace with your actual database backup command
      command = f"pg_dump -U youruser -d {database_name} -f {backup_file}" #Example for postgres (
      subprocess.run(command, shell=True, check=True)
      print(f"Backup created: {backup_file}")
    except subprocess.CalledProcessError as e:
      print(f"Backup failed: {e}")

# Example usage with an RPO of 1 hour (backups every hour)
database_name = "my_application_db"
backup_location = "/mnt/backups"

while True:
  backup_database(database_name, backup_location)
  time.sleep(3600)  # Sleep for 1 hour (3600 seconds)
```

This Python code illustrates a scheduled database backup. Although simplified, it demonstrates the concept of taking backups regularly to meet a specific RPO. The `time.sleep(3600)` corresponds to an hourly RPO. In a real-world scenario, you'd likely use a more robust scheduling mechanism and error handling.

Choosing the right RPO is a balance between business requirements (how much data loss is acceptable) and technical feasibility (how frequently can backups be performed without impacting performance and cost?). It requires a careful assessment of the application, data, and potential impact of data loss on the business.

Backup and Restore Strategies

The ability to reliably back up your data and quickly restore it is fundamental to any effective disaster recovery plan. We use various AWS services to achieve this, ensuring minimal data loss and downtime. These services offer different approaches to backup and restoration, tailored to specific data types and recovery needs.

Regular Data Backups:

The cornerstone of a good backup and restore strategy is *regular* backups. These backups act as your safety net, allowing you to revert to a previous state of your data in case of a disaster. The frequency of these backups depends heavily on your *Recovery Point Objective* (RPO) – how much data loss your business can tolerate. If you can only tolerate a few minutes of data loss, you'll need to back up far more frequently than if you can tolerate a few hours.

We implement regular data backups using several AWS services:

- **S3 (Simple Storage Service):** S3 is ideal for storing backups of static files, application code, configuration files, and even database backups. Its virtually limitless storage and high durability make it an excellent choice for long-term archival and backup.

  For example, you might use the AWS CLI (Command Line Interface) to regularly back up your website's static assets to an S3 bucket:

  ```
  aws s3 sync ./website s3://your-backup-bucket/website/ --delete
  ```

This command synchronizes the `/website` directory on your local machine with the `s3://your-backup-bucket/website/` S3 bucket. The `--delete` flag removes objects in the bucket that no longer exist locally, ensuring the backup reflects the current state of the website. S3 also supports versioning, allowing you to restore to specific points in time.

- **EBS (Elastic Block Storage) Snapshots:** EBS volumes are the persistent block storage attached to your EC2 instances. EBS snapshots are point-in-time copies of these volumes, stored in S3. They are incremental, meaning only the blocks that have changed since the last snapshot are saved, making them efficient in terms of storage and backup time.

  You can create EBS snapshots using the AWS console, the AWS CLI, or programmatically through the AWS SDKs.

  For example, using the AWS CLI:

  ```
  aws ec2 create-snapshot --volume-id vol-xxxxxxxxxxxxxxxxx --description "Daily backup of im
  ```

  This command creates a snapshot of the EBS volume with ID `vol-xxxxxxxxxxxxxxxxx`. To restore, you create a new EBS volume from the snapshot and attach it to an EC2 instance. This is a crucial process: it's the heart of recovery from instance failure.

  ```
  +-----------------+        +-----------------+        +-----------------+
  | EC2 Instance    |------->| EBS Volume      |------->| EBS Snapshot    |
  | (Running)       |        | (Attached)      |        | (Stored in S3)  |
  +-----------------+        +-----------------+        +-----------------+
                              ^
                              | Daily/Regular Backup
  ```

- **RDS (Relational Database Service) Backups:** RDS provides automated backup capabilities. It automatically creates and manages backups of your database instances. These backups are stored in S3. You can configure the backup retention period and the backup window.

  RDS also supports point-in-time recovery. You can restore your database to any point in time within the backup retention period.

  The AWS CLI example to initiate restore is:

  ```
  aws rds restore-db-instance-to-point-in-time \
    --source-db-instance-identifier mydbinstance \
    --target-db-instance-identifier mydbinstance-restored \
    --restore-time 2024-10-27T10:00:00Z
  ```

  This command restores `mydbinstance` to a new instance named `mydbinstance-restored` to the time specified. The recovery depends on the size of the Database and can take time.

  In addition to automated backups, you can also create manual snapshots of your RDS instances. These snapshots are useful for creating backups before making major changes to your database.

  ```
  +-----------------+        +-----------------+        +-----------------+
  | Application     |------->|   RDS Instance  |------->| RDS Snapshot    |
  | (Access DB)     |        | (Database)      |        | (Stored in S3)  |
  +-----------------+        +-----------------+        +-----------------+
                              ^
                              | Automated/Manual Backup
  ```

  The above shows data flow.

In summary, selecting the appropriate backup strategy depends on the data type, RPO, and RTO (Recovery Time Objective – how quickly you need to recover) requirements. Often, a combination of these strategies is used to provide comprehensive data protection. Regular testing of restore procedures is also crucial to ensure that backups are valid and can be restored successfully within the required RTO.

Multi-Region Active-Active

Multi-Region Active-Active is a disaster recovery (DR) strategy where your application runs simultaneously in multiple AWS regions. This approach aims for continuous availability, even if one entire region experiences a failure. Instead of waiting to recover, traffic is automatically routed to a healthy region.

Concept and Functionality:

Imagine you have a web application. In a traditional single-region setup, if that region goes down, your application is unavailable. With Multi-Region Active-Active, you deploy the *same* application to at least two different AWS regions (e.g., us-east-1 and us-west-2). Both regions actively serve user requests. A global load balancer (like AWS Route 53 or a third-party DNS provider) distributes traffic between these regions.

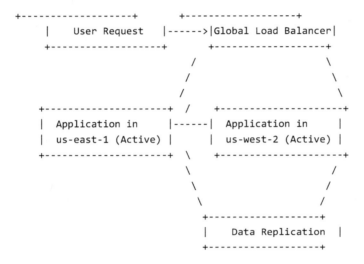

```
+------------------+        +------------------+
|   User Request   |------>|Global Load Balancer|
+------------------+        +------------------+
                     /                      \
                    /                        \
                   /                          \
+--------------------+  /  +--------------------+
| Application in     |------| Application in     |
| us-east-1 (Active) |     | us-west-2 (Active) |
+--------------------+  \  +--------------------+
                     \                      /
                      \                    /
                       \                  /
                   +------------------+
                   |  Data Replication |
                   +------------------+
```

In this diagram, user requests are directed to the Global Load Balancer, which intelligently routes them to either the application instance in the us-east-1 region or the instance in the us-west-2 region. The crucial aspect is that *both* applications are actively processing requests. Data replication between the regions ensures data consistency, which we'll discuss next.

Data Replication:

The key to a successful Multi-Region Active-Active setup is robust data replication. All changes made in one region must be synchronized to the other region(s) in near real-time. This ensures that if one region fails, the other region has the most up-to-date data.

Different types of data require different replication strategies:

- **Databases:** Use database replication features provided by your database service (e.g., RDS Multi-AZ with cross-region read replicas, DynamoDB Global Tables, or Cassandra multi-datacenter replication). DynamoDB Global Tables are a straightforward option when using DynamoDB.
- **Object Storage (e.g., S3):** S3 Cross-Region Replication (CRR) automatically replicates objects between buckets in different AWS regions.
- **Application State:** Ensure that application state is stored externally (e.g., in a distributed cache like Redis or Memcached, or in a database) and is replicated across regions. Avoid storing state locally within an application instance.

Example: DynamoDB Global Tables

```
# Example (Conceptual - AWS SDK code will vary) showing how you enable Global Tables with boto3
import boto3

dynamodb = boto3.client('dynamodb', region_name='us-east-1')

try:
    dynamodb.update_table(
        TableName='my_global_table',
        ReplicaUpdates=[
            {
                'Create': {
                    'RegionName': 'us-west-2'
                }
            }
        ]
    )
    print("Successfully enabled us-west-2 as a replica region.")
except Exception as e:
    print(f"Error enabling replica: {e}")
```

This Python example (using boto3) demonstrates how to add a replica region to a DynamoDB table, transforming it into a Global Table. In practice, you'd handle error conditions and ensure appropriate IAM permissions. The critical thing is that DynamoDB manages the replication process once configured.

Traffic Management and Failover:

A global load balancer monitors the health of the applications in each region. If it detects a failure in one region, it automatically stops sending traffic to that region and redirects all traffic to the remaining healthy region(s).

- **DNS-based Failover (e.g., Route 53):** Route 53 can be configured with health checks. If a health check fails, Route 53 can automatically update DNS records to point to the healthy region.
- **Global Load Balancers:** Some load balancers can span multiple regions and handle failover automatically.

Example: Route 53 Failover

Using AWS Route 53 you will configure primary and secondary records. The primary points to your active region, and secondary points to your DR region.

```
Record Name: example.com
Type: A (Alias)

Primary Record:
    Alias Target: ELB in us-east-1 (Active)
    Evaluate Target Health: Yes

Secondary Record:
    Alias Target: ELB in us-west-2 (DR)
    Evaluate Target Health: Yes
Failover Record Type: SECONDARY

Health Check: Created, associated with us-east-1 ELB
```

Route 53 constantly monitors the primary record (your active Elastic Load Balancer in us-east-1). If the health check fails (meaning the load balancer or the resources behind it are unhealthy), Route 53 automatically switches traffic to the secondary record, pointing to your Elastic Load Balancer in us-west-2.

Advantages:

- **Highest Availability:** Provides the best possible availability. If one region fails, the application remains available in other regions with minimal interruption.
- **Improved User Experience:** Users experience minimal downtime during failures.
- **Low RTO and RPO:** Achieves near-zero Recovery Time Objective (RTO) and Recovery Point Objective (RPO).

Disadvantages:

- **High Cost:** Most expensive DR option due to the need to run and maintain full environments in multiple regions.
- **Complexity:** More complex to set up and manage than other DR strategies, especially concerning data replication and consistency. Requires careful planning and robust automation.
- **Data Consistency Challenges:** Ensuring data consistency across regions can be difficult, especially with complex data models and high write volumes. Requires careful consideration of consistency models (e.g., eventual consistency vs. strong consistency) and potential conflict resolution strategies.

Pilot Light & Warm Standby

These are Disaster Recovery (DR) strategies that aim to minimize downtime and data loss, offering different balances between cost and recovery speed compared to a fully active-active setup. Both involve having a secondary environment ready to take over in case the primary environment fails, but they differ in their state of readiness.

Pilot Light:

Think of Pilot Light as a scaled-down version of your application's core components, always running in a secondary region. This minimal environment typically consists of the essential services needed to quickly bring the full application online. It's like the pilot light on a gas stove – a small flame always burning, ready to ignite the full burner.

- **Scaled-Down Environment:** The key here is "scaled-down." You're not running a full replica of your production environment. Instead, you have the *most critical* services running. This might include databases in a minimal configuration, core networking infrastructure, and essential application servers. Non-essential components are typically shut down.

- **Faster Recovery:** When a disaster strikes the primary region, you quickly scale up the pilot light environment to handle full production load. This involves launching additional application servers, increasing database capacity, and configuring load balancing.

- **Cost-Effective:** Because you're only running a minimal set of resources in the secondary region, Pilot Light is a more cost-effective DR strategy than Active-Active. You only pay for the full environment when you need it during a disaster.

- **Example:**

  Suppose you have an e-commerce application with a database, application servers, and a web server. In a Pilot Light setup:

  - The database might be running in a smaller instance size in the secondary region, constantly replicating data from the primary database.
  - The application servers are not running, but the necessary AMIs (Amazon Machine Images) are created and ready to be launched.
  - The web server might be running with a static "under maintenance" page.

  During a disaster, you would:

  1. Launch the application servers using the pre-built AMIs.
  2. Scale up the database to the appropriate instance size.
  3. Configure the load balancer to direct traffic to the newly launched application servers.

4. Update DNS settings to route users to the secondary region's load balancer.

```
# Example of scaling up a database instance using AWS SDK (Boto3)
import boto3

def scale_db_instance(instance_id, new_instance_type):
    rds = boto3.client('rds')
    response = rds.modify_db_instance(
        DBInstanceIdentifier=instance_id,
        DBInstanceClass=new_instance_type,
        ApplyImmediately=True # Apply changes immediately for DR scenario
    )
    print(response)

# Usage example: Scale up a db instance that is running in pilot light environment
# scale_db_instance('my-db-instance', 'db.m5.large')
```

Warm Standby:

Warm Standby is a more robust DR strategy than Pilot Light. It involves maintaining a fully functional, but scaled-down, replica of your production environment in a secondary region. Think of it like a backup generator that's always on, ready to take over immediately.

- **Pre-Configured Infrastructure:** In Warm Standby, all the components of your application – databases, application servers, web servers, etc. – are running in the secondary region. However, they are typically running at a reduced capacity compared to the primary region.

- **Faster Recovery than Pilot Light:** Because the environment is already running, failover is much faster in Warm Standby compared to Pilot Light. You simply need to scale up the resources to handle the production load.

- **Higher Cost than Pilot Light:** The trade-off for faster recovery is higher cost. You are paying for a fully functional environment in the secondary region, even though it's not actively serving production traffic.

- **Example:**

  Using the same e-commerce application example, in a Warm Standby setup:

  - The database is running in the secondary region, constantly replicating data from the primary database. It uses a smaller instance size.
  - The application servers are running, but with fewer instances than in the primary region.
  - The web servers are running and available to take traffic, likely presenting information about the disaster.

  During a disaster, you would:

  1. Scale up the database instance size.
  2. Scale up the number of application server instances.
  3. Update DNS settings to point to the secondary region's load balancer.

```
# Example of scaling up application server instances using AWS Auto Scaling
import boto3

def scale_auto_scaling_group(group_name, desired_capacity):
    autoscaling = boto3.client('autoscaling')
    response = autoscaling.update_auto_scaling_group(
        AutoScalingGroupName=group_name,
        DesiredCapacity=desired_capacity
```

```
    )
    print(response)

# Usage example to scale up an Autoscaling Group
# scale_auto_scaling_group('my-auto-scaling-group', 10)
```

Key Differences Summarized:

Here is a sketch that visually summarizes the differences:

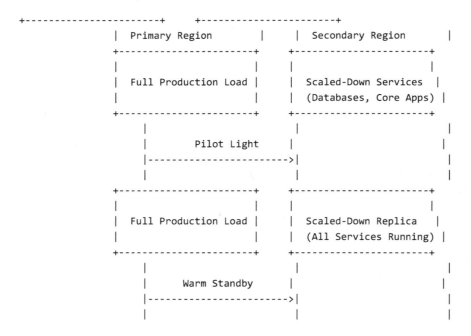

```
Cost: Pilot Light < Warm Standby < Active-Active
Recovery Time: Pilot Light > Warm Standby > Active-Active
```

Choosing Between Pilot Light and Warm Standby:

The best choice depends on your specific requirements and constraints:

- **RTO (Recovery Time Objective):** If you need to recover very quickly, Warm Standby is the better choice.
- **Cost:** If cost is a major concern, Pilot Light is the more economical option.
- **Complexity:** Pilot Light can be more complex to set up and test, as it involves automating the scaling up of the environment during failover. Warm Standby is relatively simpler.

Both Pilot Light and Warm Standby are valuable strategies for achieving disaster recovery. Understanding their strengths and weaknesses will help you choose the right approach for your application.

Chapter 24 Case Studies and Future Trends-Case Studies: How Enterprises Build on AWS

Here are 5 bullet points summarizing "Case Studies and Future Trends - Case Studies: How Enterprises Build on AWS" for your book, suitable for a single slide:

- **Real-World AWS Architectures:** Illustrate practical system design principles using enterprise case studies.

- **Scalability & Resilience Examples:** Show how specific companies achieved scalability and resilience on AWS.

- **Technology Adoption Showcases:** Demonstrate the adoption of diverse AWS services through real-world examples.

- **Problem-Solution Framework:** Present case studies outlining business problems and their AWS-based solutions.

- **Best Practices in Action:** Highlight the application of system design best practices within enterprise contexts.

Real-World AWS Architectures: A Deep Dive

This section delves into the practical application of system design principles on AWS, illustrated through real-world enterprise case studies. We will explore how companies have leveraged AWS services to build robust and scalable solutions tailored to their specific business needs. Understanding these architectures provides valuable insights into how to design and implement your own cloud-based systems effectively.

Illustrating Practical System Design Principles

The core of this section lies in dissecting actual AWS deployments to reveal the underlying design choices and their consequences. We will analyze the rationale behind selecting particular AWS services and the trade-offs involved. Let's begin with a simple example, such as a basic web application deployment on AWS:

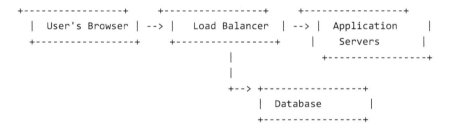

This simplified architecture shows a user accessing a web application. The Load Balancer distributes incoming traffic across multiple Application Servers, ensuring high availability and responsiveness. The Application Servers, in turn, interact with a Database to retrieve and store data. In AWS, this could translate to:

- **Load Balancer:** Elastic Load Balancing (ELB) - distributing traffic across your web servers.
- **Application Servers:** EC2 instances within an Auto Scaling Group - providing scalable compute resources.
- **Database:** Relational Database Service (RDS) - managing your database in the cloud.

Consider an e-commerce platform needing to handle fluctuating traffic. Their architecture might incorporate Auto Scaling Groups (ASG) with EC2 instances and a managed database like Amazon RDS. The ASG dynamically adjusts the number of EC2 instances based on the demand, ensuring the application remains responsive during peak shopping seasons.

Example with Code:

Let's look at a simple python example to demonstrate how one might interact with an AWS service from an application server. This snippet uses boto3, the AWS SDK for Python:

```python
import boto3

# Create an S3 client
s3 = boto3.client('s3')

def upload_file(file_name, bucket, object_name=None):
    """Upload a file to an S3 bucket

    :param file_name: File to upload
    :param bucket: Bucket to upload to
    :param object_name: S3 object name. If not specified then file_name is used
    :return: True if file was uploaded, else False
    """

    # If S3 object_name was not specified, use file_name
    if object_name is None:
        object_name = file_name

    # Upload the file
    try:
        s3.upload_file(file_name, bucket, object_name)
        print(f"File {file_name} uploaded to {bucket}/{object_name}")
        return True
    except Exception as e:
        print(e)
        return False


# Example usage
upload_file("my_local_file.txt", "my-aws-bucket", "my_s3_file.txt")
```

This simple example, when incorporated into an application running on an EC2 instance, demonstrates a practical interaction with an AWS service. The principle of secure access via IAM roles and policies applies here to restrict access based on least privilege.

Key Takeaways

- **Modularity:** AWS architectures are often built from modular components, enabling independent scaling and maintenance.
- **Scalability:** Leveraging services like Auto Scaling and Elastic Load Balancing ensures the ability to handle fluctuating workloads.
- **Resilience:** Distributing applications across multiple Availability Zones (AZs) increases fault tolerance.
- **Security:** Implementing security best practices at every layer, including network security groups, IAM roles, and encryption, is paramount.
- **Cost Optimization:** Employing techniques like right-sizing instances, using Reserved Instances, and leveraging spot instances can help reduce costs.

Understanding these principles in the context of real-world examples equips you with the knowledge to design effective and efficient AWS architectures for diverse applications.

Scalability & Resilience Examples

This section explores how real companies have successfully achieved scalability and resilience on AWS. We will dissect specific case studies to illustrate the architectural patterns, services, and configurations employed to handle fluctuating workloads and ensure continuous availability. Let's dive into practical scenarios.

Understanding Scalability:

Scalability, in essence, is the ability of a system to handle an increasing amount of work, or to be easily expanded to accommodate growth. On AWS, this typically involves automatically adjusting resources (like compute instances, storage capacity, and database connections) based on demand.

- **Vertical Scaling:** This is like upgrading the engine of your car. You're making the existing resources more powerful. On AWS, this could mean increasing the size (CPU, memory) of an EC2 instance.

  - **Example:** A small e-commerce website initially runs on a `t3.micro` EC2 instance. As traffic increases, the CPU usage consistently hits 100%. To scale vertically, they upgrade to a `t3.medium` instance with more CPU and memory.

- **Horizontal Scaling:** This is like adding more cars to your fleet. You're distributing the workload across multiple instances. On AWS, this is typically achieved using Auto Scaling Groups (ASG) and Load Balancers (LB).

  - **Example:** A popular blogging platform experiences a surge in traffic during a major news event. An Auto Scaling Group, configured with a target CPU utilization of 70%, automatically launches new EC2 instances when the existing instances become overloaded. A Load Balancer distributes the incoming traffic across these instances.

Understanding Resilience:

Resilience refers to the ability of a system to recover quickly from failures and continue operating smoothly. AWS offers various services and techniques to build resilient architectures.

- **Redundancy:** Having multiple copies of critical components. This ensures that if one component fails, another can immediately take over.

  - **Example:** A financial application stores its data in a database. To ensure redundancy, the database is deployed in a Multi-AZ (Availability Zone) configuration using Amazon RDS. If the primary database instance fails, RDS automatically fails over to a standby instance in a different Availability Zone.

- **Fault Isolation:** Designing the system so that a failure in one part doesn't cascade to other parts.

  - **Example:** A microservices architecture, where different services are responsible for specific tasks, provides fault isolation. If one service fails, it doesn't necessarily bring down the entire application.

- **Automatic Recovery:** Automating the process of detecting and recovering from failures.

  - **Example:** AWS Auto Scaling can automatically replace unhealthy EC2 instances. If an instance fails a health check, Auto Scaling terminates the instance and launches a new one.

Case Study 1: E-commerce Platform Handling Flash Sales

Problem: An e-commerce company experiences massive traffic spikes during flash sales, leading to slow response times and potential outages.

Solution:

- **Scalability:** Implement an Auto Scaling Group (ASG) for the application servers behind an Elastic Load Balancer (ELB). The ASG is configured to scale based on CPU utilization and request latency.
- **Resilience:** Deploy the application servers across multiple Availability Zones (AZs) for high availability. Use a Multi-AZ RDS instance for the database. Implement caching using Amazon ElastiCache to reduce database load.

Sketch:

```
+--------------------+
                                          |      Internet      |
                                          +--------+-----------+
                                                   |
                                          +--------V-----------+
                                          | Elastic Load Balancer |
                                          +--------+-----------+
                                                   |
                              +------------------+-----------------+
                              |                  |                 |
                              v                  v                 v
                      +--------------+  +--------------+  +--------------+
                      |  EC2 (AZ A)  |  |  EC2 (AZ B)  |  |  EC2 (AZ C)  |
                      | (ASG Member) |  | (ASG Member) |  | (ASG Member) |
                      +--------------+  +--------------+  +--------------+
                              |                  |                 |
                              +------------------+-----------------+
                                                 |
                                        +--------V-----------+
                                        |    ElastiCache     | (Optional Caching Layer)
                                        +--------+-----------+
                                                 |
                                        +--------V-----------+
                                        |    Multi-AZ RDS    |
                                        +--------------------+
```

Code Snippet (Example Auto Scaling Configuration - AWS CLI):

```
aws autoscaling create-launch-configuration \
    --launch-configuration-name my-launch-config \
    --image-id ami-0abcdef1234567890 \
    --instance-type t3.medium \
    --security-groups sg-0abcdef1234567890

aws autoscaling create-auto-scaling-group \
    --auto-scaling-group-name my-asg \
    --launch-configuration-name my-launch-config \
    --min-size 2 \
    --max-size 10 \
    --desired-capacity 2 \
    --vpc-zone-identifier subnet-0abcdef1234567890,subnet-0fedcba9876543210 \
    --target-group-arns arn:aws:elasticloadbalancing:us-east-1:123456789012:targetgroup/my-targe
```

Explanation:

- `create-launch-configuration`: Defines the template for new EC2 instances launched by the ASG.
- `create-auto-scaling-group`: Creates the ASG, specifying the minimum, maximum, and desired number of instances, the subnets to launch instances in, and the target group (Load Balancer) to register the instances with.

Case Study 2: Media Streaming Service Ensuring High Availability

Problem: A media streaming service needs to ensure uninterrupted streaming for its users, even in the face of infrastructure failures.

Solution:

- **Scalability:** Use Amazon CloudFront (CDN) to cache content closer to users, reducing latency and offloading traffic from the origin servers. Origin servers (EC2 or S3) can scale independently.
- **Resilience:** Deploy origin servers in multiple regions for disaster recovery. Use Route 53 (DNS) with failover routing to automatically redirect traffic to a healthy region if the primary region becomes unavailable.

Sketch:

```
+---------------------+
                              |        Internet         |
                              +---------+-----------+
                                        |
                              +---------V-----------+
                              |   Amazon CloudFront   | (CDN)
                              +---------+-----------+
                                        |
              +---------------------+---------------------+
              |                     |                     |
              V                     V
      +-----------+         +-----------+
      | Region 1  |         | Region 2  | (Disaster Recovery)
      +-----------+         +-----------+
              |                     |
      +-----V-----+         +-----V-----+
      | S3 Bucket |         | S3 Bucket | (Origin Server)
      +-----------+         +-----------+
            OR                    OR
      +-----V-----+         +-----V-----+
      |EC2 Instances|       |EC2 Instances|
      +-----------+         +-----------+
```

Code Snippet (Example Route 53 Failover Configuration - AWS CLI):

```
aws route53 create-health-check \
    --caller-reference $(uuidgen) \
    --health-check-config file://healthcheck.json


aws route53 change-resource-record-sets \
    --hosted-zone-id Z1ABCDEFGHIJKLMN \
    --change-batch file://failover.json
```

healthcheck.json (Example):

```
{
  "IPAddress": "192.0.2.44",
  "Port": 80,
  "Type": "HTTP",
  "RequestInterval": 30,
  "FailureThreshold": 3
}
```

failover.json (Example):

```
{
  "Changes": [
    {
      "Action": "UPSERT",
```

```
    "ResourceRecordSet": {
      "Name": "example.com",
      "Type": "A",
      "SetIdentifier": "Primary",
      "Weight": 100,
      "Region": "us-east-1",
      "ResourceRecords": [
        {
          "Value": "192.0.2.44"
        }
      ],
      "HealthCheckId": "your-health-check-id"
    }
  },
  {
    "Action": "UPSERT",
    "ResourceRecordSet": {
      "Name": "example.com",
      "Type": "A",
      "SetIdentifier": "Secondary",
      "Weight": 0,
      "Region": "us-west-2",
      "Failover": "SECONDARY",
      "ResourceRecords": [
        {
          "Value": "203.0.113.45"
        }
      ],
      "HealthCheckId": "your-health-check-id"
    }
  }
  ]
}
```

Explanation:

- `create-health-check`: Creates a health check to monitor the primary region.
- `change-resource-record-sets`: Configures Route 53 to use failover routing. The primary record set (Region 1) has a weight, and the secondary record set (Region 2) has `Failover: SECONDARY`. If the health check fails, Route 53 automatically redirects traffic to the secondary region.

These case studies highlight how AWS services can be combined to achieve scalability and resilience. The specific implementation will vary depending on the application's requirements and architecture. However, the core principles of redundancy, fault isolation, and automatic recovery remain essential for building robust and reliable systems on AWS.

Technology Adoption Showcases

This section focuses on how different companies have successfully integrated various AWS services into their operations. We will explore real-world scenarios that demonstrate the practical application of AWS technologies. Think of this as a collection of blueprints, showing how others have built on AWS, offering insights into different approaches and potential solutions for your own projects.

Each showcase will detail the specific AWS services used, the reasons behind their selection, and the benefits achieved. We'll avoid abstract discussions and instead present concrete examples of technology adoption.

Imagine a company needing to store a massive amount of data. Instead of building their own data center, they can use Amazon S3 (Simple Storage Service). S3 provides scalable and secure object storage. Another company needs to run complex calculations. They might use Amazon EC2 (Elastic Compute Cloud) to provision virtual servers on demand. Or perhaps a business wants to build a serverless application. AWS Lambda lets them run code without managing servers. These are just initial examples.

To illustrate the adoption of diverse AWS services, consider the following hypothetical scenarios presented in a structured manner:

Scenario 1: Migrating a Relational Database to the Cloud

A traditional e-commerce business, *ExampleRetail*, struggled with the scalability and maintenance of their on-premises MySQL database. They experienced frequent downtime during peak shopping seasons and had a dedicated team managing the database infrastructure. To address these issues, *ExampleRetail* decided to migrate their database to Amazon RDS (Relational Database Service) for MySQL.

- **AWS Service Adopted:** Amazon RDS (MySQL)
- **Reasoning:** RDS simplifies database administration tasks like patching, backups, and scaling. The MySQL compatibility ensured a relatively smooth migration process.
- **Benefits:** Improved uptime, reduced operational overhead (fewer database administrators needed), and the ability to easily scale database resources during peak seasons. Scalability could be implemented by modifying the instance type used for the database.

A simplified code sketch illustrates this:

```
# On-Premises (Simplified):
# - Manual server management
# - Limited scalability


# AWS RDS:
# - Managed service
# - Scalable via console/API calls (e.g., AWS CLI)
#   aws rds modify-db-instance --db-instance-identifier ExampleRetailDB --db-instance-class db.r
```

Sketch:

```
+----------------------+     Migration     +-----------------------+
| On-Premises MySQL    |------------------>|  Amazon RDS (MySQL)   |
| (Manual Management)  |                   |  (Managed & Scalable) |
+----------------------+                   +-----------------------+
```

Scenario 2: Building a Serverless API for Mobile Applications

MobileAppCo wanted to create a fast and scalable API to support their mobile application without the overhead of managing servers. They chose to build a serverless API using AWS Lambda, API Gateway, and DynamoDB.

- **AWS Services Adopted:** AWS Lambda, Amazon API Gateway, Amazon DynamoDB.
- **Reasoning:** Lambda allows them to run code without provisioning or managing servers. API Gateway handles request routing and security. DynamoDB, a NoSQL database, provides fast and scalable data storage.
- **Benefits:** Reduced operational costs (pay-per-use), automatic scaling, and faster development cycles. The entire backend can be managed via Infrastructure as Code (IaC).

A simplified code sketch illustrates this:

```
# API Gateway:
# - Receives requests from mobile app
# - Routes requests to Lambda function
```

```
# Lambda Function (Python):
# import boto3
# dynamo = boto3.client('dynamodb')
# def lambda_handler(event, context):
#   response = dynamo.get_item(TableName='MobileAppDataTable', Key={'id': {'S': event['id']}})
#   return { 'statusCode': 200, 'body': response['Item'] }

# DynamoDB:
# - Stores data in a NoSQL format
```

Sketch:

```
+-------------+     API Request     +----------------+   Invocation    +----------------+  Da
| Mobile App  |-------------------->| API Gateway    |---------------->| AWS Lambda
+-------------+                     +----------------+                 +----------------+
```

Scenario 3: Implementing Real-Time Data Processing

SensorTech collects data from thousands of sensors and needs to process it in real-time for anomaly detection. They decided to use Amazon Kinesis Data Streams to ingest the data, Amazon Kinesis Data Analytics to process it, and Amazon S3 to store the processed data.

- **AWS Services Adopted:** Amazon Kinesis Data Streams, Amazon Kinesis Data Analytics, Amazon S3.
- **Reasoning:** Kinesis Data Streams allows them to ingest a high volume of streaming data. Kinesis Data Analytics allows them to run SQL queries on the streaming data in real-time. S3 provides a cost-effective storage solution for the processed data.
- **Benefits:** Real-time insights, proactive anomaly detection, and improved operational efficiency. Ability to scale the data processing pipeline as the number of sensors grows.

A simplified code sketch illustrates this:

```
# Kinesis Data Streams:
# - Ingests data from sensors

# Kinesis Data Analytics (SQL):
# CREATE OR REPLACE STREAM "DESTINATION_SQL_STREAM" (
#     sensor_id VARCHAR(64),
#     value DOUBLE,
#     ts VARCHAR(64)
#  );
# CREATE OR REPLACE PUMP "STREAM_PUMP" AS INSERT INTO "DESTINATION_SQL_STREAM"
# SELECT STREAM sensor_id, value, ts
# FROM "SOURCE_SQL_STREAM_001"
# WHERE value > 100;

# S3:
# - Stores the output of Kinesis Data Analytics
```

Sketch:

```
+-----------+    Data Stream     +--------------------------+   Real-time Processing  +---------
| Sensors   |------------------->| Kinesis Data Streams     |------------------------>| Kine
+-----------+                    +--------------------------+                         +--------
```

These examples showcase how companies have used AWS services to solve specific problems and achieve tangible benefits. The underlying principle is to leverage the right combination of AWS technologies to meet the specific needs of the application and business. Each company needed a different combination of technologies to accomplish their goals, but they were all able to leverage AWS to achieve their objectives.

Problem-Solution Framework

This section focuses on how enterprises have used AWS to solve specific business problems. Each case study will clearly outline the initial challenge a company faced, followed by a detailed explanation of the AWS-based solution they implemented. The goal is to provide a practical understanding of how AWS can be leveraged to overcome real-world obstacles.

Framework Breakdown:

We'll structure each case study around a clear problem-solution framework. This means we'll consistently present information in the following format:

1. **The Problem:** This section will define the business challenge the enterprise faced. It will describe the pain points, inefficiencies, or limitations that motivated them to seek a solution.

2. **The Solution:** This section will detail the AWS architecture and services implemented to address the problem. It will explain how the chosen services were configured and integrated to achieve the desired outcome.

3. **The Implementation:** This section will delve into the practical steps taken to deploy the solution. It might include code snippets, configuration examples, or architectural diagrams to illustrate the implementation process.

4. **The Results:** This section will quantify the benefits achieved by implementing the AWS-based solution. It will showcase the improvements in efficiency, scalability, cost savings, or other key metrics.

Example Case Study (Hypothetical):

Let's consider a hypothetical example of an e-commerce company, "ShopFast," struggling with seasonal traffic spikes.

1. **The Problem:** ShopFast experienced significant slowdowns and outages during peak shopping seasons (e.g., Black Friday, Christmas). Their existing on-premises infrastructure couldn't handle the sudden surge in traffic, leading to lost sales and frustrated customers. They needed a solution that could dynamically scale to accommodate fluctuating demand.

2. **The Solution:** ShopFast migrated their e-commerce platform to AWS, leveraging the following services:

   - **Amazon EC2 Auto Scaling:** To automatically adjust the number of EC2 instances based on traffic demand.
   - **Elastic Load Balancing (ELB):** To distribute incoming traffic across multiple EC2 instances, ensuring high availability.
   - **Amazon RDS (Relational Database Service):** To manage their database, benefiting from automatic scaling and backups.
   - **Amazon CloudFront:** A content delivery network (CDN) to cache static content (images, videos, etc.) and reduce latency for users around the world.
   - **AWS Lambda:** for serverless functions to handle small tasks.

3. **The Implementation:**

   - **EC2 Auto Scaling:** An Auto Scaling group was configured with a minimum of 5 instances and a maximum of 50 instances. Scaling policies were set to trigger instance launches based on CPU utilization.
   - **ELB:** An ELB was placed in front of the EC2 instances to distribute traffic. Health checks were configured to automatically remove unhealthy instances from the pool.

- **RDS:** A multi-AZ RDS instance was deployed for high availability. Read replicas were created to offload read traffic from the primary database.
- **CloudFront:** Static content was cached on CloudFront edge locations, reducing the load on the origin servers (EC2 instances).
- **Lambda:** A Lambda function was created to generate thumbnails for product images on the fly.

Example Code Snippet (CloudFormation template for Auto Scaling Group):

```
Resources:
  MyASG:
    Type: AWS::AutoScaling::AutoScalingGroup
    Properties:
      LaunchConfigurationName: !Ref MyLaunchConfig
      MinSize: '5'
      MaxSize: '50'
      DesiredCapacity: '5'
      LoadBalancerNames:
        - !Ref MyLoadBalancer
      AvailabilityZones: !GetAZs ''
      Tags:
        - Key: Name
          Value: ShopFast-Web-Server
          PropagateAtLaunch: true
```

4. **The Results:** ShopFast experienced the following benefits:

- **Improved Scalability:** The platform could seamlessly handle traffic spikes without performance degradation.
- **Increased Availability:** The multi-AZ RDS deployment and ELB ensured high availability, minimizing downtime.
- **Reduced Costs:** Auto Scaling dynamically adjusted the number of EC2 instances, reducing costs during off-peak hours.
- **Enhanced Performance:** CloudFront CDN improved website loading times for users globally.
- Saved cost:Lambda provides event-driven and serverless services that avoids the need to buy costly servers and maintain that.

Sketch Diagram (Simplified Architecture):

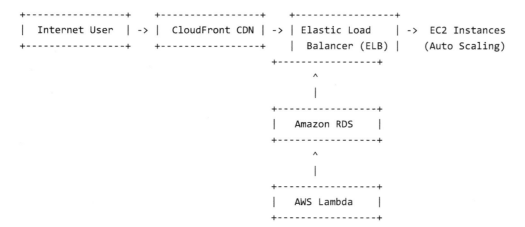

The arrows show the flow of requests. The CDN caches static content, the ELB distributes traffic, EC2 instances provide the web application and Auto scaling allows to grow the number of instance based on requirements and RDS store data and AWS Lambda allows for serverless functions to do small tasks.

By analyzing case studies through this problem-solution framework, readers will gain a deeper understanding of how AWS can be effectively used to address a wide range of business challenges. This is why real world examples are provided.

Best Practices in Action

This section focuses on demonstrating how real-world enterprises implement system design best practices when building solutions on AWS. We will move beyond theoretical discussions and examine concrete examples, illustrating how these practices are applied to solve specific business challenges.

What are Best Practices?

Before diving into case studies, it's helpful to understand what we mean by "best practices." In the context of AWS system design, these are well-established, proven techniques and approaches that contribute to systems that are:

- **Reliable:** Systems perform consistently as expected, even under stress.
- **Secure:** Systems protect data and infrastructure from unauthorized access.
- **Efficient:** Systems use resources optimally, minimizing costs.
- **Scalable:** Systems can handle increasing workloads without performance degradation.
- **Maintainable:** Systems are easy to understand, modify, and operate.

Let's look at how these practices play out in real-world scenarios.

Case Study Examples Illustrating Best Practices

Imagine a fictional e-commerce company, "ShopSphere," migrating its legacy infrastructure to AWS. Their goals are to improve scalability, enhance security, and reduce operational overhead.

Let's see how ShopSphere could implement specific best practices in different areas:

1. Infrastructure as Code (IaC)

- **Best Practice:** Define and manage infrastructure using code (e.g., AWS CloudFormation, Terraform).
- **In Action:** Instead of manually provisioning servers and configuring networks, ShopSphere uses CloudFormation templates to describe its entire AWS environment. This allows them to easily recreate the environment, automate deployments, and track changes through version control.

```
# Example CloudFormation snippet for an EC2 instance
Resources:
  MyEC2Instance:
    Type: AWS::EC2::Instance
    Properties:
      ImageId: ami-0c55b27ca097cb0c1 # Example AMI ID
      InstanceType: t2.micro
      KeyName: MyKeyPair
      SecurityGroupIds:
        - !Ref MySecurityGroup
```

Sketch:

```
+-------------------+     +-------------------+
| CloudFormation    |     | AWS Environment   |
| Template (YAML)   | --->| (EC2, S3, RDS...) |
+-------------------+     +-------------------+
      (Defines Infrastructure)  (Infrastructure Created/Managed)
```

This sketch represents how a CloudFormation template defines the desired state of the infrastructure, and AWS uses this template to create and manage resources within your AWS environment.

2. Security Best Practices

- **Best Practice:** Implement the principle of least privilege using IAM roles and policies.
- **In Action:** ShopSphere avoids granting broad permissions to its applications. Instead, each application is assigned an IAM role that grants only the necessary permissions to access specific AWS resources. For example, an application responsible for processing orders only has permission to write to the orders database and publish messages to a specific queue.

```
# Example IAM policy granting read access to an S3 bucket
{
  "Version": "2012-10-17",
  "Statement": [
    {
      "Effect": "Allow",
      "Action": "s3:GetObject",
      "Resource": "arn:aws:s3:::my-shop-bucket/"
    }
  ]
}
```

Sketch:

```
+---------------+       +--------------------+       +--------------+
| Application A | ---> |  IAM Role (Limited | ---> |  S3 Bucket   |
| (Order Proc)  |       |     Permissions)   |       |  (Order Data)|
+---------------+       +--------------------+       +--------------+

  (Requests Data)      (Controls Access)        (Provides Data)
```

This sketch shows how an application accesses an S3 bucket, but only with permissions granted through an IAM role. This limits the scope of access and improves security.

3. Scalability and Resilience

- **Best Practice:** Use Auto Scaling groups and load balancers to distribute traffic and ensure high availability.
- **In Action:** ShopSphere places its web servers behind an Application Load Balancer (ALB). The ALB distributes incoming traffic across multiple EC2 instances running in an Auto Scaling group. If one instance fails, the Auto Scaling group automatically launches a replacement. This ensures that the website remains available even during peak traffic or instance failures.

Sketch:

```
+-------+         +-------+         +-------+
| EC2   |         | EC2   |         | EC2   |
| Instance|       | Instance|       | Instance|
+-------+         +-------+         +-------+
    ^                 ^                 ^
    |                 |                 |
    +-----------------+-----------------+
                      |
          +--------------------+
          |  Auto Scaling Group|
          +--------------------+
                    ^
      +-------------------------------+
      |  Application Load Balancer     |
      +-------------------------------+
                    ^
```

```
+-----------------+
| Internet Traffic |
+-----------------+
```

This diagram illustrates how traffic is distributed across multiple EC2 instances, ensuring availability.

4. Monitoring and Logging

- **Best Practice:** Implement comprehensive monitoring and logging using services like Amazon CloudWatch.
- **In Action:** ShopSphere uses CloudWatch to monitor key metrics such as CPU utilization, memory usage, and network traffic for its EC2 instances and other AWS resources. They also collect application logs and store them in CloudWatch Logs. This allows them to quickly identify and troubleshoot performance issues or security incidents.

5. Cost Optimization

- **Best Practice:** Right-size instances, utilize Reserved Instances or Savings Plans, and leverage spot instances for non-critical workloads.
- **In Action:** ShopSphere analyzes its resource utilization patterns and right-sizes its EC2 instances to match its actual needs. They also purchase Reserved Instances for their production workloads to obtain significant cost savings compared to On-Demand pricing. For non-critical batch processing tasks, they use Spot Instances to further reduce costs.

These are just a few examples of how enterprises can apply best practices to build robust, scalable, and cost-effective solutions on AWS. Each case study will delve deeper into specific scenarios, showcasing the practical implementation of these principles and the tangible benefits they provide. Through these real-world examples, you will gain a solid understanding of how to apply system design best practices in your own AWS projects.

Chapter 25 Case Studies and Future Trends-Future of Cloud System Design and AWS Innovations

- **Real-World Application:** Case studies illustrate system design principles in practice.
- **Evolving AWS Services:** Highlighting new AWS services and features impacting future designs.
- **Serverless Architectures:** The growing role of serverless for scalability and cost efficiency.
- **AI/ML Integration:** Exploring incorporating AI/ML into system designs for automation.
- **Quantum Computing:** Discussing the potential future impact of quantum computing on cloud infrastructure.

Real-World Application: Case Studies Illustrating System Design Principles in Practice

This section delves into how the system design principles discussed throughout this chapter are applied in real-world scenarios. We'll explore several case studies, each highlighting different aspects of design and offering practical insights into the challenges and trade-offs involved in building scalable, reliable, and efficient systems.

Understanding Through Examples

Instead of abstract theory, we will examine concrete examples. These examples will demonstrate how design principles are implemented in various industries and how those principles contribute to the success of complex systems. Each case study will dissect a specific system, outlining its key components, design choices, and the reasoning behind those choices.

Case Study Structure

Each case study will follow a consistent structure to facilitate easy comparison and learning:

1. **Problem Statement:** We begin by clearly defining the problem that the system was designed to solve. This establishes the context and highlights the business requirements that drove the design process.
2. **System Architecture:** A detailed overview of the system's architecture, including its key components, their interactions, and the technologies used. A simplified diagram will often accompany this description.
3. **Design Principles Applied:** This is the core of each case study. We will identify the specific design principles that were applied in the system's design and explain how those principles contributed to the system's overall performance, scalability, reliability, and cost-effectiveness.
4. **Challenges and Trade-offs:** Real-world system design is rarely straightforward. This section acknowledges the challenges faced during the design process and the trade-offs that were made to balance competing requirements.
5. **Lessons Learned:** Each case study concludes with a summary of the key lessons learned. These lessons offer valuable insights that can be applied to future system design projects.

Illustrative Case Study: E-commerce Recommendation System

Let's consider a simplified example: designing a recommendation system for an e-commerce platform.

1. **Problem Statement:** The goal is to increase sales by suggesting relevant products to users based on their browsing history, purchase history, and other user data.

2. **System Architecture:**

- **Data Collection:** Collects user activity data (browsing, purchases, clicks).
- **Data Processing:** Cleans, transforms, and aggregates the collected data.
- **Recommendation Engine:** Uses machine learning algorithms to generate personalized recommendations.
- **Serving Layer:** Delivers the recommendations to the user interface.

```
+--------------------+      +--------------------+      +-----------------------+      +-----
|  Data Collection   |----->|  Data Processing   |----->|  Recommendation Engine |----->|  S
| (Browsing, Orders) |      | (Clean, Transform) |      |  (ML Algorithms)       |      | (Dis
+--------------------+      +--------------------+      +-----------------------+      +-----
```

3. **Design Principles Applied:**

- **Scalability:** The system must be able to handle a large number of users and products. This might involve using a distributed database and load balancing techniques.
- **Availability:** The recommendation system should be highly available to avoid disrupting the user experience. Redundancy and fault tolerance are crucial.
- **Performance:** Recommendations must be generated quickly to provide a seamless experience. Caching and optimized algorithms are essential.
- **Loose Coupling:** Decouple the recommendation engine from other services to minimize dependencies.

4. **Challenges and Trade-offs:**

- **Data Volume:** Handling a large volume of user data requires efficient storage and processing capabilities.
- **Algorithm Selection:** Choosing the right recommendation algorithm involves balancing accuracy, performance, and complexity.
- **Cold Start Problem:** Recommending products to new users with limited data is a challenge.

5. **Lessons Learned:**

   ○ Prioritize scalability from the outset.
   ○ Experiment with different recommendation algorithms to find the best fit for the specific use case.
   ○ Implement robust monitoring and alerting to detect and resolve performance issues.
   ○ Handle the cold start problem by suggesting popular items or items that are trending among similar users.

Beyond the Example

This e-commerce recommendation system case study is a simple example. Subsequent case studies will delve into more complex systems, involving:

- **Real-time data processing:** Systems that process data streams in real-time, such as fraud detection systems or social media analytics platforms.
- **Microservices architectures:** Systems built using a microservices approach, exploring the challenges and benefits of this architectural style.
- **Event-driven architectures:** Systems that rely on asynchronous communication between components using events.

By examining these real-world applications, you will gain a deeper understanding of how system design principles are applied in practice and develop the skills necessary to design robust and scalable systems of your own. The emphasis is on practical application and demonstrating the tangible impact of sound design principles.

Evolving AWS Services

Amazon Web Services (AWS) is constantly updating and expanding its suite of cloud services. This evolution has a significant impact on how we design and build systems in the cloud. Keeping abreast of these changes allows us to leverage the latest features, improve performance, reduce costs, and enhance the overall architecture of our applications. This section highlights the importance of understanding these evolving services and provides insights into how they can shape future designs.

One of the key aspects of evolving AWS services is the introduction of entirely new services. AWS regularly launches services that address emerging needs and provide innovative solutions for various challenges. For example, consider the introduction of AWS Lambda. Before Lambda, developers had to manage servers to run their code. Lambda introduced a serverless compute service, allowing developers to run code without provisioning or managing servers.

Sketch:

```
[Old Way: Servers]  --Request--> [Your Code on Server] --Response--> [User]
    |
    (You Manage Servers)


[New Way: Lambda] --Request--> [AWS Lambda] --Your Code --Response--> [User]
    |
    (AWS Manages Infrastructure)
```

This sketch shows the shift from a traditional server-based model to a serverless model enabled by Lambda. The developer no longer needs to worry about the underlying infrastructure, allowing them to focus solely on writing code.

New features are constantly added to existing AWS services. These additions can significantly alter how we use these services and the architectural patterns we employ.

For instance, consider Amazon S3 (Simple Storage Service). S3 has evolved significantly since its inception. Initially, it was a simple object storage service. Over time, AWS added features like S3 Lifecycle policies, which automate the transition of objects between different storage classes based on age. Later features include S3 Intelligent-Tiering, which automatically moves data to the most cost-effective access tier based on access patterns.

Here's a small code example to illustrate the use of S3 Lifecycle policies using the AWS CLI:

```
aws s3api put-bucket-lifecycle-configuration \
    --bucket your-bucket-name \
    --lifecycle-configuration '{
        "Rules": [
            {
                "ID": "ExpireLogFiles",
                "Prefix": "logs/",
                "Status": "Enabled",
                "Expiration": {
                    "Days": 30
                }
            }
        ]
    }'
```

This command configures S3 to automatically delete objects with the prefix "logs/" after 30 days. This automation can significantly reduce storage costs and simplify data management.

AWS frequently updates existing services to improve performance, security, or cost-efficiency. These updates might include changes to the underlying infrastructure, new pricing models, or enhanced security features.

For example, the introduction of Graviton processors (AWS's custom-designed ARM-based processors) has led to significant performance improvements and cost reductions for many workloads running on EC2 (Elastic Compute Cloud). Customers who migrated their workloads to Graviton-based instances often saw a substantial reduction in their compute costs.

These evolving services and features require a continuous learning approach. Developers and architects need to stay updated on the latest announcements, documentation, and best practices to effectively leverage these changes. AWS provides various resources for staying informed, including:

- **AWS Blogs:** Official AWS blogs regularly publish articles on new services, features, and best practices.
- **AWS Documentation:** The official AWS documentation provides detailed information on all AWS services.
- **AWS Training and Certification:** AWS offers training courses and certifications that can help you stay up-to-date on the latest AWS technologies.
- **AWS re:Invent:** The annual AWS re:Invent conference is a major event where AWS announces new services and features.

Understanding and adapting to these changes are crucial for designing robust, scalable, and cost-effective systems on AWS. By staying informed and embracing the evolving nature of AWS services, developers and architects can unlock new possibilities and build innovative solutions.

AI/ML Integration

This section delves into the integration of Artificial Intelligence (AI) and Machine Learning (ML) into system designs, specifically focusing on how these technologies can be leveraged for automation. The aim is to provide a foundational understanding of practical applications within cloud infrastructure, without assuming prior deep expertise in AI/ML.

Exploring incorporating AI/ML into system designs for automation:

System designs are evolving to incorporate AI/ML components to automate various tasks, optimize performance, and enhance decision-making. This integration moves beyond traditional rule-based systems to more adaptive and intelligent solutions. Automation through AI/ML involves using algorithms to perform tasks that typically require human intelligence, such as analyzing data, recognizing patterns, making predictions, and taking actions based on those predictions.

Consider a scenario involving infrastructure monitoring. Traditionally, monitoring systems trigger alerts based on pre-defined thresholds. For example, an alert might be generated when CPU utilization exceeds 80%. However, these static thresholds can lead to false positives (alerting when high CPU is normal during specific workloads) or false negatives (missing an issue because CPU utilization remains below the threshold, while other factors are causing performance degradation).

AI/ML can significantly improve this process. Instead of relying on fixed thresholds, an ML model can be trained on historical performance data to learn the normal behavior of the system. This model can then predict future resource usage and identify anomalies that deviate from the learned pattern. When an anomaly is detected, the system can automatically trigger alerts or even take corrective actions, such as scaling up resources or restarting failing services.

Here's a conceptual sketch of how AI/ML integrates with a monitoring system:

```
+---------------------+       +---------------------+       +---------------------+
| Infrastructure Data |------>| ML Model (Anomaly   |------>|   Alert/Action      |
| (Metrics, Logs)     |       |   Detection)        |       |   (Scale, Restart)  |
+---------------------+       +---------------------+       +---------------------+
                                         ^
                                         | Trained on Historical Data
```

This sketch illustrates that infrastructure data (metrics and logs) is fed into a trained ML model, which detects anomalies. Based on these anomalies, the system triggers alerts or takes automated actions.

Example: Anomaly Detection in a Web Application

Let's look at a more detailed example using Python and a simplified scenario. We will use the scikit-learn library, a popular machine learning library in Python, to train a simple anomaly detection model on web application request latency.

```python
import numpy as np
from sklearn.ensemble import IsolationForest

# Sample data: Web application request latency (in milliseconds)
# Assuming we have collected this data over a period.
latency_data = np.array([
    20, 22, 25, 23, 21, 18, 60,  # Anomaly around index 6
    24, 26, 28, 27, 25, 23, 22,
    19, 21, 24, 26, 25, 28, 70,  # Anomaly around index 21
    23, 20, 22, 25, 24, 27, 26
]).reshape(-1, 1)  # Reshape to a 2D array

# Train an Isolation Forest model
# Isolation Forest isolates anomalies by randomly partitioning the data.
model = IsolationForest(n_estimators=100, contamination='auto', random_state=42)
# n_estimators: Number of base estimators (trees) in the ensemble.
# contamination: The proportion of outliers in the dataset.  'auto' estimates it.
# random_state:  For reproducibility.

model.fit(latency_data) # Train the model on the latency data

# Predict anomalies: 1 for normal, -1 for anomaly
```

```
predictions = model.predict(latency_data)

# Identify the indices of anomalies
anomaly_indices = np.where(predictions == -1)

print("Anomaly Indices:", anomaly_indices[0])
# Output might be something like: Anomaly Indices: [ 6 21]

# Optionally, visualize the data with highlighted anomalies
import matplotlib.pyplot as plt

plt.figure(figsize=(10, 6))
plt.plot(latency_data, label='Request Latency')
plt.scatter(anomaly_indices[0], latency_data[anomaly_indices[0]], color='red', label='Anomaly')
plt.xlabel('Time')
plt.ylabel('Latency (ms)')
plt.title('Anomaly Detection in Web Application Latency')
plt.legend()
plt.show()
```

In this code:

- We create sample data representing request latency.
- We use `IsolationForest`, an anomaly detection algorithm.
- The model is trained on the latency data.
- The model predicts which data points are anomalies.
- We identify and print the indices of the detected anomalies.
- The optional visualization helps to see the anomalies.

This example, though simplified, demonstrates how AI/ML can be used to automatically detect anomalies in system performance, allowing for proactive intervention.

Benefits of AI/ML Integration for Automation:

- **Improved Accuracy:** AI/ML models can learn complex patterns and relationships in data, leading to more accurate predictions and better decision-making compared to rule-based systems.
- **Reduced Human Intervention:** Automation through AI/ML reduces the need for manual monitoring and intervention, freeing up human resources for more strategic tasks.
- **Scalability:** AI/ML-powered systems can scale more efficiently than traditional systems, as they can automatically adapt to changing workloads and resource demands.
- **Cost Efficiency:** By automating tasks and optimizing resource utilization, AI/ML integration can lead to significant cost savings.

In conclusion, integrating AI/ML into system designs offers significant advantages for automation, leading to more efficient, resilient, and cost-effective cloud infrastructure. By understanding these concepts, developers and system architects can begin to explore the vast potential of AI/ML for improving system performance and reducing operational overhead.

Quantum Computing: Potential Future Impact on Cloud Infrastructure

Quantum computing represents a fundamentally different approach to computation compared to classical computing. While classical computers store information as bits representing either 0 or 1, quantum computers use **qubits**. Qubits leverage quantum mechanics principles, specifically superposition and entanglement, to represent and process information.

Superposition: Imagine a coin spinning in the air. It's neither heads nor tails until it lands. A qubit, thanks to superposition, can be both 0 *and* 1 simultaneously. This allows quantum computers to explore multiple possibilities concurrently.

Sketch:

```
Classical Bit:  [0]   or   [1]  (Definite State)

Quantum Bit (Qubit):  [ 0 + 1 ] (Superposition - both 0 and 1 exist simultaneously)
```

Entanglement: Entanglement links two or more qubits together. When you measure the state of one entangled qubit, you instantly know the state of the other, regardless of the distance separating them. This correlated behavior allows for complex calculations and data processing.

Sketch:

```
Qubit A  --Entanglement--> Qubit B

Measuring Qubit A instantly reveals the state of Qubit B.
```

Impact on Cloud Infrastructure:

The implications of quantum computing for cloud infrastructure are potentially revolutionary, though still largely in the future. Here's a breakdown of potential impacts:

- **Enhanced Security:** Quantum computers pose a significant threat to current encryption methods. Many widely used encryption algorithms (like RSA) rely on the difficulty of factoring large numbers. Quantum algorithms, like Shor's algorithm, can efficiently solve this problem, potentially breaking existing encryption. Therefore, the cloud infrastructure need to adapt post-quantum cryptographic algorithms to secure the data.
- **Optimization Problems:** Cloud infrastructure providers face many complex optimization problems, from routing network traffic to scheduling resources. Quantum algorithms can provide better and faster solutions. The impact is in operational efficiency.
- **AI/ML Acceleration:** Quantum machine learning holds the potential to accelerate training and inference for AI/ML models. Quantum algorithms can speed up matrix computations and other operations crucial for machine learning.This means faster insights and better predictive capabilities for cloud-based AI services.
- **Drug discovery:** Quantum system helps in simulating molecular structure and interactions can accelarate.
- **Material Science:** In material discovery process, quantum system helps to explore complex molecular structures.
- **Financial modelling:** Financial risk analysis and options pricing can be revolutionized with high performance simulation.

Code Example (Conceptual - using a fictional Quantum Computing Library):

While building a fully functional quantum computer is still beyond the reach of most, here's a conceptual example of how quantum computing might be used to solve a simple optimization problem within cloud infrastructure – specifically, optimizing resource allocation. Please consider this as illustration purpose only.

```python
# Fictional Quantum Computing Library
import quantum_cloud_lib as qcl

# Define the problem
resources = ["CPU", "Memory", "Storage"]
tasks = ["Task A", "Task B", "Task C"]
requirements = {
    "Task A": {"CPU": 2, "Memory": 4, "Storage": 1},
    "Task B": {"CPU": 1, "Memory": 2, "Storage": 2},
    "Task C": {"CPU": 3, "Memory": 1, "Storage": 3},
```

```
}

# Define Quantum Circuit for Resource Allocation
circuit = qcl.QuantumCircuit(num_qubits=len(resources)  len(tasks))

# Initialize Quantum State with problem data
circuit.load_problem_data(requirements)

# Apply Quantum Optimization Algorithm (fictional)
circuit.apply_optimization_algorithm()

# Measure the result and get Optimal Allocation Plan
optimal_allocation = circuit.measure()

# Print the optimal resource allocation
print("Optimal Resource Allocation Plan:")
for task, allocation in optimal_allocation.items():
    print(f"{task}: {allocation}")
```

Explanation:

- The code imports a fictional quantum computing library, `quantum_cloud_lib`.
- It defines the optimization problem (resource allocation for tasks).
- It creates a quantum circuit, loads the problem data into it, applies a fictional quantum optimization algorithm, and measures the result.
- The final `optimal_allocation` variable holds the best resource allocation plan found by the quantum algorithm.

Challenges and Considerations:

Despite the promise, quantum computing faces significant challenges:

- **Hardware Development:** Building and maintaining stable, scalable quantum computers is technically challenging. Qubits are highly sensitive to environmental noise, requiring extremely low temperatures and precise control.
- **Algorithm Development:** Developing quantum algorithms that outperform classical algorithms for practical problems is an active research area.
- **Quantum Software Development:** Creating tools and programming languages for quantum computers is still in its early stages.
- **Cost:** Quantum computing resources will likely be expensive for the foreseeable future.

Conclusion:

Quantum computing's potential impact on cloud infrastructure is substantial. From enhanced security to optimized resource allocation and accelerated AI/ML, quantum computing promises to transform how cloud services are delivered and utilized. While significant hurdles remain, ongoing research and development efforts make quantum computing a critical area to watch for the future of cloud technology.